Querying Databricks with Spark SQL

Leverage SQL to query and analyze Big Data for insights

Adam Aspin

www.bpbonline.com

FIRST EDITION 2024

ISBN: 978-93-55518-019

Distributors:

BPB PUBLICATIONS
20, Ansari Road, Darya Ganj
New Delhi-110002
Ph: 23254990/23254991

MICRO MEDIA
Shop No. 5, Mahendra Chambers,
150 DN Rd. Next to Capital Cinema,
V.T. (C.S.T.) Station, MUMBAI-400 001
Ph: 22078296/22078297

DECCAN AGENCIES
4-3-329, Bank Street,
Hyderabad-500195
Ph: 24756967/24756400

BPB BOOK CENTRE
376 Old Lajpat Rai Market,
Delhi-110006
Ph: 23861747

To View Complete BPB Publications Catalogue Scan the QR Code:

Published by Manish Jain for BPB Publications, 20 Ansari Road, Darya Ganj, New Delhi-110002 and Printed by him at Manipal Technologies, Manipal

www.bpbonline.com

About the Author

Adam Aspin is an independent business intelligence consultant based in the United Kingdom. He has worked in Business Intelligence and analytics for over 25 years, and now focuses on Power BI. During this time, he has developed several dozen BI and analytics systems based on several different data platforms. Adam has been working with Databricks since it was first introduced, and has helped to deliver several analytical projects for multiple clients across Europe based on this technology.

Adam is a graduate of Oxford University. He has applied his skills for a range of clients in finance, banking, utilities, telecoms, construction, and retail. He is the author of a number of books, Querying MySQL, Querying MariaBD, Querying SQL Server, Querying Databricks with Spark SQL among others.

About the Reviewer

Max Mogenis is an accomplished professional in the data world. He has been focused on data architecture, data systems and professional consulting services for 30 plus years. Currently, he is serving as a Databricks Program lead and Enterprise Data Architect. Outside of work, he is passionate about motorcycles and traveling the globe.

Acknowledgement

My deepest gratitude goes yet again to the BPB production team for managing this, our sixth book, through the rocks and shoals of the publication process.

When delving into the arcane depths of technical products, it takes much work to maintain sight of the main objectives of a book. Fortunately, Max Mogenis, the technical reviewer, has worked unstintingly to help me retain focus on the purposes of this book. He has also shared his considerable experience of Databricks in the enterprise and has helped me immensely with his comments and suggestions.

Finally, my deepest gratitude has to be reserved for the two people who have given the most to this book. They are my wife and son, who have always encouraged me to persevere, providing all the support and encouragement that anyone could want. I am extremely lucky to have both of them.

Preface

Data is the lifeblood of the enterprise. Whether "Big Data" or the data stored in classic databases, it is queried using a variant of **Structured Query Language** (**SQL**). So, simply put, SQL is key to data analysis. A mastery of SQL will help you to delve deep into the data that is stored in corporate databases. You can apply SQL to analyse the data and then present it in a clearly understandable form.

Databricks lets you use its flavour of SQL to query the data that this platform contains. This means that SQL can usually serve a vital role in preparing the data for final delivery, irrespective of the output application that you are using to present your analysis. Most end-user tools have an option for entering SQL to help derive meaning from the underlying data sources. Consequently, a knowledge of SQL can help you analyse data faster and more clearly. The aim of this book is to give you the necessary mastery of SQL, and specifically the Databricks flavour of SQL (known as SparkSQL) to enable you to get the most out of your data, and to deliver the insights that will drive your competitive advantage.

Who this book is for

This book is there to help anyone who wants to know more about using SQL to deliver analysis. This means that you could be:

- A data analyst
- A student
- A database developer
- An accountant
- A business analyst

Or indeed anyone who needs to deliver accurate analytics from the data stored in Databricks.

Why Databricks

Databricks is one of the world's best-selling and widely used data repositories. It follows that learning the Databricks flavour of SQL (called SPARK SQL) and the basics of the Databricks database has the potential to be a career-enhancing move. As the data store for innumerable corporate databases, this mature and impressive system is used to power data analysis across the globe.

However, SPARK SQL is, fortunately, in proximity to the SQL used by rival databases. So learning *Databricks SQL* will set you on the path to applying SQL query techniques in most of the available SQL databases that are currently deployed.

What this book will bring you

This book was written to help the reader become proficient in querying databases using SQL. It is designed to help you to master a language that can seem arcane or even weird at first sight. To overcome any initial reticence that you may have, it progresses step by step through all the core concepts and techniques that you need to master. This way, you learn the essential keywords needed to query Spark SQL databases progressively without *information overload.*

To make SQL comprehensible we have chosen to introduce each new concept or keyword individually, so that you can learn each element in isolation. As the book progresses you see how SQL keywords can be combined to extend the power of SQL as you learn to create ever more powerful queries.

However no one queries databases purely for fun. So each query that you apply in this book also has a purely practical purpose. Therefore, you also see how to develop real-world queries that deliver essential data analysis. These queries can then be adapted to your own requirements using your own data.

How to read this book

This book has been designed to be read to use it in several different ways, depending on your knowledge of SQL and your real-world requirements.

SQL Novices

If you are a complete beginner, then you can begin with Chapter 1 and progress through the book until you feel that you have attained a level of SQL skills that match your needs. The book is designed to be a complete SQL querying course that allows readers with no previous SQL experience to gain the skills and experience that they need.

Refreshing your knowledge

If you are coming back to SQL after a while away, then you should probably skim through the first few chapters until you start meeting techniques and approaches that are less obvious. Then you can slow down and concentrate on progressing through the book and consolidating and refreshing your knowledge.

In-Depth querying

If your needs are more advanced, then you can probably skip Chapters 1 through 8 and start from Chapter 10. If necessary, you can use the next few chapters to provide inspiration on how best to solve your specific problems. You can then take a deep dive into Parts III and IV to make sure that your advanced SQL querying knowledge is up to mark.

Transferring SQL knowledge from another flavor of SQL

You may prefer to speed read the first few chapters to make sure that you are clear on the differences between SPARK SQL and the version of SQL that you have come from. You can then concentrate on progressing through the remainder of the book to acquire a thorough grounding in querying Spark SQL.

Solving specific issues

If you have been using SQL for a while but need some guidance to help you solve new kinds of query challenges then you can use this book as a collection of "recipes".

In this case we suggest that you refer to the Solutions List that follows the table of contents. Here you can find most of the individual sections of this book grouped by their functional focus. You can then use the examples given as a basis for solving your own query requirements.

The structure of this book

The book is set out in three parts. Each corresponds to a level of SQL querying knowledge that you can use depending on your requirements.

Part I

This first part of the book is aimed at true Spark SQL beginners. It presumes no previous knowledge of SQL or Spark SQL and helps you progressively to acquire the core knowledge that is required to carry out basic SQL queries.

It consists of the following **nine** chapters:

Chapter 1: Writing Basic SQL Queries

Chapter 2: Filtering Data

Chapter 3: Applying Complex Filters to Queries

Chapter 4: Simple Calculations

Chapter 5: Aggregating Output

Chapter 6: Working with Dates in Databricks

Chapter 7: Formatting Text in Query Output

Chapter 8: Formatting Numbers and Dates

Chapter 9: Using Basic Logic to Enhance Analysis

Part II

The second part of this book concentrates on teaching you how to handle sets of data.

It consists of the following **seven** chapters:

Chapter 10: Using Multiple Tables When Querying Data

Chapter 11: Using Advanced Table Joins

Chapter 12: Subqueries

Chapter 13: Derived Tables

Chapter 14: Common Table Expressions

Chapter 15: Correlated Subqueries

Chapter 16: Datasets Manipulation

Part III

The third part of this book aims to extend your SQL knowledge so that you can use it to solve real-world analytical problems.

It consists of the following **five** chapters:

Chapter 17: Using SQL for More Advanced Calculations

Chapter 18: Segmenting and Classifying Data

Chapter 19: Rolling Analysis

Chapter 20: Analysing Data Over Time

Chapter 21: Complex Data Output

The sample data and sample queries

To help you learn SQL the sample data is available on the BPB website. This way you can practice SQL querying using the data that we have elaborated to help you learn SQL.

Code Bundle and Coloured Images

Please follow the link to download the
Code Bundle and the *Coloured Images* of the book:

https://rebrand.ly/yfha2jw

The code bundle for the book is also hosted on GitHub at **https://github.com/bpbpublications/Querying-Databricks-with-Spark-SQL**. In case there's an update to the code, it will be updated on the existing GitHub repository.

We have code bundles from our rich catalogue of books and videos available at **https://github.com/bpbpublications**. Check them out!

Errata

We take immense pride in our work at BPB Publications and follow best practices to ensure the accuracy of our content to provide with an indulging reading experience to our subscribers. Our readers are our mirrors, and we use their inputs to reflect and improve upon human errors, if any, that may have occurred during the publishing processes involved. To let us maintain the quality and help us reach out to any readers who might be having difficulties due to any unforeseen errors, please write to us at :

errata@bpbonline.com

Your support, suggestions and feedbacks are highly appreciated by the BPB Publications' Family.

Piracy

If you come across any illegal copies of our works in any form on the internet, we would be grateful if you would provide us with the location address or website name. Please contact us at **business@bpbonline.com** with a link to the material.

If you are interested in becoming an author

If there is a topic that you have expertise in, and you are interested in either writing or contributing to a book, please visit **www.bpbonline.com**. We have worked with thousands of developers and tech professionals, just like you, to help them share their insights with the global tech community. You can make a general application, apply for a specific hot topic that we are recruiting an author for, or submit your own idea.

Reviews

Please leave a review. Once you have read and used this book, why not leave a review on the site that you purchased it from? Potential readers can then see and use your unbiased opinion to make purchase decisions. We at BPB can understand what you think about our products, and our authors can see your feedback on their book. Thank you!

For more information about BPB, please visit **www.bpbonline.com**.

Join our book's Discord space

Join the book's Discord Workspace for Latest updates, Offers, Tech happenings around the world, New Release and Sessions with the Authors:

https://discord.bpbonline.com

Table of Contents

CHAPTER 1
Writing Basic SQL Queries

Introduction

Welcome to Databricks and the new world of data analysis that you are about to experience. As you are standing on the threshold of this voyage into the realm of serverless analytics, you could be feeling a little apprehensive. Well, do not worry; your journey will be as simple and comprehensible as possible. This chapter will start you on your adventure, first by outlining the software that you will be using and then by explaining what Databricks is. Then, it will show you how to take an initial look at the data itself. As you progress, you will learn how to be more selective about the data that you analyze.

It may seem obvious, but you will need some data in an accessible dataset before you can start your analysis. Throughout this book, you will be developing your analytical skills with the aid of a sample dataset named *Prestige Cars*. This dataset contains a small amount of data concerning sales of vehicles by a fictitious British car reseller. If you want to try the examples in this chapter, you will have to download the sample data from the BPB website and install it into a version of Databricks. So, it follows that now could be a good time to set up the sample dataset as described in *Appendix A* unless you have already done so. Of course, you can install the sample data only if Databricks is already available. So, if you are not in an enterprise environment where Databricks is already accessible, you will need to set up an account for the Databricks community edition before anything else.

Structure

In this chapter, you will learn about the following topics:

- Databricks
- The Databricks Web interface
- Getting started with Databricks notebooks
- Cells
- Spark SQL
- Databricks databases (schemas) and tables
- Activating a database
- Displaying the data in a table
- Help writing SQL
- Limiting the number of records displayed
- Displaying data from a specific field
- Finding the columns in a table
- Displaying data from a specific set of fields
- Modifying the field name in the output
- Removing duplicates from query output
- Sorting data
- Sorting data in reverse order
- Applying multiple sort criteria
- Running SQL queries
- Displaying the available tables
- Finding all the views in a database
- Resizing book cells
- Overriding the 1,000-row output limit

Assuming that you have all the prerequisites in place, it is time to move on to the core focus of this chapter and start querying Databricks data.

Objectives

In this chapter, you will learn how to:

- Query Databricks databases using Databricks notebooks
- List the contents of tables
- Select only certain fields in tables to display
- Display only a few records from a table
- Give columns new names in your query output
- Sort your output

NOTE: If you know a little about SQL and if you have a basic knowledge of databases, then feel free to skip past the first few sections of this chapter (or even the first few chapters) until you find the parts that are new to you. If this is not the case, it is preferable to start from the beginning and provide all the information that you are likely to need to get the most out of your SQL learning experience.

Databricks

Databricks is a cloud data platform that delivers serverless analytics. This means that all the data and processing take place in the cloud (currently, Amazon Web Services, Microsoft Azure, or Google Cloud). All the analytics and data querying that you will do is carried out in a Web browser. Unlike traditional databases, Databricks does not load data into a database but stores data in files in a cloud-based data lake—hence the term *serverless analytics*.

Another area where Databricks breaks with the traditional database paradigm is by separating data storage from processing. This approach allows for much greater scalability and the ability to handle huge amounts of data-making Databricks is a leader in the area of Big Data.

The technical approaches that underpin Databricks are extremely complex, but fortunately, the Databricks interface hides virtually all the complexity. All you have to do is load data (or access data that is already loaded) and start querying.

The Databricks Web interface

To start querying data in Databricks, you first need to log on. If you have a login to an enterprise version of Databricks, then you will have been given a corporate login to use. If not (and assuming that you have created a community account), then all you need to do is to enter the following URL in your Web browser:

https://community.cloud.databricks.com/login.html

This will take you to the Databricks startup page, as shown in *Figure 1.1*:

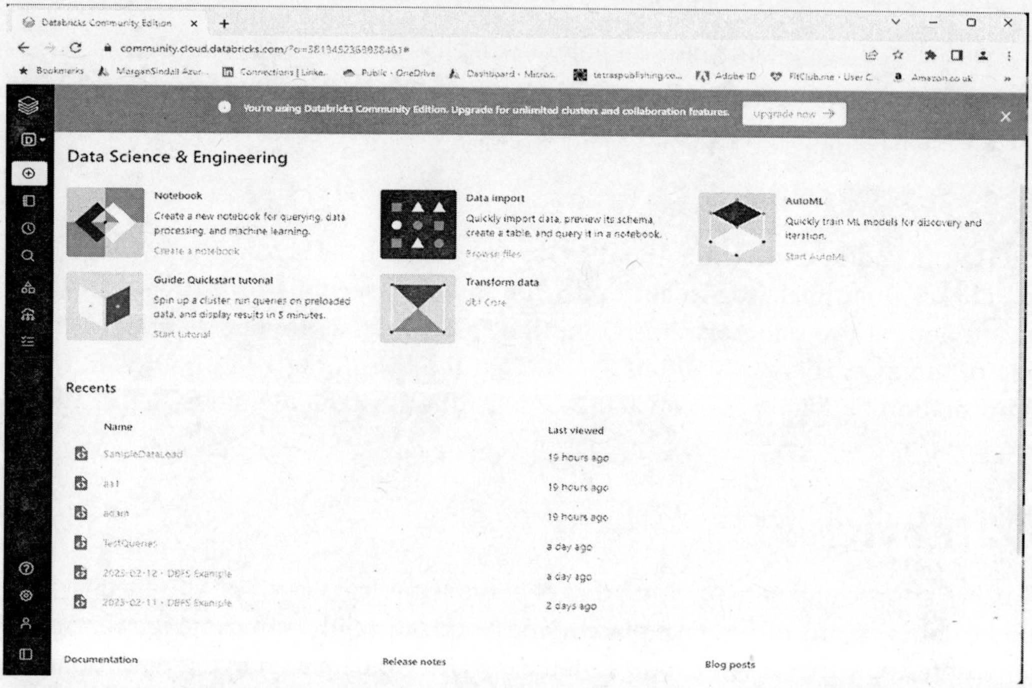

Figure 1.1: *The Databricks startup page*

Hover over the left sidebar to expand it. This is the main *menu* where you can find all the core Databricks options. You can see this in *Figure 1.2*:

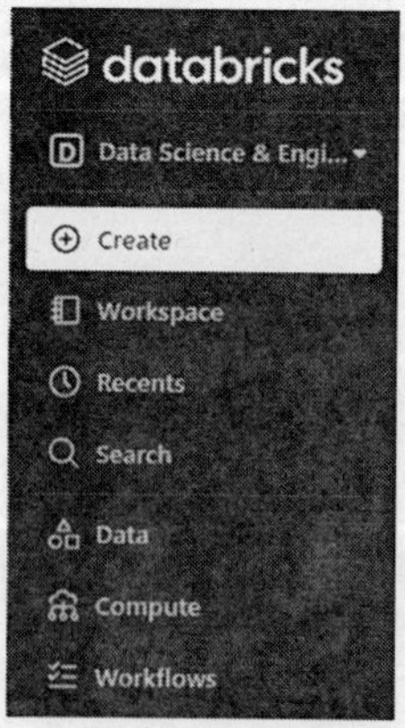

Figure 1.2: *The Databricks main menu*

NOTE: This book is only focused on one aspect of Databricks-querying data with Spark SQL. Consequently, there are huge swathes of Databricks that we will not be looking at. If you need to delve into other aspects of the platform, then the Databricks documentation is a good place to start.

Getting started with Databricks notebooks

Interaction with data in Databricks takes place in Databricks notebooks. You can consider these to be a kind of programming window where you will write your code to analyze and return data. The first thing to do is to create a new notebook. To create a new notebook, follow the following steps:

1. Hover over the plus symbol in the left pane and select **Notebook** in the popup pane. You can see this in *Figure 1.3*:

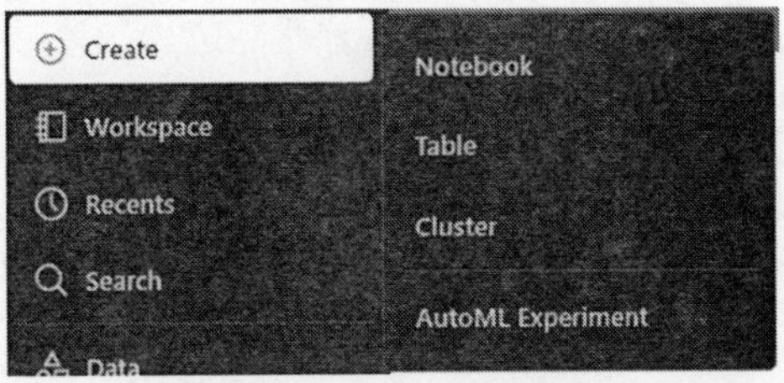

Figure 1.3*: The Create pane*

2. In the dialog that appears, enter a name for your notebook, ensure that the default language is set to SQL, and choose the cluster that you will be using to compute results. You can see this in *Figure 1.4*:

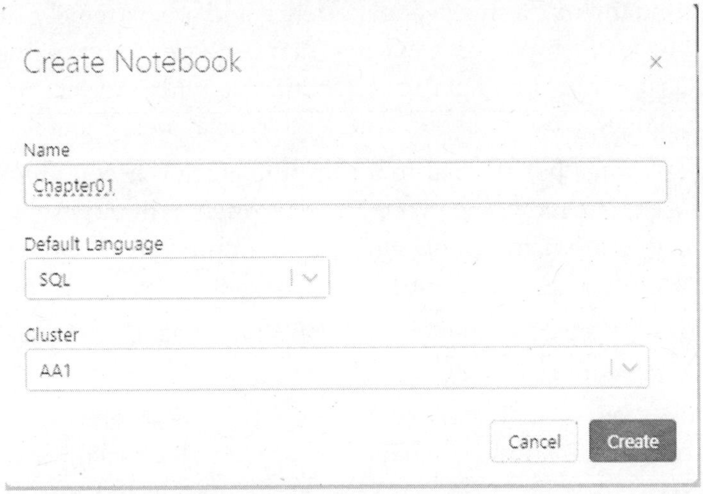

Figure 1.4*: The Create Notebook dialog*

3. Click **Create**, and a new notebook will be created. You can see this in *Figure 1.5*:

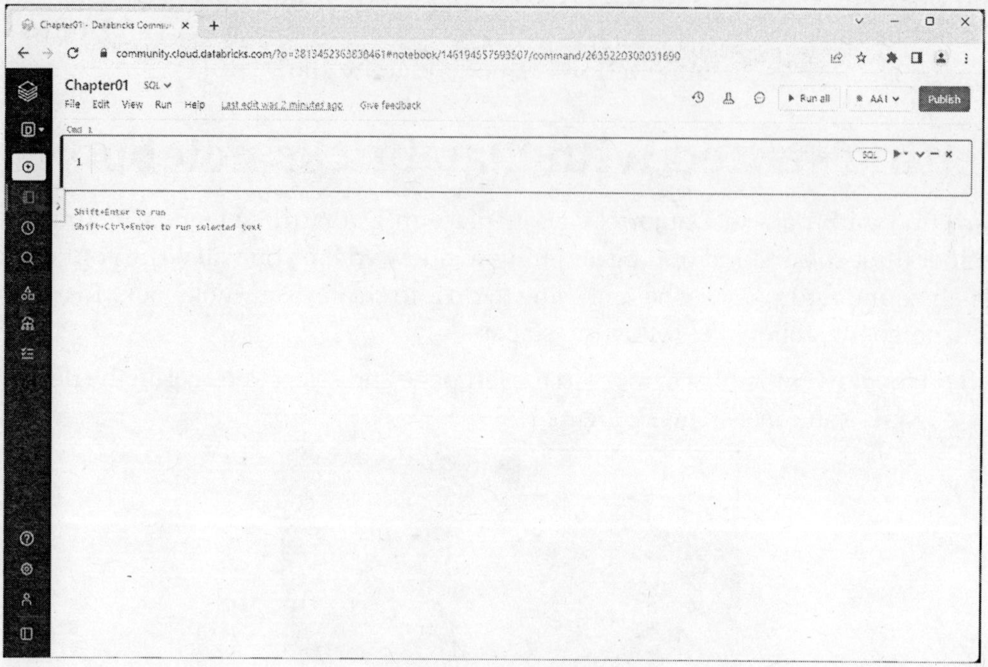

Figure 1.5: *A Databricks Notebook*

4. It is as simple. You can now start typing in SQL code to query your data.

Tricks and traps

Notebooks are fundamental to the user experience and are extremely simple to use. Their simplicity belies their power, however. As the idea is to start using Spark SQL to query data, it is probably best not to overwhelm you with interface considerations for the moment. Nonetheless, to begin, you need to be aware of that.

- A notebook must be attached to a compute cluster. If you are working in a corporate environment, then your IT department will indicate which cluster to use. If you are using the Databricks Community edition, then you will need to set up a cluster and connect this cluster to your notebooks.
- Notebooks are saved automatically. You do not have to manually save the code that you enter in a notebook.
- Notebooks can contain code written in SQL, Python, Scala, or R. The notebook needs to know which language you will be using to process code. In our case, this will be SQL, which is why you selected SQL as the default

language. You can change the default language at any time by clicking on the language popup at the top of the notebook.

- A workbook name can contain virtually any combination of letters, numbers, spaces, and even special characters.
- Workbooks are stored in Workspaces, which are a kind of container for your (or your colleagues') interactions with Databricks.

Cells

All the SQL that you write to query data in Databricks will be written in a cell inside a notebook. You can create as many cells as you like and can reorder them inside the notebook. Cells can be copied and deleted, and each cell can run code in any of the languages that Databricks uses.

This allows notebooks to become complex programs, where the code contained in sequences of cells can be run from end to end. For the moment, it is easiest (at least when starting out with Databricks notebooks) to use a single cell for your SQL and replace the cell contents with the code that you are writing for each code sample in the book.

NOTE: In a corporate environment (but not, unfortunately, when using the community edition of Databricks), you will also see an option for SQL Warehouse in the menu bar on the left. This also lets you enter SQL commands and also offers a powerful SQL editor. The results will, in any case, be the same as those when using notebooks to write SQL queries.

Spark SQL

Databricks lets you use several languages to manipulate data. This book (as you can guess from the title) focuses on only one of these languages-Structured Query Language or SQL. The version of SQL that Databricks uses is known as Spark SQL. Databricks itself is built on top of the Spark open-source technology stack. It is a full-fledged and robust variant of SQL that you can use to extract and shape data stored in Databricks datalakes. Spark SQL will generally be referred to simply as SQL in this book.

Databricks databases (schemas) and tables

As you have decided to learn and use Spark SQL queries to analyze data stored in Databricks, you need to know a few of the basic concepts that underpin SQL and databases, to begin with. This is how Databricks classifies the data that you will be querying in Spark SQL:

- At the lowest layer are the files that contain data. As far as the sample data you will be using is concerned, these are simple comma-separated lists.
- These lists are attributed to a metadata layer (a conceptual overlay) that gives each file a recognizable structure. This structure is called a table. All the rows in a table consist of the same number of columns. So, a table is really nothing more than a well-structured list—rather like the ones that you have probably encountered in Excel.
- Tables are grouped (logically, at least) into databases or, as Databricks prefers to call them, schemas.

To resume, then, a Databricks database (or schema) is a collection of lists (tables) containing columns (fields) of data in a set of rows (records). These elements can then be accessed independently or joined together to deliver the analysis you are looking for.

Conceptually, a database looks something like as shown in *Figure 1.6:*

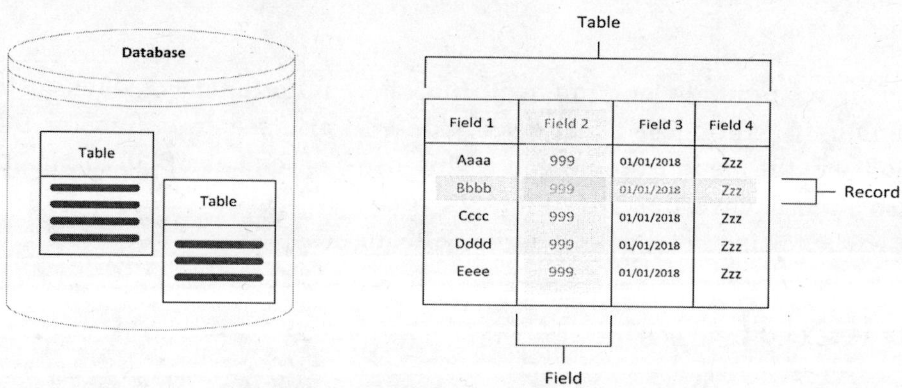

Figure 1.6: *Conceptualizing data in Databricks*

It is worth grasping from the outset that Databricks does not copy the source files into tables like a traditional database does. The data remains in the source files. What Databricks does is it adds an internal overlay to the data in the files so that the data can be accessed as if it were in a database, and so can use SQL (the classic database query language) to query the data.

NOTE: Please note that all the exercises in this book use Databricks's default database. The sample data is visible in the default database in the Databricks Community edition.

Activating a database

Before running any queries, you need to ensure that your book is using the correct database. To switch to (or to keep using) the default database where the sample data is stored, simply enter the following command in a workbook cell:

```
USE DATABASE default;
```

Then press *Ctrl + Enter* to run the command. Databricks will simply display **OK** beneath the cell to indicate that the database is active.

Displaying the data in a table

For your first query, let us suppose firstly that you have loaded the sample data as described in *Appendix B* and that you want to see the details of vehicles sold by Prestige Cars Ltd:

1. In a blank book cell, type in the following short piece of SQL:

   ```
   SELECT  *
   FROM    allsales;
   ```

2. Press the *Ctrl + Enter* to run the code and show the results. The results will appear under the code, as shown in *Figure 1.7:*

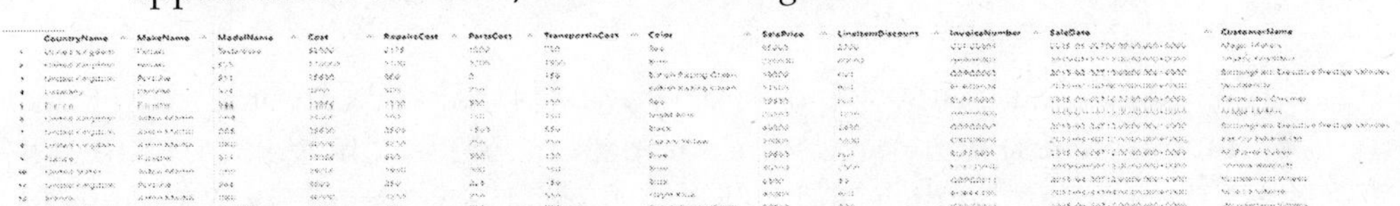

Figure 1.7: *Displaying all the data in a table with SELECT **

How does it work

In just four words, you have said to Databricks, *Show me the complete contents of the* **AllSales** *table, including all the rows and all the columns of data*. All you needed to know was which table you wanted to look at. SQL did the rest.

This code snippet is incredibly simple—four words in all—but that is enough to show you how SQL works in practice. If you issue the right command, then you will get back the data you want to see. The point of the command is to let you see everything that is stored in a table of data.

Of course, you will need to know which table contains the data you want to display when you are dealing with your own data. If you are working in an enterprise environment, this may involve talking to the people in your organization who developed or maintained the databases. Alternatively, there may be documentation that you can read to find the information you require.

If there is no one you can ask and no documentation available, then you can still acquaint yourself with the data by running the `SELECT * FROM` clause with each data table that you can find in Databricks. However, before doing this, it is best to continue a little further in this book and learn how to limit the number of records outputs by a query. Later in this chapter, you will learn how to display all the tables in a database.

So, what exactly have you done here? Let us take a closer look at what you have written. *Figure 1.8* breaks down the SQL statement into its constituent parts:

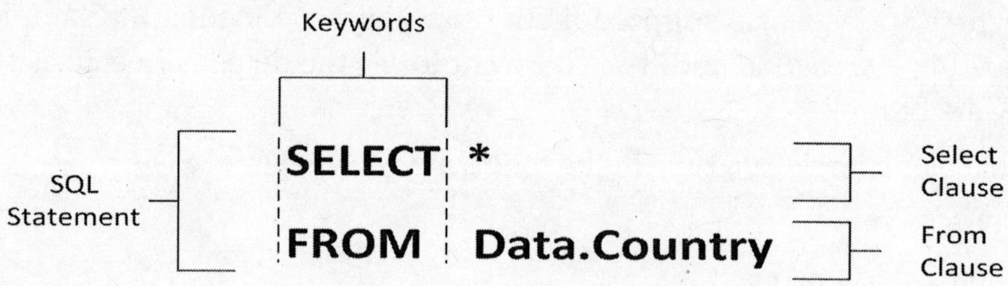

***Figure 1.8:** The anatomy of a simple SQL statement*

These constituent parts are as follows:

- **Keywords**: SQL is built using a set of keywords that you combine to produce commands. These commands (or snippets or phrases, if you want to call them that) are in English and follow a fairly rigorous syntax. Learning to understand and apply the *grammar* of SQL is what this book is all about.
- **Clauses**: These are a set of short phrases composed of keywords and data elements that make up a SQL statement.

Tricks and traps

This was a simple SQL command, but the following are nonetheless a few key points that you will need to remember:

- As mentioned previously, Databricks can contain (or host, if you prefer) dozens of databases. This means you always *have* to tell Databricks which database you want to interrogate. When using the community edition, it is simpler to use the default database. In a corporate environment, you should probably *not* use the default database.
- If you do not indicate the correct database to use, Databricks will either return no data at all or, worse, return the wrong data from another database.

- *Ctrl + Enter* runs (or executes if you prefer) the SQL code that you have typed or copied into a book cell. There are other ways to run a query that you will learn a little later in this chapter.
- You can click inside the table of data returned by a query to scroll left and right or up and down through the data.
- It can happen (even when you are an experienced data analyst) that executing a query, returns nothing more than an irritating error message like the following:

```
Error in SQL statement: AnalysisException: Table or view not found:
allsales; line 1 pos 14;.
```

- This probably means you have not specified correctly which database you want to query or that you have simply mistyped the table name.
- In this book, the data tables that you need to use will be explained as you meet them. Here you have seen the first of the small set of tables that make up the sample data. As its name suggests, the AllSales table contains the details of cars that have been sold by *Prestige Cars Ltd*.
- By default, only 1,000 rows are output from a query. This can be overridden, as you will learn a little later in this chapter.
- Under the output data, you can also see how long it took to process the data, when it was last refreshed, the number of rows returned by the query, and how long since the query was run.

Help writing SQL

While Databricks books cannot write SQL for you, they can help you enter the names of tables, fields, and SQL keywords. As an example, clear the contents of the current cell and then do the following:

1. Start typing **`SELECT`**.
2. After three characters, press the *Tab* key.
3. You will see that the book has found only one word, that is, a keyword or table or field name (the **`SELECT`** keyword), and has completed the word for you. To continue the example, clear the contents of the current cell and then *Enter*:

```
SELECT * FROM al
```

4. Now press the *Tab* key. You will see a popup menu with any possible elements beginning with **`al`** that you could use, as shown in *Figure 1.9:*

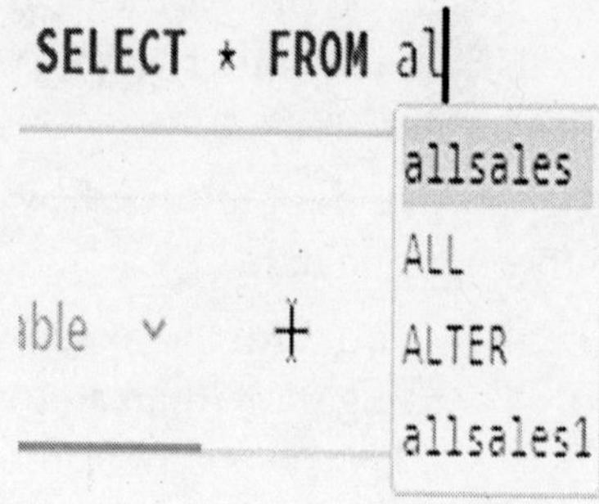

Figure 1.9: The choice of available elements using autoprompt

5. Click the required item in the list, and it will be added to the SQL code.

Limiting the number of records displayed

Databricks tables can contain millions—or even billions—of records. Each time you run a query, all the records you see are sent from the server to the querying application. It follows that displaying all the rows in a huge table can place an unnecessary strain on the server that stores the data and on the network that connects the server to your workstation. So, in the real world, it is a good idea to display only a small number of records when examining a table. This is particularly true when looking at a table for the first time.

Fortunately, SQL has a way of limiting the number of rows returned by a query. This is nothing more than a simple extension of the command that you used in the previous section. Here you can see how to tweak a piece of SQL code to display only a few records in the query output.

Delete any SQL that might be in the query window (or open a new query window), and enter the following code snippet:

```
SELECT   *

FROM     allsales

LIMIT    5;
```

Run the SQL code by pressing *Ctrl + Enter*.

How does it work

Executing this command will display all the columns in the table—but only the first five records. This will look like the output shown in *Figure 1.3* (limited to the first five rows).

You may well be wondering which records you are seeing when you ask SQL to display only five rows (or indeed any other number or records). The answer is that you might not even see the same set of records when you run this command at different times. Databricks does not necessarily return the first (or last) five records that were added to a table. Neither does it display the last five to be updated, viewed, or printed.

This apparently minor question reveals an important fact about Databricks data. Records are stored in any order (or, at least, as they were loaded). However, there is no immediate way of telling, in a table, whether the data is stored in any sequence-nor does it matter to SQL. Remember this when querying tables, and never trust the data to be returned in any specific order unless you have asked for this to happen. How to do this is explained later in this chapter.

Tricks and traps

The following are a few points that are worth mentioning at this juncture:

- There are several ways to run the SQL code in a query window. Pressing *Ctrl + Enter* is only one method. Another is to select **Run→Run** Cell from the **Workbook** menu. Yet another alternative is to click the small triangle at the top right of the workbook cell and click on **Run Cell.**
- You can enter the keywords and the table and column names in either uppercase or lowercase or even a mixture of the two. In this book, however, we will always enter keywords in uppercase to help them stand out in the code snippet. Hopefully, this will make them easier to learn.
- You do not have to write queries in a purely linear fashion, starting with the **SELECT** clause and continuing to the end of the query. You can start with any part of the query and build it up as you want.

Displaying data from a specific field

A Databricks table can contain hundreds of columns. Most of the time, you will want to display data from only a few of the available columns in a table. The next piece of SQL shows how you choose a single column to display instead of all the available columns in a table. Specifically, it shows how to list only the customer names as follows:

```
SELECT CustomerName
FROM   allsales;
```

Executing this piece of code (using any of the techniques that were pointed out at the end of the previous section) will show you something similar to the output shown in *Figure 1.10:*

	CustomerName
1	Magic Motors
2	Snazzy Roadsters
3	Birmingham Executive Prestige Vehicles
4	WunderKar
5	Casseroles Chromes
6	Le Luxe en Motion

Figure 1.10: *Choosing a column from a table*

How does it work

By replacing the star (or asterisk if you prefer) in your SQL with a specific column name, you have told Databricks that it is this column—and this column only—that you want to display. This example also makes the point that SQL is an extremely modular and extensible language, and you can easily extend or modify a simple command to make it more specific.

Of course, this approach relies on your knowing the exact name of a column and also typing it exactly as it appears in the table. Fortunately, Databricks has ways of displaying column names and using them in your SQL, as you will discover in the next section.

Tricks and traps

Even simple SQL commands have their subtleties. When listing data, you need to remember the following:

- You can write short SQL commands like this one on a single line if you prefer. Alternatively, you could write the following instead of placing each clause on a separate line:

  ```
  SELECT CustomerName FROM allsales;
  ```

This is entirely a question of personal choice. As we are presuming that you are new to SQL, we will keep the core SQL statements on separate lines in this book to accentuate the underlying logic of the language. In your queries, you can write the SQL any way you want, as long as it works. All that Databricks wants is that the *grammar* of the command is technically accurate and that keywords are separated by spaces or returns.

Finding the columns in a table

You may well be wondering how on Earth you can be expected to remember all the columns in each table so that you can type them into your SQL queries. Fortunately, Databricks Workbooks can help you here by displaying all the columns in a table in a single click.

Displaying the columns in a table is really easy. All you have to do (in an empty cell in a workbook) is type the following command:

```
DESCRIBE allsales;
```

You should see something like the output shown in *Figure 1.11* (you may see fewer rows for the moment):

	col_name	data_type	comment
1	CountryName	string	null
2	MakeName	string	null
3	ModelName	string	null
4	Cost	int	null
5	RepairsCost	int	null
6	PartsCost	string	null
7	TransportInCost	int	null
8	Color	string	null
9	SalePrice	int	null
10	LineItemDiscount	string	null
11	InvoiceNumber	string	null
12	SaleDate	timestamp	null
13	IsRHD	boolean	null
14	DateBought	timestamp	null
15	CustomerName	string	null
16	SalesDetailsID	int	null
17	StockCode	string	null
18	BuyerComments	string	null
19	MakeCountry	string	null
20	TotalSalePrice	double	null
21	Town	string	null
22	PostCode	string	null
23	Country	string	null
24	IsReseller	boolean	null
25	IsCreditRisk	boolean	null
26	CountryISO3	string	null
27	LineItemNumber	int	null
28	Address1	string	null

***Figure 1.11:** Displaying the columns in a table*

When you display the list of columns in a table, you can also see some more technical information concerning the type of data that the column contains. We will explain what datatypes are in later chapters.

SQL writing style

You can format the SQL that you write using multiple styles. You may prefer to write short SQL statements on a single line. Alternatively, you may find it clearer if you place the core keywords such as **SELECT**, **FROM**, and **ORDER BY** on separate lines. The choice is yours.

All you have to remember is that keywords must be separated by a space, a tab character, or a line break. Otherwise, the presentation of your SQL is entirely up to you.

Displaying data from a specific set of fields

SQL does not limit you to displaying all the fields—or only one field—from a table. You can choose not only the fields from a table that you want to display but also the order in which they will appear in the output from the query. The following piece of code shows you how to select two fields (**CountryName** and **Sales Region**) from another table in the database—the **Country** table:

```
SELECT CountryName, CustomerName

FROM   allsales;
```

Executing this piece of code will show you something similar to the output in *Figure 1.12:*

	CountryName	CustomerName
1	United Kingdom	Magic Motors
2	United Kingdom	Snazzy Roadsters
3	United Kingdom	Birmingham Executive Prestige Vehicles
4	Germany	WunderKar
5	France	Casseroles Chromes
6	United Kingdom	Magic Motors
7	United Kingdom	Birmingham Executive Prestige Vehicles
8	United Kingdom	Eat My Exhaust Ltd
9	France	M. Pierre Dubois

Figure 1.12: *Displaying multiple fields from the Country table*

How does it work

Here again, you have extended the base SQL that you used at the start of the chapter. Specifically, you have developed the `SELECT` statement to include the field names containing the data that you want to view. All you had to do was to separate each field name with a comma and place the field names in the order that you want to see their data in the output from left to right.

Tricks and traps

There is only one major trick to remember when listing a specific set of fields:

- Remember not to add a comma after the final field in a list of fields in the `SELECT` clause.

Columns or fields

Whereas spreadsheets prefer the term *columns*, databases tend to use the word *fields*. So, despite the fact that we have used the term column up until now, in this chapter, we will switch to using the term field from now on. Both words, however, describe the same thing and can generally be used interchangeably.

Modifying the field name in the output using aliases

Many datasets have cryptic—or frankly incomprehensible—field names. While, as an analyst or data guru, you might get used to this, it is not always a good idea to present information to users in a way that makes the data harder to understand than is necessary. So, SQL allows you to output the data under a different field header to enhance readability. In this example, you will display the country field under another name. Start by taking a look at the following code snippet and then at the output it returns in *Figure 1.13:*

```
SELECT CountryName, CountryISO3 AS IsoCode FROM allsales;
```

	CountryName	IsoCode
1	United Kingdom	GBR
2	United Kingdom	GBR
3	United Kingdom	GBR
4	Germany	DEU
5	France	FRA
6	United Kingdom	GBR
7	United Kingdom	GBR
8	United Kingdom	GBR

Figure 1.13: *Changing a field name using an alias*

How does it work

In the query output, the original field name is replaced by the name you have chosen—**`IsoCode`** in this example. This technique is called *aliasing*; you are giving the field another name in the query. Applying an alias has no effect at all on the underlying data and does not change the underlying field name. What it does do is apply a different (and ideally more comprehensible) name in the query output.

Tricks and traps

Aliases have their own particular set of rules that must be adhered to if they are to work correctly. Essentially you need to remember the following points:

- You may have noticed that all the table and field names that have been used so far contain neither spaces nor special (that is, non-alphanumeric) characters. This is because SQL requires you to specify the names of what it calls objects—that is, fields and tables, among other things—in a specific way. However, we do not want to make things appear over-complicated here, so as a starting point, let us just say you are better avoiding all non-alphanumeric characters when creating an alias for a field.
- If you want to add a space or special characters to an alias (suppose in the example used in this section, you want to see **ISO Code** as the field heading), then you must place the alias inside backquotes. That is, you can write the following to add a space to the alias **`IsoCode`** that you want to use instead of the real field name:

```
SELECT CountryName, CountryISO3 AS `Iso Code` FROM allsales;
```

In practice, many data people advise that you avoid spaces and nonstandard characters if you can, as this can get painful when writing complex queries. To encourage this, we have stuck to aliases without spaces or non-alphanumeric characters in this book.

- An alias cannot be more than 122 characters long.
- Aliases *can* contain underscores.
- You can also add an alias *without* the AS keyword using the following code:

  ```
  SELECT CountryName, CountryISO3 `Iso Code` FROM allsales;
  ```

However, we prefer not to use this technique and so will not be taking this approach when aliasing columns:

- Backquotes are also known as backticks.
- Backquotes are not the same as single quotes. There are cases in SQL when they may be used interchangeably-but aliases with spaces, or special characters *must* use backquotes, *not* single or double quotes.
- You cannot use double quotes or single quotes in aliases.

Removing duplicates from query output

As befits a company that sells its products across the globe, the CEO of Prestige Cars needs to know where its presence is felt the most. It follows that she wants you to produce a list of the countries where the company's customers can be found. A quick look at the all-sales table reveals a **Country** field that you can use to list countries.

Here is the SQL that will produce the list you require:

```
SELECT DISTINCT  CountryName

FROM             allsales;
```

This query returns the results shown in *Figure 1.14:*

	CountryName
1	Germany
2	France
3	Belgium
4	United States
5	Italy
6	Spain

Figure 1.14: *Returning distinct elements from the data*

How does it work

This query applies the **DISTINCT** keyword to remove any duplicates from the list of countries.

The new aspect of this example is the **DISTINCT** keyword. This keyword is incredibly useful because it removes all duplicates from the query output before you even see the query results.

Undo and redo

A Databricks workbook is like many other desktop applications and Web interfaces in that you can undo changes and redo them if you want to.

Ctrl + *Z* will undo one or more modifications.

Ctrl + *Y* will redo modifications that you have undone.

Sorting data

Now that you can select the fields that contain the data you want to see in the sequence that you want to see them, you probably also want to sort the data. For example, you might want to sort car sales by increasing the sale price. To do this, just run the following snippet and take a look at the numbers in the **SalePrice** field in *Figure 1.15*. They are now sorted from lowest to highest.

```
SELECT    MakeName, ModelName, SalePrice
FROM      allsales
ORDER BY  SalePrice;
```

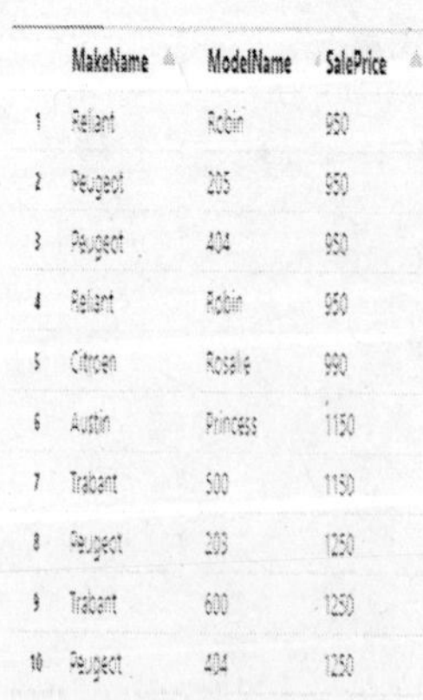

	MakeName	ModelName	SalePrice
1	Reliant	Robin	950
2	Peugeot	205	950
3	Peugeot	404	950
4	Reliant	Robin	950
5	Citroen	Rosalie	990
6	Austin	Princess	1150
7	Trabant	500	1150
8	Peugeot	203	1250
9	Trabant	600	1250
10	Peugeot	404	1250

Figure 1.15: Sorting data in ascending order

How does it work

To sort the data returned by a query, just add the **ORDER BY** keyword (it is considered to be a single keyword even if it is really two words) after the **FROM** clause of the SQL command. Then you add the field that you are sorting the data on. This creates an **ORDER BY** clause.

Equally important is that writing SQL is all about making simple extensions to existing code. So, you do not have to produce instant reams of code that work the first time. You can start with a small snippet of code, test it, and then extend it until it does exactly what you want it to do.

Tricks and traps

The following are several key points to remember here:

- The **ORDER BY** keyword can also be used on text (in which case it sorts in alphabetical order), on numbers (where it sorts from lowest to highest), or on dates (in which case it places the dates in from earliest to latest).
- If you want, you can add the **ASC** keyword after the sort field name to force an **ORDER BY** statement to sort the data in ascending order. However, Databricks sorts of data in ascending order out of the box. So, the result would be the same even if you wrote the following:

  ```
  SELECT * FROM allsales ORDER BY SalePrice ASC;
  ```

- If you test this, you will see the same result that you saw when you added the **ASC** keyword to the **ORDER BY** clause in the SQL snippet at the start of this section. Techies refer to this as the default sort order.
- If you find that reiterating field names in the **ORDER BY** clause is somewhat laborious, then you can always apply a shortcut. Instead of using a field name, you can use a number to represent it. So, you could write the SQL query at the start of this section as follows:

  ```
  SELECT    MakeName, ModelName, SalePrice
  FROM      allsales
  ORDER BY  3;
  ```

The number that you use in the **ORDER BY** clause stands for the position of the field in the **SELECT** clause of the SQL statement. So in this example, 1 represents **IsoCode** (aliased as **IsoCode**), 2 mean **CountryName** (the second field in the **SELECT** clause), and so on.

NOTE: We will use keywords to describe core Databricks terms even when the *keyword* consists of several individual words.

Sorting data in reverse order

As you saw in the previous example, data can be sorted from lowest to highest really quickly and easily. You can also sort data from highest to lowest (or Z to A). Changing the sort order is as simple as replacing the **ASC** (short for ascending) keyword that you just met with the **DESC** (short for descending) keyword. You can see this in the output shown in *Figure 1.16*, which is the result of the following code snippet that sorts the country names in reverse order of **SalePrice**:

```
SELECT     MakeName, ModelName, SalePrice

FROM       allsales

ORDER BY   SalePrice DESC;
```

	MakeName	ModelName	SalePrice
1	Ferrari	Enzo	395000
2	Ferrari	Enzo	365000
3	Bugatti	57C	365000
4	Bugatti	57C	355000
5	Bugatti	57C	345000
6	Bugatti	57C	335000
7	Ferrari	F50	310000
8	Lamborghini	Jarama	305000

Figure 1.16: *Sorting data in alphabetical order*

How does it work

Switching the sort order is as easy as adding the **ASC** keyword to the end of the **ORDER BY** clause or replacing the **DESC** keyword with the **ASC** keyword at the end of the **ORDER BY** clause of a SQL command. Using **DESC** forces SQL to sort the results from highest to lowest (if they are numbers), Z to A (if they are text), or latest to earliest (if they are dates).

Applying multiple sort criteria

Larger data sets can require that you sort data according to multiple criteria. Suppose, for instance, that you want to list all the cars sold first by country, then by make (per country), and finally by model if there are several makes sold for a specific country.

This is easy to do in SQL because it is a simple extension of the techniques that you have seen in the previous two sections. Take a look at the following code snippet:

```
SELECT    CountryName, MakeName, ModelName
FROM      allsales
ORDER BY  CountryName, MakeName, ModelName;
```

Executing this query will return output similar to that shown in *Figure 1.17*:

	CountryName	MakeName	ModelName
1	Belgium	Alfa Romeo	Giulia
2	Belgium	Alfa Romeo	Spider
3	Belgium	Aston Martin	Rapide
4	Belgium	Aston Martin	Vantage
5	Belgium	Noble	M600
6	Belgium	Peugeot	205

Figure 1.17: *Sorting sales using multiple fields*

How does it work

Sometimes, you will be faced with a table where some fields contain the same data elements repeated several times. A telephone directory is like this. You may have many pages of people named Smith, although nearly all may have different first names. Even if the last name and the first name are the same, they may have different middle initials. In these cases, you need to sort the data on successive fields so that (to continue the telephone directory analogy) you sort first by last name, then by first name, and finally by middle initial.

Entering several fields after the **`ORDER BY`** keyword tells SQL to sort the data progressively on the fields you entered. In this example, it means the following:

- First, by the country.
- Then, by the make (if there is more than one record with the same country).
- Finally, by the model (if there is more than one record with the same country and make).

All you have to do is enter the field names separated by a comma in the **`ORDER BY`** clause.

Tricks and traps

Applying a multiple-sort order has its own specific set of core requirements. These include the following:

- While there may be technical limits to the number of fields you can sort on, in practice, you do not need to worry and can extend the field list that you use in the `ORDER BY` statement to include as many fields as you want.
- In this example, you used the same fields in the `SELECT` statement that you used in the `ORDER BY` statement. This is not compulsory in SQL because there is no obligation in a basic SQL query to display the same fields that you use for ordering the data. However, when you are testing your SQL skills (or ensuring that the data looks like you think it should), it can be a good idea to use the same groups of fields in both clauses. This way, you can see whether the output is what you expect.
- Sorting query results requires a lot of computing horsepower when you are dealing with large tables running on small clusters. We recommend that you sort data only if it is really necessary.
- As was the case for `SELECT` clauses, you should not add a comma after the final field name in the `ORDER BY` clause.

Running SQL queries

So far in this chapter, you have always run queries in the time-honored way by pressing *Ctrl + Enter* or selecting **Run=>Cell** from the book menu. Databricks does, however, offer you several ways to run SQL queries. These methods are explained in *Table 1.1:*

Scope	Menu option	Keyboard Shortcut
Cell	**Run Cell**	*Shift + Enter*
All cells	**Run All**	*Shift + Alt + Enter*
Part of the cell (selected text)	**Run Selected Text**	*Ctrl + Shift + Enter*
All previous cells	**Run All Above**	*Shift + Alt-Up* Arrow
All following cells	**Run All Below**	*Shift + Alt-Down* Arrow

***Table 1.1:** Code execution scope*

Displaying the available tables

All the data in Databricks is stored in files but accessed in SQL using tables. A Databricks database can consist of dozens—or even hundreds—of tables of data that have been carefully designed and created by database professionals. The first thing that you will have to do when faced with any database that is new to you is to take a look at the tables it contains. To do this, enter the following Spark SQL in a blank cell:

```
SHOW TABLES;
```

You should see something like the list of tables shown in *Figure 1.18:*

	database	tableName	isTemporary
1	default	allsales	false
2	default	budget	false
3	default	country	false
4	default	customer	false
5	default	make	false
6	default	marketinginformation	false
7	default	model	false
8	default	pivottable	false
9	default	sales	false
10	default	sales2015	false
11	default	sales2016	false
12	default	sales2017	false
13	default	sales2018	false
14	default	salesbycountry	false
15	default	salescategory	false
16	default	salesdetails	false

***Figure 1.18:** Displaying the tables contained in a database*

As this sample database is small, it contains only a handful of tables. As you progress through this book, you will learn what data each table contains.

Finding all the views in a database

One of the aims of this book is to introduce you progressively to the essential objects you will need to learn to manipulate when querying data.

Apart from tables, one kind of Databricks object that you need to know about is the view. Quite simply, although all data is stored in tables, you could frequently find yourself querying not only tables but views as well. Views are a way of looking at data that filter or combines data in some way, essentially making life easier for users by doing some of the work for you.

In SQL queries, you can treat views exactly as if they were tables. The first thing to know is how to find the views in a database. Fortunately, this is similar to what you just did when looking at the database tables:

```
SHOW VIEWS;
```

Resizing book cells

When you start using a book, you will only see the first few records of the data that is output. Although you can scroll down (and right) in the table of data returned by a query, you can also resize a table vertically by dragging the bottom right corner of the table up and down.

Overriding the 1,000-row output limit

By default, Databricks books only display the top 1,000 records returned by a query. If a query returns more than 1,000 records, you can choose to override this setting by clicking on the **Truncated data** popup at the bottom of the output data and selecting Click to re-execute with maximum result limits. You can see this in *Figure 1.19*. However, you need to be wary of doing this with massive datasets:

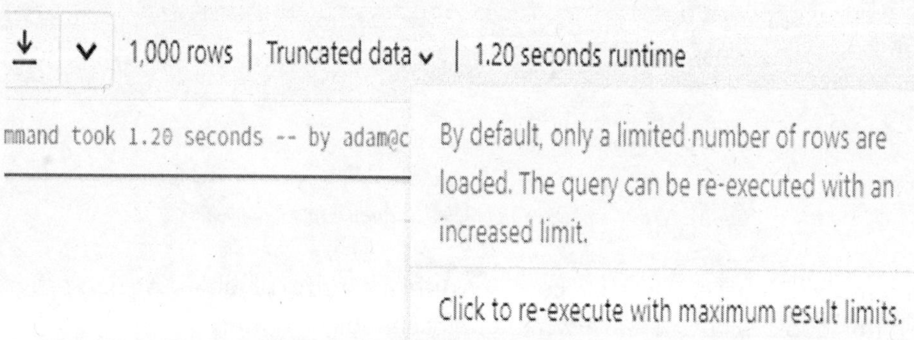

***Figure 1.19:** Overriding the result limits*

Conclusion

This chapter demonstrated how to perform elementary SQL queries. You saw how to open a Databricks book and connect to a specific database. Then you see how to dig into some of the tables that make up a database and take a look at the data they contain.

You then learned how to be a little more selective when outputting data and, consequently, to choose which fields to display from a query. You also saw how to limit the number of records that a query returned as well as how to sort the data.

All in all, you have already made vast strides toward the basic analysis of Databricks data. With this knowledge safely acquired, it is time to move on to the next step: filtering data. This is what you will be looking at in the upcoming chapter.

Core knowledge learned in this chapter

SQL is a language that is built on a collection of core concepts and a set of clearly defined keywords. Using all of these correctly—and understanding exactly what they can and cannot do—is what learning to use SQL is all about. To help you build up your SQL vocabulary, we will always recapitulate any new concepts and keywords that you have met at the end of each chapter. The following table displays the fundamental keywords that you have learned to use in this chapter:

Concept	Description
Database	A database is a structured way of storing data following a clear set of rules.
Table	A table is a coherent unit of data storage.
Field	A field is a homogenous data definition for a column of data.
Record	A row of data elements is made up of fields.
`SELECT`	This is one of the essential SQL keywords, and you will probably use it in just about every SQL command that you will ever write. It means to *isolate and display*.
`FROM`	This is another core keyword. It tells the database which tables you want to look at.
`LIMTT`	This keyword restricts the number of rows that a query displays. You can set either a precise number of records to show or a percentage of the total number of records in a table.
`AS`	This keyword lets you display a field under another name. It is called aliasing a field.
`*`	The star (or asterisk) keyword means *everything*. Yes, this is also a keyword, even if it is only a single character. Using this avoids you having to know what the names of the fields in a table are.
`ORDER BY`	This keyword combination sorts the output from a query using the selected field or fields as the sort keys.
`ASC`	Adding this keyword to an ORDER BY clause sorts the data in ascending order.
`DESC`	Adding this keyword to an ORDER BY clause sorts the data in descending order.
`SHOW TABLES`	Lists all the tables in a database.
`SHOW VIEWS`	Lists all the views in a database.
`DESCRIBE`	Displays the columns in a table and their datatypes.

CHAPTER 2
Filtering Data

Introduction

All over the world, the amount of data that people and organizations create and store is growing at an ever-increasing rate. Seeing the wood for the trees is becoming ever more complex but ever more necessary. You need to be able to filter your data to deliver relevant and valuable information from the multitude of facts and figures in the many tables that make up your database.

Structure

In this chapter, you will learn about the following topics:

- Filtering text
- Applying multiple text filters
- SQL writing style
- Excluding an element
- Using multiple exclusion filters
- Filtering numbers over a defined threshold
- Filtering numbers under a defined threshold

- Filtering on values up to and including a specific number
- Filtering on a range of values
- Using Boolean filters (true or false)

Objectives

This chapter introduces you to the core techniques to extend your queries so that you are delivering the information you want. As you might expect, filtering data has existed as long as databases have existed. Consequently, you can apply various methods to restrict the data returned by a query. Sometimes there could be several ways to get the same result, so we occasionally have an alternative solution to the problems. However, our primary focus is introducing the core techniques to apply to the queries to obtain the correct and reliable output.

You will take away the following key points from this chapter:

- Finding records containing one or more pieces of text.
- Finding rows that do not contain a specific piece of text.
- Using numbers as thresholds to filter output.
- Using ranges of numbers to filter results.
- Finding records that match a yes/no criterion.

Data scientists often talk about the logic of data. This is because databases are (most often) the result of logical design, and consequently, querying them requires a coherent and structured approach. This does not mean you need an advanced degree in philosophy or mathematics to analyze data with SQL. All you need is a little rationality and some practice. This chapter will encourage you to use both as you take your first steps in filtering data.

Filtering text

Imagine that a new marketing director has just arrived at Prestige Cars. First, she wants to know how the color of cars varies by each model sold. More precisely, she wants a report displaying all the models' Prestige cars has sold in a specific color. This means you can get off to a good start by applying more specific filters to your data. As the **AllSales** table contains a color column, you can quickly see which models of what color the company has ever sold. The following short piece of SQL delivers this:

```
SELECT DISTINCT ModelName, Color
```

```
FROM            allsales
WHERE           Color = 'Red';
```

Enter (or copy and paste) this query into the query window and run it. The result will be as shown in *Figure 2.1:*

	ModelName	Color
1	Phantom	Red
2	355	Red
3	280SL	Red
4	Princess	Red
5	404	Red
6	DB5	Red
7	TR6	Red

***Figure 2.1:** A simple equality filter*

How does it work

This query introduces the **`WHERE`** clause, possibly the most useful keyword in the SQL lexicon. A **`WHERE`** clause requires you to enter what data element you want to find in which column. In this example, this means that the **`Color`** field in the **`allSales`** table contains the element **`Red`**. This is done by specifying the following:

A field name, in this example, is the **`color`** column.

`=` The equals operator tells SQL that you are looking for an exact match to an element.

The element to find in this case is **`red`**.

As you are looking for a text element (color is not a number), you must enclose the text that you are looking for in quotes. These can be single or double quotes, which lets Databricks know you are looking for a string of characters (text if you prefer) and not a number. We tend to use single quotes in my Databricks SQL queries, but this is simply a question of habit.

You must add the **DISTINCT** keyword you first encountered in *Chapter 1: Basic SQL Queries*. Using this keyword ensures you see only one example of each red model and avoid repeating records for any red models sold several times.

Tricks and traps

As this is the first time you applied a filter using the **WHERE** keyword, note the following important points:

- Any field contained in tables you assembled in the **FROM** clause can be used to filter data. The field that appears in the **WHERE** clause does not have to be present in the **SELECT** clause.
- Although humans can see instantly that a text is not a number, SQL does not find it so easy. So, you must always remember to enclose the text in single or double quotes when writing SQL, and this is especially necessary when using a **WHERE** clause.
- Databricks is case-sensitive. Consequently, you must enter the color you are filtering on exactly as it appears in the data. This means that **RED**, **red**, and **Red** are three different words (or filters) to Databricks. You will learn how to filter data without case sensitivity in *Chapter 3: Applying Complex Queries to Filters*.

Applying multiple text filters

The new marketing director liked your initial sales analysis for a specific color. So, she has returned with a second request. She wants you to extend the previous query so that she can get an idea of all models ever stocked in **Red**, **Green**, or **Blue**. The following SQL will do this for you:

```
SELECT    ModelName, Color
FROM      allsales
WHERE     Color IN ('Red', 'Green', 'Blue');
```

If you execute this query, you should see something like the output shown in *Figure 2.2*:

	ModelName	Color
1	Testarossa	Red
2	355	Blue
3	944	Red
4	911	Blue
5	DB5	Blue
6	944	Blue
7	944	Green
8	Testarossa	Green
9	280SL	Red
10	Giulia	Red

Figure 2.2: Filtering on multiple criteria for a single column

How does it work

This query extends the **WHERE** clause by adding the new keyword **IN**. This keyword lets you enter a list of elements you want to filter, such as colors. Each element must, if it is text, be in single quotes and then separated by a comma from each element in the list. The entire list must then be enclosed in parentheses. There is no real limit to the number of elements that you can add to a list while filtering data. In this example, however, you only see vehicles that are **Red**, **Green**, or **Blue**. When using an **IN** clause like this, the elements that you are filtering on must all be contained in the same field.

Tricks and traps

It is probably worth noting the following important point. You can enter multiple elements in an **IN** clause over many lines. So, the **IN** clause could have been written like the following:

```
IN (
      'Red'
     ,'Green'
     ,'Blue'
     )
```

SQL writing style

You have probably noticed that we have adopted a certain way of writing queries in SQL. The approach is to write all keywords in uppercase and begin each major phrase, such as **SELECT**, **FROM**, and **ORDER BY**, indented in the left margin.

Indeed, there are as many ways of writing SQL as there are data analysts and database programmers. So do not feel that you must stick to this style. You can write your SQL in lowercase, uppercase, or any case.

We do advise, nonetheless, that you try and keep your SQL looking clean and readable. When you have written a query and obtained the results you were hoping for (or, better, results that shine a new light on your data), it is easy to forget that the slightly crumpled code you crafted could be hard to understand at a later date. A little effort spent making the code look more elegant can help you understand it better now and maintain it more easily.

Excluding an element

The marketing director is on a roll. The more she digs into the data, the more ideas she comes up with. Her latest intuition is to look at all sales except **Ferraris**. Fortunately, SQL lets you exclude an element from the results when filtering data so that you can output a list of all the ever sold except for a specific car. The following SQL snippet does just that:

```
SELECT      DISTINCT MakeName
FROM        allsales
WHERE       MakeName <> 'Ferrari'
ORDER BY    MakeName;
```

Running this code will return a list, as shown in *Figure 2.3*:

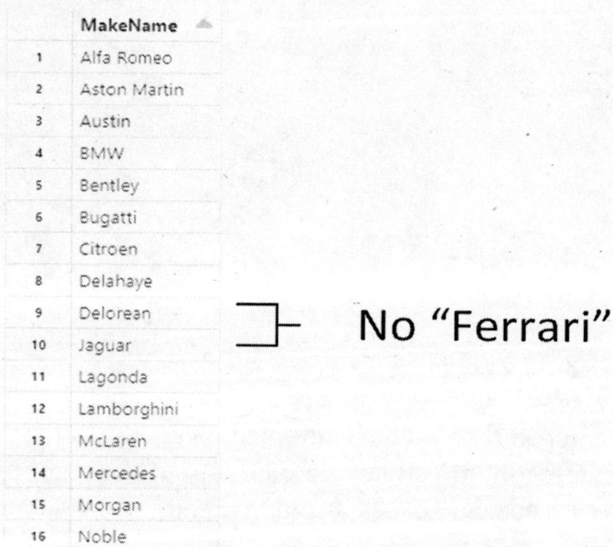

	MakeName
1	Alfa Romeo
2	Aston Martin
3	Austin
4	BMW
5	Bentley
6	Bugatti
7	Citroen
8	Delahaye
9	Delorean
10	Jaguar
11	Lagonda
12	Lamborghini
13	McLaren
14	Mercedes
15	Morgan
16	Noble

Figure 2.3: Applying an exclusion filter

How does it work

In this query, you applied a filter on a field (the make field in this example). However, you specified that the filter is used to exclude, rather than include, the element you specify. This is done by using the <> (or *not equal*) operator. This operator is the opposite of the equal operator you saw in the previous section and effectively means *anything but*. It will exclude any item you specify from the results, such as **Ferrari**. Any field in the table in the **FROM** clause can filter data.

As you can see, sorting the list alphabetically has helped you understand the output. Equally, showing each makes only once, thanks to the judicious use of the **DISTINCT** keyword, makes the result clearer and more understandable.

Tricks and traps

When excluding a single element from a list, there is one variation that you might find interesting and one important reminder:

- As an alternative to using <> in the **WHERE** clause, you can use **!=** instead to signify not equals and consequently exclude it from the output. The **WHERE** clause in the example would look like the following:

  ```
  WHERE MakeName != 'Ferrari'
  ```

- Once again, any text used in a **WHERE** clause must be enclosed in single quotes. Numbers, however, should be entered without any quotes at all.

Using multiple exclusion filters

An excited marketing director now wants even more data to power her research. This time she wants a list of all the sold cars except **Porsche**, **Aston Martin**, and **Bentley**. It is possible (and not difficult) to exclude a selection of elements from a list in SQL. Look at the following code to see how to display a list of vehicles that excludes a specific list of makes:

```
SELECT      DISTINCT MakeName
FROM        allsales
WHERE       MakeName NOT IN ('Porsche', 'Aston Martin', 'Bentley')
ORDER BY    MakeName;
```

If you run this code, you should see something like the output shown in *Figure 2.4*:

	MakeName
1	Alfa Romeo
2	Austin
3	BMW
4	Bugatti
5	Citroen
6	Delahaye
7	Delorean
8	Ferrari

Figure 2.4: *Applying an exclusion filter using multiple criteria*

How does it work

As you can see (if you scroll through the query output), the cars you specified in this SQL's **`NOT IN`** clause are nowhere to be seen in the results.

This query is like the last one (and, to some extent, the one before). In this query, the **`WHERE`** clause contains a list of elements (in parentheses, comma-separated, and with each text element enclosed in single quotes), but the **`IN`** keyword has been extended to read **`NOT IN`**. The outcome is that any element in the list between the parentheses after **`NOT IN`** will not appear in the result set.

Tricks and traps

The following is one important point to be aware of:

- When you write queries to filter data, you must decide whether including or excluding a specific list of elements in a dataset is easier. In most cases, it is best to reduce coding to a minimum because this reduces the risk of error. So, if you have a shorter list of items to exclude than to include, it is probably better to choose an exclusion list.

Filtering numbers over a defined threshold

Your reputation as an analytics guru is spreading throughout the company. Now it is the turn of the finance director to arrive at your desk with a request. He wants to get an idea of the higher-value cars that are in stock or have been sold; more specifically, he wants to see a list of all cars with a purchase price of more than £50,000.

This request is a reminder that filtering data is not always a question of defining exact matches. This is especially true where numbers are concerned. The following query will do this:

```
SELECT    ModelName, Cost

FROM      allsales

WHERE     Cost > 50000;
```

If you run the preceding code, you should see something like the output in *Figure 2.5*, where all vehicle costs are more than £50,000:

	ModelName	Cost
1	Testarossa	52000
2	355	176000
3	DB6	60800
4	Flying Spur	64400
5	355	135600
6	Testarossa	156000
7	355	125200
8	Virage	98872

Figure 2.5: *Using a numeric comparison filter*

How does it work

In this example, you queried the **`allSales`** table using a **`WHERE`** clause on the cost field, which applied the greater-than operator (**>**) followed by a value used in the comparison. This, in effect, told SQL to *give me the costs greater than 50,000*. As you can see, the figure used for the comparison is not formatted in any way.

NOTE: The most important thing to remember when using numbers to filter data is that a figure does not need to be enclosed in single quotes like text does.

Tricks and traps

The following is one specific thing to note about the greater-than-operator:

- The greater-than operator (**>**) means exactly what it says. This query will not return any records where the vehicle cost is exactly £50,000; only those with at least £50,000.01, that is, greater than 50,000.

Filtering numbers under a defined threshold

As a variation on the previous example, let us imagine you want to look at cars that are or have been in stock where the cost of any spare parts was below a certain threshold. The following piece of SQL returns this information:

```
SELECT      ModelName, Cost, PartsCost

FROM        allsales

WHERE       PartsCost < 1000;
```

If you run this code, you will see the output as shown in *Figure 2.6*, where the parts cost less than £1,000:

	ModelName	Cost	PartsCost
1	911	15600	0
2	924	9200	750
3	944	15960	500
4	DB4	23600	750
5	DB6	60800	750
6	911	15680	500
7	DB5	29200	500
8	944	6800	225

***Figure 2.6**: Using a less-than-comparison filter*

How does it work

This example tweaks the previous one to apply a slightly different filter. This time you are looking at vehicles where the cost of spare parts was less than £1,000. All this was done by using the field you want to use as a basis for the comparison, the less-than operator (the < symbol), and a value.

Tricks and traps

The following are a couple of things to remember when filtering using numbers.

- When filtering this figure, you did not need to include the parts cost in the output. However, it can be a good practice to include the fields you use in a **WHERE** clause in the initial output, as this enables you to sanity-check the query results. Once you are satisfied that the results are accurate, you can remove the field you filter from the **SELECT** clause.
- You must *never* format a number you use in the **WHERE** clause to filter output. You always enter the number without a thousand separators or currency symbols, and the number must be entered raw for the filter to work.

Filtering on values up to and including a specific number

Still looking at our stock of vehicles past and present. Let us imagine that the finance director wants to look at all cars where the repair cost was up to (and including) £500.00. Writing the following SQL snippet will let you deliver the analysis that he wants to see:

```
SELECT      ModelName, RepairsCost
FROM        allsales
WHERE       RepairsCost <= 500;
```

Running this code will deliver the output shown in *Figure 2.7*, where all repair costs are less than or equal to £500:

	ModelName	RepairsCost
1	924	500
2	DB4	500
3	944	250
4	Flying Spur	500
5	944	500
6	Giulia	400
7	XK150	390

Figure 2.7: *Using a less-than-or-equal-to-comparison filter*

How does it work

This example is a variation on the last one and shows that the less-than and greater-than operators can be amended to make them *or equal to* by adding the equal sign. This will start the comparison with the figure (or letters) used. As you can see from the results of the query, records containing the figure that is used as the upper threshold in the `WHERE` clause (500) are included in the result set.

Tricks and traps

You might want to note the following trick with the greater-than or lesser-than operators:

- You can add the equal sign to either the greater-than (>) or lesser-than (<) operator to convert it to, respectively, greater than or equal to and lesser than or equal to.

Filtering on a range of values

You can also filter results so that a range of data is returned. Let us look at an example of this by setting up a query to list vehicles where the parts cost is between a lower and an upper threshold. This lets you answer a request from the CEO for a list of all makes of cars that prestige cars have sold where the parts cost is between £1,000 and £2,000. The following is the SQL to do this:

```
SELECT      DISTINCT MakeName

FROM        allsales

WHERE       PartsCost BETWEEN 1000 AND 2000

ORDER BY    MakeName;
```

If you run this query, you will see the output shown in *Figure 2.8*:

	MakeName
1	Alfa Romeo
2	Aston Martin
3	Bentley
4	Ferrari
5	Jaguar
6	Lagonda
7	Lamborghini
8	Morgan
9	Noble
10	Porsche
11	Rolls Royce

***Figure 2.8:** Using a range comparison filter*

How does it work

In this query, the **WHERE** clause is in two parts:

First: The BETWEEN operator followed by the figure for the lower threshold in your filter.

Finally: The AND operator followed by the figure for the upper threshold in the filter.

The overall result is that using the **BETWEEN** and **AND** operators in a **WHERE** clause lets you specify a range of data to filter on.

Tricks and traps

The **BETWEEN** and **AND** operators are extremely powerful when applied to filters. However, several aspects of their use require close attention. These include the following:

- **BETWEEN ... AND** can also be used with text. If you use letters rather than numbers, you can limit the output across an alphabetical range.
- You must begin a **BETWEEN...AND** filter with the lower threshold and end with the upper threshold. If you reverse the threshold figures, the query will likely return nothing.
- As you can see from this example (and, indeed, is the case in any other code using a **WHERE** clause), you do not have to place the field used in the **WHERE** clause in the **SELECT** statement. Of course, you can repeat the *filter* field in the **SELECT** clause if you want to be sure that no data has been returned that does not meet the criteria you have entered. Doing this when developing and testing queries can be advisable, and then removing it once you have the correct result.
- If you prefer, you can write this kind of **WHERE** clause using the <= (less than or equal to) and >= (greater than or equal to) operators. The **WHERE** clause in this example, rewritten using these operators, would look like the following:

  ```
  WHERE       PartsCost >= 1000 AND PartsCost <= 2000
  ```

  As you can see, this approach requires you to *repeat the field name* in the clause. However, when you write a filter that defines a range to exclude using greater than or equal to and lesser than or equal to, you do *not* have to enter the lowest threshold value first. In other words, this piece of SQL would work equally well:

  ```
  WHERE       PartsCost <= 2000 AND PartsCost >= 1000
  ```

Using Boolean filters (true or false)

Sometimes a column may contain only a simple true or false value. Filtering on fields is easy, but it requires you to know that data like this is stored as true or false. In the **allSales** table, a field named **IsRHD** is one of these fields. The following code snippet shows how you can use it to display all the right-hand drive models that prestige cars have ever sold:

```
SELECT     DISTINCT MakeName, ModelName

FROM       allsales
```

```
WHERE      IsRHD = TRUE
ORDER BY   MakeName, ModelName;
```

If you execute this query, you will see the output shown in *Figure 2.9*:

	MakeName	ModelName
1	Alfa Romeo	1750
2	Alfa Romeo	Giulia
3	Alfa Romeo	Giulietta
4	Alfa Romeo	Spider
5	Aston Martin	DB2
6	Aston Martin	DB4
7	Aston Martin	DB5
8	Aston Martin	DB6
9	Aston Martin	DB9
10	Aston Martin	Rapide
11	Aston Martin	Vanquish
12	Aston Martin	Vantage
13	Aston Martin	Virage
14	Austin	Cambridge
15	Austin	Lichfield
16	Austin	Princess

Figure 2.9: *Using a Boolean filter in a WHERE clause*

How does it work

We have queried the **allSales** table to get a list of vehicles sold. To finish, we have added the **DISTINCT** keyword to ensure that no duplicates are returned and the **ORDER BY** clause to output the result alphabetically to make it easier to read. The final tweak is to ensure that the **WHERE** clause only allows records that contain an **IsRHD** field with a value of **TRUE** indicating that this vehicle is right-hand drive.

The interesting aspect of this query is that it is adapted to a specific type of SQL data. The data type used in the **IsRHD** column is called a Boolean data type, and it only holds values of **TRUE** or **FALSE**, although a Boolean field might, possibly, accept empty (or NULL) values as well. However, we will examine these subtleties in *Chapter 3: Applying Complex Filters to Queries.*

Tricks and traps

As we have introduced a new SQL concept, there are, inevitably, a few key points to retain.

- If you wanted to reverse this query to show only left-hand drive cars, which are stored in the **allsales** table with the **IsRHD** column set to false, you would tweak the **WHERE** clause to read as follows:

```
WHERE        IsRHD = FALSE
```

- You can also write Boolean filters in any of these ways:

```
WHERE        IsRHD = "no"
WHERE        IsRHD = "YES"
WHERE        IsRHD = "n"
WHERE        IsRHD = "Y"
WHERE        IsRHD = 1
WHERE        IsRHD = 0
WHERE        IsRhd = "TRUE"
WHERE        IsRhd = "FALSE"
WHERE        IsRhd IS TRUE
WHERE        IsRhd IS FALSE
```

- If you use **YES**, **no**, **Y**, or **n** in a **WHERE** clause to filter on a Boolean value, then you *must* place the text in single or double quotes. They can, however, be in upper- or lowercase.

Conclusion

This chapter has taken you much further into the world of SQL querying. Where before you could select only tables and columns, now you can delve deep into the data itself and output only the rows that interest you.

First, you learned the importance of the **WHERE** clause and how to use the power of spark SQL to choose to display only certain records. You saw how to select text and numbers, including ranges of numbers and figures above or below a specified value.

Finally, you learned to filter on true or false (or Boolean) values.

Core knowledge learned in this chapter

This has been quite a full and intense chapter. The following are the keywords you saw in this chapter:

Concept	Description
`WHERE`	This essential keyword starts every clause that allows you to filter data in a query.
`IN`	This keyword lets you enter a series of words or numbers that must exist in a column if the data for a record is to be displayed.
`<>`	This operator selects data that does not equal a specified word, phrase, or number.
`!=`	This operator also selects data that does not equal a specified word, phrase, or number.
`NOT IN`	This keyword combination excludes any records where a column does not contain one of a series of words or numbers.
`>`	This operator filters on numbers or letters less than a specified figure.
`<`	This operator filters on numbers or letters that are more than a specified figure.
`>=`	This operator filters on numbers or letters more than or equal to a specified figure.
`<=`	This operator filters on numbers or letters that are less than or equal to a specified figure.
`BETWEEN…AND`	This operator allows you to set a range (usually of figures) to filter a data set.
`IS TRUE`	This operator filters on Boolean (true or false) columns where the column value is set to *true*.
`IS FALSE`	This operator filters on Boolean (true or false) columns where the column value is set to *false*.

CHAPTER 3
Applying Complex Filters to Queries

Introduction

Filtering data is at the heart of SQL. You often must apply multiple filters simultaneously to extract what you seek. This means learning to apply multiple levels of logic to filter criteria to achieve the desired result. The logic you need may be quite simple or possibly quite advanced. However, it will always be built using the same approach and similar methods.

Structure

In this chapter, we will cover the following topics:

- Using either/or filters
- Using multiple separate criteria concurrently
- Using multiple filters and an exclusion
- Filtering on both text and numbers simultaneously
- Applying complex alternative filters at the same time
- Removing case-sensitivity in filters
- Using wildcard searches

- Forcing case-insensitivity in wildcard filters
- Using wildcards to exclude data
- Applying alternative wildcard patterns
- Using a specific part of the text to filter data
- Filtering NULLs or nonexistent data
- Searching using regular expressions

Objectives

In this chapter, you will extend the knowledge that you acquired in the previous chapter by learning how to use SQL filters to:

- Search for data on alternative criteria.
- Apply separate criteria simultaneously to narrow down a search.
- Use simple logic to apply multiple criteria in more complex searches.
- Use wildcard data searches to find a value that is only part of a field.
- Filter data on a specific part of a field.
- Find NULL (or empty) data.
- Applying regular expressions for complex searches.

Using either/or filters

The CEO has just sent you an e-mail. She needs to narrow her analysis to conduct an in-depth review of either **Red** or **Ferrari** car sales. A request like this makes the point that not all data searches are as simple as those you saw in *Chapter 2: Filtering Data*. On many occasions, you will probably want to create more complex queries that require either of them to be met. The following code snippet shows how to select data where either of two possible conditions is true:

```
SELECT     DISTINCT MakeName, Color

FROM       allsales

WHERE      Color = 'Red' OR MakeName = 'Ferrari';
```

This query will show something like the output in *Figure 3.1*:

	MakeName	Color
1	Triumph	Red
2	Ferrari	Silver
3	Ferrari	Black
4	Ferrari	Night Blue
5	Peugeot	Red
6	Jaguar	Red
7	Alfa Romeo	Red

Figure 3.1: *Filtering on alternative criteria*

How does it work

This example introduces a fundamental SQL keyword **OR**. This keyword lets you apply alternative filter conditions. You have queried the **allSales** table using a **WHERE** clause that filters on a certain color or a specified make. This query shows that when looking for elements in different columns, you must use the **OR** keyword in the **WHERE** clause. From the **WHERE** clause, you must always be extremely precise and indicate which column applies which specific filter.

Tricks and traps

When meeting a vital new concept for the first time, you need to take away a few key notions:

- This kind of query will return more results than the more restrictive filters you saw in *Chapter 2: Filtering Data,* as it implies a wider search, given that it is an either/or selection.
- An OR query like this will return data when either of the two conditions is true or even when both are true. However, a record where both conditions are true (that is, where the make is **Ferrari** and the color is red) will not appear twice.
- Each part of the **WHERE** clause follows the logic you saw in *Chapter 2: Filtering Data*. So, the text is enclosed in single or double quotes, as is normal when filtering text data.
- The technical name for a filter like this is a logical or.
- You can add as many **OR** operators to a query as you want. However, you must repeat the column name for each filter you apply, even if the filters apply to the same column.

Using multiple separate criteria concurrently

The CEO wants to build on your query results and conduct a narrower search. She wants to look for a red `Ferrari` only. You can deliver the required result with only a small tweak to the code that you just wrote:

```
SELECT          MakeName, Color, SaleDate, SalePrice

FROM            allsales

WHERE           Color = 'Red' AND MakeName = 'Ferrari';
```

Running this query should show something like *Figure 3.2*:

	MakeName	Color	SaleDate	SalePrice
1	Ferrari	Red	2015-01-02T08:00:00.000+0000	65000
2	Ferrari	Red	2017-09-20T04:33:00.000+0000	155000

Figure 3.2: *Searching for simultaneous criteria*

How does it work

This query is like the previous one. So, let us just look at the differences. In this example, OR has been replaced by **AND**. This tells SQL that both criteria must be met for a record to pass the filter. Records, where the vehicle is a red Ferrari, will appear in the output.

Tricks and traps

You are likely to use the **AND** keyword frequently in your SQL career. So, it is worth noting the following points:

- The **AND** operator will narrow down the search considerably, as all filter conditions must be met for a record to be allowed through to the output.
- A query can have multiple criteria that are applied to filter the data. You can add as many **AND** clauses to the **WHERE** clause as you like.
- The technical name for a filter like this is "logical **AND**".

Using multiple filters and an exclusion

Until now, when using multiple selection criteria, you have looked at limited selections using only two elements. Now, you have been asked to find all makes except Bentleys, where the cars are **`Red`**, **`Green`**, or **`Blue`**. You are lucky that SQL can help you create more complex filters that can apply these criteria easily. To see how this kind of complex query is written, look at the following piece of SQL:

```
SELECT      DISTINCT MakeName, Color

FROM        allsales

WHERE       Color IN ('Red', 'Green', 'Blue')

            AND MakeName != 'Bentley';
```

Running this query will return the output as shown in *Figure 3.3*:

	MakeName	Color
1	Citroen	Green
2	Triumph	Red
3	Lamborghini	Blue
4	Mercedes	Green
5	Aston Martin	Blue
6	Peugeot	Red

***Figure 3.3:** Combining multiple selections with an exclusion*

How does it work

This query shows you that you can combine any filtering techniques you have seen in this chapter and the previous one if they help you attain the required result. This filter mixes the **`IN`** operator to filter on a chosen selection of colors (red, green, or blue) but excludes all Bentleys from the result, whatever the color.

This query applies the following two conditions:

1. **First**: It itemizes a list of colors that the vehicle can be.
2. **Second**: It extends the criteria with an **`AND`** clause to add a second condition that excludes Bentley as the make.

The resulting output is a list of all makes except **Bentley** if the cars are red, green, or blue.

Tricks and traps

We have only two points to note here:

1. You can use **<>** or **!=** to exclude an element in a **WHERE** clause.
2. We added the **DISTINCT** keyword to the **SELECT** clause to produce a shorter results list by excluding duplicates.

Filtering on both text and numbers simultaneously

Sometimes you want to filter data so that a certain condition is always met, and then a second criterion must also be met. The second criterion can apply different, alternative criteria to other fields. For example, the request from the finance director to see a report containing all the red cars ever bought where their repair cost or the cost of spare parts exceeds £1,000.00. The following SQL snippet shows this type of query in action:

```
SELECT      ModelName, Color, PartsCost, RepairsCost

FROM        allsales

WHERE       Color = 'Red'

            AND (PartsCost > 1000 OR RepairsCost > 1000);
```

Executing this piece of SQL will return a list, as shown in *Figure 3.4*:

	ModelName	Color	PartsCost	RepairsCost
1	Testarossa	Red	1500	2175
2	944	Red	500	1360
3	XK120	Red	500	1100
4	355	Red	750	2000
5	Rapide	Red	750	1360
6	DB9	Red	750	1490

Figure 3.4: Nested criteria

How does it work

This query reads the **allSales** table and then specifies that only red cars must be the output. It extends the filter with a second criterion to select data using another condition that must be met on either of the two columns.

The parentheses used to enclose the second part of the filter (after the **AND** operator) are an important part of the **WHERE** clause. Placing part of the **WHERE** clause inside parentheses means the following:

- First, any of the conditions inside the parentheses must be true.
- Second, the condition outside the parentheses must also be true.

So, the resulting filter is essentially in two parts:

- **Not only**: The color field must contain the red text.
- **As well as**: The parts cost must be over £1,000.00, *or* the repair cost must be over £1,000.00.

The filter says: For every red car, see whether the parts or the repair cost is over 1,000. If both these criteria are met, the record containing this data will appear in the result set.

Tricks and traps

When writing queries that provide alternative filters, there are a few key points to take away:

- It is vital to place any alternatives (in this example, it means the cost of spares or the repair cost) inside parentheses. The query will be interpreted as any red car or any repair cost over £1,000.00 or any parts cost over £1,000.00. Not doing this will return a completely different result set.
- If the parts and the repair cost exceed £1,000, the filter will work, as it needs only one filter to match to function correctly. Once one filter condition is met, SQL does not care if others are met. However, a record that meets all the alternative criteria will **not** appear multiple times in the output. It just means that the minimal conditions for the row to be allowed into the result set have been met.
- In this example, we deliberately avoided using the **DISTINCT** keyword in the **SELECT** clause. This way, the query output delivered the complete list of vehicles matching the required criteria.

Applying complex alternative filters at the same time

There could be days in your career as a data analyst when you will wonder why (and how) people can dream up the requests they send you. Take, for instance, this suggestion from the finance director: *I want to see all red, green, or blue Rolls-Royce Phantom-or failing that, any vehicle where both the parts cost and the repair cost are over £5,500.00.*

You are, yet again, in luck because SQL queries can be tailored to filter data down to an extremely fine level of detail. Suppose you need to see either of the following categories of sales:

- Red, Green, or Blue Rolls-Royce Phantoms.
- Sales where both the parts and repair costs are over 5,500.

We realize that this may seem to be a strange thing to ask—but believe me, we have seen more peculiar requirements in the past. In any case, the following is the code that can satisfy the request:

```
SELECT DISTINCT  ModelName, Color, PartsCost, RepairsCost

FROM        allsales

WHERE            (Color IN ('Red', 'Green', 'Blue')

                   AND

                   ModelName = 'Phantom')

                 OR

                (PartsCost > 5500 AND RepairsCost > 5500);
```

If you run this piece of SQL, you will see a data set as shown in *Figure 3.5*:

	ModelName	Color	PartsCost	RepairsCost
1	F50	Silver	7900	9250
2	Phantom	Red	750	500
3	57C	Red	7500	9250
4	Phantom	Green	2200	1490
5	Phantom	Green	1500	5500

***Figure 3.5:** Complex nested criteria*

How does it work

This piece of SQL has two parts, each on either side of the central `OR` keyword. The filter applies to both the parts of the `WHERE` clause independently and then returns any records that match either (or both) conditions. It is as if there are two separate filters in action, each independent of the other.

To ensure that each side of the `OR` clause does exactly what you want, you must enclose each in parentheses. This way, the filter consists of the following three elements:

1. **A first condition**: That defines the acceptable color and model.
2. **The OR operator**: That tells SQL to apply either the first criterion or the second.
3. **A second condition**: That sets a specific cost threshold for either of the two fields.

As this `WHERE` clause is a little more complex, you might want to look at *Figure 3.6*, which explains how it works more visually:

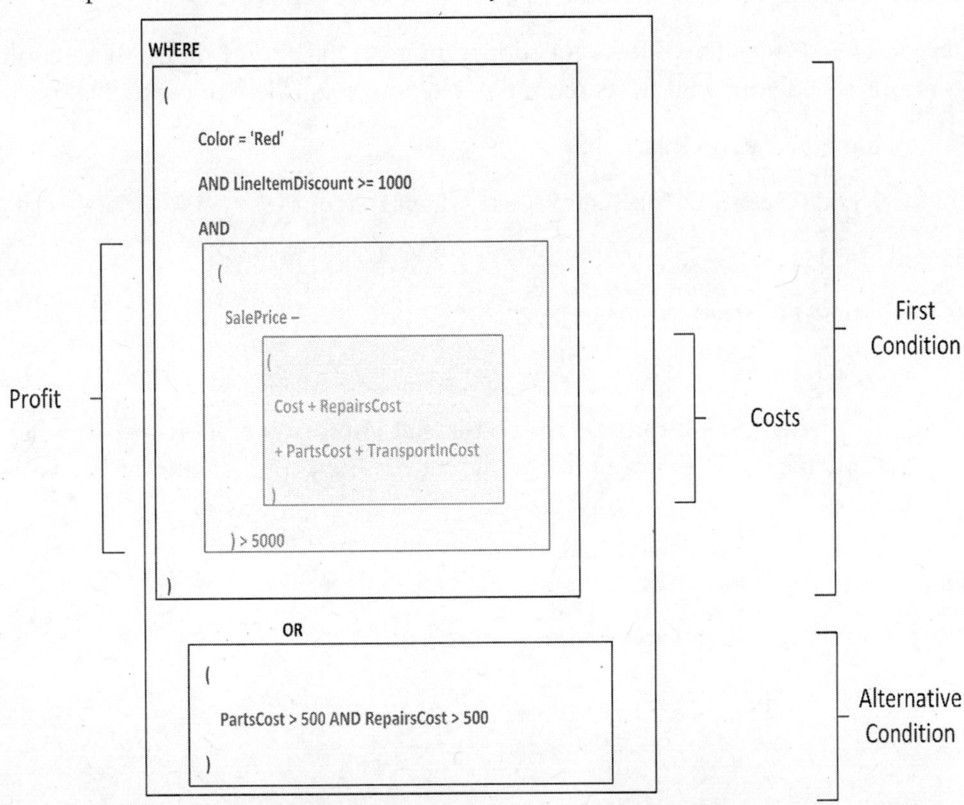

***Figure 3.6:** The anatomy of a complex WHERE clause*

Tricks and traps

These kinds of complex filters come with their own set of variations and caveats. You need to remember the following:

- You can write the **WHERE** clause as a single line if you prefer so that it reads as follows:

  ```
  WHERE (Color IN ('Red', 'Green', 'Blue') AND ModelName = 'Phantom')
  OR (PartsCost > 1500 OR RepairsCost > 1500)
  ```

- This is purely a question of presentation. However, you may find that separating the **WHERE** clause over several lines makes it easier to read and understand because a multi-line format enhances the fact that there are two separate aspects to the filter, each on a separate side of the **OR** keyword.
- Once again, if both filter conditions are met, the filter will work because it needs only one of them to match to succeed. SQL does not care if others are met if one filter condition is met.

Removing case-sensitivity in filters

Databricks is case-sensitive. However (depending on the source data), there could be occasions when you want to search for an element regardless of capitalization.

The following SQL can do this:

```
SELECT      ModelName, Color, PartsCost ,RepairsCost
FROM        allsales
WHERE       UPPER(Color) = 'DARK PURPLE'
ORDER BY    ModelName;
```

Running this piece of SQL produces the result that you can see in *Figure 3.7*, where all the dark purple vehicles are returned, whatever the capitalization of the word purple is:

	ModelName	Color	PartsCost	RepairsCost
1	135	Dark Purple	750	1360
2	350SL	Dark Purple	500	660
3	350SL	Dark Purple	457	2000
4	911	Dark Purple	750	500
5	Continental	Dark Purple	750	1490
6	DB9	DARK PURPLE	500	500
7	Dino	Dark Purple	1500	2175

Figure 3.7: A WHERE clause that performs a case-insensitive search

How does it work

This short query outputs the four fields that you can see in the **SELECT** clause. However, it is the **WHERE** clause that adds something new.

- **First**: You begin a WHERE clause.
- **Second**: You wrap the field name that you are searching (for example, color) inside the **UPPER()** function.

Finally, you add an equal's operator and enter the text that you are looking for in uppercase.

The **UPPER()** function converts the contents of the field it encloses to uppercase inside the filter action. As you are comparing the field for the query, now in uppercase, to a text you entered in uppercase, you are effectively canceling out any case sensitivity for this part of the filter. This is because you compare an uppercase text to filter uppercase field content.

This query introduced a fundamentally new concept of Databricks functions. As this is the first time you are using a function in Databricks, you need to know a little about Databricks functions and what they do:

- A function modifies the element that it is applied to. This element is often a field, meaning that the function will be applied to every record in the table for the field it is applied to.
- Simple functions like the **UPPER()** function used here are applied to a single field by placing the field name inside the parentheses that follow the function name.
- The field name (or other element enclosed inside the parentheses) is called a **parameter**.
- Databricks has a wealth of built-in functions that help you query data, and you will be meeting many of them throughout the rest of this book.

Tricks and traps

The following points are worth noting at this juncture:

- You must apply the **UPPER()** function to each field from which you want to remove case sensitivity.
- Altering the case sensitivity of the filter does not alter the field contents. You can see this in *Figure 3.7*, where all the colors are a mixture of uppercase and lowercase characters.

Using wildcard searches

Returning a list of data is nearly always easy when everything (including the data) is perfect. In the real world, however, this is not always the case. Maybe the data was incorrectly entered, or you cannot remember how it was spelled. Sometimes it could be a combination of both of these circumstances. You are reminded of this when the receptionist comes to your desk with a request for some help. She knows that prestige cars have a customer with **Peter** (or was that **Pete**?) somewhere in their name, and you need to find this person in the database. Fortunately, SQL has a few solutions to help you filter a little more approximately. One example is given in the following piece of SQL:

```
SELECT      CustomerName

FROM        allsales

WHERE       CustomerName LIKE '%Pete%';
```

Running this query will return the output as shown in *Figure 3.8*:

	CustomerName
1	Peter McLuckie
2	Honest Pete Motors
3	Peter McLuckie
4	Honest Pete Motors
5	Peter Smith
6	Peter McLuckie
7	Peter McLuckie
8	Honest Pete Motors
9	Honest Pete Motors

Figure 3.8: Wildcard filtering

How does it work

This code searched the customer table for any element in the **CustomerName** field containing the characters **Pete**. Consequently, it found **Pete** and **Peter** and would have found **Peter**, Pete's Sake, or any text containing **Pete**.

This kind of search is called a wildcard filter, and it requires you to adhere to a few basic principles:

- Wildcard searches require you to use the **LIKE** operator.
- As we are searching inside a text field, the text must be enclosed in single quotes, as was the case in all queries that you saw previously that searched on text-based fields.
- The percentage symbol (**%**) means *any character or characters*. This symbol is called a wildcard in this context.
- You must place any percentage symbols *inside* the quotes.

In other respects, a wildcard search is like a filter applied to any text-based column. The only real difference is using the **%** character to widen the range of elements that Databricks can return.

Tricks and traps

Wildcard searches are powerful, but you do have to take care while using them. The following are some examples:

- When using these kinds of searches, you must know that the filter is still case-sensitive. So, entering any of the following will not work:

  ```
  LIKE '%pete%'
  ```

  ```
  LIKE '%PETE%'
  ```

- If you want to locate a few characters anywhere inside a field, place the wildcard (the percentage symbol) on either side of the text you seek.
- If you are certain the records you are looking for have a field that begins with the text that you are using to filter the result (Pete in this example), then you can alter the **WHERE** clause so that it looks like this:

  ```
  WHERE        CustomerName LIKE 'Pete%'
  ```

- As you can see, the wildcard is entered only after the search text. This, in effect, tells SQL that the field to look for begins with Pete can have any text after this but nothing before.
- If the records that you are looking for have a field that ends with the text that you are using to filter the result (Pete in this example), then you can alter the **WHERE** clause so that it looks like this:

  ```
  WHERE        CustomerName LIKE '%Pete'
  ```

  This code tells SQL to find records where the **CustomerName** field ends with **Pete** however many characters precede the text that you are looking for.

- Wildcards will apply to letters, numbers, or even symbols; they are not limited to alphabetical letters. However, they are mostly used when filtering text-based data.

- You can add multiple wildcard characters in a filter like the following:

  LIKE '%Pete%S%'

This will return the output as shown in *Figure 3.9*:

	CustomerName
1	Peter Smith
2	Peter Smith
3	Peter Smith
4	Pete Spring

Figure 3.9: *Complex wildcard filtering*

Essentially, this wildcard filter means:

- Any initial characters (or none) followed by
- The word Pete followed by
- Any other characters (or none) followed by
- An S followed by
- Any other characters (or none)

Forcing case-insensitivity in wildcard filters

Sometimes you may want Databricks to apply a non-case-sensitive search when using wildcard filters. The following short piece of SQL shows that this is extremely easy to do:

```
SELECT MakeName

FROM allsales

WHERE MakeName ILIKE '%L%';
```

Running this piece of code produces the result as shown in *Figure 3.10*:

	MakeName
1	Bentley
2	Alfa Romeo
3	Bentley
4	Alfa Romeo
5	Bentley
6	Bentley
7	Alfa Romeo
8	Lamborghini
9	Lamborghini
10	Alfa Romeo

Figure 3.10*: A WHERE clause that performs a case-insensitive search when using a wildcard*

How does it work

Making a wildcard search case sensitive simply means replacing the `LIKE` keyword with the `ILIKE` keyword.

In this specific example, you are returning makes with an `L` or an `l` in the marque's name. In this example, using the `ILIKE` operator with wildcard symbols before and after the `L` means that the uppercase or lowercase `L` can be anywhere in the make name.

Tricks and traps

The following point is important when carrying out case-sensitive searches when using a wildcard:

- If you want to exclude a character and retain case-insensitivity, you can negate the filter using the **`NOT`** operator. So, for instance, you could write code like the following to find makes without an `L` in the name:

  ```
  SELECT * FROM allsales WHERE MakeName NOT ILIKE '%L%';
  ```

Using wildcards to exclude data

There could be occasions when you want to use wildcards to exclude data from the query output. Suppose, for instance, you want to produce a list of all the customers except those with **`Pete`** in their name. The following SQL extends the code from a previous example to do exactly this:

```
SELECT      DISTINCT CustomerName
FROM        allsales
WHERE       CustomerName NOT LIKE '%Pete%';
```

Running this query will show the kind of result that you can see in *Figure 3.11*:

	CustomerName
1	Matterhorn Motors
2	Mme Anne Duport
3	SuperSport S.A.R.L.
4	Pierre Blanc
5	London Executive Prestige Vehicles
6	Alex McWhirter
7	Raimondo Delattre
8	Prestige Imports
9	Autos Sportivos
10	Andy Cheshire
11	Convertible Dreams

***Figure 3.11:** Excluding data by applying a wildcard*

How does it work

Preceding the **LIKE** operator with the **NOT** keyword reverses the filter logic. This means that in this query, at least every customer will be displayed unless their name contains the characters **Pete**. You can verify this by scrolling down through the result set. You will see that no customer with *Pete* in their name is present. We included the **DISTINCT** keyword to ensure a list of unique customers.

Applying alternative wildcard patterns

Some filtering will require you to define and apply multiple wildcard patterns to return a wider data set based on various wildcards. Although you can achieve this using the **OR** operator that was described earlier in this chapter, there is a much simpler way to achieve this outcome, as you can see in the following piece of SQL:

```
SELECT      DISTINCT MakeName, ModelName, Color
FROM        allsales
WHERE       Color LIKE SOME ('%ed%', '%el%')
ORDER BY    MakeName, ModelName;
```

This code delivers the output as shown in *Figure 3.12*:

	MakeName	ModelName	Color
1	Alfa Romeo	Giulia	Red
2	Aston Martin	DB4	Canary Yellow
3	Aston Martin	DB5	Red
4	Aston Martin	DB6	Canary Yellow
5	Aston Martin	DB6	Red
6	Aston Martin	DB9	Red
7	Aston Martin	DB9	Canary Yellow
8	Aston Martin	Rapide	Red

***Figure 3.12:** Applying multiple wildcards*

How does it work

This code extends the use of the **`LIKE`** keyword that you used previously, and this time, it applies multiple wildcards. Essentially, all you do is to:

- Add the **`SOME`** keyword after the **`LIKE`** keyword.
- Place alternative wildcard elements inside parentheses, with each wildcard element separated by a comma from the previous one.

SQL will then use any of the wildcard elements to filter the data. Any records that match any of the wildcard elements will appear in the output.

Tricks and traps

There are a few things that you need to be aware of:

- **`ILIKE`** also accepts multiple wildcard elements in the same way that **`LIKE`** does.
- You can add as many wildcard elements as you like if they are separated inside the parentheses and commas.
- You can produce the same output with SQL like:

```
SELECT     DISTINCT MakeName, ModelName, Color
FROM       allsales
WHERE      Color LIKE '%ed%'
           OR
           Color LIKE '%el%'
ORDER BY   MakeName, ModelName;
```

Using a specific part of the text to filter data

Just as you glanced at the clock at the end of the day, the finance director appeared beside your desk with a strange demand. He informs you that the account number field is structured so that you can identify the country of sales from certain characters at a specific point in the field. So, he wants you to use this to isolate all the sales made to French customers.

Put another way, he means, *I have a field where each character or certain character has a specific meaning, and the field always has the same number of characters with the same subgroups of meaningful characters*. This data includes a bank account or certain social security numbers (or other identity codes). In these cases, you want to specify that a certain number of characters can be anything at all, but others (at a specific place in the field) have a meaning you want to filter on.

The **`InvoiceNumber`** field of the sales table is one of these fields. It is defined like the following:

- The left three characters indicate the currency of sale
- Characters 4 and 5 indicate the destination country
- The last three characters provide a sequential invoice number

This approach is explained more graphically in *Figure 3.13*:

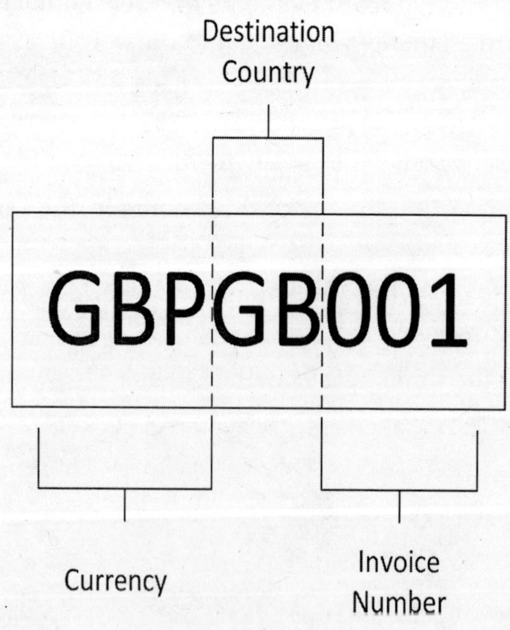

***Figure 3.13:** Structured fields*

The invoice number **GBPGB001** tells you that this sale was made in pounds sterling to a client in the **United Kingdom**, and the invoice no is **001**.

If you are faced with a structured field, you can search on parts of the field to isolate certain records. In this example, the following SQL returns vehicles sold to **France**, whatever the currency and the invoice number are:

```
SELECT DISTINCT   ModelName, InvoiceNumber
FROM              allsales
WHERE             InvoiceNumber LIKE '___FR%';
```

Running the preceding query (and specifically using three underscores in the **WHERE** clause before the **FR%**) will return the output in *Figure 3.14*:

	ModelName	InvoiceNumber
1	XJ12	EURFR089
2	F50	EURFR151
3	XK150	EURFR170
4	355	EURFR186
5	TR5	EURFR313
6	57C	EURFR221

Figure 3.14: *Wildcard searches in structured fields*

How does it work

This piece of SQL uses wildcards to filter a field. More precisely, it uses the underscore character as a single-character wildcard. So, the **WHERE** clause in this sample says this:

- **First**: Find any three characters on the left of the field (specified by the three underscores).
- **Then**: Filter on **FR**.
- **Finally**: Do not filter on any other characters to the end of the text (let anything through, no matter how many characters). The percentage symbol represents this.

When faced with structured, coded texts in data fields, knowing what each subset of characters means in the field is vital. Providing that you know this, you can then filter on any part of the text, as you did here.

Tricks and traps

While filtering on a specific part of a field is not difficult, it helps to remember the following points when you do this:

- Where there is a strict coding scheme, such as a bank account number, you can use the underscore wildcard to replace a single character or a specified number of characters. However, there must be one character, at least if you use an underscore, unlike the percentage wildcard, which means zero to any number of characters.
- You can use the underscore wildcard anywhere in a search pattern and even use it several times. For instance, you could also have written this **WHERE** clause as follows:

  ```
  WHERE      InvoiceNumber LIKE '___FR____'
  ```

  This pattern will find any initial three, FR, and four final characters.
- The wildcard searches (using % or _) can be slow on large data sets. If your work will entail carrying out lots of searches like these on massive tables, you need to talk to your database administrator to see if they can speed up searches. If you have no one to help you, you can find plenty of advice on the Web explaining how to accelerate text searches in Databricks.
- **ILIKE** also accepts the underscore as a single wildcard character. **ILIKE** will, however, not apply a case-sensitive search.

Filtering NULLs or nonexistent data

Finding data is easy if the data is present; however, real-world databases can contain missing data elements. Indeed, the marketing director has noticed that the corporate database is missing some clients' postcodes (ZIP codes). So, she has asked for a list of all customers without this vital information.

Fortunately, SQL can handle empty data fields easily. So, you use the following short piece of SQL to deliver the report that will make the man from the marketing department very happy:

```
SELECT   CustomerName, PostCode

FROM     allsales

WHERE    PostCode IS NULL;
```

Running this query will return the output shown in *Figure 3.15*:

	CustomerName	PostCode
1	WunderKar	null
2	Casseroles Chromes	null
3	M. Pierre Dubois	null
4	Sondra Horowitz	null
5	Vive La Vitesse	null
6	M. Pierre Dubois	null
7	La Bagnole de Luxe	null

***Figure 3.15:** Finding NULL fields*

How does it work

Nonexistent data is handled in specific ways in SQL because empty fields are considered special. Indeed, any missing or empty data element is even given a particular name, called a **NULL** value by SQL.

We must be up-front and admit that dealing with **NULL** values can get tricky. So, rather than explaining everything you need to know about them in one fell swoop, we prefer to introduce the techniques you will need to know as required during this book.

For now, you need to know that you can filter on **NULL** values using the IS keyword followed by the word **NULL**. This will allow you to isolate data on nonexistent elements.

To begin your acquaintance with NULLs, you should take note of the following points:

- Although Databricks notebooks display the word **NULL** in the query output, this indicates that the field is blank. The field itself contains nothing at all and certainly not the word **NULL**.
- If you need to filter on records that contain data-any data-in a specific field, you can use SQL like the following:

  ```
  SELECT   CustomerName, PostCode
  FROM     allsales
  WHERE    PostCode IS NOT NULL;
  ```

  As you can see, any nonempty elements can be displayed by negating the **IS NULL** command and instead writing **IS NOT NULL**.
- As SQL uses the equal operator for other filters, you could be tempted to write code like the following:

  ```
  WHERE    PostCode = NULL
  ```

However, you need to be aware that this will not work correctly, and it will always return a blank record set. So, you could be lured into a false sense of security and believe there are no empty items in a dataset when this is far from the case.

- **NULL** really does mean an empty field. SQL is very two finicky about this. If users have entered spaces or even a couple of single quotes (which are invisible to the eye but mean that the field is not strictly empty), then **IS NULL** will not catch these fields.
- As an alternative to writing **IS NULL**, you can also use the **ISNULL()** function like the following:

```
SELECT   CustomerName
FROM     allsales
WHERE    ISNULL(PostCode);
```

- As an alternative to writing **IS NOT NULL**, you can also use the **ISNOTNULL()** function like the following:

```
SELECT   CustomerName
FROM     allsales
WHERE    ISNOTNULL(PostCode);
```

- To find fields containing a space, you can use SQL like the following (using single or double quotes):

```
WHERE    PostCode = ' '
```

- To find fields containing a blank (an empty string), you can use SQL like the following (using single or double quotes):

```
WHERE    PostCode = ''
```

Searching using regular expressions

The marketing director has come up with a final challenge for you. She wants to look for all customers whose name begins with **Pe** and ends with **g**.

Fortunately, you know that Databricks can apply regular expressions when filtering data, and you write the following piece of SQL to produce the result shown in *Figure 3.16*:

```
SELECT   CustomerName
FROM     allsales
WHERE    CustomerName REGEXP '^Pe.*g$';
```

	CustomerName
1	Pete Spring

***Figure 3.16**: Using regular expressions to filter data*

How does it work

Sometimes you may need to apply quite complex filters to the data in a table. You could be looking for e-mails that do not match a valid e-mail format or social security numbers that are not correct, for instance.

In cases like these, Databricks can help you by using regular expressions in the `WHERE` clause of an SQL query. Regular expressions are a text filtering and verification technique that has been around for a very long time and is used in many different programming languages, databases, and applications.

Regular expressions are a vast subject which can be extremely complex. So, what we will be doing here is to introduce you to one of the ways that you can use regular expressions in Databricks. If you need to study regular expressions in depth, we suggest that you look at one of the many excellent Web or print resources that can explain this technique in detail.

Anyway, in this example, we use the following approach:

- **First**: In the `WHERE` clause, enter the field to which you want to apply a regular expression.
- **Second**: Enter the `REGEXP` keyword.
- **Finally**: Enter the regular expression pattern in quotes.

Tricks and traps

You need to know the following points when using regular expressions in Databricks:

- Regular expressions can be combined with other filtering techniques in the `WHERE` clause.
- You can enclose the regular expression pattern in either single or double quotes.
- Regular expression patterns can be fiendishly complex. As even a cursory overview of regular expressions could take several chapters.

Conclusion

This chapter took you much further into the world of SQL filtering. You saw how to apply either/or filters and define multiple cumulative conditions using the data from different fields in a SQL query. Moreover, you also saw how to apply more complex logic to force Databricks to apply certain conditions but not others or to combine conditions to deliver the result you wanted. Finally, after learning how to conduct fuzzy searches using wildcards or regular expressions, you learned that you could apply filter conditions to certain field parts and even filter on nonexistent (or `NULL`) data.

Core knowledge learned in this chapter

These are the keywords that you saw in this chapter:

Concept	Description
`AND`	This logical operator forces a filter to meet two conditions if a record is to be displayed in the output.
`OR`	This logical operator allows a filter to let data through to the result if either filter condition is met.
`NOT`	The logical operator reverses the logic of a filter.
`LIKE`	This keyword lets you look for the partial contents of a column when filtering records, and it is case-sensitive.
`ILIKE`	This keyword lets you look for the partial contents of a column when filtering records without case sensitivity.
`SOME`	This keyword is used with `LIKE` or `ILIKE` to allow multiple wildcard patterns in a `WHERE` clause.
`%`	This operator is used with the `LIKE` keyword to filter the partial contents of a column and can represent any characters—or none.
`_`	This operator is used with the `LIKE` keyword to filter the partial contents of a column, and it represents any single character.
`<>`	This operator excludes an element from a query.
`!=`	This operator excludes an element from a query.
`IS NOT NULL`	This operator finds only `NULL` (blank or empty) values.
`ISNOTNULL()`	This function finds only `NULL` (blank or empty) values.
`IS NULL`	This operator finds only values that are not `NULL` (blank or empty).
`ISNULL()`	This function finds only values that are not `NULL` (blank or empty).
`REGEXP`	This keyword applies a regular expression search to filter output data.

CHAPTER 4
Simple Calculations

Introduction

SQL is not limited to merely finding and filtering data. It can also carry out calculations that range from elementary math to relatively advanced statistical operations. An essential aspect of writing SQL queries is learning to apply math to the core data to deliver increased insight and analysis.

Structure

In this chapter, we will cover the following topics:

- Doing simple math
- Examining data types in SQL tables and views
- Isolating sections of formulas when applying math
- Calculating ratios
- Increasing values by a defined percentage
- Ordering the output of calculations
- Handling missing data
- Filtering on a calculation

- Using complex calculated filters
- Operator precedence

Objectives

This chapter will show you how to perform simple math on the numeric data in Databricks data tables. Once you have mastered the basics, you should be able to build on this knowledge to enhance your SQL queries to deliver all kinds of numerical analysis.

More specifically, you will see how to:

- Perform basic arithmetic.
- Create formulas that force Databricks to perform calculations in the right order.
- Identify numeric fields in tables.
- Handle missing (or **NULL**) numeric data.
- Use calculations to filter data.

None of this is difficult, so now is the time to learn to use SQL to practice your math.

Doing simple math

The finance director is fuming. He cannot find a spreadsheet that tells him the exact cost of every car sold, including any repairs, parts, and transport costs. Inevitably this becomes something that you must deal with. So, let us see how to calculate the total cost of each vehicle sold. A quick look at the **AllSales** table shows that four columns itemize cost elements, the purchase cost of the vehicle, and the cost of repairs, parts, and transport. The following code snippet shows how you can add them together to produce the cost of sales on the fly in SQL:

```
SELECT   MakeName, ModelName
         , Cost + RepairsCost + PartsCost + TransportInCost AS TotalCost
FROM     allsales;
```

Executing this code returns the output shown in *Figure 4.1*:

	MakeName	ModelName	TotalCost
1	Ferrari	Testarossa	56425
2	Ferrari	355	185650
3	Porsche	911	16410
4	Porsche	924	10600
5	Porsche	944	17970
6	Aston Martin	DB4	25000

Figure 4.1: Adding up the data from several columns

How does it work

This code snippet takes the **`allsales`** table as the basis of the information you need to analyze the sales data.

As you can see, adding up the data in a set of columns is as simple as entering the columns as part of a **`SELECT`** clause with a plus (+) operator between each column name. The key element is that all the columns must contain numeric data.

So, although Databricks is a kind of database, it can perform various calculations. These range from the elementary to the complex. Although the math you used to determine the cost of sales is not particularly demanding, it is a useful introduction to basic calculations you can apply to your data using SQL.

Tricks and traps

As we introduce a new concept in SQL, there are perhaps inevitably a few key points to retain when carrying out elementary calculations:

- As a matter of principle, we have added an alias to the calculated column that is returned to avoid it using the actual SQL code as the column name, as it would if you did not give it an alias. Removing the alias gives output as shown in *Figure 4.2*:

	MakeName	ModelName	(((Cost + RepairsCost) + PartsCost) + TransportInCost)
1	Ferrari	Testarossa	56425
2	Ferrari	355	185650
3	Porsche	911	16410
4	Porsche	924	10600
5	Porsche	944	17970

Figure 4.2: Not aliasing calculated columns

- Calculations in Databricks are like carrying out arithmetical operations in Excel (or any other spreadsheet). In SQL, you define the calculation once for a column or a set of columns rather than for a cell reference. It will be applied to every row in the query output without you having to copy the formula down over hundreds of rows as you would have to in a spreadsheet.
- Remember to place commas at the fields' start or end when writing your SQL. You can add them to the end or the start of lines; it is all the same as SQL. This is why the second line of this example begins with a comma (and this is why there is no comma at the end of the first line).

Examining data types in SQL tables and views

When using SQL to carry out calculations, it is fundamental that the columns you reference contain numbers and not strings of characters. It takes only a single column in a calculation to contain some text for the calculation not to work for that row and for a **`NULL`** to be output instead of the expected result.

You need to be careful when choosing the columns you can and cannot use when performing calculations in SQL. Fortunately, data tables contain reliable indications of which columns can only store numbers. Columns like this are known as having numeric data types. Generally, database designers will have used them to contain numeric data that you can use in your calculations.

In *Chapter 1: Basic SQL Queries*, you saw how to discover the fields (or columns, if you prefer) a table or a view contains. This technique has the added advantage of letting you see the data type of each column so that you can build your calculations safely and reliably.

You saw that the columns you used in the query in the previous section (**`Cost`**, **`RepairsCost`**, **`PartsCost`**, **`TransportInCost`**, **`SalePrice`**, and **`LineItemDiscount`**) are all one of the two following data types:

- **`Int`**
- **`Double`**

This is good news because these are two of Databricks's numeric data types. The following are other numeric data types:

- **`Float`**
- **`Decimal`**
- **`Tinyint`**

- **Smallint**
- **Bigint**

If the columns you want to use in a calculation are any of these data types, your calculation should not give you a **NULL** result for the record.

There are, inevitably, many other Databricks data types. Still, we prefer to introduce them as needed rather than overwhelm you with technical details this early in your SQL querying career.

Isolating sections of formulas when applying math

Now let us return to the finance director's analysis of costs. He was pleased with your cost of sales calculation; however, he wants you to subtract this from the sale price to give the net margin. The piece of code that follows delivers exactly what he is looking for. As you can see, it groups certain elements inside parentheses to isolate parts of the formula so that they are calculated independently of the rest:

```
SELECT   MakeName, ModelName
         ,SalePrice - (Cost + RepairsCost + PartsCost + TransportInCost)
         AS GrossMargin
FROM     SalesByCountry;
```

If you run this code, you should get the output in *Figure 4.3*:

	MakeName	ModelName	GrossMargin
1	Ferrari	Testarossa	8575
2	Ferrari	355	34350
3	Porsche	911	3090
4	Porsche	924	900
5	Porsche	944	1980
6	Aston Martin	DB4	4500

Figure 4.3: *Nesting calculations to guarantee precedence in SQL math*

How does it work

Even simple arithmetic may require that certain calculation elements be worked out before others. Adding parentheses around the cost elements guarantees that the fields containing the vehicle costs will be added together before subtracting the resulting figure from the sales price. We realize that this may seem obvious and that you are probably used to creating calculations like this in Excel. However, from the start, we prefer to clarify that all calculations in Databricks can be nested in parentheses like this to force an order of precedence in your arithmetic. This way, certain parts of the calculation are carried out before others.

Tricks and traps

As simple as the math is, the following are a couple of key points to note:

- Nesting fields inside parentheses to force the order of calculations is always safer than trusting a computer to get things right every time. Additionally, adding parentheses to nest calculation elements can help you clarify your logic, especially when you return to it weeks or months later.
- Any calculation should have a meaningful alias. This, too, can help you better understand the logic when you look at it again in days to come.

Calculating ratios

The finance director is increasingly excited that SQL can apply the math he needs for his analyses. So, now he wants you to give him a list containing the cost-to-sales ratio (also known as the cost of goods sold ratio or the cost of sales to revenue ratio). As this is quite simply the gross profit (that you calculated in the previous section) divided by the sale price, the SQL for this is as follows:

```
SELECT   MakeName, InvoiceNumber,

         (SalePrice - (Cost + RepairsCost + PartsCost

          + TransportInCost))

          / SalePrice AS RatioOfCostsToSales

FROM     AllSales;
```

When you run this code, Databricks gives you the output as shown in *Figure 4.4*:

	MakeName	InvoiceNumber	RatioOfCostsToSales
1	Ferrari	GBPGB001	0.131923076923077692
2	Ferrari	GBPGB002	0.156136363636363
3	Porsche	GBPGB003	0.1584615384615384 6
4	Porsche	EURDE004	0.0782608695652174
5	Porsche	EURFR005	0.0992481203007518 8
6	Aston Martin	GBPGB006	0.152542372881355 94
7	Aston Martin	GBPGB007	0.1080808080808080 8

Figure 4.4: *Calculating a ratio*

How does it work

As you have already seen addition and subtraction, now is a good time to move on to simple division in SQL. This formula is a three-step process.

- **First**: It adds up the total costs per vehicle (the field names nested inside the inner parentheses).
- **Second**: It subtracts the cost of sales from the sale price. This calculation is contained in the outer parentheses and is the gross margin.
- **Finally**: It divides the gross margin by the sale price to return the cost ratio per vehicle.

The result is that you see the ratio of costs to sale for every vehicle sold. For now, the result has no formatting applied, and consequently, it looks much as it probably would in a spreadsheet. We fully realize that raw data can be hard to read. However, we will look at formatting output in *Chapter 10: Using Multiple Tables When Querying Data* and *Chapter 21, Complex Data Output,* so that you can concentrate on the calculation techniques for the moment.

Increasing values by a defined percentage

To finish your tour of elementary math in SQL, let us imagine that the sales director wants to test the margin improvement if you increased the sale prices by 5% but kept the costs the same. The SQL formula is shown as follows:

```
SELECT (SalePrice * 1.05)

       - (Cost + RepairsCost + PartsCost + TransportInCost)

       AS ImprovedSalesMargins

FROM   SalesByCountry;
```

When you execute this code, you should get something like the result shown in *Figure 4.5*:

	ImprovedSalesMargins
1	11825.00
2	45350.00
3	4065.00
4	1475.00
5	2977.50
6	5975.00

***Figure 4.5**: "What if" calculations in SQL*

How does it work

This formula extends the gross margin calculation you created earlier and multiplies the sale price by 5%. It is a what-if projection. In practice (and just as you would in a spreadsheet), this means the following:

- **First**: Take the existing formula and add the asterisk (*****) as the multiplication operator after the **`SalePrice`** field.
- **Second**: Type in 1.05 to *hard-code* the 5% increase (100% and 5%, literally).
- **Third**: Nest this projected sale price calculation in parentheses to ensure that it is calculated correctly—and separately—from the rest of the formula.
- **Finally**: The cost elements are added together, and these fields are also enclosed in parentheses to guarantee that this calculation is carried out independently of the remainder of the formula. Then the total cost is subtracted from the increased sale price to increase the margin.

This formula teaches you to mix static values and fields in SQL formulas. To extend the spreadsheet analogy we have been using in this chapter, you can mix references and values in a formula in SQL just as you can in Excel.

Ordering the output of calculations

Knowing even the most basic math in SQL can help you unlock real insights. For example, let us see how using the knowledge and SQL techniques you have seen in this chapter can produce the list of the 50 most profitable sales in percentage. The following is the SQL code to deliver this:

```
SELECT     MakeName
           ,(SalePrice - (Cost + RepairsCost + PartsCost
             + TransportInCost))
           / SalePrice AS Profitability
FROM       SalesByCountry
ORDER BY   Profitability DESC
LIMIT 50;
```

Executing this code should return the data shown in *Figure 4.6* (and if you scroll through the output, you will see that it contains only 50 records):

	MakeName	Profitability
1	Aston Martin	0.18701470199841536
2	Lamborghini	0.183921568627451
3	Lamborghini	0.18319148936170213
4	Ferrari	0.18178082191780823
5	Bugatti	0.18164179104477612
6	Ferrari	0.1814

***Figure 4.6:** Sorting on a calculated column*

How does it work

This formula combines many techniques you have seen in this chapter and previous chapters.

- **First**: It calculates the ratio of costs to sales as described previously.
- **Second**: It orders the output by this ratio (which you have aliased, meaning you can now use the alias to sort the results).

- **Third**: It finishes by limiting the number of rows returned to 50 using the `LIMIT` keyword.
- **Finally**: The **`ORDER BY`** keyword—with **`DESC`** to specify that the sort is from greatest to smallest figure—presents the data in descending order, and the 50 records are output once the sort order has been applied.

The useful trick here is to mix the `LIMIT` and **`ORDER BY`** keywords. As you request that the data be output from the most profitable to the least profitable sale, the top 50 will be the 50 most profitable sales.

In this example, we have deliberately chosen not to display all the 50 records the query returns. However, you can scroll through the result set in the query window to check that only 50 records are displayed.

Tricks and traps

There is one major point to note when you are sorting the result of a calculation:

- When sorting the output in a query, you can sort on the column alias you have applied to a calculation. If you do not apply an alias, you must repeat the calculation in the **`ORDER BY`** clause to sort on the calculation. In other words, if you had not specified that the calculated column was named profitability, then you would have had to create an **`ORDER BY`** clause like the following:

```
ORDER BY (SalePrice - (Cost + RepairsCost + PartsCost
           + TransportInCost))
           / SalePrice DESC
```

NULLs

The calculations you tried on the sample database worked smoothly. However, this may not be true in the real world of less-than-perfect data. This is because we have, up until now, glossed over a database concept that lies in wait to trap the unwary. This potential problem is called NULL handling.

Fields (columns if you prefer) can contain no data at all in some cases. For instance, the **`RepairsCost`** column could be nothing for a particular vehicle. In this case, the value contained in the data table would be **`NULL`**. In database terms, this means *I don't know what this value is*. It is a techie way of saying *nothing*.

It simply means there is no corresponding value and that **`NULL`** will be output for this column if you write a query that selects this record.

However, things get complicated if you try to calculate on a record where one or more of the numeric values you use contains a **NULL**. If this is the case, then the entire calculation will return **NULL**. In effect, all the calculation is invalid, and nothing at all is calculated. It is almost as if a **NULL** has a contagious effect that infects the entire calculation that contains it.

This can be extremely troublesome in practice, as it is probably not what you expect. Indeed, suppose you are used to spreadsheet calculations where an empty cell makes virtually no difference (unless you try to divide a value by it). In that case, this result probably comes as a most unwelcome surprise.

Handling missing data

The sales director has lost her sunny optimism, and she has stormed over to your desk and asked how it can be possible that a top-of-the-range sports car can cost nothing. To prove her point, she scrolls down the output from the query you wrote to calculate gross margin (in the second SQL calculation at the start of this chapter) and points at the records, as shown in *Figure 4.7*:

340	Aston Martin	Virage	18800
341	Aston Martin	DB9	16910
342	Aston Martin	DB6	9091
343	Trabant	600	-1082
344	Triumph	TR5	900
345	Alfa Romeo	Giulietta	390
346	Citroen	Rosalie	-300
347	Reliant	Robin	-1210
348	Ferrari	Daytona	null

Missing Value

Figure 4.7: *The effect of NULLs on a calculation*

Unfortunately, this is the effect that a **NULL** has produced in a calculation. One car does not have a repair cost. However, instead of ignoring this or treating it as a zero, SQL invalidates the whole calculation for that record.

There is a safeguard that you can apply to your calculations to prevent NULLs from distorting the results you were expecting. The solution involves wrapping numeric fields inside the SQL **NVL()** function to convert any **NULL** values in a field to another value that you specify. When handling NULLs in calculations, this nearly always means replacing the **NULL** with a zero.

To show you how this can be done, here is the SQL from the previous section using the **NVL()** function to prevent errors from creeping into the calculation this time:

```
SELECT   MakeName, ModelName
         ,Cost + RepairsCost + NVL(PartsCost, 0)  + TransportInCost
         AS TotalCost
FROM     allsales;
```

This code now returns the record as shown in *Figure 4.8*:

348	Ferrari	Daytona	121900

***Figure 4.8:** Using the NVL() function*

How does it work

This query still uses the **`allsales`** table. It is almost identical to the query used at the start of this chapter; the only difference is that the **`PartsCost`** field (that contains **`NULL`** values) is wrapped in the **`NVL()`** function so that any NULLs will be converted to zeros. Thus, the calculation will work correctly for every record (as zero does not affect an arithmetical calculation).

You have seen a few functions in previous chapters. The **`NVL()`** function works like the functions you have already met, with one major difference. The **`NVL()`** function needs you to place two elements inside the parentheses.

- **A field or value**: In this case, it is the numeric field that can contain NULLs.
- **A replacement value**: In this case, it is a 0 (zero).

When you enclose the **`PartsCost`** field inside the **`NVL()`** function, you say, *If the* **`PartsCost`** *field contains a* **`NULL`**, *then use a zero instead.* This way, the calculation will add a zero to the costs you are adding up instead of making the calculation fail for any record with a **`NULL`** in the PartsCost field.

NOTE: You can, of course, wrap any numeric field used in a calculation in the `NVL()` function as a simple precaution against Databricks returning a `NULL` value rather than the result that you were expecting.

Tricks and traps

As you will be using more SQL functions in this chapter, you need to be aware of a few core principles that underlie their use are as follows:

- The elements inside the parentheses of any function are called parameters that you pass into the function. The first parameter that the **`NVL()`** function requires is the field to which it must be applied, and the second parameter (after the comma) is the number to apply if the field is **NULL**.

- In most cases, the parameters you use in functions are compulsory. You will all get an error message if you do not add a parameter.
- Geeks call using a parameter in a function like this *parameter passing*.

Filtering on a calculation

It is hard to argue that there is no more fundamental business metric than profitability. So, it will come as no surprise to learn that Prestige Cars Ltd.'s CEO wants to know the net profit on sales. She particularly wants to see a list of sales for all vehicles making a profit of more than £5,000.00. This SQL snippet shows you how to keep her happy:

```
SELECT     DISTINCT MakeName, ModelName, SalePrice
FROM       allsales
WHERE      SalePrice -
             (Cost + RepairsCost + NVL(PartsCost, 0)
              + TransportInCost) > 5000;
```

If you execute this piece of SQL, you will see data like the output as shown in *Figure 4.9*:

	MakeName	ModelName	SalePrice
1	Porsche	911	33600
2	Lamborghini	Diabolo	255000
3	Delorean	DMC 12	99500
4	Ferrari	Mondial	155000
5	Porsche	959	66500
6	Ferrari	F40	250000

***Figure 4.9:** Filtering on a calculation*

How does it work

SQL can also use calculations in **WHERE** clauses to filter data. As our data does not contain the figure for the net profit, we must calculate this metric on the fly if we want to use it as a filter criterion.

This query shows how to use calculated data to filter the data returned by a SQL query. The SQL calculates the net profit by adding all the costs and then deducting this figure from the sale price. If the result exceeds 5,000, then the record is displayed.

Tricks and traps

The one point you need to take away from this example is as follows:

- You do not have to add the calculation used in a **WHERE** clause to a **SELECT** clause. However, it can be useful to start by adding the calculation to the output so that you can verify the result.

Using complex calculated filters

It is late in the day, and you are thinking of heading home. Just as your eyes drift toward the door, the sales director rushes with a seemingly unending request for data. She wants a list of all cars made, and models sold where the profit exceeds £5,000.00, the car is red, and the discount is greater than or equal to £1,000.00, or the repairs cost and the parts cost is greater than £500.00.

This query is an extension of the code used in the previous example. So, you can build on your previous experience and discover that even seemingly complex requests often require nothing more than a well-thought-out **WHERE** clause to deliver the required result. The code you need is given as follows:

```
SELECT     DISTINCT MakeName, ModelName
FROM       allsales
WHERE      (Color = 'Red' AND LineItemDiscount >= 1000
           AND (SalePrice - (Cost + RepairsCost + PartsCost
                            + TransportInCost)) > 5000)
        OR (PartsCost > 500 AND RepairsCost > 500);
```

Running this query should show something like *Figure 4.10*:

	MakeName	ModelName
1	Bentley	Mulsanne
2	Rolls Royce	Ghost
3	Ferrari	F50
4	Bugatti	57C
5	Jaguar	Mark V
6	Lamborghini	400GT

***Figure 4.10:** A complex query filtering on several fields and a calculation*

How does it work

This query applies the `WHERE` clause to the `allSales` table to filter records where:

- `Either`: The color of the vehicle is red, the discount is greater than £1,000.00, and the net profit is over £5,000.00
- `Or`: The parts and repair cost is greater than £500.00

As you can see, this query focuses on the `WHERE` clause. Inside this clause, it is worth paying particular attention to the parentheses that are used. The filters on either side of the `OR` operator are enclosed in parentheses. This means all the conditions inside the parentheses must be true for the filter to be successful. Consequently, the parts cost must be more than 500, as must the repair cost for a sale to make the grade. Alternatively, all three conditions for the other filter (red, the discount of 1,000 or more, and profit of at least 5,000) must be met for the record to make it through to the final output.

The only potentially tricky aspect of this query is the way you must nest criteria inside parentheses to obtain the result you are looking for. This can take some practice, but the effort is well worth it. Of course, if you have any experience writing formulas using Microsoft Excel or other databases, you are probably already used to this concept. Breaking filter requirements into logical, isolated steps is a key part of learning to write efficient SQL.

Tricks and traps

Complex `WHERE` clauses can become easier to understand and simpler to write if you remember the following points:

- When you must produce complex `WHERE` clauses, it may help to begin by isolating the *levels* of the logic over several lines, as you can see in *Figure 4.11:*

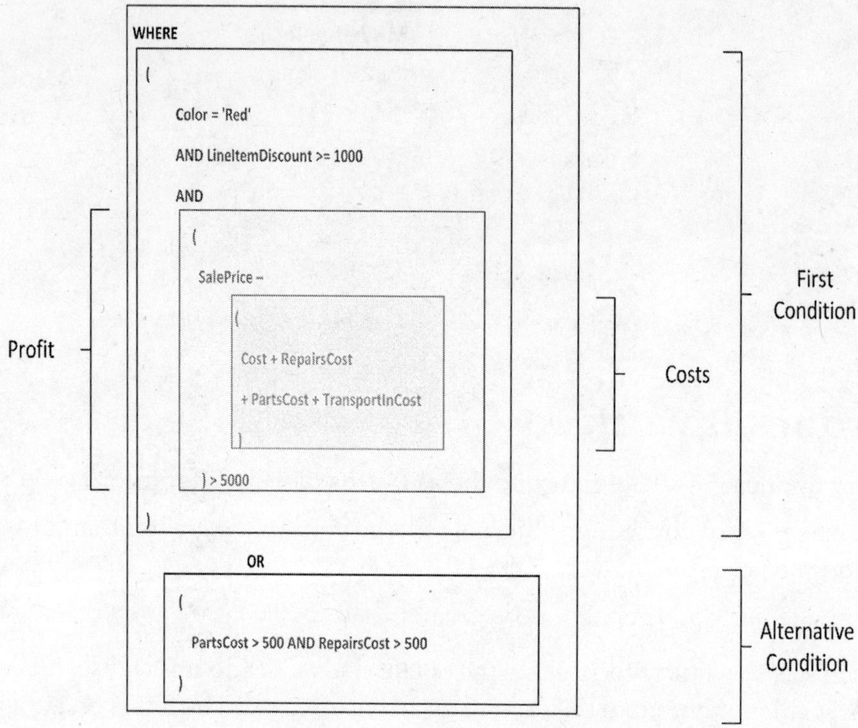

Figure 4.11: Nesting parentheses

- Even a complicated query is a series of parts you assemble to apply a criteria-based filter. Our advice when faced with complex queries is to break them down into their constituent elements and understand what is required before writing SQL code.
- It can help if you first try to write out the filter as *pseudo-code*, that is, more as a description of the required logic than an exact and accurate piece of SQL. This can help you to understand the underlying requirements of the filter and how to:
    - Create all the individual comparison elements that make up the whole.
    - Group the filter elements so that they respect the final logic that is required.
- In this query, we chose not to add the fields used in the WHERE clause to the query output. You can add them to check that the filter works if you desire.

Operator precedence

When adding calculations, you need to be aware that there is a strict order of precedence for mathematical operators. These are outlined in *Table 4.1*:

Operator	Level of precedence
* (Multiplication), / (Division), % (Modulo)	1
+ (Positive), - (Negative), + (Addition), + (Concatenation), - (Subtraction)	2
=, >, <, >=, <=, <>, !=, !>, !< (Comparison operators)	3

***Table 4.1**: Operator precedence*

Conclusion

In this chapter, you saw how SQL can carry out simple arithmetic. You learned how to perform basic math using the data in fields and values you add to your code to perform calculations across multiple rows and columns in a few lines of code. You also saw how to pre-empt errors when the source data contains NULLs or when attempting to divide by zero in a calculation.

You have already made vast strides toward the basic analysis of Databricks data. With this knowledge safely acquired, it is time to move on to the next step aggregating data to deliver totals, subtotals, and other simple calculations. This is what you will be looking at in the next chapter.

Core knowledge learned in this chapter

These are the fundamental keywords you have learned to use in this chapter:

Concept	Description
`+`	This is the arithmetical addition symbol; it adds two elements (fields or values).
`-`	This is the arithmetical subtraction symbol; it subtracts two elements (fields or values).
`*`	This is the arithmetical multiplication symbol; it multiplies two elements (fields or values).
`/`	This is the arithmetical division symbol; it divides two elements (fields or values).
`NVL()`	This converts `NULL` (or empty) values into a value that can be used in your calculations.
`Parentheses`	Parentheses are used in calculations to force certain parts of a formula to be calculated before others.

CHAPTER 5
Aggregating Output

Introduction

Analyzing data consists of much more than just selecting records from a database. There is no denying that you must start by choosing the right columns from the suitable tables, joining the tables correctly, and filtering the data accurately. However, SQL starts to deliver true insights when you begin to aggregate data so that you can see the high-level figures that drive your business.

Structure

In this chapter, we will cover the following topics:

- Calculating table totals
- Using calculated aggregations
- Using grouped aggregations
- Using multiple levels of grouping
- Calculating averages
- Counting grouped elements
- Counting unique elements

- Displaying upper and lower numeric thresholds
- Aggregating across multiple columns
- Aggregating across columns and rows
- Filtering groups
- Filtering on aggregated results
- Selecting data based on aggregated results as well as specific filter criteria
- Sorting by aggregated results
- Finding elements where every Boolean value is true

Objectives

It is worth looking at how SQL can aggregate metrics. This is because it is particularly good at returning totals, averages, and many analytical insights with little time and effort. In this chapter, you will start to explore the basic techniques you can use to apply aggregations to your data and deliver insight straight from the database. More specifically, you will learn how to:

- Generate grand totals
- Group elements with aggregate totals
- Count categories of elements
- Find maximum and minimum values
- Calculate averages
- Select data using aggregated results
- Filter data on aggregated values

So, without further ado, it is time to discover how SQL can aggregate data in many ways at multiple levels to deliver the analysis you need.

Calculating table totals

To begin with (and you guessed it, following a call from the finance director), suppose that you want to calculate the total cost of all the vehicles that Prestige Cars Ltd has ever stocked. The SQL code looks like the following:

```
SELECT      SUM(Cost) AS TotalCost

FROM        allsales;
```

Running this query gives the results shown in *Figure 5.1*:

	TotalCost
1	17574360

Figure 5.1: *Using the SUM() function to calculate the total for a field*

How does it work

Adding up a column of figures is easy to do in SQL. You can use the **`SUM()`** function on any numeric field in a table to get the total of the values in the column. In this example, the **`SUM()`** function was applied to the cost field stock table. The result is simply the total sum of all the available figures in the cost field (or column, if you prefer) of the stock table. You did wrap up the name of the field you wanted to add inside the parentheses that are part of the **`SUM`** function. This simple modification was all that Databricks needed to return the total rather than the detail for each record.

Tricks and traps

As this is the first time you have used a function to aggregate data, you need to be aware of the following essential points:

- **`SUM()`** is what is known as an aggregation function. It returns a single value for a calculation across a set of values (a field in this case). This makes it different from the functions you have seen in this book. Until now, any function was applied to each record in a table. Functions like **`SUM()`** do not work at such a detailed level and cannot show the detail of each row, and they exist only to provide a high-level aggregation of values.
- The **`SUM()`** function requires numeric values to work. If you try calculating the total of a text field, Databricks will return an error message.
- Providing an alias for aggregation functions is always a good idea because SQL will never display a name for an aggregated column unless you provide one. Instead, it will add the column heading **`SUM(Cost)`**.

Using calculated aggregations

Muttering that he is too busy to copy formulas down over hundreds of records in a spreadsheet, the finance director has tasked you to calculate the aggregate sales, cost, and gross profit for all vehicles sold. Fortunately, you can use multiple aggregate expressions in the same query. The following is the SQL statement that does this:

```
SELECT        SUM(Cost) AS TotalCost
             ,SUM(SalePrice) AS TotalSales
             ,SUM(SalePrice) - SUM(Cost) AS GrossProfit
FROM         allsales;
```

Executing this query gives the results displayed in *Figure 5.2*:

	TotalCost	TotalSales	GrossProfit
1	17574360	21977950	4403590

***Figure 5.2:** Calculating the total for several fields using SUM()*

How does it work

This code snippet shows you that you can return the total for any numeric field from any table in a query. As a final touch, this code calculates aggregations by subtracting the total purchase cost from the total sale price.

As the SQL makes clear, you can apply aggregation functions such as `SUM()` to several columns and then apply calculations to the aggregated value just as you did to non-aggregate fields in the previous chapter.

Tricks and traps

You will like a couple of cool features when using aggregation functions. So, be aware of the following:

- One great feature of the `SUM()` function (which applies to all the aggregation functions you will meet in this chapter) is that it handles `NULL` values without affecting the result. If you remember, a `NULL` in a calculation will make the result `NULL` too. However, any number of NULLs in a column that you aggregate using `SUM()` will not cause any difficulties, unlike when applying normal SQL math.
- It is important to wrap each numeric column inside its `SUM` function when calculating aggregated values. In theory, you could have expressed the calculation as follows:

  ```
  SUM(SalePrice - Cost)
  ```

  If you try, the preceding code may appear to work at first sight. However, it is not guaranteed to work in all circumstances. This is because `NULL` values in a column are handled without difficulty by the `SUM()` function only if *each column* is wrapped inside its `SUM()`. So, this approach could return an erroneous result if a field has `NULL` values.

- If you need the output from a calculation more than once, you must repeat the calculation each time. You cannot refer to a calculation as you can in a spreadsheet.

Using grouped aggregations

The sales manager has just emailed you a simple request for data. She wants the aggregate cost for each model of car. The next piece of SQL shows you just how easy this is to segment your data this way with SQL:

```
SELECT     ModelName, SUM(Cost) AS TotalCost
FROM       allsales
GROUP BY   ModelName;
```

If you run this query, you should see the results as shown in *Figure 5.3*:

	ModelName	TotalCost
1	944	127640
2	205	3920
3	400GT	116000
4	Silver Seraph	287560
5	Spider	38480
6	Plus 4	14800
7	Alpina	17200
8	Lichfield	24080
9	Giulietta	73752
10	924	112032

Figure 5.3: Grouping aggregated results using **GROUP BY**

How does it work

The previous two examples *Using calculated aggregations* and *Using grouped aggregations*, showed you that SQL could calculate the total for a column in one or more tables easily and quickly. In practice, however, you will probably want to analyze results broken down into separate categories. In this query, you joined the model and stock tables (so that you could see the model's name, not just a code) and output the model's name and the total cost. Then you added a new keyword—**GROUP BY**—to the end of the SQL statement. Simply adding another field that is not being aggregated (usually a text field) to the **GROUP BY** clause is enough for Databricks to calculate the total for each element in the field that is *not* wrapped in an aggregate function.

It is normal to add the field you are grouping to the **SELECT** statement to see which figure corresponds to which aggregated element.

Tricks and traps

There is only one potential trap for the unwary in code that groups data.

- Any nonaggregate fields in the **SELECT** clause (the ones that are not enclosed in aggregation functions such as **SUM**) must be repeated in the **GROUP BY** clause. If you do not do this, then Databricks will complain by showing an error message such as the one shown in *Figure 5.4*:

```
Error in SQL statement: AnalysisException: grouping expressions sequence is empty, and 'spark_catalog.default.allsales.ModelName' is not an agg
regate function. Wrap '(sum(spark_catalog.default.allsales.Cost) AS TotalCost)' in windowing function(s) or wrap 'spark_catalog.default.allsale
s.ModelName' in first() (or first_value) if you don't care which value you get.;
Aggregate [ModelName#1152, sum(Cost#1153) AS TotalCost#2338L]
+- SubqueryAlias spark_catalog.default.allsales
   +- Relation spark_catalog.default.allsales[CountryName#1150,MakeName#1151,ModelName#1152,Cost#1153,RepairsCost#1154,PartsCost#1155,Transport
InCost#1156,Color#1157,SalePrice#1158,LineItemDiscount#1159,InvoiceNumber#1160,SaleDate#1161,IsRHD#1162,DateBought#1163,CustomerName#1164,Sales
DetailsID#1165,StockCode#1166,BuyerComments#1167,MakeCountry#1168,TotalSalePrice#1169,Town#1170,PostCode#1171,Country#1172,IsReseller#1173,...
4 more fields] parquet
```

Figure 5.4: Missing **GROUP BY** *error message*

- Fortunately, this is one of the more understandable error messages. It simply tells you to ensure that any fields you output using the **SELECT** clause must be either in the **GROUP BY** clause or wrapped in an aggregation function if they are numeric. The following code, for instance, would produce an error:

  ```
  SELECT ModelName, SUM(Cost) AS TotalCost FROM allsales
  ```

Using multiple levels of grouping

Fired up by the analysis you have provided so far, the finance director wants you to dig deeper into the data and compare the total purchase cost for every make and model of vehicle sold. This is easier than you think, as the following code illustrates:

```
SELECT     MakeName, ModelName, SUM(Cost) AS TotalCost
FROM       allsales
GROUP BY   MakeName, ModelName
ORDER BY   MakeName, ModelName
;
```

Executing this query should return the results in *Figure 5.5*:

	MakeName	ModelName	TotalCost
1	Alfa Romeo	1750	10820
2	Alfa Romeo	Giulia	71756
3	Alfa Romeo	Giulietta	73752
4	Alfa Romeo	Spider	38480
5	Aston Martin	DB2	365152
6	Aston Martin	DB4	225360
7	Aston Martin	DB5	240272

Figure 5.5: *Grouping on multiple fields*

How does it work

This SQL snippet shows that you can extend the grouping principle by adding as many non-aggregated fields as you want to a query. Each field that you add to the `SELECT` clause (and to the `GROUP BY` clause) will entail a deeper level of detail in the output, giving you a hierarchical analysis of your data.

As you can see in the results from the query, the total sales appear for each model by make. So, grouping data on multiple fields creates a hierarchy in the output. This hierarchy corresponds to the order in which the fields are entered in the `GROUP BY` clause. In other words, the first field (`MakeName`) is the topmost level in the hierarchy, and then `ModelName` is the second level.

Tricks and traps

Grouping on multiple fields comes easily with a little practice. Nonetheless, it can help to remember the following:

- It is important to add the fields you are aggregating in a coherent order in both the `SELECT` and `GROUP BY` clauses. This is because your users will perceive the output as a logical hierarchy. In practice, this means starting with the highest level on the left and working down through successive lower levels of data. This is because users probably expect a model to be a subdivision of a make of a car and not the reverse.
- Although you do not have to apply the same order for the fields you use to segment data in the `SELECT` and `GROUP BY` clauses, it is generally best to keep

them identical for the person viewing the data. This is because it can become extremely confusing if you sort the data using one kind of sequence and then display the fields in another. The actual hierarchy is defined by the fields in the **GROUP BY** clause, whatever the sequence of the fields in the **SELECT** clause.

- Once again, adding an alias to any field resulting from an aggregation will avoid a column name that is merely SQL code.
- Do not add aliases in the **GROUP BY** clause; Databricks will only give an error message.

Calculating averages

An essential business metric is the average cost of goods bought. So, it was inevitable that the finance director would want to see the average purchase price of every make and model of car ever bought. Fortunately, SQL makes this kind of calculation easy, as the following piece of code illustrates:

```
SELECT      MakeName, ModelName
            ,AVG(Cost) AS AverageCost
FROM        allsales
GROUP BY    MakeName, ModelName;
```

Running this query should return the results shown in *Figure 5.6*:

	MakeName	ModelName	AverageCost
1	Bentley	Mulsanne	62580
2	Rolls Royce	Ghost	63780
3	Triumph	TR3A	31600
4	BMW	E30	26800
5	Ferrari	F50	202920
6	Bugatti	57C	269600
7	Alfa Romeo	Spider	7696
8	Jaguar	Mark V	23780
9	Lamborghini	400GT	116000
10	Mercedes	280SL	30890.285714285714

Figure 5.6: Calculating the average purchase price using the AVG() function

How does it work

This code snippet introduces another aggregation function **AVG()**. As its name implies, the **AVG()** function calculates the average of the values in a column.

Any required fields that will be used to group the data are added to the **SELECT** and **GROUP BY** clauses. Finally, the **AVG()** function is wrapped around the cost field and added to the **SELECT** clause to calculate the average purchase price of every make and model.

Tricks and traps

One thing may surprise you when grouping and aggregating with Databricks is as follows:

- Although you may see output sorted as expected when using a **GROUP BY** clause as there is no guarantee that this will always be the case. So, to be sure, you should always add an **ORDER BY** clause.

Counting grouped elements

The CEO has stated categorically that any business must be able to see briefly how many items have been sold per product category. In the case of Prestige Cars Ltd., this means visualizing the number of cars sold by make and model. SQL can answer these kinds of questions with consummate ease, as the following SQL snippet shows:

```
SELECT      MakeName, ModelName

            ,COUNT(SalesDetailsID) AS NumberofCarsSold

FROM        allsales

GROUP BY    MakeName, ModelName

ORDER BY    MakeName, ModelName;
```

Running this query should return the results as shown in *Figure 5.7*:

	MakeName	ModelName	NumberofCarsSold
1	Alfa Romeo	1750	2
2	Alfa Romeo	Giulia	8
3	Alfa Romeo	Giulietta	7
4	Alfa Romeo	Spider	5
5	Aston Martin	DB2	8
6	Aston Martin	DB4	7
7	Aston Martin	DB5	6

Figure 5.7: *Counting cars by model using the COUNT() function*

How does it work

The SQL aggregation functions are not limited to adding up columns of numbers, and you can also count the number of records that make up a subset of data. So, this piece of SQL introduces the **COUNT()** aggregation function. As its name implies, it counts the number of rows in a group of records rather than adding up any figures.

The trick in this piece of SQL is to use the same grouping element in the **GROUP BY** clause as in the **SELECT** clause. So, as we have used the make and model fields in the **SELECT** clause, we must do the same in the **GROUP BY** clause.

Tricks and traps

Although the **COUNT()** function works in a virtually identical way to the **SUM()** and **AVG()** functions you have already seen, there are nonetheless a few things to be aware of.

- Sometimes all you want to do is to find the total number of rows in a table. Perhaps you are looking at a large table and want an idea of its size. Should this be the case, then the SQL is extremely simple. Just use the following to return the total number of records in a table:

  ```
  SELECT COUNT(*) FROM Stock
  ```

- You could be tempted to use **COUNT(*)** when analyzing data, but adding the field name that interests you between the parentheses when using the **COUNT()** function is advisable. This is because **COUNT(*)** will count all rows whether they contain the data, and **COUNT(Cost)** will count only the records with a cost figure, and the two results could be different.
- The trick in SQL that counts the number of elements is to use the same grouping elements in the **GROUP BY** clause as in the **SELECT** clause. As we have used the make and model in the **SELECT** clause, we must also use them in the **GROUP BY** clause.
- The **COUNT()** function can be applied to text and numeric fields.

Counting unique elements

There could be occasions when you need to analyze a dataset and deduce the number of specific and individual elements it contains instead of the total number of rows. You discovered this when the sales director appeared at your desk and asked for the number of different countries Prestige Cars has ever sold vehicles to.

Fortunately, SQL makes this kind of high-level investigation easy; it can be done in a couple of lines of code, like in the following code snippet:

```
SELECT  COUNT(DISTINCT CountryName) AS CountriesWithSales

FROM    allsales;
```

Running this query will show the results in *Figure 5.8*:

	CountriesWithSales
1	8

Figure 5.8: *Counting unique values in a list*

How does it work

In this query, you use the **`SalesByCountry`** view you met earlier as the data source. You are using the **`COUNT()`** function to return several records and specify that you want to see the number of records in which the **`CountryName`** field contains data.

However, you have added the **`DISTINCT`** keyword inside the parentheses for the **`COUNT()`** function. Instead of getting the total number of records where there is a country, you are returning the number of unique countries in the **`CountryName`** field.

Displaying upper and lower numeric thresholds

Data analysis is frequently about identifying limits and thresholds. At least, this is what the sales manager seems to think because she wants you to identify the largest and smallest sale prices for each model of car sold. SQL makes it easy to perform analyses of the limits of datasets, as you can see from the following piece of SQL:

```
SELECT       ModelName
             ,MAX(SalePrice) AS TopSalePrice
             ,MIN(SalePrice) AS BottomSalePrice
FROM         allsales
GROUP BY     ModelName;
```

If you execute this query, you will see the results in *Figure 5.9*:

	ModelName	TopSalePrice	BottomSalePrice
1	944	19950	7500
2	205	3950	950
3	400GT	145000	145000
4	Silver Seraph	139500	99950
5	Spider	12500	5650
6	Plus 4	18500	18500

Figure 5.9: *Using the MAX() and MIN() functions to show the maximum and minimum values for a data group*

How does it work

The **FROM** clause in this query ensures that you are looking at the correct table for sales and can access the model names. Then, you use **SELECT** to specify the model's name and the sale price (twice, one for each aggregation function). However, you have applied the **MAX()**, and **MIN()** functions on the **SalePrice** field to calculate the maximum and minimum, respectively. Finally, any non-aggregated fields you placed in the **SELECT** clause are added to the **GROUP BY** clause.

Tricks and traps

As simple as they are, the **MAX()** and **MIN()** functions require a few comments.

- You can extend the principle by adding further fields to the **SELECT** and **GROUP BY** clauses to drill down into a finer level of analytical detail, as you saw previously in the section *Using calculated aggregations*.
- If you apply a series of aggregation functions to the same field, you must repeat the field name for each function used.

Aggregating across multiple columns

Analyzing data can also mean the maximum and minimum values across multiple columns. Imagine, for instance, that the CEO of Prestige Cars wants to discover the biggest (and smallest) value for each sale of either the cost of repairs or transporting vehicles. SQL makes this easy using the **GREATEST()** and **LEAST()** aggregate functions. You can see them in use in the following SQL:

```
SELECT      MakeName, ModelName, SaleDate, InvoiceNumber
           ,RepairsCost, TransportInCost
           ,GREATEST(RepairsCost, TransportInCost) AS GreatestCost
           ,LEAST(RepairsCost, TransportInCost) AS LeastCost
FROM        allsales;
```

This piece of SQL gives the result that you can see in *Figure 5.10*:

	MakeName	ModelName	SaleDate	InvoiceNumber	RepairsCost	TransportInCost	GreatestCost	LeastCost
1	Ferrari	Testarossa	2015-01-02T08:00:00.000+0000	GBPGB001	2175	750	2175	750
2	Ferrari	355	2015-01-25T12:00:00.000+0000	GBPGB002	5500	1950	5500	1950
3	Porsche	911	2015-02-03T10:00:00.000+0000	GBPGB003	660	150	660	150
4	Porsche	924	2015-02-16T08:00:00.000+0000	EURDE004	500	150	500	150
5	Porsche	944	2015-01-02T10:33:00.000+0000	EURFR005	1360	150	1360	150
6	Aston Martin	DB4	2015-03-14T12:00:00.000+0000	GBPGB006	500	150	500	150
7	Aston Martin	DB5	2015-03-24T12:00:00.000+0000	GBPGB007	2500	550	2500	550

Figure 5.10: Aggregating across multiple columns

How does it work

Aggregating across multiple columns is as simple as using the **GREATEST()** or **LEAST()** aggregate functions where, previously, you would have used **MAX()** or **MIN()**. However, instead of adding a single column inside the parentheses, add a comma-separated list of columns. In this case, we are returning the largest and smallest values from the **RepairsCost** and **TransportInCost** columns, whichever column contains the largest or smallest values.

We have added the **RepairsCost** and **TransportInCost** fields to the query output, making it easier to understand how this query works. This lets you see that the **GREATEST()** and **LEAST()** functions have isolated the largest and smallest values from these columns in each row.

Tricks and traps

The following are few points to note down:

- The output data is not grouped as when using the **MAX()** and **MIN()** functions. Indeed, the query returns all the records from the **allsales** table.
- All the columns referenced inside the **GREATEST()** and **LEAST()** aggregate functions must be the same datatype.
- All the columns referenced inside the **GREATEST()** and **LEAST()** aggregate functions must be separated by a comma.
- There is no practical limit to the number of columns you can enclose inside the **GREATEST()** and **LEAST()** functions when aggregating across columns.

Aggregating across columns and rows

You can extend the aggregation across columns to aggregate across both columns and rows if you need to add grouping to the output. You can see the code that delivers this in the following SQL snippet:

```
SELECT    MakeName, ModelName
          ,MAX(GREATEST(RepairsCost, TransportInCost, PartsCost))
          AS GreatestCost
          ,MIN(LEAST(RepairsCost, TransportInCost, PartsCost))
          AS LeastCost
```

```
FROM      allsales
GROUP BY  MakeName, ModelName;
```

This piece of SQL gives the result that you can see in *Figure 5.11*:

	MakeName	ModelName	GreatestCost	LeastCost
1	Bentley	Mulsanne	2000	550
2	Rolls Royce	Ghost	1490	500
3	Triumph	TR3A	970	550
4	BMW	E30	550	500
5	Ferrari	F50	9250	1950
6	Bugatti	57C	9250	1950
7	Alfa Romeo	Spider	500	150
8	Jaguar	Mark V	2000	150
9	Lamborghini	400GT	9250	1950
10	Mercedes	280SL	1360	150

***Figure 5.11:** Aggregating across columns and rows*

How does it work

This SQL works at two levels:

1. **First**: All the columns you wish to scan to find the largest and smallest values in a record are wrapped inside the **`GREATEST()`** and **`LEAST()`** functions.
2. **Second**: The **`GREATEST()`** and **`LEAST()`** functions are wrapped in, respectively, the **`MAX()`** and **`MIN()`** functions.

Finally, any fields that are required in the output are added to the **`GROUP BY`** clause.

So, what the query does is to find, for each row, the largest and smallest values from the **`RepairsCost`**, **`TransportInCost`**, and **`PartsCost`** columns (whichever column contains the largest or smallest values for each record) and then uses these row values to find the largest or smallest value for the resulting columns.

Tricks and traps

There is only one point to make is given as follows:

- You do not need to add a **`GROUP BY`** clause if all you want are the largest and smallest figures. That is, you could write SQL like the following:

```
SELECT  MAX(GREATEST(RepairsCost, TransportInCost)) AS GreatestCost
        ,MIN(LEAST(RepairsCost, TransportInCost)) AS LeastCost
FROM    allsales;
```

To return results, refer to *Figure 5.12*:

	GreatestCost	LeastCost
1	9250	140

***Figure 5.12:** A total from aggregating across columns and rows*

Filtering groups

The sales director was pleased with your ability to aggregate results using all the available data in a database. So, she wants you to push the envelope and filter the data so that she can see how many red cars have been sold by make. SQL will let you do this, and you can build on the knowledge you have acquired so far in this chapter by applying any of the filtering techniques you saw in previous chapters.

As an example, here is how to count the cars sold in a specific color:

```
SELECT      MakeName, COUNT(SalePrice) AS CarsSold

FROM        allsales

WHERE       Color = 'Red'

GROUP BY    MakeName;
```

This code returns the output shown in *Figure 5.13*:

	MakeName	CarsSold
1	Peugeot	1
2	Jaguar	5
3	Trabant	3
4	Austin	1
5	Mercedes	1
6	Alfa Romeo	1

***Figure 5.13:** A calculated aggregation with a filter applied*

How does it work

This code snippet returns the number of cars sold using the technique you saw in the section *Using grouped aggregations* of this chapter. What is new is the **`WHERE`** clause, which is applied just as you would use it in any other query. Remember that the **`WHERE`** clause must be placed before the **`GROUP BY`** clause, or you will get an error message.

Filtering on aggregated results

As part of the company's worldwide sales drive, the sales director wants to focus Prestige cars' marketing energies on the countries where you make the most sales. This section shows you how to show the data only for countries where more than 50 cars have been sold. To start with, look at the following SQL snippet:

```
SELECT      CountryName, COUNT(SalesDetailsID) AS NumberofCarsSold

FROM        allsales

GROUP BY    CountryName

HAVING     COUNT(SalesDetailsID) > 50;
```

Running this code gives the output in *Figure 5.14*:

	CountryName	NumberofCarsSold
1	France	69
2	United Kingdom	164

***Figure 5.14:** Applying a filter to an aggregation*

How does it work

Occasionally, you will need to use an aggregation to filter data. You want to calculate an aggregated value and use this metric to filter a dataset. In cases like these, you need to apply a filter that is not a straight comparison with a value stored in a table, as in the preceding example.

What is interesting in this query is the **HAVING** clause. It is here that the aggregate filter is applied. This clause says, *allow aggregated output into the result set only where there are more than 50 source records (sales) in the aggregate source set.* It counts the number of sales (identified by the **SalesDetailsID** value of each sale) for each element in the **GROUP BY** clause (the country) and then only returns rows where the country that you have grouped on has more than 50 sales.

The **HAVING** clause acts like a filter at an aggregate level on the selected data, and the **WHERE** clause operates at the level of each record. The **HAVING** clause filters data on an aggregated value and the number of sales made for each aggregated element once the record-level filters have been applied.

If you want to convince yourself that this technique works, run the query without the **HAVING** clause. This will return the number of sales for all countries.

Selecting data based on aggregated results as well as specific filter criteria

The sales director has surpassed herself. This time she has left a note with what looks like a complicated request. She wants to know the clients who have not only bought at least three cars but where each of the three vehicles generated a profit of at least £5,000.00. So, before getting anxious about it, let us consider what question is being asked. Her demand could be translated as follows: *find all car sales making more than £5,000 in profit. Now group them by customer. And display only customers with at least three cars making at least this much profit.*

This sounds more complicated than it is. So, before your eyes glaze over, look at the following SQL:

```
SELECT     CustomerName, COUNT(SalesDetailsID) AS NumberofCarsSold
FROM       allsales
WHERE      (SalePrice
             - (
                  Cost + NVL(RepairsCost,0) + PartsCost
                  + TransportInCost)
                ) > 5000
GROUP BY   CustomerName
HAVING     COUNT(SalesDetailsID) >= 3;
```

Running this code gives the output as shown in *Figure 5.15*:

	CustomerName	NumberofCarsSold
1	SuperSport S.A.R.L.	7
2	Pierre Blanc	3
3	Prestige Imports	5
4	Convertible Dreams	4
5	Screamin' Wheels	7
6	Antonio Maura	6
7	Vive La Vitesse	9
8	Honest Pete Motors	7
9	M. Pierre Dubois	3
10	Le Luxe en Motion	4

Figure 5.15: *A calculated aggregation with both a HAVING clause and a WHERE clause*

How does it work

Once again, the **FROM** clause merely guarantees that you can access all the fields needed to answer the query (that is, you have selected the correct table). The **SELECT** clause merely says you want to list the customer's name and the number of vehicles sold to that customer. As this is an aggregation query, the field you use to break down the data (customer name) must also appear in the **GROUP BY** clause.

The power of this query resides in using the following two types of filters applied in sequence:

1. A classic **WHERE** clause for a nonaggregate (record-level) filter.
2. An aggregate filter in a **HAVING** clause.

Each of these performs a separate and distinct function in the query in a specific order:

- **First**: The **WHERE** clause calculates the individual margin for each sale and allows only those records that match this criterion through to the next (grouping) stage.
- **Finally**: The **HAVING** clause takes the resulting filtered records that have been grouped and aggregated and applies a second filter level. This time only groups with at least three elements (three cars making more than £5,000.00 profit) are let through into the query output.

The main thing to remember with queries like the one applied here is that SQL has a strict filter priority applied by SQL, which will apply a **WHERE** clause *before* it applies a **HAVING** clause.

Tricks and traps

As you are meeting a new concept and a new keyword for the first time, you need to be wary of a couple of potential issues that must be managed carefully when you are using the **HAVING** clause:

- Note that we used the **NVL()** function described in the previous chapter when calculating the profit for each car sold. Had we not used this function, Databricks would have returned a **NULL** rather than the profit for any car with a **NULL** value in the **RepairsCost** field.
- The order of the clauses in the SQL statement is extremely important when applying a **HAVING** clause to the code. You must always place the **HAVING** clause after the **GROUP BY** clause and before the **ORDER BY** clause (if there is one).

Query analysis

We cannot deny that SQL can get complicated sometimes. However, it is never more than an accumulation of techniques and keywords that must apply to deliver a result. So, if you are faced with a seemingly difficult challenge, the approach should always be to break the question down into its smallest parts and then try a sequential approach, something like the following:

What tables are needed? Without the source data, there is nothing that you can do. So you could be best by beginning with the **FROM** clause to ensure you can access all the columns you need from all the required tables.

What output is required? Choose the columns you want to see in the result—and set up any necessary calculations.

What aggregations? If you need aggregations, you should add them—and ensure that the **GROUP BY** clause contains any non-aggregated fields that you have placed in the **SELECT** clause.

How are you filtering data? Then you should apply any filters that you need to exclude data that is not relevant to your analysis. Remember to break down the filter into its smallest parts and build it up slowly and coherently.

Any aggregated filters? Use the **HAVING** clause if you are filtering on the result of an aggregation.

Is the output sorted? Finally, an **ORDER BY** clause sorts the output.

Sorting by aggregated results

The CEO wants to see what drives the company's bottom line. More specifically, she wants to isolate the three most lucrative models sold so that she can focus sales efforts on those brands. Aggregation queries can be used to help you to analyze and prioritize your data. A classic example is when you want to see what brings in the most money. The following short piece of SQL illustrates this:

```
SELECT      MakeName
FROM        allsales
GROUP BY    MakeName
ORDER BY    SUM(SalePrice) DESC
LIMIT 3;
```

Executing this code snippet gives the output as shown in *Figure 5.16*:

	MakeName
1	Ferrari
2	Aston Martin
3	Bugatti

Figure 5.16: *Using LIMIT, ORDER BY, and GROUP BY to segment data*

How does it work

This query groups the output data and shows you can add an **`ORDER BY`** clause to sort the output. Interestingly you can sort an aggregated field whether it is present in the **`SELECT`** clause or not. The **`LIMIT`** keyword can be used in aggregation queries too.

To encourage you to persevere with SQL, consider the potential value of the information and concise and efficient query returns. You can see where your company is making money, and this, after all, is worth a little effort on the SQL learning curve.

Finding elements where every Boolean value is true

Occasionally, you have to isolate data where every Boolean flag is true. In the case of Prestige cars, the CEO wants to see if the steering wheel's position influences sales for color. So, she has asked you to show vehicle colors and specify if only right-hand drive models are sold in that color.

The following simple SQL handles this elegantly:

```
SELECT    Color, BOOL_AND(IsRHD) AS AllRightHandDrive
FROM      allsales
GROUP BY  Color;
```

Running this code snippet gives the output as shown in *Figure 5.17:*

	Color	AllRightHandDrive
1	Dark Purple	true
2	Silver	false
3	Green	false
4	British Racing Green	false
5	Blue	false

Figure 5.17: *Displaying output using the BOOL_AND() function*

How does it work

Wrapping any Boolean column in the **BOOL_AND()** function will return:

- **TRUE** if all the elements in the data subset are set to **TRUE**.
- **FALSE** if any element in the data subset is set to **FALSE**.

In practice, it only takes a single record to be flagged as **FALSE** in the data for the **BOOL_AND()** function to return **FALSE**. Essentially, this is a method for finding attributes where every flag is set to **TRUE**.

To make this clearer, take a look at the following SQL that shows the distribution of right-hand drive vehicles for colors:

```
SELECT      Color, IsRHD
FROM        allsales
GROUP BY    Color, IsRHD
ORDER BY    Color, IsRHD;
```

You can see the output in *Figure 5.18:*

	Color	IsRHD
1	Black	false
2	Black	true
3	Blue	false
4	Blue	true
5	British Racing Green	false
6	British Racing Green	true
7	Canary Yellow	false
8	Canary Yellow	true
9	DARK PURPLE	true
10	Dark Purple	true
11	Green	false
12	Green	true

Figure 5.18: *Distribution of right hand drive vehicles for colors*

As you can see, Dark Purple is the only color where all vehicles are right-hand drive. Consequently, applying the **BOOL_AND()** function to the **IsRHD** field returns true—as shown in *Figure 5.17*.

Tricks and traps

When using the `BOOL_AND()` function, you need to be mindful that:

- The `BOOL_AND()` function will only work on Boolean columns.
- You cannot use `BOOL_AND()` in a `WHERE` clause.
- If you use `BOOL_AND()`, you must add a `GROUP BY` clause.

Conclusion

This chapter has introduced you to the vast potential of SQL to calculate aggregations. You saw how to group data into separate segments and return totals, counts, maxima, and minima for these segments in a few lines of code.

Then, you learned how to use calculations alongside aggregations to perform deeper analyses. You also saw how to filter data using aggregation functions to isolate certain data elements.

Finally, you saw how to combine aggregation functions with some of the functions you saw in previous chapters to deliver in-depth commercial analysis.

Core knowledge learned in this chapter

The following are the keywords you learned in this chapter:

Concept	Description
`SUM()`	This function returns the total for a column of numbers and will also calculate the total for or for each data segment where grouping is applied.
`GROUP BY`	This phrase tells Databricks that you want to segment results into groups of elements.
`COUNT()`	This function tells you how many records there are in a table or for each data segment.
`COUNT(DISTINCT)`	This function tells you how many individual records there are in a table.
`MAX()`	This function returns the largest value in a column of numbers for each data segment.
`MIN()`	This function returns the lowest value in a column of numbers for each data segment.

Concept	Description
`GREATEST()`	This function works across multiple columns to find the largest value in each row for the selected columns.
`LEAST()`	This function works across multiple columns to find the smallest value in each row for the selected columns.
`HAVING`	This clause filters the data on aggregate values (unlike the `WHERE` clause, which filters individual records).
`BOOL_AND()`	This function
`BOOL_OR()`	This function

Join our book's Discord space

CHAPTER 6
Working with Dates in Databricks

Introduction

Most data analysis has a time component. You could want to look at sales for a certain day, month, or year. Perhaps you must compare margins with the previous year or the preceding month. Indeed, the list of possible questions that need answering when analyzing data over time is virtually infinite. It follows that it is important to understand how Databricks handles dates. Indeed, it can rapidly become essential to master the techniques you need to apply when adding a time element to your analysis.

Structure

In this chapter, we will cover the following topics:

- Dates in Databricks
- Using a range of dates to filter data
- Finding data for a given quarter
- Filtering data by weekday
- Finding records for a specific week of the year
- Aggregating data by the day of the week in a given year

- Analyzing data by day of the year
- Grouping data by the full weekday
- Displaying cumulative data over a period of months to a specific date
- Displaying cumulative data over 90 days up to a specific date
- Displaying the data for the previous three months

Objectives

Databricks delivers a range of solutions for analyzing data over time. The possibilities are as far-reaching as the analytical requirements you could face. This chapter introduces how to deal with dates in data analysis because this will prepare you for the real-world challenges you may face when analyzing data over time.

Handling time analysis (or querying dates in data if you prefer) is a vast subject. As you are still taking your first steps with SQL, we will not attempt to answer every imaginable question on this subject in one chapter. However, we will try to provide you with a basic understanding of how Databricks can be used as the basis for deep insights into how data evolves over time.

This involves learning how to:

- Filter by a specific date
- Filter by a range of dates
- Isolate data by year, month, week, and day
- Aggregate values over time
- Handle relative dates
- Handle SQL date data types and avoid common pitfalls

We would like to make clear from the start that—for the moment at least—we are using date and time as interchangeable concepts for the most part in this chapter. For the moment, we will be dealing only with dates as you learn to analyze data over time. In *Chapter 20: Analyzing Data Over Time*, you will see how to deal with the hours and minutes that make up the time element of certain data elements. However, bringing the date element to the fore when analyzing data matters, so this is what we will be examining in this chapter.

Dates in Databricks

In *Chapter 4: Simple Calculations*, we touched briefly on datatypes in Databricks, where you saw that numbers ideally must be stored as a numeric datatype. As there are datatypes for numeric values, there are datatypes for dates. They are as follows:

- **Date**: Date datatypes contain the date, day, month, and year. They do not contain any time elements such as hours or seconds.
- **Timestamp**: Timestamp datatypes contain not only the date but also hours, minutes, seconds, and possibly time zone information.

In an ideal world, the source data has been loaded into Databricks in such a way that Databricks tables can recognize dates as valid date or timestamp data types. Alternatively, a data engineer has converted the raw source data into the appropriate date or timestamp data types. Unfortunately, in some cases, the source data may not have been converted, and dates have been left as strings (or just text, if you prefer). If you encounter this when dealing with your data, you must look at *Chapter 20: Analyzing Data Over Time* to discover ways to extract dates from strings.

Fortunately for us on our Spark SQL learning trajectory, the sample data for Prestige Cars has defined all dates as Timestamps. So these contain date and time elements. Also, the Databricks tables based on the source files recognize any date or date/time fields as Timestamps. So you will not have to worry about converting strings to valid dates.

Filtering records by date

Suppose the sales director wants to see the list of cars bought on July 25, 2015. The following SQL code will do that:

```
SELECT      MakeName, ModelName, DateBought
FROM        allsales
WHERE       TO_DATE(DateBought) = '2015-07-25';
```

Run the preceding code, and you will see the output as shown in *Figure 6.1*:

	MakeName	ModelName	DateBought
1	Jaguar	XJS	2015-07-25T12:00:00.000+0000
2	Aston Martin	DB6	2015-07-25T12:00:00.000+0000
3	Porsche	944	2015-07-25T12:00:00.000+0000

Figure 6.1: *Using dates in a WHERE clause to filter on a date*

How does it work

You can easily filter on any date or timestamp field to show when an event took place. You do this by applying a **WHERE** clause, just as you would do for text or numbers.

The interesting thing is how you represent the data in the **WHERE** clause. There are the following three main aspects to this:

1. **Quotes**: The date is enclosed in single quotes as if it were text.
2. **Date specification**: The date should be YYYY-MM-DD—thus, four digits for the year, then two digits for the month (including a leading zero for months 1–9), and then two digits for the day (including a leading zero for days 1–9). The dash is required as a separator element to separate the year from the month or the day, and the complete date *must* be enclosed in single or double quotes.
3. **Time truncation**: As the source data contains both date and time elements (as shown in *Figure 6.1*), you need to *remove the time element* when filtering on dates. Otherwise, SQL will filter on the date and the time-and as the date that you entered as part of the **WHERE** clause has no time element, it will not match the date and time in the **SaleDate** column.

Wrapping a field name in the **TO_DATE()** function strips out the time element in the underlying data and allows you to filter uniquely on the date part of the data. As you can see from *Figure 6.1*, this does not prevent the output from showing the complete data and time elements stored in the data table.

Otherwise, this is a standard **WHERE** clause. It uses the equal operator to specify that you are looking to filter data on a specific date.

Tricks and traps

As you are just beginning to learn how to handle dates in SQL queries, there are inevitably key elements that you must retain. The following are the major starting points:

- When entering dates, you can use other operators besides the equal operator (=). For instance, you can use >= (greater than or equal to) to list all records from—and including—a specific date. To list data up to and including a specific date, you can use the <= (less than or equal to) operator. For dates before or after a given date, you can use the < (less than) or > (greater than) operator.
- When entering dates in the YYYY-MM-DD format, you must add leading zeroes for the day and the month. So you cannot enter a date like the following:

```
WHERE       TO_DATE(DateBought) = '2015-7-25';
```

- An alternative to entering a date in the YYYY-MM-DD format is to use the **MAKE_DATE()** function to specify a date. If you chose to use **MAKE_DATE()**, the previous SQL snippet would look like the following:

```
SELECT     MakeName, ModelName, DateBought
FROM       allsales
WHERE      TO_DATE(DateBought) = MAKE_DATE(2015,07,25);
```

- The **MAKE_DATE()** function requires that you enter the year as the first parameter, the month as the second parameter, and the day as the final parameter. As with all functions in Databricks, these parameters (or elements, if you want to think of them this way) are separated by a comma. The advantage of using the **MAKE_DATE()** function to specify a date is that you do not need to add leading zeroes to the day and month parameters if you do not want to. In other words, you could enter something like the following:

```
WHERE      TO_DATE(DateBought) = MAKE_DATE(2015,7,25)
```

- An alternative way of stripping out the time element from a timestamp field is to apply the **CAST()** function to a string like the following:

```
WHERE CAST(DateBought AS DATE) = MAKE_DATE(2015,07,25);
```

- Formatting dates used in query output are described in *Chapter 7: Formatting Text in Query Output*.

Date datatypes in tables

The filter you applied in the previous section will only work correctly if the field(s) you use for date filters is in one of Databricks's data types. If the field is a string (a text), you must enter the date exactly as it is typed in the table and hope there are no typos in any of the data, or the query will not work properly. Also, sorting and filtering by date will not yield the expected results.

Fortunately, the fields containing date information in the Prestige cars dataset have been designed correctly, containing dates and times. However, when you are querying other datasets, you are probably best advised to check the data types of any fields that look like they hold dates or date and time data.

Using a range of dates to filter data

Pleased with your initial answer to her request, the sales director wants a list of all the cars bought between June 30, 2016, and July 31, 2016. The following SQL shows how to do the following:

```
SELECT     MakeName, ModelName, DateBought
```

```
FROM        allsales
WHERE       TO_DATE(DateBought) BETWEEN '2016-06-30' AND '2016-07-31';
```

Figure 6.2 shows the output from the preceding piece of SQL:

	MakeName	ModelName	DateBought
1	Porsche	944	2016-06-30T12:00:00.000+0000
2	Porsche	911	2016-07-03T12:00:00.000+0000
3	Alfa Romeo	Giulia	2016-07-03T12:00:00.000+0000
4	Ferrari	Testarossa	2016-07-05T12:00:00.000+0000
5	Ferrari	355	2016-07-07T12:00:00.000+0000
6	Porsche	959	2016-07-08T12:00:00.000+0000
7	Porsche	928	2016-07-09T12:00:00.000+0000

***Figure 6.2:** Filtering on a range of dates using the BETWEEN operator*

How does it work

Once again (with the `FROM` clause duly configured to include the required table), you can apply a `WHERE` clause to filter on dates, this time outputting all the records where the sale date was in the range specified in the `WHERE` clause. As you can see from the previous SQL snippet, you are using the `BETWEEN...AND` clause that you met in *Chapter 2: Filtering Data* to select a date range.

Tricks and traps

Dealing with date ranges means you must be precise, specifically as far as the following are concerned:

- When you use the **`BETWEEN`** and **`AND`** keywords, SQL will include the start and end dates in the range that your defined range. For this particular query, that means from June 30, 2016, to July 31, 2017, inclusive.
- If you are using **`BETWEEN...AND`** in a date range query, you must place the start date before the end date and not vice versa. If you reverse these elements and write the filter as follows:

  ```
  WHERE TO_DATE(DateBought) BETWEEN '2015-07-31' AND '2015-06-30'
  ```

  it will return no results, even if you are certain there are records for the specified date range.
- If you enter an invalid date in the **`WHERE`** clause (say June 31), no results will be returned.

- You can also enter date ranges using the **<=** and **>=** operators. Using these, the **WHERE** clause for the query in this example would be as follows:

```
WHERE DateBought <= '20175-07-31' AND DateBought >= '2016-06-30'
```

- Using the **<=** and **>=** operators, you can enter the upper and lower threshold values in any order. So the previous code snippet could be entered as follows:

```
WHERE DateBought >= '2016-06-30' AND DateBought <= '20175-07-31'
```

Finding the number of days between two dates

The finance director is keen to make sure that cars do not stay on the firm's books too long. He says that they tie up expensive capital. So, he wants a list of the makes and models and the number of days each vehicle remained unsold on the lot. After a few minutes, you deliver the following piece of code:

```
SELECT
             MakeName
            ,ModelName
            ,DateBought
            ,SaleDate
            ,DATEDIFF(SaleDate, DateBought) AS DaysInStock
FROM        allsales;
```

Executing the preceding code snippet gives the output as shown in *Figure 6.3*:

	MakeName	ModelName	DateBought	SaleDate	DaysInStock
1	Ferrari	Testarossa	2015-01-01T12:00:00.000+0000	2015-01-02T08:00:00.000+0000	0
2	Ferrari	355	2015-01-10T12:00:00.000+0000	2015-01-25T12:00:00.000+0000	15
3	Porsche	911	2015-01-29T12:00:00.000+0000	2015-02-03T10:00:00.000+0000	4
4	Porsche	924	2015-02-14T12:00:00.000+0000	2015-02-16T08:00:00.000+0000	1
5	Porsche	944	2015-01-01T12:00:00.000+0000	2015-01-02T10:33:00.000+0000	0
6	Aston Martin	DB4	2015-03-05T12:00:00.000+0000	2015-03-14T12:00:00.000+0000	9

Figure 6.3: *Using the DATEDIFF() function to calculate the difference in days between two dates*

How does it work

This SQL introduces the **DATEDIFF()** function. This function allows you to calculate the number of days between two dates. The **DATEDIFF()** function needs the following two elements (or parameters to give them their technical name) to display the number of days between two dates:

1. **First**: The **end** date for the calculation. In this example, you want to end the period with the vehicle's sale date using the field **SaleDate**. This parameter, too, must be in a format that Databricks can recognize as a date. So the parameter must be either a date or timestamp field, generated using the **TO_DATE()** function or a text that Spark SQL can recognize as a valid date.
2. **Second**: The **start** date for the calculation. This means defining the initial date in the calculation, which is the **DateBought** field. This must be in a format that Databricks can recognize as a date.

Tricks and traps

The **DATEDIFF()** function is not difficult to apply to SQL queries. However, you do need to be aware of a few key aspects of its use, which are given as follows:

- You must enter the end date as the first parameter and the start date as the second parameter. If you do not, the number of days the function returns will be negative.
- **DATEDIFF()** can only count days.
- The dates you use in the **DATEDIFF()** function must also be entered in a way that lets Databricks recognize them as being dates. In other words, they must be entered as a valid date data type. This means referring to fields that are date data types (as is the case in this example) or entering dates in a valid date format (which you can see in the next example).
- It is best to add an alias to the function, as Databricks will never try to guess a column name when a function is used. If you do not add an alias, the column header will display part (or all) of the code.
- You can test the **DATEDIFF()** function independently of the rest of the query in a code snippet or use a fixed date as one or both of the date parameters that you apply to the function like the following:

  ```
  SELECT DATEDIFF('2015-08-15', '2015-07-01')
  ```

  This code will return the days between the two dates you specify.

Aggregating data over a date range

Suppose your sales manager wants to know the average daily purchase amount over six months. After a few minutes of thought, you come up with the following code snippet:

```
SELECT      SUM(Cost)
            / DATEDIFF('2015-12-31', '2015-07-01')
              AS AverageDailyCost
FROM        allsales
WHERE       DateBought BETWEEN '2015-07-01' AND '2015-12-31';
```

You can see what the preceding code delivers in *Figure 6.4*:

	AverageDailyCost
1	4191.366120218579

Figure 6.4*: Calculating a daily average using the number of days between two dates with the DIFFDATE() function*

How does it work

You saw that Databricks can determine the number of days between two dates, which can be extended to calculate the average purchase price over days.

The SQL filters the date range used for the calculation from July 1, 2015, to December 31, 2015. This date range is defined in the **WHERE** clause.

The SQL applies the **SUM()** function to the **SELECT** clause to calculate the total cost of all vehicles. This will apply only to vehicles bought between the two dates specified in the WHERE clause. Then, the **DATEDIFF()** function is used again in the **SELECT** clause to calculate the number of days between the two dates. Finally, the SQL divides the total purchase price by the number of days. The result is then displayed as the single figure that the query returns.

The **DATEDIFF()** function calculates the days between two dates. In this example, the following two dates are hard-coded into the **DATEDIFF()** function:

1. **The start date**: It is entered as 2015-07-01 because, in this example, you want to start the evaluation period on July 1, 2015.
2. **The end date**: It is entered as 2015-12-31 because you want to end the evaluation period on December 31, 2015.

Filtering by year

As Prestige cars have been selling for several years, the finance director wants to isolate the sales for a specific year. SQL makes this easy, as the following code shows:

```
SELECT      MakeName, ModelName, YEAR(SaleDate) AS YearOfSale
FROM        allsales
WHERE       YEAR(SaleDate) = 2015
ORDER BY    MakeName, ModelName;
```

Running the preceding SQL delivers the output as shown in *Figure 6.5*:

	MakeName	ModelName	YearOfSale
1	Alfa Romeo	Giulia	2015
2	Aston Martin	DB4	2015
3	Aston Martin	DB5	2015
4	Aston Martin	DB5	2015
5	Aston Martin	DB6	2015
6	Aston Martin	DB6	2015
7	Aston Martin	DB6	2015

***Figure 6.5:** Using the YEAR() function on a date field*

How does it work

This query uses the **`YEAR()`** function to extract the year from the date in the **`WHERE`** clause so that you can specify which year to filter. Although it is perhaps not strictly necessary, we have added this same function to the **`SELECT`** clause as well so that you can then confirm, visually, that the year that interests you is being returned by the query. As you can observe, the **`YEAR()`** function extracts the year element from a date or timestamp field, irrespective of the month and day of the month. As is the case with all SQL functions, you can use this function in any part of the query. Applying it to the **`WHERE`** clause means that it is used to filter on the year.

We have added an **`ORDER BY`** clause to this piece of SQL to structure the output and remind you that this can be done in any query you are writing.

Tricks and traps

There are only a few points to make, which are given as follows:

- The **`YEAR`** function outputs (or returns in geek-speak) the year as a number. This means that when using **`YEAR`** in a **`WHERE`** clause, you do not need to enter the year in single quotes.
- The **`YEAR`** function strips out any time parts of the date and the month and day elements leaving only the year.
- When writing and testing the query, you can always begin by adding any fields you use in the **`WHERE`** clause to the **`SELECT`** clause. Once you are satisfied that the SQL is working correctly, you can remove these fields from the

SELECT clause unless you need to display the data. So your final query could read the following:

```
SELECT      MakeName, ModelName
FROM        allsales
WHERE       YEAR(SaleDate) = 2015
ORDER BY    MakeName, ModelName;
```

- An alternative to the **YEAR()** function is the **EXTRACT()** function. The two are interchangeable, but you may occasionally come across Databricks SQL that uses the **EXTRACT()** function, so it is best to know it exists. If you were to use the **EXTRACT()** function, the previous SQL snippet would look like the following:

```
SELECT       MakeName, ModelName
            ,EXTRACT(YEAR FROM SaleDate) AS YearOfSale, saledate
            ,SalePrice
FROM        allsales
WHERE       EXTRACT(YEAR FROM SaleDate) = 2015;
```

- The **EXTRACT** function requires the following three parameters:
  - (i). The date element to isolate (this can be **YEAR**, **MONTH**, **DAY**, or **WEEKDAY**). When using **DATE_PART()**, you *must* place the date element you wish to isolate in quotes.
  - (ii). The **FROM** keyword.
  - (iii). The date or timestamp field to use as a data source.
- Yet another alternative to the **YEAR()** function (that you might see in existing Databricks SQL code) is the **DATE_PART()** function. In the following code, the SQL used previously with the **YEAR()** function replaced by the **DATE_PART()** function:

```
SELECT        MakeName, ModelName, DATE_PART('YEAR', SaleDate) AS
YearOfSale, saledate
            ,SalePrice
FROM        allsales
WHERE       DATE_PART('YEAR', SaleDate) = 2015;
```

- The **DATE_PART()** function requires the following two parameters:
  - (i) The date element to isolate (this can be YEAR, MONTH, DAY, or WEEKDAY).
  - (ii) The date or timestamp field to use as a data source.

Filtering records over a series of years

Now that he has the sales lists for 2015, the finance director wants to look at the data for 2015 and 2016. Fortunately, SQL does not limit you to analyzing data for a single year, as the following query makes clear:

```
SELECT DISTINCT MakeName, ModelName, YEAR(SaleDate)
                AS YearOfSale
FROM            allsales
WHERE          YEAR(SaleDate) IN (2015, 2016)
ORDER BY        YearOfSale, MakeName, ModelName;
```

Run the preceding query and get the output shown in *Figure 6.6*. You will have to scroll down the output to see the change in the year of sale.

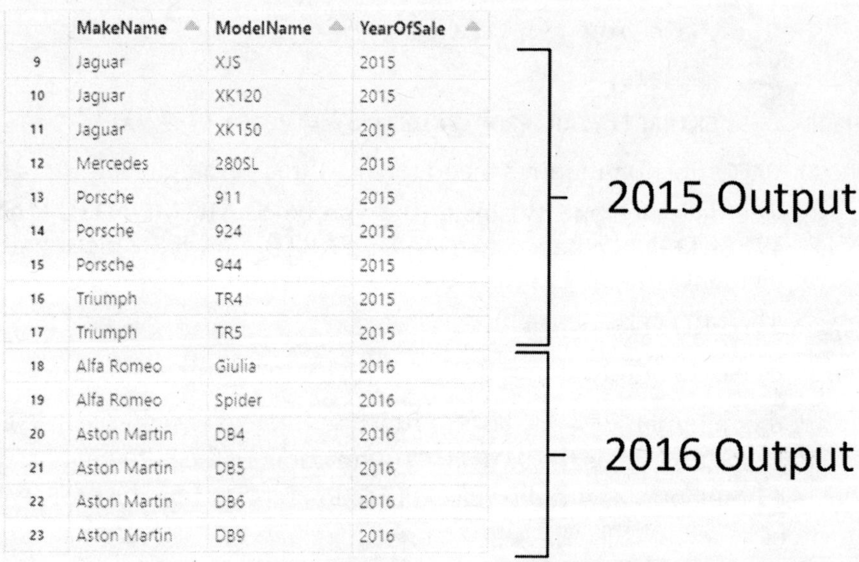

	MakeName	ModelName	YearOfSale
9	Jaguar	XJS	2015
10	Jaguar	XK120	2015
11	Jaguar	XK150	2015
12	Mercedes	280SL	2015
13	Porsche	911	2015
14	Porsche	924	2015
15	Porsche	944	2015
16	Triumph	TR4	2015
17	Triumph	TR5	2015
18	Alfa Romeo	Giulia	2016
19	Alfa Romeo	Spider	2016
20	Aston Martin	DB4	2016
21	Aston Martin	DB5	2016
22	Aston Martin	DB6	2016
23	Aston Martin	DB9	2016

***Figure 6.6:** Filtering on a series of years using the IN keyword*

How does it work

This query is essentially driven by a **WHERE** clause that tells Databricks to filter the results so that only data for 2015 to 2016 is returned. This is done using an `IN` keyword, as you did in *Chapter 3: Complex Filters*. As with the previous queries that used the `IN` keyword, each filter element is separated by a comma from the other elements, and the complete list is enclosed in parentheses.

Finally, the results are sorted by year, make, and model. However, to sort by the year, you need, once again, to apply the **YEAR()** function to the **SaleDate** field in the **ORDER BY** clause.

Tricks and traps

To make things easier when you are writing your queries to isolate data over time, you may want to pay attention to the following key points:

- If you wish to use a function in the **ORDER BY** clause, then you **must** add a column alias to the field that has a function applied, and then you must use the alias in the **ORDER BY** clause and not repeat the code used. So the following code will not work.

```
SELECT DISTINCT MakeName, ModelName, YEAR(SaleDate)
FROM            allsales
WHERE          YEAR(SaleDate) IN (2015, 2016)
ORDER BY       YEAR(SaleDate), MakeName, ModelName;
```

- You can enter as many years as you like in an **IN** function just remember to separate each year with a comma (**,**). As was the case when filtering on a single year, the **YEAR()** function uses figures, so no single quotes are needed.
- You can enter the years in an **IN** function in any order. So you could enter the years as follows:

```
WHERE YEAR(SaleDate) IN (2016, 2015)
```

- When filtering over a range of years, you might prefer to avoid entering each year individually and use the **BETWEEN...AND** syntax in the **WHERE** clause to specify a range of years, like the following:

```
WHERE YEAR(SaleDate) BETWEEN 2013 AND 2016
```

- You must repeat the **YEAR()** function in a SQL query every time you extract the year from a date or datetime field. This kind of function can be applied to most parts of SQL queries. You can see this in the preceding code snippet, where the **YEAR()** function is used in both the **SELECT** and **WHERE** clauses.

Find sales for a specific day of the month

Date analysis in Databricks can go down to the level of days. This makes it easy to find, for example, which days of the month produce the highest sales. This is applied in the following code snippet, which introduces the **DAY()** function.

```
SELECT      DAY(SaleDate) AS DayOfSale
            ,SUM(SalePrice) as SalesPerDayOfMonth
```

```
FROM        allsales
GROUP BY    DAY(SaleDate)
ORDER BY    SalesPerDayOfMonth DESC;
```

You can see the output from the preceding query as shown in *Figure 6.7*:

	DayOfSale	SalesPerDayOfMonth
1	15	2159230
2	31	1900470
3	1	1886740
4	10	1485650
5	25	1286040
6	30	1214370

Figure 6.7: *Filtering on a series of years using the IN keyword*

How does it work

This piece of SQL wraps the **`SaleDate`** field in the **`DAY()`** function. As its name implies, this function extracts the day (the number of days in the month) from the **`SaleDate`** field.

Once you have this element from a date, adding it to the **`SELECT`** clause (where it is given an alias) and a **`GROUP BY`** clause (to allow aggregation of the sales figures) is easy. Then as a final twist, you can sort by the cumulative sales per day to discover that the 15th of the month is the best day to sell used cars.

Tricks and traps

We need to note a couple of points, which are given as follows:

- The **`DAY()`** function can only be applied to **`DATE`** or **`TIMESTAMP`** columns (or texts converted to dates, using the **`TO_DATE()`** function).
- You can also isolate the day element from a **`DATE`** or **`TIMESTAMP`** column using code like the following:

  ```
  EXTRACT (DAY FROM SaleDate)
  ```

- Alternatively, you can isolate the day element from a **`DATE`** or **`TIMESTAMP`** column like the following:

  ```
  DATE PART('DAY', SaleDate)
  ```

Isolating data for a specific year and month

The CEO is convinced that some months are better for sales than others. She has asked for the sales for July 2015 to check out her hunch. Fortunately, SQL lets you be as precise as you like when querying for data. If you want to list the vehicle sales for a certain month each year, you could use the following code:

```
SELECT      MakeName, ModelName, SaleDate
FROM        allsales
WHERE       YEAR(SaleDate) = 2015
            AND MONTH(SaleDate) = 7;
```

Execute the preceding code snippet, and you will see the cars displayed as shown in *Figure 6.8*:

	MakeName	ModelName	SaleDate
1	Alfa Romeo	Giulia	2015-07-12T10:00:00.000+0000
2	Jaguar	XK150	2015-07-15T12:00:00.000+0000
3	Jaguar	XJS	2015-07-25T12:00:00.000+0000
4	Aston Martin	DB6	2015-07-25T12:00:00.000+0000

Figure 6.8: *Using the YEAR() and MONTH() functions to filter output*

How does it work

The **`MONTH()`** function isolates the month part of a date. More precisely, it returns or filters on the number of month in the year. So, January is 1, February is 2, and so on, until 12 (December). As you can combine the **`YEAR()`** and **`MONTH()`** functions in a **`WHERE`** clause, limiting the output data to a specific month and year is not difficult. However, you do have to filter on the year and the month separately. This is why the query required you to say, and *I want the year 2015* ***and*** *the month of July*.

Tricks and traps

For the sake of completeness, it is worth knowing that you can replace the **`MONTH()`** function with the **`EXTRACT()`** or **`DATE_PART()`** functions using code like the following:

```
AND EXTRACT(MONTH FROM SaleDate) = 7
```

or,

```
AND DATE_PART('MONTH', SaleDate) = 7
```

Finding data for a given quarter

The CEO was disappointed about the sales in July 2015, so now she wants to see sales for the entire third quarter of 2015. SQL can recognize calendar quarters (or trimesters) too. Refer to the following code snippet:

```
SELECT     MakeName, ModelName, SaleDate

FROM       allsales

WHERE     QUARTER(SaleDate) = 3

          AND YEAR(SaleDate) = 2015;
```

Figure 6.9 shows you what happens when you run this code. As you can see, all the moths in the output are in the third quarter of the year:

	MakeName	ModelName	SaleDate
1	Alfa Romeo	Giulia	2015-07-12T10:00:00.000+0000
2	Jaguar	XK150	2015-07-15T12:00:00.000+0000
3	Jaguar	XJS	2015-07-25T12:00:00.000+0000
4	Aston Martin	DB6	2015-07-25T12:00:00.000+0000
5	Triumph	TR4	2015-08-02T08:00:00.000+0000
6	Triumph	TR5	2015-09-05T12:00:00.000+0000
7	Porsche	924	2015-09-15T10:00:00.000+0000
8	Jaguar	XK120	2015-09-15T12:00:00.000+0000

Figure 6.9: *Filtering on the calendar quarter with the QUARTER() function*

How does it work

The **QUARTER()** function isolates the calendar quarter of the year. Consequently, the months of January through March are quarter 1, the months of April through June are quarter 2, the months of July through September are quarter 3, and the months of October through December are quarter 4. The number of the quarter can be used in the **SELECT** or **WHERE** clauses. In this example, the result is that only sales for the third quarter of 2015 are returned.

The **QUARTER()** function is applied to the **SaleDate** field in this query. Consequently, it returns the calendar quarter for each sale. This will inevitably be a number between 1 and 4. Then the **WHERE** clause looks for the third quarter of the date of sale, or, more precisely, says this: *The quarter of the* **SaleDate** *field equals three.* So, you will see sales for the third quarter only. As you want to limit the result to the third quarter of a specific year (and not just any third quarter of every year for which there is data), you must extend the **WHERE** clause by specifying the year to filter on.

Tricks and traps

The **QUARTER()** function is really simple to use. The following are the only things to remember:

- The **QUARTER()** function will work only if the field that you use as the parameter for the **QUARTER()** function is one of the date data types.
- You do not have to specify a year, but it is probably best to narrow down the search to sales for a quarter in a specific year.
- You can, if you prefer, use the **EXTRACT()** or **DATE_PART()** functions instead of the **QUARTER()** function, like the following:

  ```
  EXTRACT(QUARTER FROM SaleDate)

  DATE_PART('QUARTER', SaleDate)
  ```

Filtering data by weekday

When analyzing sales, you may want to isolate all purchases for a weekday. SQL can do this using code like the following:

```
SELECT     MakeName, ModelName

FROM       allsales

WHERE      WEEKDAY(SaleDate) = 6

           AND YEAR(SaleDate) = 2016;
```

Running the preceding code snippet produces output as shown in *Figure 6.10*:

	MakeName	ModelName
1	Lamborghini	Countach
2	Lamborghini	Diabolo
3	Bentley	Flying Spur
4	Porsche	928
5	Triumph	TR6
6	Triumph	GT6

***Figure 6.10:** Finding all the vehicles sold on a specific day of the week*

How does it work

The **WEEKDAY()** function lets you isolate the weekday for a date. It returns the weekday as a number, where 0 is Monday, 1 is Tuesday, 2 is Wednesday, 3 is Thursday, 4 is Friday, 5 is Saturday, and 6 is Sunday. Knowing this allows you to use the **WEEKDAY()** function in a **WHERE** clause to filter by day of the week.

Once again, in this example, you have narrowed the search to a specific year as a separate part of the **WHERE** clause.

Tricks and traps

There is only a small key point to note, which are given as follows:

- You can use the **EXTRACT()** or **DATE_PART()** functions instead of the **WEEKDAY()** function, like the following:

  ```
  EXTRACT(WEEKDAY FROM SaleDate)
  DATE_PART('WEEKDAY', SaleDate)
  ```

Finding records for a specific week of the year

The sales director has announced he would like to look at the sales for a specific week. SQL helps you to do this by filtering data by week. You can see an example in the following SQL:

```
SELECT      MakeName, ModelName, SaleDate
FROM        allsales
WHERE       WEEKOFYEAR(SaleDate) = 6
            AND YEAR(SaleDate) = 2017
ORDER BY    SaleDate;
```

Execute the preceding code, and you will get the results as shown in *Figure 6.11*:

	MakeName	ModelName	SaleDate
1	Ferrari	Enzo	2017-02-07T08:00:00.000+0000
2	Ferrari	Enzo	2017-02-08T01:01:00.000+0000
3	Alfa Romeo	Giulietta	2017-02-09T05:01:00.000+0000
4	Austin	Lichfield	2017-02-10T11:02:00.000+0000
5	Triumph	TR6	2017-02-12T04:02:00.000+0000

Figure 6.11: *Using the WEEKOFYEAR() function to isolate the week of the year*

How does it work

This code sample selects all records where the sale occurred in the 6th week of the year. As this function is used in a **`WHERE`** clause, you are filtering the data so that only sales records for Week 6 are returned-as you can see from the **`SaleDate`** field in the output. As calendar years start on different days, the weeks will not correspond to the same date range for every year.

Tricks and traps

When using **`WEEKOFYEAR()`**, you must remember the following points:

- **`WEEKOFYEAR()`** can be used virtually anywhere in a SQL query. This means you can apply it in the **`SELECT`** clause, for instance, to see the weeks or weekdays when sales took place.
- You can replace **`WEEKOFYEAR()`** with **`EXTRACT(WEEKOFYEAR FROM SaleDate)`**.

Aggregating data by the day of the week in a given year

The HR manager needs to see how sales vary across days of the week. He has explained that he needs to forecast staff requirements for busy days. So, let us suppose he wants to see the weekdays where Prestige cars made the most sales in 2015. The following piece of SQL code will just do that:

```
SELECT      WEEKDAY(SaleDate) AS DayOfWeek
           ,SUM(SalePrice) AS Sales
FROM        allsales
WHERE      YEAR(SaleDate) = 2015
GROUP BY   WEEKDAY(SaleDate)
ORDER BY   SUM(SalePrice) DESC;
```

If you run the preceding code, you will get the table as shown in *Figure 6.12*:

	DayOfWeek	Sales
1	6	403695
2	3	306950
3	4	231140
4	1	186000
5	5	154150
6	0	107100
7	2	31940

Figure 6.12: *Grouping output by day of the week using the WEEKDAY() function*

How does it work

This code returns the seven days of the week and the aggregate sales per weekday. It uses the **`WEEKDAY()`** function in the following two ways in this query:

1. **First**: The **`WEEKDAY()`** function is used in the **`SELECT`** query to specify the number of days of the week that you want to isolate in the query.
2. **Second**: The **`WEEKDAY()`** function is used again in the **`GROUP BY`** clause. This ensures that the data is aggregated at the level of the day of the week.

The **`WHERE`** clause filters on a specific year (2015). Finally, for good measure, the query sorts the aggregated output by sales value from highest to lowest. This makes it clear which days have the greatest sales over a year.

Tricks and traps

Analyzing data over time has its traps, as well as a few things you might need to know are given as follows:

- You can group output on a function like **WEEKDAY()**, just as on any field. You could also sort on a function like this if you needed to use code like the following:

```
SELECT      WEEKDAY(SaleDate) AS DayOfWeek
           ,SUM(SalePrice) AS Sales
FROM        allsales
WHERE       YEAR(SaleDate) = 2015
GROUP BY    WEEKDAY(SaleDate)
ORDER BY    WEEKDAY(SaleDate);
```

- You cannot replace **WEEKDAY()** with **EXTRACT(WEEKDAY FROM SaleDate)**.

Analyzing data by day of year

Sometimes a clue to driving sales can be found in unexpected places. At least, when the CEO asks you for a list of sales for each day in a particular year, this is what you assume. Happily, SQL makes this easy, as you can see in the following short piece of SQL that introduces the **DAYOFYEAR()** function:

```
SELECT      DAYOFYEAR(SaleDate) AS DayOfYear
           ,SUM(SalePrice) AS Sales
FROM        allsales
WHERE       YEAR(SaleDate) = 2017
GROUP BY    DAYOFYEAR(SaleDate)
ORDER BY    SUM(SalePrice) DESC;
```

You can see the output from the preceding SQL as shown in *Figure 6.13*:

	DayOfYear	Sales
1	97	515500
2	263	454500
3	39	395000
4	212	380500
5	38	365000
6	305	359000
7	184	335000
8	130	329000
9	90	313940
10	89	305000

***Figure 6.13**: Grouping output by day of year*

How does it work

This code isolates the day of the year from all the sale dates and then aggregates the sales for each day of that year. It uses the **DAYOFYEAR()** function in the following two places to output the day of the year:

- **First**: The **DAYOFYEAR()** function is used in the **SELECT** query to specify the number of days of the year that you want to isolate in the query.
- **Second**: The **DAYOFYEAR()** function is used again in the **GROUP BY** clause. This ensures that the data is aggregated at the level of the day of the year.

In this example, the output data is sorted on the number of sales. However, you could just as easily sort the data by the day of the year like the following:

```
SELECT      DAYOFYEAR(SaleDate) AS DayOfYear
            ,SUM(SalePrice) AS Sales
FROM        allsales
WHERE       YEAR(SaleDate) = 2017
GROUP BY    DAYOFYEAR(SaleDate)
ORDER BY    DAYOFYEAR(SaleDate);
```

Grouping data by the full weekday

The HR manager liked the information you just gave him about weekday sales. However, he would prefer to see the days of the week written out in full and not just have them appear as numbers in the output. After a couple of simple modifications, your SQL now looks like the following:

```
SELECT      DATE_FORMAT(SaleDate, "EEEE") AS Weekday
            ,SUM(SalePrice) AS Sales
FROM        allsales
WHERE       YEAR(SaleDate) = 2015
GROUP BY    DATE_FORMAT(SaleDate, "EEEE")
ORDER BY    SUM(SalePrice) DESC;
```

If you execute the preceding code, you will get the table as shown in *Figure 6.14*:

	Weekday	Sales
1	Sunday	403695
2	Thursday	306950
3	Friday	231140
4	Tuesday	186000
5	Saturday	154150
6	Monday	107100
7	Wednesday	31940

Figure 6.14: *Grouping output by day of the week using the DATE_FORMAT() function*

How does it work

Displaying the day of the week as a number can be a little brutal. So, Spark SQL has a function that can humanize the output. So, to display the actual weekday, you can tweak the first line of the query so that it looks like the following:

```
SELECT      DATE_FORMAT(SaleDate, "EEEE") AS DayOfWeek
```

Using the **DATE_FORMAT()** function, the weekday appears as the weekday text. As you can see, the **DATE_FORMAT()** function also takes two parameters: first, the field to be displayed differently, and second, code to specify how the date must appear in the output. These codes are given in *Table 6.1*.

Format code	Description	Example
d	Number of days in month	9
dd	Number of days in month with a leading zero, if a single figure	09
M	Numeric month	6
MM	Numeric month with a leading zero; if a single figure	06
MMMM	Full name of month	July
MMM	Abbreviated name of month	Jul
yy	Year as two digits	23
yyyy	Year as four digits	2023
E or EE or EEE	Abbreviated day of week name	Tue
EEEE	Full day of week name	Tuesday
G or GG or GGG	AD / BC	AD
GGGG	Anno Domini	Anno Domini

***Table 6.1:** Date formats*

Any field used in the **SELECT** or **ORDER BY** clause that is not an aggregate function must also be present in the **GROUP BY** clause as it is used in the **SELECT** clause. So the **DATE_FORMAT()** function must appear here, as well. In other words, you cannot write SQL like the following without returning an erroneous result:

```
SELECT      DATE_FORMAT(SaleDate, "EEEE") AS Weekday
            ,SUM(SalePrice) AS Sales
FROM        allsales
WHERE       YEAR(SaleDate) = 2015
GROUP BY    SaleDate
ORDER BY    SUM(SalePrice) DESC;
```

In this SQL snippet, the output is aggregated according to one date grouping but displays data according to a different date.

Tricks and traps

There are only a few points to note down, which are given as follows:

- The **DATE_FORMAT()** function can output date elements in many other ways, as you can see from *Table 6.1*.
- If you were to sort on the **DATE_FORMAT()** function, the weekdays would appear alphabetically. To display the aggregated data appearing in the traditional order of the days of the week, you need to sort to on the **WEEKDAY()** function like the following:

```
SELECT      DATE_FORMAT(SaleDate, "EEEE") AS Weekday
           ,SUM(SalePrice) AS Sales
FROM       allsales
WHERE      YEAR(SaleDate) = 2015
GROUP BY    DATE_FORMAT(SaleDate, "EEEE")
           ,WEEKDAY(TO_DATE(SaleDate))
ORDER BY   WEEKDAY(TO_DATE(SaleDate));
```

- In this case, it is worth noting that as you are sorting on the **WEEKDAY()** function but displaying the output from the **DATE_FORMAT()** function, you have to add both to the **GROUP BY** clause. If you run the preceding code, you will get the table as shown in *Figure 6.15*:

	Weekday	Sales
1	Monday	107100
2	Tuesday	186000
3	Wednesday	31940
4	Thursday	306950
5	Friday	231140
6	Saturday	154150
7	Sunday	403695

Figure 6.15: *Sorting aggregated data on the day of the week*

Displaying cumulative data over a period of months to a specific date

As the Prestige Cars sales director is manically focused on the sales trends, you have been sent a request to produce a list of all the sales over an exact period of months. Fortunately, SQL makes this easy, as you can see in the following code snippet:

```
SELECT     SUM(SalePrice) AS CumulativeSales

FROM       allsales

WHERE      SaleDate BETWEEN DATEADD(MONTH, -2, '2018-07-25')

           AND '2018-07-25';
```

Executing the preceding code will return the output as shown in *Figure 6.16*:

	CumulativeSales
1	668755

Figure 6.16: *Displaying cumulative data using the DATEADD() function*

How does it work

There is no need to reach for a calendar and work out the exact date two months previously; SQL can do this for you using the **DATEADD()** function.

Using the **DATEADD()** function like this in the **WHERE** clause means that you are saying this: *Filter on a date range between a specified date (July 25, 2018) and two months previous to that date.*

The **DATEADD()** function needs the following three elements or parameters to work.

- **First**: The time element that you want to calculate—days, months, quarters, years, and so on. You want to see several months in this example, so **MONTH** is used.
- **Second**: The actual number of months (or whatever time element you use in your query). If you are going back in time—as we are here, to look back over two months—you need to enter –2 (preceding the figure with a minus sign) to make it clear to SQL that the date is past.
- **Third**: The date for the number of days to be added to—or subtracted from. Once again, entering this in the YYYY-MM-DD format is more reliable—and always in single quotes.

Tricks and traps

As you would probably expect, **DATEADD()** does come with a couple of important points that you need to remember when you are using it and those points are given as follows:

- Forgetting the minus sign before the number of days in the **DATEADD()** function would show the sales for the 90 days *after* the specified date.
- The **DATEADD()** function can calculate periods using more than just days. If needed, you can define that number as months, quarters, or years. *Table 6.2* shows the main elements that you add as the first parameter of a **DATEADD()** function to specify the type of period you are using:

Element	Definition	Example
YEAR	Year	DATEADD(YEAR, -1, '2017-07-25')
MONTH	Month	DATEADD(MONTH, -2, '2017-07-25')
DAY	Day	DATEADD(DAY, -90, '2017-07-25')
QUARTER	Quarter	DATEADD(QUARTER, -1, '2017-07-25')

Table 6.2: *DATEADD() elements*

Displaying cumulative data over 90 days up to a specific date

The HR manager has emailed another request. He needs to calculate the final bonus of a salesperson who is leaving the company and consequently needs to see the accumulated sales made by this staff member in the 90 days up to July 25, 2017. SQL can do this (and we will imagine it is for the salesperson who sells Jaguars for Prestige Cars). So, to see her sales for the 90 days up to the specified date, you would write SQL like the following:

```
SELECT      SUM(SalePrice) AS CumulativeJaguarSales

FROM        allsales

WHERE       TO_DATE(SaleDate) BETWEEN DATE_SUB('2017-07-25', 90)

           AND '2017-07-25'

            AND MakeName = 'Jaguar';
```

Run the preceding piece of SQL code, and you will see the output as shown in *Figure 6.17*:

	CumulativeJaguarSales
1	109000

Figure 6.17: Using the DATE_SUB() function to specify a period relative to a date

How does it works

What is new here is how a period is defined in the **WHERE** clause. In this case, when subtracting an exact number of days, you use the **DATE_SUB()** function.

The **DATE_SUB()** function needs the following two parameters to work:

- **First**: The date for the number of days to be added to—or subtracted from. Once again, entering this in the YYYY-MM-DD format is more reliable—and always in quotes. This can, of course, be a column that contains data that can be interpreted as a date by Databricks.
- **Second**: The actual number of days (or whatever you use in your query). If you are going back in time—as we are here, to look back over 90 days—you need to enter **90**.

Tricks and traps

You may find a couple of points useful when using the **DATE_SUB()** function, which are given as follows:

- It is, technically, possible to use a negative number as the second parameter of the **DATE_SUB()** function. However, using the **DATEADD()** function is almost always simpler. So, to add 90 days to a date, you can write SQL like this:

  ```
  WHERE    TO_DATE(SaleDate) BETWEEN '2017-07-25' AND DATE_SUB('2017-07-25', -90)
  ```

- **DATE_SUB()** only subtracts days from a date. It cannot be tweaked to subtract other date elements.

Displaying the data for the previous three months

Suppose you want to see the rolling sum of car sales for each make sold during the previous three months up to and including the current date. The following piece of SQL code can do it for you:

```
SELECT     MakeName, SUM(SalePrice) AS CumulativeSales
```

```
FROM        allsales
WHERE       CAST(SaleDate AS DATE)
            BETWEEN ADD_MONTHS(CURRENT_DATE, -3)
            AND CURRENT_DATE
GROUP BY    MakeName
ORDER BY    MakeName ASC;
```

Running the preceding code will not deliver any output with the Prestige cars dataset. However, you can test this approach using your data.

How does it work

This code snippet introduces two new date functions, the **`CURRENT_DATE()`** and **`ADD_MONTHS()`**.

In spark, SQL **`CURRENT_DATE()`** means *now*. So, this query will always display data relative to the day it is run. If you run it today, you will see data up to today's date. Run it tomorrow, and the data will be different because the rolling total now ends on a different date.

`ADD_MONTHS()` does exactly what its name suggests; it adds several months to a date. This function requires the following two parameters:

1. **First**: This can be a date that you enter in the YYYY-MM-DD format (a hard-coded date), a field that can be interpreted as a date, or a **`TIMESTAMP`** field.
2. **Second**: Several months to add to the date. If you enter a negative number, the months are subtracted from the date.

This query does the following:

- **First**: It aggregates the total sales for each make, using a **`SUM`** on the **`SalePrice`** field and a **`GROUP BY`** on the **`MakeName`** field so that you see the total sales by make.
- **Second**: It limits the data to the last three months using the **`ADD_MONTHS()`** function and specifies that the period covers *now until three months previously* using the **`BETWEEN...AND`** function to define a range to filter on.
- **Third**: It presents the results in alphabetical order of make using the **`MakeName`** field in the **`ORDER BY`** clause.

Tricks and traps

There are a couple of useful things that you need to understand about the **ADD_MONTHS()** function, which are given as follows:

- **ADD_MONTHS()** adjusts to the number of days in the month. So, if you set the date as March 31 and use the following SQL Databricks will output February 28:

  ```
  ADD_MONTHS('2017-03-31', -1)
  ```

- You can also use the **DATEADD()** function to add or subtract months to or from a date. In this case, the SQL would look like the following:

  ```
  WHERE      TO_DATE(SaleDate) BETWEEN DATEADD(MONTH, -3, '2017-07-
  25')
             AND '2017-07-25'
  ```

- The **CURDATE()** function can be used interchangeably with **CURRENT_DATE()**.

Finding the current system date

If you want to check the current date and time, then a single line of SQL code can do this for you, which is as follows:

```
SELECT CURRENT_DATE();
```

Running the preceding code will return the date your Databricks assumes to be the current date.

Tricks and traps

The parentheses after the **CURRENT_DATE()** function are optional. You can also enter the following SQL code to return the current date:

```
SELECT CURRENT_DATE;
```

Conclusion

This chapter has taken you on a whirlwind tour of the core date functions you will need when analyzing how data evolves over time. You have discovered how to query data for a specific date or a range of dates. You have seen that you can look at data over years, quarters, weeks, months, or days. Indeed, you learned how to analyze data to date and how to compare data with previous time periods.

Analyzing data over time is such a vast subject that we can only scratch the surface in a single chapter of all that you can do. However, you can rest assured that you will see many more ways of handling date and time data in *Chapter 20: Analyzing Data Over Time*. In the upcoming chapter, you will learn how to modify text output in Spark SQL queries.

Core knowledge learned in this chapter

These are the keywords that you learned in this chapter:

Concept	Description
`DATEDIFF()`	This function finds the number of days, months, years, and so on between two given dates.
`CAST()`	This function converts a date time data type to a date.
`YEAR()`	This function isolates the year part of a date.
`MONTH()`	This function isolates the month part of a date.
`DAY()`	This function isolates the day part of a date.
`QUARTER()`	This function returns the quarter, weekday, and so on for a date.
`DAYOFYEAR()`	This function isolates the day in the year for a date.
`WEEKDAY()`	This function isolates the day of the week for a date.
`WEEKOFYEAR()`	This function isolates the week in the year for a date.
`DATE_FORMAT()`	This function formats a date in a specific way.
`DATEADD()`	This function adds or subtracts several days, months, years, and so on, to or from a given data and finds the date in the future or the past.
`ADD_MONTHS()`	Adds or subtracts a specified number of months to or from a date.
`CURRENT_DATE()`	This function finds the current date.
`DATE_SUB()`	Adds or subtracts a specified number of days to or from a date.

Join our book's Discord space

Join the book's Discord Workspace for Latest updates, Offers, Tech happenings around the world, New Release and Sessions with the Authors:

https://discord.bpbonline.com

CHAPTER 7
Formatting Text in Query Output

Introduction

A large part of SQL code is written purely to delve into mounds of data and return carefully chosen and filtered output. However, this is not the whole picture. Sometimes you will need your SQL skills to tweak the presentation of the data you deliver. This chapter explains how to take the text returned by a query and make the output easier to read and more meaningful. It also explains how to filter output using only part of the data in a text field.

Structure

In this chapter, we will cover the following topics:

- Enhancing the output from SQL queries
- Avoiding NULLs in text-based data
- Concatenating and grouping
- Extracting the first few characters from a field
- Filtering records based on the part of a field
- Filtering data using specific characters at a given position inside a field

Objectives

After understanding the technical focus of the previous chapters, it is time to learn some presentation techniques. You may not need these approaches on all occasions, but there are bound to be times when you must select not just a column of data but part of a column. Perhaps, you will need to amalgamate two or more columns into one. Maybe you will need to convert the contents of a column to lowercase or simply add some extra text to the contents of a column.

Presenting your data is, then, the subject of this chapter. After all, delivering clear and understandable analysis is your aim. It follows that knowing how to polish the final delivery is every bit as fundamental as the initial analysis.

Adding text to the output

Sometimes you may want to list some data and add repetitive text to the output. Suppose, for instance, you want to add the word **Customer** before each customer name in a query. You can do this using the following code:

```
SELECT 'Customer: ' || CustomerName AS Customer

FROM   allsales;
```

Executing the preceding piece of code will give you a result as shown in *Figure 7.1*:

	Customer
1	Customer: Magic Motors
2	Customer: Snazzy Roadsters
3	Customer: Birmingham Executive Prestige Vehicles
4	Customer: WunderKar
5	Customer: Casseroles Chromes
6	Customer: Magic Motors

***Figure 7.1:** Adding text to the output from a column*

How does it work

Any text you like can be added to the data in an output column. However, so that SQL knows you are adding extra text, not a SQL keyword, you must place the additional text in single quotes. Then you use the double pipe (||) operator to append the variable data column. Of course, you can start with the column name and then add some fixed text afterward if you prefer.

Tricks and traps

Although this technique is relatively simple, you should know a couple of things, which are given as follows:

- Additional text can be placed in either single or double quotes.
- Adding an alias when adding text to a single field is considered good practice, or Databricks will display the source SQL for the column as the column header.
- Any additional text can be in single or double quotes. So the **`SELECT`** clause could read as follows:

  ```
  SELECT "Customer: " || CustomerName AS Customer
  FROM   allsales;
  ```

- You can use most printable characters (such as spaces) in the text you add to a column name. Just ensure that any text is inside the quotes.
- If you want to add a single quote to the complementary text, double up on any quotes used. So, to add the text **`Yesterday's Sales`**, the SQL will look like the following:

  ```
  SELECT 'Yesterday''s Sales for ' || CUSTOMERNAME
  FROM    Data.SalesByCountry;
  ```

Adding text to numbers

Occasionally numbers are just not enough. You need to enhance them by adding some explanatory text. SQL lets you do this. The following short snippet code shows how to do this:

```
SELECT 'Sold For:' || SalePrice AS SoldFor
FROM   allsales;
```

Running the preceding SQL will return the output in *Figure 7.2*, which is what you expect to see:

	SoldFor
1	Sold For:65000
2	Sold For:220000
3	Sold For:19500
4	Sold For:11500
5	Sold For:19950
6	Sold For:29500
7	Sold For:49500

***Figure 7.2:** Adding text to a numeric field*

How does it work

The double-pipe operator concatenates (or joins) data from several columns into a single output column.

Amalgamating columns

Many datasets, by definition, fragment data into small, independent pieces. Yet when you want to output data, you frequently need to join data from two or more columns into one piece of information. This technique is called concatenation and can be applied to any data type column.

Look at the following code snippet:

```
SELECT CustomerName, Address1 || ' ' || Town || ' '
          || PostCode AS FullAddress
FROM   allsales;
```

Executing the preceding code returns the output in *Figure 7.3*:

	CustomerName	FullAddress
1	Magic Motors	27, Handsworth Road Birmingham B1 7AZ
2	Snazzy Roadsters	102, Bleak Street Birmingham B3 5ST
3	Birmingham Executive Prestige Vehicles	96, Aardvark Avenue Birmingham B2 8UH
4	WunderKar	null
5	Casseroles Chromes	null
6	Magic Motors	27, Handsworth Road Birmingham B1 7AZ
7	Birmingham Executive Prestige Vehicles	96, Aardvark Avenue Birmingham B2 8UH
8	Eat My Exhaust Ltd	29, Kop Hill Liverpool L1 8UY

***Figure 7.3:** Concatenating data from several columns*

How does it work

Using the double pipe (||), the operator takes the data from another column and appends it to the end of the column that you have already added to a **SELECT** clause. You then add any separator text (spaces, commas, and so on) that you want to add to make the result more readable. As you saw in the previous section, any text you add to a query must be in single quotes.

Tricks and traps

The following are some of the tricks and traps you need to know:

- As you are, by definition, using data from several fields, SQL cannot know what name to give to the resulting column. So, it is best to add an alias when concatenating data.

Avoiding NULLs in text-based data

If you take a closer look at the output shown in *Figure 7.3*, you will see many records that show **NULL** as the result of joining address, town, and **PostCode** fields. If you look at the data in these fields in the customer table, you will notice that there is data for at least one of these fields for clients, such as **WunderKar**, and when the fields are concatenated, they show nothing at all. Once again, null propagation is occurring and affecting the output.

Fortunately, SQL can apply the same solution to this problem you used in *Chapter 4: Simple Calculations*. Look at the following SQL snippet that is adapted from the initial code in the previous example:

```
SELECT CustomerName, NVL(Address1, '') || ' ' || NVL (Town, '') || ' '
                     || NVL (PostCode, '') AS FullAddress
FROM   allsales;
```

The result will now look like the output as shown in *Figure 7.4*:

	CustomerName	FullAddress
1	Magic Motors	27, Handsworth Road Birmingham B1 7AZ
2	Snazzy Roadsters	102, Bleak Street Birmingham B3 5ST
3	Birmingham Executive Prestige Vehicles	96, Aardvark Avenue Birmingham B2 8UH
4	WunderKar	AlexanderPlatz 205 Berlin
5	Casseroles Chromes	29, Rue Gigondas Lyon
6	Magic Motors	27, Handsworth Road Birmingham B1 7AZ
7	Birmingham Executive Prestige Vehicles	96, Aardvark Avenue Birmingham B2 8UH
8	Eat My Exhaust Ltd	29, Kop Hill Liverpool L1 8UY
9	M. Pierre Dubois	14, Rue De La Hutte Marseille
10	Sondra Horowitz	10040 Great Western Road Los Angeles
11	Wonderland Wheels	57, Grosvenor Estate Avenue London E7 4BR

***Figure 7.4**: Adding the NVL() function to avoid NULL propagation*

How does it work

A **NULL** value in any field, even if it is a text field, will propagate a **NULL** value into all the other fields you concatenate it with. This will result in a **NULL** being output. This is the same effect you saw previously for numbers in *Chapter 4: Simple Calculations*. However, we imagine this is not what you expected and certainly not what you want to see in the result.

The solution is the same for both letters and numbers. If you suspect a column contains NULLs, enclosing the field name in the **NVL()** function is best advised. This function requires:

First, the field containing possible **NULL** values you want to trap and replace with another character.

Second, the replacement character can be a blank space or an empty character (as in this example), in which case two single quotes will do the trick.

Tricks and traps

Make sure that you retain the following point when using the **NVL()** function, as it is important:

- If you apply **NVL()** to a text field, you must set the replacement character as a text. So, even if you replace **NULL** with a number, this must be in quotes.

Concatenating and grouping

The sales director now wants a list of all the different make and model combinations sold with the total sale price for each combination. However, they want to display the make and model in the same column this time. As they hover near your desk, you can quickly produce the following piece of SQL to deliver what they want:

```
SELECT      MakeName || ', ' || ModelName AS MakeAndModel
            ,SUM(SalePrice) As TotalSold
FROM        allsales
GROUP BY    MakeName ||', ' || ModelName;
```

Running the preceding query produces the output in *Figure 7.5*:

	MakeAndModel	TotalSold
1	Ferrari, 355	1191450
2	Alfa Romeo, Spider	48100
3	Porsche, Boxster	22500
4	Lamborghini, Countach	127150
5	Citroen, Rosalie	10190
6	Austin, Princess	11900

***Figure 7.5:** Grouping on concatenated fields*

How does it work

When using a **GROUP BY** clause, it is vital to include all the fields in the **SELECT** clause in the **GROUP BY** clause if these fields are not part of an aggregation function such as **SUM()**. This means you must copy the fields from the **SELECT** clause to the **GROUP BY** clause, as we did in the preceding SQL snippet.

Tricks and traps

There is one variation on a theme you can use when grouping aggregated fields, hich is given as follows:

- You do not need to add the fields used in the **SELECT** clause exactly as they are concatenated. That is, you could write the **GROUP BY** clause like te following:

  ```
  GROUP BY    MakeName, ModelName
  ```

Adding multiple pieces of text to numbers

You may want to combine data from text and numeric fields in a single element. For instance, add the word **Sales** before the sale price and a currency indicator afterward. The following SQL shows you how this can be done:

```
SELECT      CONCAT('Sales: ', TotalSalePrice ,' GBP')

            AS SalePriceInPounds

FROM        allsales;
```

Running the preceding code gives the results as shown in *Figure 7.6*:

	SalePriceInPounds
1	Sales: 65000.0 GBP
2	Sales: 220000.1 GBP
3	Sales: 19500.0 GBP
4	Sales: 11500.0 GBP
5	Sales: 19900.0 GBP
6	Sales: 29500.0 GBP

Figure 7.6: *Adding text to the output from a numeric field using the CONCAT() function*

How does it work

As you saw previously, SQL will not let you just assemble the contents of various fields by stringing them together or even add descriptive text to numbers without a little tweaking. Another way to output dates or numbers with boilerplate text is to use the **CONCAT()** function. This lets you join multiple fields and text to produce the desired output. However, if you have multiple fields to join together, then the **CONCAT()** function can be much easier to use. Just make sure you separate each text or field with a comma and place all text in quotes.

Tricks and traps

The **CONCAT()** function can be incredibly useful. You can take full advantage of it if you bear the following points in mind:

- Normally, you do not worry about formatting numbers in SQL like in Excel or reporting software. Indeed, you must leave numbers unformatted; otherwise, they will be considered text by Databricks. However, there could be cases where you need to format numbers (albeit to a limited extent). One way to do this is to append text to a number.

- Note that you can include spaces inside the single quotes around the text you are appending to the figures (the GBP) to enhance the final appearance of the output.
- This example shows only three elements inside the **`CONCAT()`** function, but you can add multiple fields and text.
- The **`CONCAT()`** function will also handle date data types.
- A useful advantage of using the **`CONCAT()`** function is that it handles NULLs flawlessly. So, even if one or more of the fields that you apply contains a **`NULL`**, this will not cause the final output to become a **`NULL`**. In other words, **`NVL()`** is superfluous if you are using the **`CONCAT()`** function.

Converting text to uppercase

Databricks can store alphabetical data in either uppercase or lowercase characters. However, the sales director wants a list of all the customer names in uppercase for a mail merge operation. As there will inevitably be times when you want to standardize the output without having to worry about how the data itself is stored, the following SQL code can do this for you:

```
SELECT      UPPER(CustomerName) AS Customer
FROM        allsales;
```

Running the preceding query gives the results as shown in *Figure 7.7*:

	Customer
1	MAGIC MOTORS
2	SNAZZY ROADSTERS
3	BIRMINGHAM EXECUTIVE PRESTIGE VEHICLES
4	WUNDERKAR
5	CASSEROLES CHROMES
6	MAGIC MOTORS

Figure 7.7: *Converting the text in a field to uppercase using the UPPER() function*

How does it work

Applying the **`UPPER()`** function to the **`CustomerName`** field ensures that every customer name output by the query will appear in uppercase. The **`UPPER()`** function requires at least one field as its parameter.

Tricks and traps

The following are a few suggestions of things you might need to be aware of when using the **`UPPER()`** function:

- Using any function means that SQL will not deduce the column name (even if it seems obvious). So, you will have to add an alias if you want the query output not to display the actual SQL code for any columns you convert to uppercase.
- This function will not affect any nonalphabetic characters in a field. So, numbers and punctuation will not change.
- This function is purely decorative and does not affect whatsoever on the underlying data. If the customer's name is stored in lowercase in the database, it will stay that way.
- You can apply the **`UPPER()`** function to multiple fields at once if you need to do so. So, you could write SQL like the following:

  ```
  SELECT     UPPER(Color || ' ' || InvoiceNumber)
  FROM       allsales;
  ```
- You can also use the **`UCASE()`** function to produce the same output.

Converting text to lowercase

Just as you can convert text (or strings, to give them their technical definition) to uppercase, you can convert them to lowercase. Look at the following code:

```
SELECT     LOWER(ModelName) AS Model
FROM       allsales;
```

Executing the preceding query gives the output as shown in *Figure 7.8*:

	Model
45	countach
46	diabolo
47	mondial
48	911
49	360
50	giulia

***Figure 7.8:** Converting strings to lowercase using the LOWER() function*

How does it work

Applying the **`LOWER()`** function to the **`ModelName`** field ensures that every vehicle model output by the query will appear in lowercase. This will not affect the way that the original data is stored and will produce the same result whether the original data in the source table is in lowercase, uppercase, or a mixture of the two. As you can see, numbers are not affected by this function.

Tricks and traps

- If you prefer, you can also use the **`LCASE()`** function to produce the same output like the following:

```
SELECT     LCASE(ModelName) AS Model
FROM       allsales;
```

Converting text to initial capitals

If you need to ensure visual conformity when outputting text, you can also force the display of initial capitals using SQL like the following:

```
SELECT     INITCAP(ModelName) AS Model
FROM       allsales;
```

Executing the preceding query gives the output as shown in *Figure 7.9*:

	Model
1	Testarossa
2	355
3	911
4	924
5	944
6	Db4
7	Db5
8	Db6

Figure 7.9: *Converting strings to initial capitals using the INITCAP() function*

Tricks and traps

The **`INITCAP()`** function does exactly what it implies—it converts the first letter to a capital. However, it also sets all other letters in each word to lowercase, which does not affect numbers.

Extracting the first few characters from a field

Sometimes text can be too long. At least this is what the marketing director thinks, as it wants to show the make names as acronyms using the first three letters of each make in a catalog of products. Fortunately, SQL lets you choose to output only a few characters of longer text, as you can see in the following code excerpt:

```
SELECT     ModelName || ' (' || LEFT(MakeName, 3) || ')' AS MakeAndModel

FROM       allsales;
```

Running the preceding query gives the results as shown in *Figure 7.10*:

	MakeAndModel
1	Testarossa (Fer)
2	355 (Fer)
3	911 (Por)
4	924 (Por)
5	944 (Por)
6	DB4 (Ast)

Figure 7.10: *Using the LEFT() function to extract a specific number of characters from the left of a string*

How does it work

SELECT clause not only concatenate strings from two fields (**ModelName** and **Make**) but also adds brackets to the result. The **LEFT()** function ensures that only the three leftmost characters from the make field are used when creating the make and model composite name.

The **LEFT()** function works like the following:

- **First**: Enter the field name containing the data from which you want to extract a few characters, followed by a comma.
- **Second**: Enter the number of characters to extract from the field as the second part of the **LEFT()** function.

Tricks and traps

When using functions like **`LEFT()`**, you need to be mindful of the following:

- Functions like **`LEFT()`** require two parameters. A comma separates each parameter inside the parentheses.
- The **`LEFT()`** function requires you to specify the field you are extracting characters from and then the number of characters you want to display. It is important to respect the order of these two elements (field first and then the number of characters) when you use the **`LEFT()`** function.
- Text functions are frequently used as part of a more complex formatting requirement. As you go through this chapter, remember that you can combine multiple text functions in many ways to get the output you are looking for.
- **`LEFT()`** requires an alias like most functions because it will not deduce the column name in the output header row.

Displaying the three characters at the right of the text

Sometimes you must isolate a series of characters from the right end of a field. In Prestige Cars' system, for instance, the finance director wants you to select the three characters at the right of the invoice number as these indicate the sequential number for the invoice. The SQL to do this is as follows:

```
SELECT     RIGHT(InvoiceNumber, 3) AS InvoiceSequenceNumber

FROM       allsales

ORDER BY   InvoiceSequenceNumber;
```

Running the preceding query returns the results as shown in *Figure 7.11*:

	InvoiceSequenceNumber
1	001
2	002
3	003
4	004
5	005
6	006

Figure 7.11: *Extracting characters from the right of a string using RIGHT()*

How does it work

The **RIGHT()** function ensures that only a specified number of characters from the right of the **InvoiceNumber** field are displayed. Any characters to the left of these characters (however, many there are) are discarded. The **RIGHT()** function is pretty much like the **LEFT()** function, and only it operates at the other end of the text in a field. You specify the field you are using as the base data and then give the number of characters to extract from the right of the field.

Another thing you did here is to sort the data on the output from the **RIGHT()** function. There are the following two ways of doing this:

- **Either**: Specify the same function—**RIGHT(InvoiceNumber, 3)**—that you used in the **SELECT** statement in the **ORDER BY** clause.
- **Or**: Use the alias in the **ORDER BY** clause, as we did here.

Tricks and traps

Our comments on using functions like **RIGHT()** or **LEFT()** largely concern sorting the data. These are as follows:

- Using the alias to sort data is often a lot simpler than rewriting the function that produced the output data.
- If you are sorting the data by a subset of the contents of a field, then you must either use the alias from the **SELECT** clause or rewrite the function in the **ORDER BY** clause. If you use the field name alone, you will probably not get the expected output as you are not sorting on the same criteria. So, using the following SQL will give the output that you can see in *Figure 7.12*:

```
SELECT      RIGHT(InvoiceNumber, 3) AS InvoiceSequenceNumber
FROM        allsales
ORDER BY    InvoiceNumber;
```

	InvoiceSequenceNumber
1	074
2	125
3	132
4	171
5	171

Figure 7.12: Misleading output when not using the same function in the SELECT and ORDER BY clauses

Displaying a given number of characters at a specific place in the text

In the Prestige Cars IT system, the fourth and fifth characters of the invoice number indicate the country where the vehicles were shipped. Knowing this, the sales director wants to extract only these characters from the invoice number field to analyze destination countries. The following is the SQL to do this:

```
SELECT     SUBSTRING(InvoiceNumber, 4, 2) AS DestinationCountry
FROM       allsales;
```

If you execute the preceding query, you will see the data as shown in *Figure 7.13*:

	DestinationCountry
1	GB
2	GB
3	GB
4	DE
5	FR

Figure 7.13: *Extracting a fixed number of characters from inside a field using SUBSTRING()*

How does it work

If you are always extracting a fixed number of characters from the same starting point in the text of a field, then **`SUBSTRING()`** is the function to use. This function takes the following three parameters (or needs three pieces of information) to work correctly:

1. **First**: Indicate the field you are working on.
2. **Second**: The number of characters from the left where you want to extract text.
3. **Third**: Provide the number of characters to extract commencing at the starting point defined in the preceding parameter.

As with all functions, each parameter is separated from the others by a comma. This function can seem unwieldy at first glance, and *Figure 7.14* explains it more visually:

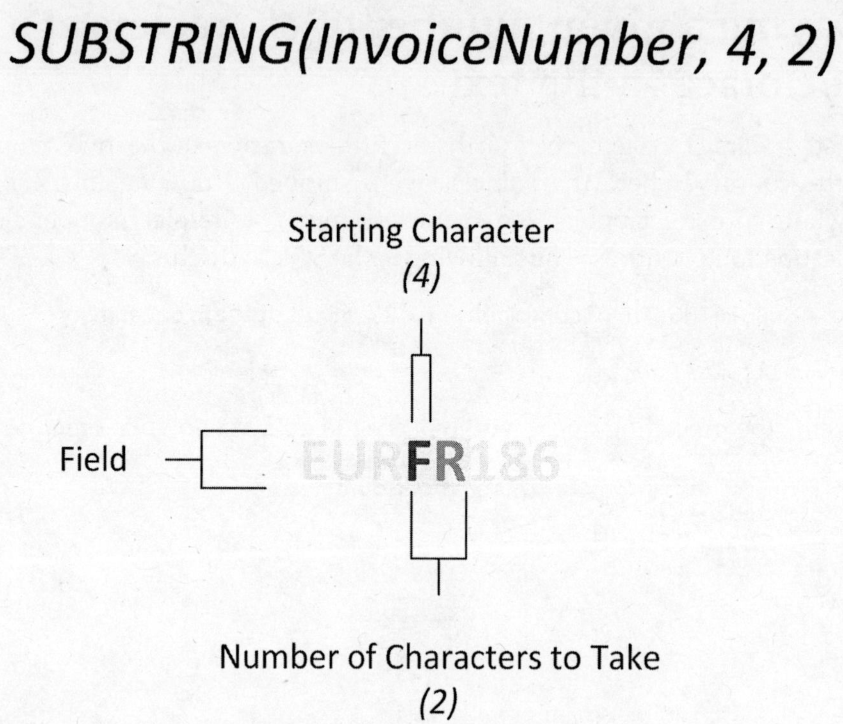

Figure 7.14: *The anatomy of a SUBSTRING() function*

Tricks and traps

The following are a couple of important points to retain here:

- It is vital to respect the order in which you enter the parameters (starting point and number of characters) when using the **`SUBSTRING`** function, or you are likely to get only gibberish returned.
- A few functions require more than one or two parameters to be supplied, so **`SUBSTRING`** is, fortunately, more of an exception than a rule.

Replacing NULLs with the contents of another field

You probably do not want to present empty fields in the table that you are outputting. In cases like this, you can replace NULLs with a fixed value using the **`NVL()`** function that you discovered in *Chapter 4: Simple Calculations* and also saw earlier in this chapter. However, you may prefer to adopt an approach that says:

- If the main field is `NULL`, use the contents of a second field (if the field contains anything).
- If the second field is `NULL`, use the contents of a third field (if this field contains anything).

This logic can be implemented using the **`COALESCE()`** function that you can see in use in the following piece of SQL:

```
SELECT     COALESCE(PostCode, Address1, Town)

FROM       allsales;
```

This SQL gives the result as shown in *Figure 7.15*:

	coalesce(PostCode, Address1, Town)
1	B1 7AZ
2	B3 5ST
3	B2 8UH
4	AlexanderPlatz 205
5	29, Rue Gigondas
6	B1 7AZ
7	B2 8UH
8	L1 8UY

Figure 7.15: Replacing NULL field elements with data from alternate fields

How does it work

`COALESCE()` requires a comma-separated list of fields. So, all you have to do is to present Databricks with a choice of fields (in the order that you want them used), and SQL will:

- Use the first field if it contains data for this record.
- Use the second field if it contains data for this record and the first field is **`NULL`**.
- Use the third field if it contains data for this record and the first and second fields are **`NULL`**.
- And so on, until the last field you specified is tested to determine whether it contains data.

Tricks and traps

Please note the following important point when using the **COALESCE()** function:

- **COALESCE()** can be fussy about data types. Essentially this means that all the fields you place in the list of fields inside **COALESCE()** should be the same data type or similar types of data (all numeric or all date or all string).
- Not adding an alias meant that the actual SQL code for the **COALESCE()** field became the column header.

Filtering records based on the part of a field

In the Prestige Cars database, the invoice number field always begins with three characters that indicate the payment currency (even if all the invoices are in pounds sterling). This allows you to produce a list of sales in a specified currency which is great, as the sales director has requested a list of sales where the invoice was paid in euros. The SQL that can do this is mercifully simple.

```
SELECT      InvoiceNumber, TotalSalePrice
FROM        allsales
WHERE       LEFT(InvoiceNumber, 3) = 'EUR'
```

Executing the preceding query gives the results as shown in *Figure 7.16*:

	InvoiceNumber	TotalSalePrice
1	EURDE004	11500
2	EURFR005	19900
3	EURFR009	19600
4	EURFR136	45000
5	EURFR013	8950
6	EURFR015	22950
7	EURFR018	75500

Figure 7.16: *Using a string function in a WHERE clause*

How does it work

This approach allows you to filter the **InvoiceNumber** field and output only those records where the three leftmost characters are **EUR**.

Here you are using a string function in the **WHERE** clause of a SQL query. This function is applied as it would be in a **SELECT** clause. In this particular case, the **LEFT()** function is used. The first parameter is the field from which you want to extract part of the data (the **InvoiceNumber** field). The second parameter is the number of characters to extract (three in this case). The value returned from the function is used to filter the data.

Tricks and traps

Note the following:

- You can use a function in a **WHERE** clause without using it in the **SELECT** clause.
- You can use the full field you are filtering in the **SELECT** clause without affecting the **WHERE** clause in any way.
- You might want to add the function you use in the **WHERE** clause to the **SELECT** clause initially (with or without the filter) to see whether the function gives the expected result.

Filtering data using specific characters at a given position inside a field

The sales director wants to see all the cars shipped to France but made in Italy. Fortunately, the invoice number definition used by Prestige Cars guarantees that the fourth and fifth characters contain the two-character code of the country where the car was shipped. So, you can use this information to extract a list of vehicles delivered to one country—and use another field to add a second field to restrict the country of manufacture. The SQL to do this is as follows:

```
SELECT      InvoiceNumber, TotalSalePrice

FROM        allsales

WHERE       SUBSTRING(InvoiceNumber, 4, 2)  = 'FR'

            AND MakeCountry = 'ITA';
```

Running the preceding query gives the results as shown in *Figure 7.17*:

	InvoiceNumber	TotalSalePrice
1	EURFR031	2550
2	EURFR107	169500
3	EURFR121	365000
4	EURFR122	395000
5	EURFR151	255950
6	EURFR186	155000

Figure 7.17: *Using SUBSTRING() and a standard comparison operator in a WHERE clause*

How does it work

This example clarifies that a `WHERE` clause can contain multiple criteria for comparisons and for more complex filters using functions. Here you are using a `WHERE` clause to filter the `InvoiceNumber` field where the fourth and fifth characters are `FR` (to isolate cars delivered to France), as well as using a country to specify that the car was built in Italy.

The `WHERE` clause of this query is where the action takes place. Its anatomy is as follows:

- **First**: The `SUBSTRING()` function is applied. The first parameter (the field name) is `InvoiceNumber` in this example. The second parameter, the number of characters from the left where the extraction will begin, is set to 4. Then the number of characters to extract at this point in the text is set to two. The filter is then defined as the two characters `FR` (for France).
- **Second**: An `AND` operator is added to the `WHERE` clause to add a second filter element to the query.
- **Finally**: The `MakeCountry` field is set to `ITA` (for Italy). Of course, this means knowing that the `MakeCountry` field uses ISO three-character acronyms to represent countries, but this is part and parcel of the need to know your data before you can use it.

Conclusion

This chapter gave you an overview of some core techniques you can apply to your code to adjust the presentation of text-based data. You saw how to extract part of a text column and convert text from uppercase to lowercase and vice versa. You also learned how to mix text and numbers in a single column.

These techniques enable you to use and shape the data to go beyond merely listing columns of data. Armed with the knowledge you have acquired in this chapter, you can query Databricks data and present it in a more meaningful and understandable way to your users.

Core knowledge learned in this chapter

These are the keywords and concepts you learned in this chapter:

Concept	Description
`UPPER()`	This function converts any text into uppercase characters. Numbers and symbols are not affected by this function.
`LOWER()`	This function converts any text into lowercase characters. Numbers and symbols are not affected by this function.
`INITCAP()`	This function converts any text into lowercase characters and the first character of each word into uppercase. Numbers and symbols are not affected by this function.
`LEFT()`	This function extracts a defined number of characters from the left of a string.
`RIGHT()`	This function extracts a defined number of characters from the right of a string.
`STR()`	This function converts a number to text to be used as a string of characters in a piece of SQL.
`SUBSTRING()`	This function extracts a defined number of characters from a string, beginning at a specified number of characters from the left of the string.
`COALESCE()`	This function replaces a NULL with the contents of another field.
`Concatenation`	This technique joins the output from two or more columns into a single output field.

CHAPTER 8
Formatting Numbers and Dates

Introduction

SQL will always attempt to present numbers at the most detailed level possible. This could mean displaying more decimals than you need. Equally, it may display dates in a way that you (or the users you deliver the output to) find a little clunky. So, you need to be able to format numbers and dates in ways that make the data more readable and intuitively understandable. This chapter covers a range of techniques that will help you achieve these objectives.

Structure

In this chapter, we will cover the following topics:

- Removing the decimals from the output
- Rounding a field up to the nearest whole number
- Rounding a value to the nearest whole number
- Rounding a value up or down to the nearest thousand
- Banker's rounding
- Displaying a value in a specific numeric format

- Displaying a value in a specific currency
- Outputting a date in a specific date format
- Presenting the time in a specific format

Objectives

You may often need to alter the output of your queries to improve their presentation. For instance, you may want to remove the decimals from the output or apply a specific number format. Alternatively, you need to display a date in a certain way, as in Excel.

This chapter introduces the basic formatting techniques which you would find essential when enhancing the presentation of your query results. So, while these techniques do not alter the accuracy of the output, they can make it considerably easier to understand.

NOTE: Formatting dates and numbers convert them into text, meaning SQL can no longer calculate a formatted number or date. So, you should always format numbers and dates once you are sure this is the final result of a query once any calculations have been applied.

Removing the decimals from the output

In some reports, you do not need decimals. So, SQL lets you remove them from output data easily. Look at the following snippet, which applies this technique to the Sale Price field:

```
SELECT    TotalSalePrice, FLOOR(TotalSalePrice) AS SalePriceRoundedDown
FROM      allsales;
```

Applying this query gives the results in *Figure 8.1*. We have kept the original untouched data as the output from the **FLOOR()** function so that you can see the difference when the function is applied.

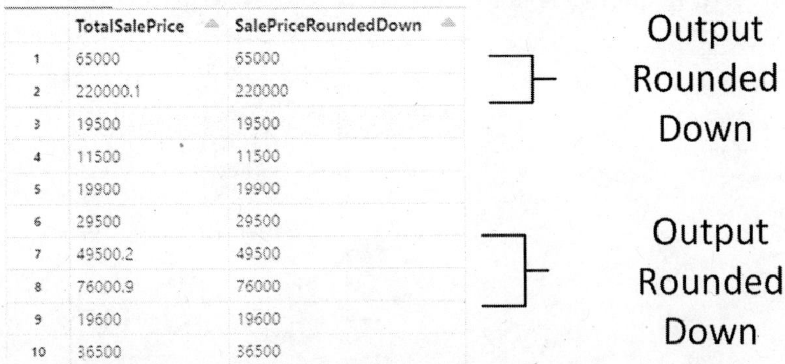

	TotalSalePrice	SalePriceRoundedDown
1	65000	65000
2	220000.1	220000
3	19500	19500
4	11500	11500
5	19900	19900
6	29500	29500
7	49500.2	49500
8	76000.9	76000
9	19600	19600
10	36500	36500

***Figure 8.1**: Truncating decimals from a number using the FLOOR() function*

How does it work

The **`FLOOR()`** function can remove the decimals from a column of figures. No rounding is applied; the numbers are simply stripped off the decimal part. If the number does not contain any decimals, then it simply stays the same.

Tricks and traps

You must remember one main factor when applying the **`FLOOR()`** function, which is given as follows:

- The **`FLOOR()`** function can be applied only to numeric data types.

Rounding a field up to the nearest whole number

Just as you can round numbers down, you can also round them up in SQL. The following code snippet shows you how to do this to the **`TotalSalePrice`** field:

```
SELECT      TotalSalePrice, CEILING(TotalSalePrice) AS SalePriceRoundedUp
FROM        allsales;
```

Running the preceding query gives the results as shown in *Figure 8.2*:

	TotalSalePrice	SalePriceRoundedUp
1	65000	65000
2	220000.1	220001
3	19500	19500
4	11500	11500
5	19900	19900
6	29500	29500
7	49500.2	49501
8	76000.9	76001
9	19600	19600
10	36500	36500

Figure 8.2: *Rounding up a decimal number to the next highest whole number using the CEILING() function*

How does it work

The **`CEILING()`** function removes the decimals from the figures you output but rounds the number up to the next highest whole number (or integer if you prefer the term). We have included the original data in the output so that you can compare the two versions of the numbers. In the real world, you would probably display only one version of the data in the output.

Tricks and traps

In the same case as with the **`FLOOR()`** function, the following is true when using the **`CEILING()`** function:

- The **`CEILING()`** function can be applied only to numeric data types.

Rounding a value to the nearest whole number

If you want to round decimals up or down to the nearest whole number, Databricks has the **`ROUND()`** function to do this, as the following SQL snippet makes clear:

```
SELECT      TotalSalePrice, ROUND(TotalSalePrice, 0) AS SalePriceRounded

FROM        allsales;
```

Running the preceding query shows you both the original and rounded values, as you can see in *Figure 8.3*:

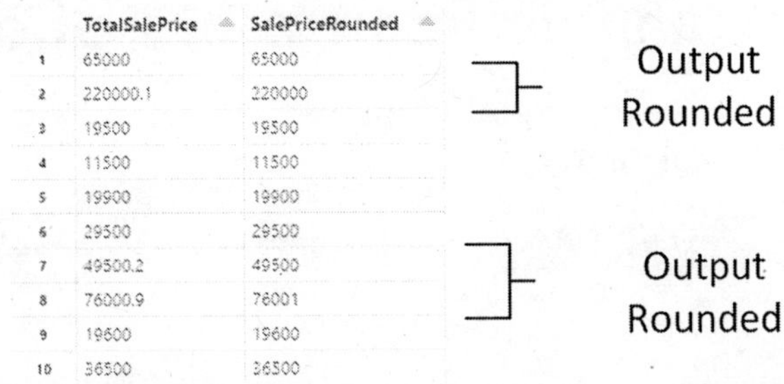

***Figure 8.3**: Applying the Round function to numeric output*

How does it work

When used this way, the **ROUND()** function rounds up or down to the nearest whole number, whether higher or lower. As you can see from *Figure 8.3*, where you can compare the sale price to the rounded sale price, you can round numbers both up and down.

The **ROUND()** function needs you to add a parameter that indicates how many decimal places the number is rounded to. Using a 0 as the second parameter means no decimals, effectively removing the decimals from the field used as the first parameter.

Tricks and traps

The following are a few comments to note down here:

- Exporting a rounded output to a spreadsheet (or any other application) and then calculating the total for the column can produce rounding errors (compared to calculating the total for a column where no rounding has been applied), as the decimals have been limited or removed definitively.
- You can treat the second parameter in the **ROUND()** function as optional. If you simply apply a **ROUND()** function to a field, it will round to the nearest integer as if you had added a zero as the second parameter. So you could write SQL like the following to produce the same output that you can see in *Figure 8.3*:

  ```
  SELECT    TotalSalePrice, ROUND(TotalSalePrice) AS SalePriceRounded
  FROM      allsales;
  ```

- To round to a specific number of decimals, you use a positive number as the second parameter of the **ROUND()** function. The following code shows how to round to two decimals:

  ```
  ROUND(SalePrice, 2)
  ```

Rounding to a specific number of decimals

You can also round output to a specific number of decimals using the **`ROUND()`** function. The following SQL does exactly this.

```
SELECT      TotalSalePrice, ROUND(TotalSalePrice, 2) AS SalePriceRounded
FROM        allsales;
```

Running the preceding query returns the output that you can see in *Figure 8.4*:

	TotalSalePrice	SalePriceRounded
1	65000	65000
2	220000.1	220000.1
3	19500	19500
4	11500	11500
5	19900	19900

***Figure 8.4**: Rounding to two decimals*

It is important to note that rounding to a fixed number of decimals will not alter the way that numbers are displayed (in other words it does not forma the output). However, the underlying data now contains only the defined number of decimals.

Rounding a value up or down to the nearest thousand

You may want to round up or down to thousands when dealing with large figures. SQL can do this easily, as the following code snippet shows:

```
SELECT      SalePrice, ROUND(SalePrice, -3)
                AS SalePriceRoundedToThousand
FROM        allsales;
```

Executing the preceding query gives you the original data and the rounded output, as you can see in *Figure 8.5*:

	SalePrice	SalePriceRoundedToThousand
1	65000	65000
2	220000	220000
3	19500	20000
4	11500	12000
5	19950	20000
6	29500	30000
7	49500	50000

***Figure 8.5**: Rounding to the nearest thousand*

How does it work

The **ROUND()** function takes the following two parameters:

- **First**: The numeric field whose output you want to modify.
- **Second**: The type of rounding to be applied. This can be a positive or negative number. A positive number affects the number of decimals, and a negative number affects the integer values (the whole number).

In this example, the **SalesDate** field is rounded to the nearest thousand. This happens because the second parameter used in the **ROUND()** function is negative. Consequently, the rounding is applied to the nearest thousands in this case. You can even set this to be tens, hundreds, thousands, millions, or billions if you want.

The negative number you use as the second parameter indicates how the number is rounded. *Table 8.1* shows how you applied the number in the left column as the second parameter of the **ROUND()** function to obtain the result described in the right column:

Parameter	Effect
-1	Rounds to the nearest 10
-2	Rounds to the nearest 100
-3	Rounds to the nearest 1,000
-4	Rounds to the nearest 10,000
-5	Rounds to the nearest 100,000

***Table 8.1**: Rounding up numbers*

You can continue and round to millions or billions if you want. However, the parameter represents the number of zeros in the rounded result. If you are looking only at rounding to a decimal value, then you simply make the second parameter of the **ROUND()** function a positive number.

Tricks and traps

There is only one point to be aware of when using the **ROUND()** function, which is given as follows:

- If you leave out the second parameter (and the comma that precedes it), then the **ROUND()** function simply removes the decimals from the field.

Banker's rounding

The **ROUND()** function you saw is simple to apply and ruthlessly efficient. Nonetheless, this function may not suit all circumstances, and this is because it rounds up when the decimal figure is 5 or more. Sometimes you may want to round down when the decimal is 5 (or less).

This approach—often known as banker's rounding—can be achieved simply by using the **BROUND()** function like the following.

```
SELECT     TotalSalePrice, BROUND(TotalSalePrice, 0) AS SalePriceRounded

FROM       allsales

ORDER BY   TotalSalePrice;
```

In this case, any decimals between 0 and 5 are rounded down.

Tricks and traps

There are only two important points to be aware of when using the **BROUND()** function, which are given as follows:

- Like the **ROUND()** function, the **BROUND()** function takes an optional second parameter. If you leave out the second parameter (and the comma that precedes it), then the **ROUND()** function simply removes the decimals from the field.
- As was the case for the **ROUND()** function, a positive number as the second parameter affects the rounding for the number of decimals, and a negative number affects the rounding for the integer values (the whole number).

Displaying a value in a specific numeric format

The sales director wants you to make some of the reports you send directly from Databricks look slightly easier to read (as she puts it). So, she wants you to present data with a thousand separators and two decimals. Fortunately, Databricks makes this kind of presentation easy, as the following code snippet shows:

```
SELECT      FORMAT_NUMBER(cost, "#,###.00") AS UKCostPrice

FROM        allsales

ORDER BY    stockcode;
```

Executing the preceding query gives you the formatted output, as shown in *Figure 8.6*:

	UKCostPrice
1	20,000.00
2	15,600.00
3	6,040.00
4	17,200.00
5	66,072.00
6	146,000.00
7	47,600.00

Figure 8.6: Formatting numbers for readability

How does it work

This query introduces the **FORMAT_NUMBER()** function. This function requires two parameters. They are as follows:

- **First**: The numeric field to format.
- **Second**: The placeholder codes to define the presentation of the numbers plus any text to precede or follow the formatted figures. This must all be enclosed in quotes.

In this specific case, the cost field from the stock table is stored as a number without any thousand separators or the specific number of decimals (there could be between 0 and 4 decimals for this field). So, to make the output more palatable to the eye, the **FORMAT_NUMBER()** function is used. This function does the following two things:

- **First**: It adds a thousand separators every three figures to the left of the decimal point.
- **Second**: It limits the number of decimals to display to two.

The format codes that you can apply are given in *Table 8.2*:

Format code	Description
`0`	Compulsory number
`#`	Optional number
`,`	Thousands separator
`.`	Decimal

***Table 8.2:** Number formats*

You can add text to the output before or after the numbers. To get a better idea of how the format codes are used and the results that they give, look at *Table 8.3*:

Format code	Output	Explanation
`#.0`	9950.0	Any numbers to the left of the decimal with one number after the decimal point.
`#.00`	9950.00	Any numbers to the left of the decimal with two decimals.
`#,###.00`	9,950.00	Any numbers (with thousands of separators if the number is greater than 1,000) to the left of the decimal with two decimals.
`EUR #,###.00`	EUR 9,950.00	A text to the left of the numbers and any numbers (with thousands of separators if the number exceeds 1,000) to the left of the decimal with two decimals.
`GBP #.0 CR`	EUR 9950.0 CR	A text to the left of the numbers, any numbers to the left of the decimal point (without a thousand separator), two decimals and a text to the right of the single decimal.

***Table 8.3:** Sample number formats*

Tricks and traps

We have only a couple of comments to note here:

- As is the case with virtually all columns involving a function, adding a column alias is generally a good idea.

- You can also format the output from a calculation using the **`FORMAT_NUMBER()`** function. So you could write code the following code:

```
SELECT      FORMAT_NUMBER(Partscost + RepairsCost, "#,###.00") AS
RawCost
FROM        allsales
ORDER BY    stockcode;
```

- You cannot switch the display of the thousand's separator and decimal point to local or national styles (such as the European use of the comma as the decimal point and the period as the thousands separator).
- Format codes can be wrapped in either single or double quotes. So the SQL used in the initial code sample in this section could read as follows:

```
SELECT      FORMAT_NUMBER(cost, '#,###.00') AS RawCost
FROM        allsales
ORDER BY    stockcode;
```

Displaying a value in a specific currency

The sales director is in a hurry and says she will not have the time to format the data you sent her. Therefore, she wants you to output a list of vehicle sales that can be immediately presented to the CEO. She wants the output to include thousands of separators, two decimals, and a British pound symbol.

You can do this, too, as the following short SQL example shows:

```
SELECT      MakeName, ModelName
            ,FORMAT_NUMBER(SalePrice, "GBP #,###.00")
            AS SterlingSalePrice
FROM        allsales
ORDER BY    MakeName, ModelName, SterlingSalePrice DESC;
```

Running the preceding query gives the results in *Figure 8.7*, where the result appears in pounds sterling:

	MakeName	ModelName	SterlingSalePrice
1	Alfa Romeo	1750	GBP 9,950.00
2	Alfa Romeo	1750	GBP 3,575.00
3	Alfa Romeo	Giulia	GBP 8,695.00
4	Alfa Romeo	Giulia	GBP 6,950.00
5	Alfa Romeo	Giulia	GBP 6,000.00
6	Alfa Romeo	Giulia	GBP 25,000.00
7	Alfa Romeo	Giulia	GBP 2,550.00
8	Alfa Romeo	Giulia	GBP 17,500.00

Figure 8.7*: Formatting numbers as British pounds*

How does it work

It is worth noting that if you are using SQL output directly, not as a source for another program like Excel, then you may want to produce formatted output that is easier for your public to understand. However, Databricks is not naturally a presentation tool. Consequently, a little work can be necessary to produce polished output directly from a SQL query.

Formatting numbers in this way generally implies a two-pronged approach given as follows:

- **First**: Use the `FORMAT_NUMBER()` function to display the number with the required number of decimals and the thousands separator.
- **Second**: Add a text representing the currency before or after the codes for the numeric representation.

Tricks and traps

It is important to remember that Spark SQL is, at its heart, a query language and not a presentation tool. So, you need to consider the following when delivering formatted output:

- It is probably obvious that no exchange rate conversion is taking place here. All that happens is that the figures are formatted in pounds just as you would in Excel.
- You can add any text before or after the formatted numbers. So, you can use ISO currency specifications or units of distance or weight if you need to.

- If you intend to use the output from a query in another application, then you should not format figures unless you are sure they will not be used in downstream calculations.
- Alternatively, you may prefer to use the **CONCAT()** function to add a currency unit before or after the formatted figure, like the following:

```
SELECT CONCAT("£ ", FORMAT_NUMBER(SalePrice, "#,###.00")) FROM
allsales
```

Outputting a date in a specific date format

Suppose you need to send a list of data to the CEO that contains a date, and you need that date to be in the specific format that she has requested (first the day, then the abbreviation for the month, and finally the year in four figures in this occurrence). The following SQL will do that for you:

```
SELECT      InvoiceNumber

           ,DATE_FORMAT(SaleDate, 'd M y') AS SaleDate

FROM        allsales;
```

Running the preceding query gives the results as shown in *Figure 8.8*:

	InvoiceNumber	SaleDate
57	GBPGB050	15 6 2016
58	EURFR051	15 6 2016
59	EURFR051	15 6 2016
60	EURFR051	15 6 2016
61	GBPGB052	1 7 2016
62	EURES192	1 11 2017

***Figure 8.8:** Outputting a date in a specific format using the DATE_FORMAT() function*

How does it work

If you want to display a date in a wide range of possible formats, you can use the **DATE_FORMAT()** function to display dates in the precise format you require. The **DATE_FORMAT()** function takes a date or timestamp field and forces the result to be output in one of the many date and time formats that Databricks can deliver.

The `DATE_FORMAT()` function takes the following two input parameters:

- **First**: The field you want to convert. This must be a date, datetime field, or field that Databricks can convert to a datetime data type. The `SaleDate` field suits the purpose here.
- **Second**: The internal code that indicates the output format. This must be enclosed in quotes.

As with all functions, you just need to ensure you enter the parameters (or elements, if you prefer) in the correct order, from left to right.

The code format you apply will always consist of one or more placeholder codes and possibly separator characters enclosed in single or double quotes.

Table 8.4 lists the possible date format codes you can use and combine to present dates. Please remember that capitalization of these codes is important:

Format code	Description	Example
`d`	Number of days in month	9
`dd`	Number of days in month with a leading zero, if a single figure	09
`M`	Numeric month	6
`MM`	The numeric month with a leading zero; if a single figure	06
`MMMM`	Full name of the month	July
`MMM`	Abbreviated name of the month	Jul
`yy`	Year as two digits	23
`yyyy`	Year as four digits	2023
`E` or `EE` or `EEE`	Abbreviated day of week name	Tue
`EEEE`	A full day of week name	Tuesday
`G` or `GG` or `GGG`	AD/BC	AD
`GGGG`	Anno Domini	Anno Domini

***Table 8.4:** Date formats*

Do not worry about ever trying to learn these codes. In all probability, you will only ever need a few of them, and you will almost certainly end up remembering the ones you use most often. If you need a complete list of all the possible codes, they are available on the Databricks website. As creating date format codes can appear to be a little daunting at first sight, *Table 8.5* contains a set of sample date formats to give you a few ideas as to how to create your date formats:

Format code	Example
`DATE_FORMAT(SaleDate, ' dd MMM yyyy')`	25 Jul 2018
`DATE_FORMAT(SaleDate, ' EEEE, dd MMMM yyyy')`	Saturday, 25 July 2015
`DATE_FORMAT(SaleDate, ' yyyyMMdd')`	20180725
`DATE_FORMAT(SaleDate, ' dd/MM/yy')`	25/07/18

Table 8.5*: Sample date formats*

Tricks and traps

The following are a few things to note when formatting dates:

- This approach will work only if the field is a valid datatype or can be converted to a date, and if this is not the case, SQL will return a NULL.
- If you use the **`DATE_FORMAT()`** function, you are, in effect, converting the date to text. Consequently, you may no longer be able to carry out date calculations once the field has been formatted.
- You must respect the capitalization of the format codes when you write your output formats for dates.
- You can use either single or double quotes to enclose the format codes you apply.
- The complete set of required format codes must be placed inside quotes, and you should not enclose each element inside separate quotes.
- You can add any separators between the format codes, hyphens, slashes, spaces, and so on.

Presenting the time in a specific format

You can decide how to present time elements as you can format dates in Databricks. Indeed, you do this using the same function (but with different formatting codes) that you learned in the previous section, as the following SQL snippet shows:

```
SELECT     InvoiceNumber
           ,DATE_FORMAT(SaleDate, "HH mm") AS SaleTime
FROM       AllSales;
```

Running the preceding query gives the results as shown in *Figure 8.9*:

	InvoiceNumber	SaleTime
1	GBPGB001	08 00
2	GBPGB002	12 00
3	GBPGB003	10 00
4	EURDE004	08 00
5	EURFR005	10 33
6	GBPGB006	12 00
7	GBPGB007	12 00

***Figure 8.9**: Outputting a date in a specific format using the DATE_FORMAT() function*

You apply a time format to a datetime or time field exactly as you applied it to a date field in the previous section.

- **First**: Enter the field you want to convert and a comma.
- **Then**: Enter the internal code that indicates the time format that you want to apply (in quotes) and the right parenthesis.

Table 8.6 lists most of the possible time format codes that you can use to present dates and times:

Format code	Description	Example
h	Hour	0…23
hh	Hour	1..12
m	Minutes	00..59
mm	Seconds	00..59
a	AM or PM	PM
S	Microseconds	000000..999999
kk	Hour in24 hour clock	23
a	Time	hh:mm:ss followed by AM or PM
z	Time zone name	GMT

***Table 8.6**: Time formats*

Tricks and traps

The same comments are applied to time formatting as applied to the formatting dates:

- You can use either single or double quotes to enclose the format codes you apply.
- The format codes must be placed inside quotes—not each element.
- You can add any separators between the format codes—hyphens, slashes, spaces, colons, text, and so on.

- You can combine date and time formatting, of course. To display the date and time, you could combine formatting codes like the following:

```
DATE_FORMAT(SaleDate, 'dd/MM/yyyy hh:mm')
```

- The capitalization of format codes is extremely important.

Conclusion

This chapter showed you some of the core techniques you can use to alter how numbers and dates are output from a SQL query. You learned how to round numbers up and down by rounding by tens, hundreds, and even thousands. Then, you saw how to apply a thousand separators and define the number of decimals. Finally, you saw how to present dates and numbers in various ways using custom formats.

Core knowledge learned in this chapter

The followings are the keywords and concepts you learned in this chapter:

Concept	Description
`FLOOR()`	This function rounds numbers down to the nearest integer.
`CEILING()`	This function rounds numbers up to the nearest integer.
`ROUND()`	This function rounds numbers to integers—and factors of 10.
`BROUND()`	This function rounds numbers to integers—and factors of 10 while rounding down from 5.
`DATE_FORMAT()`	This function alters how a date (and time, if available) is presented in the output.
`FORMAT_NUMBER()`	This function applies an output format to numbers and dates either from a predefined list or according to a user-defined format.

Join our book's Discord space

Join the book's Discord Workspace for Latest updates, Offers, Tech happenings around the world, New Release and Sessions with the Authors:

https://discord.bpbonline.com

CHAPTER 9
Using Basic Logic to Enhance Analysis

Introduction

Accurate data selection is a good first step in the effective analysis. However, there may be times when you are faced with so much data that it is difficult to detect the nuggets of information hidden in all the columns and rows of facts and figures. To prevent you from missing key details, Databricks can highlight the records that stand out from the rest and give you greater control over your data, which is done using the basic logical functions of Spark SQL.

Structure

In this chapter, the following topics will be discussed:

- Generating an alert when a value is too high
- Shortening text and adding ellipses to indicate truncation
- Designing complex calculated alerts
- Creating key performance indicators
- Classifying a series of elements without the necessary categories present in your data
- Creating ad hoc category groupings

- Applying multiple ad hoc categories
- Categorizing data using nested classifications
- Choosing elements from a list
- Placing nulls at the start or end of a list

Objectives

Applying logic in a SQL query generally involves testing data for the characteristics that interest you and either flagging any records that need to be investigated further or handling the output in specific ways depending on the result of a logical process. This can mean applying different scenarios depending on the values in a field or excluding data based on a logical test.

Logic tests are, essentially, limited only by your requirements and imagination. In this chapter, we will introduce you to some techniques you can apply to use SQL to do some heavy lifting when analyzing data.

Generating an alert when a value is too high

Keeping track of costs is an essential part of any business. Suppose the finance director of Prestige Cars Ltd. wants a report that flags any car ever bought where the cost of the parts was greater than the cost of repairs. The following code does this by adding an extra column to the list of parts and repairs costs that draws your attention to any potential anomalies:

```
SELECT      Cost, RepairsCost, PartsCost
            ,IFF(PartsCost > RepairsCost, 'Cost Alert!', NULL)
            AS CostAnalysis
FROM        allsales;
```

Running the preceding query gives the results as shown in *Figure 9.1*:

	Cost	RepairsCost	PartsCost	CostAnalysis
1	52000	2175	1500	null
2	176000	5500	2200	null
3	15600	660	0	null
4	9200	500	750	Cost Alert!
5	15960	1360	500	null
6	[illegible]	500	750	Cost Alert!

Figure 9.1: *Using conditional logic and the IFF() function to test output*

How does it work

This short piece of SQL introduces the **IFF()** function. This function is another of the three-parameter functions in SQL, and it requires the following:

- **First**: A test is to be carried out. Normally, this consists of comparing the data in a column with either a fixed value or the data in another column. In this example, the test sees whether the data in the **PartsCost** column is of a higher value than the data in the **RepairsCost** column for each record.
- **Second**: A result that is displayed if the test proves true (in the preceding in this example, the parts that mean a parts cost is greater than the repair cost). This can be text, a number, a calculation, or nothing, and so on. In this example, you are displaying the text **Cost Alert!** Because the result is a text in this case, it must be in single or double quotes.
- **Finally**: A result that appears if the test proves false (in this example, that means a parts cost less than or equal to the repair cost). This part of the function can also be text, a number, a calculation, or indeed nothing at all. In this example, you want to show nothing, so the **NULL** keyword is used because that means *nothing* in this context.

The following figure shows you how this works more graphically:

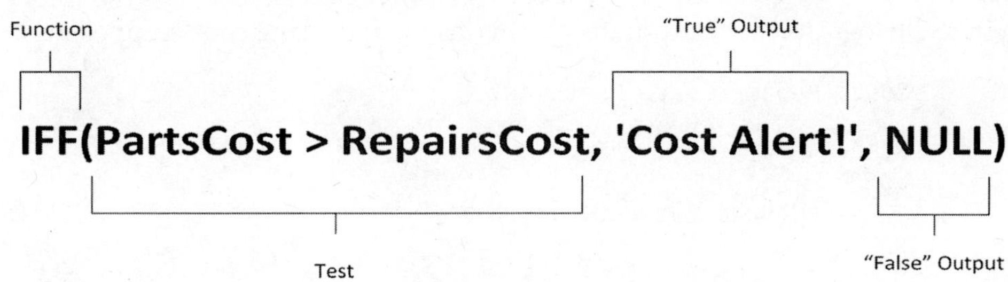

Figure 9.2: *The anatomy of an IFF() expression*

Tricks and traps

IFF() expressions can be a powerful addition to your SQL armory. However, when using them, you will always have to bear the following key points in mind:

- If you wanted to show something other than a blank cell in the output (the word **OK**, for instance), you could use the **IFF()** function in the following way instead:

  ```
  IFF(PartsCost > RepairsCost, 'Alert', 'OK')
  ```

- You can consider the test that is the first parameter of an **IFF()** function as being a mini **WHERE** clause to some extent. This is because you apply the same comparative logic in the test parameter as in a **WHERE** clause. In this case, the result must return an outcome that SQL can interpret as true or false.

- An **IFF()** function is not limited to just displaying text; it can also carry out calculations in the second and third parts of the function. So you could write SQL like the following to cut the parts cost in half if it is greater than the cost of the repair:

```
SELECT      Cost, RepairsCost, PartsCost
            ,IFF(PartsCost > RepairsCost, 'Cost Alert!', PartsCost
* 0.5)
           AS AdjustedPartsCost
FROM       allsales;
```

Shortening text and adding ellipses to indicate truncation

The sales director wants some customer feedback. She knows that the sales database has comments from clients in it, but she does not need or want to display all the text. She only wants to show the first few characters and then use ellipses to indicate that the text has been shortened. This way, she can always extract the full comment later. Applying SQL logic to your output can do this, as the following code snippet shows:

```
SELECT      Cost, RepairsCost, PartsCost
            ,IFF(
                 LEN(BuyerComments) < 25
                 ,BuyerComments
                 ,LEFT(BuyerComments, 20) + ' ...'
                ) AS Comments
FROM        allsales;
```

Running the preceding query gives the results as shown in *Figure 9.3*:

	Cost	RepairsCost	PartsCost	Comments
5	15960	1360	500	null
6	23600	500	750	null
7	39600	2500	1500	FAbulous motor!
8	60800	3250	750	null
9	15680	890	500	null
10	29200	1950	500	null

Figure 9.3: *Applying conditional logic to alter output using the IFF() function*

How does it work

An **IFF()** function tests the contents of a column. However, instead of comparing one value with another, it calculates the number of characters in the column for each record using the **LEN()** function. This function simply calculates the number of letters or numbers in a string. In the output shown in *Figure 9.3*, if there are less than 25 characters in the field, its output is full. If not, only the first 20 characters are allowed into the result, with three dots (an ellipsis) appended to them. This way, you can be certain that you will never see more than 25 characters when displaying the buyer's comments.

This example's point is to clarify that the output from an **IFF()** function need not just be hard-coded text, as you saw previously. An **IFF()** function will let you use database fields as the output for true and false parameters.

Designing complex calculated alerts

This time the sales director has left you stunned. She wants you to look at the profit on each car sold and flag any sale where the profit figure is less than 10% of the purchase price while, at the same time, the repair cost is at least twice the parts cost. However, this request illustrates that you frequently need to isolate specific cases from the rest of the data when analyzing datasets.

In practice, this often means that any tests you apply to your data can be more complex than those you have seen in this chapter. It is possible to use functions like **IFF()** to carry out quite logical complex tests and to return a value depending on the outcome of those tests. The following SQL is an example:

```
SELECT      Cost, RepairsCost, PartsCost
```

```
        ,IFF(
             (SalePrice -
               (Cost + LineItemDiscount
                        + PartsCost
                        + NVL(RepairsCost, 0)
                        + TransportInCost
                  )
              )
              < (SalePrice * 0.1)
              AND (RepairsCost * 2) > PartsCost
           ,'Warning!!'
           ,'OK'
            ) AS CostAlert
FROM    allsales;
```

Executing the preceding SQL gives the results as shown in *Figure 9.4*:

	Cost	RepairsCost	PartsCost	CostAlert
1	52000	2175	1500	Warning!!
2	176000	5500	2200	Warning!!
3	15600	660	0	OK
4	9200	500	750	OK
5	15960	1360	500	OK

Figure 9.4: More complex logical tests using IFF()

How does it work

The **`IFF()`** function tests the sales and costs for every vehicle sold and flags any sales where the profit is less than 10% of the purchase price, and the repair costs are at least double the parts cost. All this is done in the first part of the **`IFF()`** function.

The preceding example shows that an **`IFF()`** function can be as complex as you need it to be and include nested parentheses like a **`WHERE`** clause.

In a complex **IFF()** function, it is the first parameter of the test that is usually complex. The actual output can be quite simple. In this example, the test is in the following two parts:

1. The calculation of the profit percentage.
2. The calculation of the repairs to parts ratio.

This can be broken down into the following four steps:

1. **First**: The net profit is calculated (as you have done previously in this book) by subtracting the total of all the cost elements from the sale price.
2. **Second**: 10% of the sale price is calculated. This, too, is enclosed inside its own set of parentheses.
3. **Third**: The SQL then compares the net profit to 10% of the sale price.
4. **Finally**: The code then multiplies repair costs by a factor of two (which is isolated from the rest of the test by being placed in parentheses) and compares this to the parts cost.

If both these tests are true, the **IFF()** function will display a **Warning** as its output.

Tricks and traps

When designing complex tests using the **IFF()** function, it can help to remember the following:

- If you want to try a complex **IFF()** function, you can always start by using the test part of the **IFF()** statement in the **WHERE** clause. This will allow you to see the filter effect of the test code. Then, once you are sure the code does exactly what you want, you can place it inside an **IFF()** function in the **SELECT** statement.
- Using parentheses efficiently can be a real boon when building complex tests (the first parameter of an **IFF()** function) in SQL. More specifically, they can help you isolate separate aspects of the test to concentrate on each unit separately.
- The tests act like a small **WHERE** clause, and they can use the same logical operators **AND**, **OR**, and **NOT** that you first saw in *Chapter 3: Complex Filters*.
- As the final output does not show the profit figure, you may want to add this, at least when testing the query. This will let you ensure that the logic is correct.

Creating key performance indicators

As a final flourish for the dashboard that she wants to present to the board of directors, the sales manager wants to create a set of **Key Performance Indicators** (**KPIs**). This involves defining the output from the analysis as good, bad, or acceptable.

This kind of request illustrates that not all tests on your data can give simple black-or-white results. Sometimes you may require a more nuanced answer and must output three or more states that categorize the output.

The following piece of SQL is designed for precisely this kind of eventuality:

```
SELECT      Cost, RepairsCost, PartsCost
           ,IFF(
                (SalePrice -
                      (Cost + LineItemDiscount - PartsCost
                       + RepairsCost + TransportInCost)
                 ) < SalePrice * 0.1
                   ,'Warning!!'
               ,IFF(
                    (SalePrice -
                          (Cost + LineItemDiscount - PartsCost
                           + RepairsCost + TransportInCost)
                     ) < SalePrice * 0.5, 'Acceptable'
                    , 'OK'
                   )
               ) AS CostAlert
FROM        allsales;
```

Running the preceding query gives the results as shown in *Figure 9.5*:

	Cost	RepairsCost	PartsCost	CostAlert
1	52000	2175	1500	Acceptable
2	176000	5500	2200	Warning!!
3	15600	660	0	OK
4	9200	500	750	OK
5	15960	1360	500	OK
6	23600	500	750	Acceptable

Figure 9.5: *Nested logic tests using IFF()*

How does it work

This type of query probably looks more complicated than it is. It is called a nested **`IFF()`** statement because you place one **`IFF()`** function inside another. What it does is as follows:

- **First:** It calculates the sale price minus all the associated costs (the net margin) and then compares the result to the price multiplied by 10%. If the margin is lower than 10% of the sale price, the function displays a **Warning** and goes no further.
- **Then:** If the costs exceed the calculated sale price, it calculates the net margin and then compares the result to the price multiplied by 150%. If the margin is lower than 50% of the sale price, the function displays **Acceptable**. This is realistic; by definition, the margin is already more than 10% of the costs at least—but less than 50%. If not (meaning we have a margin of more than 50%), it displays **OK**.

Figure 9.6 clarifies this concept, showing the progression through the tests from the lowest to the highest value:

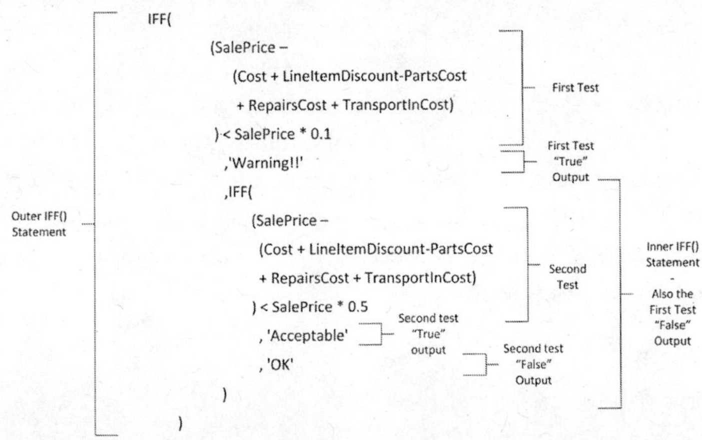

Figure 9.6: *The anatomy of a nested IFF() expression*

A nested **IFF()** function like this is extremely logical and will try to stop the tests as fast as possible. So, when writing them, you want to ensure that you have defined a clear progression through the various parts of the test. This nearly always means beginning with the lowest value for the comparison (110% in this example) and then progressing to the next level in the comparison (150% here), and so on. If you make the succession of tests coherent and progressive, they will probably be easier to write and both simpler to understand and easier to correct if there are errors. It will also make updating the test easier if you return to it months later.

Tricks and traps

Designing successive nested tests in SQL is both an art and a science. You might want to consider the following points:

- The hard part of writing nested **IFF** statements is getting the parentheses right. This can take a little practice, so be patient if you are starting down this route.
- If you have spent time writing nested **IF** statements in Excel, then you are probably familiar with this technique because it is similar in Databricks.
- There is no technical limit to nesting **IFF** statements; however, it can become hard to write the SQL correctly if you nest beyond three or four levels. So, it is advisable to use **CASE** statements (described in the following section) if your requirements become challenging and require these many levels of nesting.

Classifying a series of elements without the necessary categories present in your data

The finance director needs to manage exchange rate risk. So, he wants you to add each client's currency area to a printout. Unfortunately, the database does not have a field that holds the currency area. Moreover, you cannot modify the data structures to add a new category to the database. The following SQL shows how you can carry out this kind of operation to extend your analysis by superposing an ad hoc categorization on an existing dataset:

```
SELECT     CountryName

           ,CASE CountryName

              WHEN 'Belgium' THEN 'Eurozone'
```

```
            WHEN 'France' THEN 'Eurozone'
            WHEN 'Italy' THEN 'Eurozone'
            WHEN 'Spain' THEN 'Eurozone'
            WHEN 'United Kingdom' THEN 'Pound Sterling'
            WHEN 'United States' THEN 'Dollar'
            ELSE 'Other'
        END AS CurrencyRegion
FROM        Country;
```

Running the preceding query gives the results as shown in *Figure 9.7*:

	CountryName	CurrencyRegion
1	Belgium	Eurozone
2	France	Eurozone
3	Germany	Other
4	Italy	Eurozone
5	Spain	Eurozone
6	United Kingdom	Pound Sterling
7	United States	Dollar
8	China	Other
9	India	Other
10	Switzerland	Other

***Figure 9.7:** Using a CASE statement to add categories*

How does it work

The Prestige Cars database may not contain currency areas, but it contains each client's country. Fortunately, there are not too many of them. This means you can write some SQL to check the country name, and then, depending on the country, the output can be one of the following:

- Eurozone
- Pound sterling
- Dollar

You do this with a CASE statement. This statement does the following:

- **First**: Define the field to test by adding it after the word **`CASE`**. In this example, the test is extremely brief, and it is simply **`CASE CountryName`**, which is all required.

- **Second**: List all the possible outcomes; for example, *If the country is [whatever the country], then output the following....* This is done by entering the **`WHEN`** keyword and the output you want to see. In this example, the output is text enclosed in single quotes. Moreover, you can add as many **`WHEN`** clauses as you want to a **`CASE`** statement.
- **Third**: Say what is to happen if none of the tests is true; in other words, what must be output if the database does not contain a country in your list? This is done by entering the **`ELSE`** keyword, followed by the output you want to see in this case.
- **Finally**: Add the **`END`** keyword and preferably a column alias.

This example is carrying out a simple equality test. All you are doing is comparing the contents of a field with a list you enter and telling SQL what to do when a match is found.

To make this a little clearer, look at *Figure 9.8*:

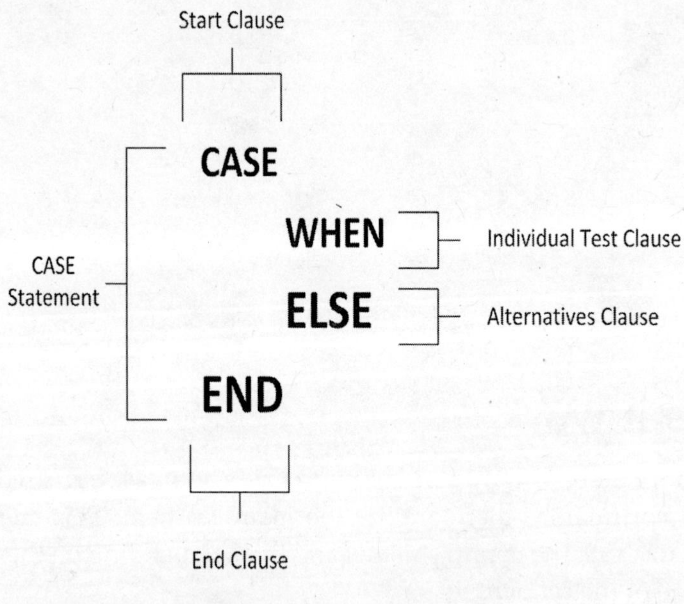

***Figure 9.8:** The anatomy of a CASE expression*

Tricks and traps

You need to bear the following in mind when using **`CASE`** statements:

- A **`CASE`** statement (a bit like a nested **`IFF()`** statement) will exit (that is, return an output value) at the first possible opportunity. So, if several elements in your list can cause the statement to match a value, it will take only the first one that it comes to when going down through the list. Any others will not count and will not be applied to the data.

Creating ad hoc category groupings

The finance director is overjoyed that you solved his previous problem and were able to add currency areas to the output. So, he wants to take this one step further and has asked you for a report that counts car makes according to the geographical zone where they were built.

Fortunately, you can extend the use of **CASE** statements to group and aggregate data even when you are adding categories that do not exist in the underlying database, as the following piece of SQL illustrates:

```
SELECT    CASE
            WHEN MakeCountry IN ('ITA', 'GER', 'FRA') THEN 'European'
            WHEN MakeCountry = 'GBR' THEN 'British'
            WHEN MakeCountry = 'USA' THEN 'American'
            ELSE 'Other'
          END AS SalesRegion
          ,COUNT(SalesDetailsID) AS NumberOfSales
FROM       AllSales
GROUP BY   CASE
            WHEN MakeCountry IN ('ITA', 'GER', 'FRA') THEN 'European'
            WHEN MakeCountry = 'GBR' THEN 'British'
            WHEN MakeCountry = 'USA' THEN 'American'
            ELSE 'Other'
          END;
```

Executing the preceding query gives the output as shown in *Figure 9.9:*

	SalesRegion	NumberOfSales
1	European	159
2	British	188
3	American	1

Figure 9.9: Using a CASE function to group data

How does it work

This code snippet lets you add a custom grouping element not contained in the source data. However, at its heart, it uses the same identical `CASE` statement twice:

- **First**: In the `SELECT` clause, to output the new grouping element (European, British, American, or other).
- **Second**: In the `GROUP BY` clause, to group and aggregate the output using the same categorization.

In this example, the `CASE` statement is structured slightly differently from how it was used in the previous example. The field that is tested appears in each `WHEN` clause, not only after the `CASE` keyword. Although this may seem a little longer-winded, applying is much simpler. As you can see, you no longer must detail every possible individual comparison separately, as you can now use the `IN` function to enter lists of alternatives. This makes shorter code easier to understand and maintain, even if you must repeat the field name you are testing.

Otherwise, this SQL is perfectly normal and uses a `COUNT()` aggregation function to give the total number of sales from the source table.

Tricks and traps

The following are two points to note when using `CASE` statements (in either the `SELECT` or `GROUP BY` clause).

- As in the previous example, the `CASE` statement ends with an `ELSE` clause (to handle any categorizations you have not thought of) and the `END` keyword (to tell SQL that the `CASE` statement is finished).
- Do not add an alias to the `CASE` statement in the `GROUP BY` clause.

Applying multiple ad hoc categories

Applying categories that no one thought of when the database was being built is normal in the world of SQL. However, user requests are quite complex, requiring you to provide clever SQL. As a case in point, the sales director wants you to create a category built on two complementary analyses, categorizing purchasers by type and geography. Refer to the following SQL:

```
SELECT     CustomerName
           ,CASE
           WHEN IsReseller = 0 AND Country
                                 IN ('IT', 'DE', 'FR', 'ES', 'BE')
                   THEN 'Eurozone Retail Client'
           WHEN IsReseller = 0 AND Country IN ('GB')
                   THEN 'British Retail Client'
           WHEN IsReseller = 0 AND Country IN ('US')
                   THEN 'American Retail Client'
           WHEN IsReseller = 0 AND Country IN ('CH')
                   THEN 'Swiss Retail Client'
           WHEN IsReseller = 1 AND Country
                                   IN ('IT', 'DE', 'FR', 'ES', 'BE')
                   THEN 'Eurozone Reseller'
           WHEN IsReseller = 1 AND Country IN ('GB')
                   THEN 'British Reseller'
           WHEN IsReseller = 1 AND Country IN ('US')
                   THEN 'American Reseller'
           WHEN IsReseller = 1 AND Country IN ('CH')
                   THEN 'Swiss Reseller'
          END AS CustomerType
FROM        Customer;
```

If you run the preceding query, you should see the output as shown in *Figure 9.10*:

	CustomerName	CustomerType
1	Magic Motors	British Reseller
2	Snazzy Roadsters	British Reseller
3	Birmingham Executive Prestige Vehicles	British Reseller
4	WunderKar	Eurozone Reseller
5	Casseroles Chromes	Eurozone Reseller
6	Le Luxe en Motion	Swiss Reseller
7	Eat My Exhaust Ltd	British Reseller

Figure 9.10: *Complex evaluation using CASE statements*

How does it work

This code analyzes two fields to decide whether a client is a reseller and, if so (or not), which geographical area they belong to. It does this using a **CASE** statement, but this must be structured in a slightly different way from the approach that you saw earlier in this chapter. This time, you must specify each of the fields that you are using to test data in each **WHEN** clause instead of once only after the **CASE** keyword. This approach may seem a little laborious, but its key advantage is that every individual in the **WHEN** clause can contain its own specific logic that is separate from the **WHEN** clauses. In this example, the combinations of reseller status and country are used to define a series of overall categories: Eurozone Retail Client, British Retail Client, American Retail Client, Swiss Retail Client, Eurozone Reseller, British Reseller, American Reseller, and Swiss Reseller.

Tricks and traps

Complex case statements like this one entail being aware of the following key points:

- If tracking all these variations on a theme becomes difficult, you can organize **CASE** statements into nested subgroups, as seen in the section *Categorizing data using nested classifications*.
- You can format the **WHEN** clause as you see fit. We placed the **WHEN...THEN** clauses on separate lines to make the code easier to understand. However, there is nothing to stop you from writing the following, for instance, with all the SQL on a single line:

  ```
  WHEN IsReseller = 1 AND Country = 'USA' THEN 'American Reseller'
  ```
- When there is only one element to test in the **WHEN** clause, you can use equal (=) rather than **IN**.

Categorizing data using nested classifications

The sales director wants you to flag various customers by their credit status and geographical region. The following piece of SQL explains how to do that, but slightly differently from the way you saw in the previous example. To make custom categorizations easier to understand, you can nest the elements you are examining into structured hierarchies to make the concept and the code easier to comprehend. To appreciate this approach, take a look at the following SQL:

```
SELECT      CustomerName
            ,CASE
                WHEN IsCreditRisk = 0 THEN
                         CASE
                             WHEN Country IN ('IT', 'DE', 'FR'
                                             ,'ES', 'BE')
                                 THEN 'Eurozone No Risk'
                             WHEN Country IN ('GB')
                                 THEN 'British No Risk'
                             WHEN Country IN ('US')
                                 THEN 'American No Risk'
                             WHEN Country IN ('CH')
                                 THEN 'Swiss No Risk'
                         END
                WHEN IsCreditRisk = 1 THEN
                         CASE
                             WHEN Country IN ('IT', 'DE', 'FR'
                                             ,'ES', 'BE')
                                THEN 'Eurozone Credit Risk'
                             WHEN Country IN ('GB')
```

```
                          THEN 'British Credit Risk'
                        WHEN Country IN ('US')
                          THEN 'American Credit Risk'
                        WHEN Country IN ('CH')
                          THEN 'Swiss Credit Risk'
               END
          END AS RiskType
FROM       Customer;
```

Running the preceding query gives the results as shown in *Figure 9.11*:

	CustomerName	RiskType
1	Magic Motors	British No Risk
2	Snazzy Roadsters	British Credit Risk
3	Birmingham Executive Prestige Vehicles	British No Risk
4	WunderKar	Eurozone No Risk
5	Casseroles Chromes	Eurozone No Risk
6	Le Luxe en Motion	Swiss Credit Risk
7	Eat My Exhaust Ltd	British No Risk
8	M. Pierre Dubois	Eurozone No Risk
9	Sondra Horowitz	American No Risk
10	Wonderland Wheels	British No Risk
11	London Executive Prestige Vehicles	British Credit Risk
12	Glittering Prize Cars Ltd	British No Risk
13	La Bagnole de Luxe	Eurozone No Risk

***Figure 9.11:** Nested CASE statements*

How does it work

This SQL query has an outer and an inner group of **CASE** statements.

- **First**: The outer statement looks at the **IsCreditRisk** field. It begins by saying: *When the credit risk is absent, move on to the inner* **CASE** *statement (and carry out further tests on the country). Then, if the customer poses a credit risk (that is, the field is true or contains a 1 for this kind of field), continue processing with another separate* **CASE** *statement and test the country.*
- **Then**: The inner statement, in either case, looks at the country and applies separate tests. Only if the outer and inner tests give a positive result (for

instance, if a customer is not a credit risk and the country is **Britain**) will one of the outcomes be returned **British No Risk** in the event of a British risk-free customer.

Tricks and traps

We have only a couple of comments to make about nested **CASE** statements, which are given as follows:

- In this example, the inner **CASE** statements were nearly identical, containing the same tests on the country. This approach is specific to this example and will not always be the case in practice.
- In the customer table, the **IsCreditRisk** field is numeric, not Boolean. Consequently, you must use a 1 or a 0 when filtering data. If the **IsCreditRisk** field were Boolean, the SQL would read as follows:

  ```
  WHEN IsCreditRisk = true THEN
  ```

Choosing elements from a list

Sometimes you may have to categorize data by looking up values in a custom list. Databricks lets you look up values from a custom hard-coded list you create using the **DECODE()** function.

You can see the first example of the **DECODE()** function on the following piece of SQL. In this example, the **DECODE()** function compensates for the fact that the dataset does not contain the full name of the country where the vehicle was manufactured. To get around this, the **DECODE()** function takes the three-letter code that provides the country of manufacture and *looks up* the full country name.

```
SELECT     MakeName, MakeCountry
          ,DECODE(MakeCountry
                  ,'ITA' ,'Italy'
                  ,'FRA' ,'France'
                  ,'GBR' ,'Great Britain'
                  ,'USA' ,'United States'
                  ,'GER' ,'Germany'
                ) AS FullMakeCountryName
FROM       allsales;
```

Running the preceding query gives the output as shown in *Figure 9.12*:

	MakeName	MakeCountry	FullMakeCountryName
1	Ferrari	ITA	Italy
2	Ferrari	ITA	Italy
3	Porsche	GER	Germany
4	Porsche	GER	Germany
5	Porsche	GER	Germany
6	Aston Martin	GBR	Great Britain

***Figure 9.12:** Using DECODE() to select elements for display*

How does it work

The **`DECODE()`** function works like the following:

- **First**: The database field used for the lookup is specified as the first **`DECODE()`** parameter.
- **Then**: A series of *key / Value* data pairs are added as further parameters to **`DECODE ()`**. This set of value pairs can be a simple two-column list. The first column contains a key (a value that will be compared with the value found in the database record) then the element from the second column will be output by the SQL.
- **Finally**: A default value is optionally added. This will be used if a key value is not found in the list.

You can see a more visual explanation of the **`DECODE()`** function in *Figure 9.13*:

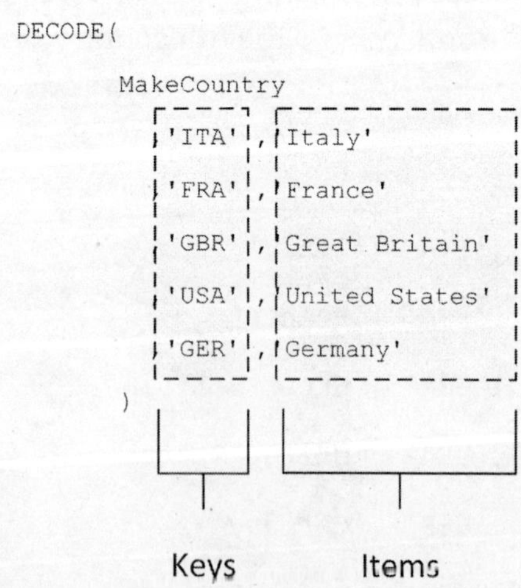

***Figure 9.13:** The DECODE() function explained*

Tricks and traps

You need to be aware that the **DECODE()** function comes with a few minor restrictions, which asre given as follows:

- If the list does not contain the key elements you are referencing in the source data column, then **DECODE()** will return a **NULL**.
- You can avoid **NULL** being returned if the key values used by the **DECODE()** function do not include the database value by adding a final default value to the list of items inside the parentheses. If you wanted to display the word *unknown* in the eventuality that a database value returned none of the countries listed inside the **DECODE()** function, the SQL could look like the following:

```
DECODE(MakeCountry
                  ,'ITA' ,'Italy'
                  ,'FRA' ,'France'
                  ,'GBR' ,'Great Britain'
                  ,'USA' ,'United States'
                  ,'GER' ,'Germany'
                  ,'Unknown'
                 ) AS FullMakeCountryName
```

- The key value used for the lookup can be a number, string, or Boolean (true or false) value.
- As an example of **DECODE ()** using a numeric value for the key value is as follows:

```
SELECT     MakeName
          ,DECODE(MakeID
                  ,1 ,'Red Dragon'
                  ,2 ,'Amazing EV'
                 ) AS Car
FROM       make;
```

Running the preceding query gives the output as shown in *Figure 9.14*:

	MakeName	Car
1	Ferrari	Red Dragon
2	Porsche	Amazing EV
3	Lamborghini	null
4	Aston Martin	null
5	Bentley	null

***Figure 9.14**: Using DECODE() to reference numbers in a list of values to return*

- As an example of **DECODE ()** using a boolean value for the key value is as follows:

```
SELECT     MakeName, IsRHD
          ,DECODE(IsRHD
                  ,true ,'Right Hand Drive'
                  ,false ,'Left Hand Drive'
                ) AS SteeringSide
FROM       allsales;
```

Running the preceding query gives the output as shown in *Figure 9.15*:

	MakeName	IsRHD	SteeringSide
1	Ferrari	true	Right Hand Drive
2	Ferrari	true	Right Hand Drive
3	Porsche	true	Right Hand Drive
4	Porsche	true	Right Hand Drive

***Figure 9.15:** Using DECODE() to reference TRUE or FALSE in a list of values to return*

- You can use single or double quotes for strings inside a **DECODE ()** function.

Placing nulls at the start or end of a list

The sales director has presented you with a quandary. She requested a sales list by increasing the value of discounts, which you duly delivered. However, as there was a large number of sales where no discount was applied, Databricks began the list with the **NULL** values for the **LineItemDiscount** field because NULLs are considered by Spark SQL to be smaller than any numerical value.

However, this is not what the sales director wants. She wants a list that begins with the smallest values and places any empty (non-discounted) sales at the bottom.

This is where a little SQL logic can assist you, as the following code snippet shows:

```
SELECT      *
FROM        SalesByCountry
ORDER BY    CASE WHEN LineItemDiscount IS NULL THEN 1 ELSE 0 END
            ,LineItemDiscount
```

Running the preceding code will return the output as shown in *Figure 9.16*:

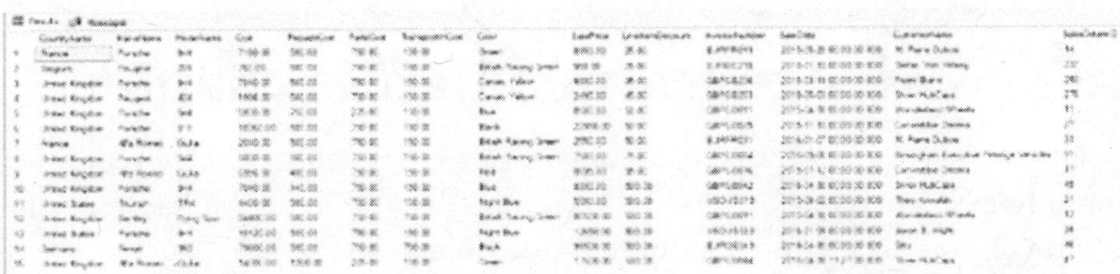

***Figure 9.16:** Using a CASE statement to place NULL values at the end of a list*

How does it work

The trick to handling **NULL** values in a sort order is to add a sort key that isolates the **NULL** values and then sorts the non-NULL values first.

The following is what the **ORDER BY** clause has done here:

- **First**: An initial sort of element is applied using a **CASE** statement. In Figure 9-16, this piece of logic says, *If the* **LineItemDiscount** *field contains a* **NULL**, *consider it to contain a 1; otherwise, consider any value as a 0*. So, the first sort key is, effectively, a 1 or a 0, meaning that NULLs are 1s, and so appear after all the 0s (in effect, after any numeric values).
- **Second**: The **ORDER BY** clause sorts on the **LineItemDiscount** field once the sort on the **NULL** fields has been applied.

Tricks and traps

We have only one comment to make about these kinds of **CASE** statements, which is as follows:

- You can simply place the **NULL** values at the top or bottom of the output by switching the 1 and 0 values in the **CASE** statement. So, to place the NULLs at the top of the list, you would write the following:

```
ORDER BY    CASE WHEN LineItemDiscount IS NULL THEN 0 ELSE 1 END
```

Conclusion

In this chapter, you saw how to classify data according to your criteria. You also learned how to use SQL to apply logical tests to data. This meant using functions such as **IFF()** and **CASE** to evaluate logical conditions. This technique implied testing the contents of one or more fields to decide on an outcome.

Core knowledge learned in this chapter

This chapter showed you how to test data for exceeding thresholds you define for showing unexpected characteristics. You saw that a little logic applied to a query could help you to see through a mountain of data and focus your attention on the outliers and anomalies that can be of real interest.

You learned the following keywords in this chapter:

Concept	Description
IFF()	This function allows you to test output and apply one or another outcome.
CASE	This function can test multiple data states and apply a choice of outcomes.
WHEN	This keyword is used with a CASE statement that lets you apply a test to data.
ELSE	This keyword is used with a CASE statement that lets you apply an outcome for untested cases.
DECODE()	This function is used to select an element from a list based on an initial value.

CHAPTER 10
Using Multiple Tables When Querying Data

Introduction

Now that you are at ease with the basics of querying, it is time to extend your SQL knowledge by examine how to analyze data stored across multiple tables. Databricks is not a database in the classic sense of the term, where data is virtually always broken down into many separate tables that you link together to deliver the results you are looking for. However, the data loaded into Databricks may come from a traditional relational database where the data is stored across multiple tables, or the source data may have been broken down into separate data tables. Whatever the reason, querying data from several tables at once is so fundamental to Spark SQL that you need to master these techniques reasonably early in your SQL apprenticeship.

Structure

In this chapter, we will cover the following topics:

- Joining tables
- Joining multiple tables
- Join subtleties
- Using table aliases

- Joining many tables
- Visualizing databases
- Querying across databases

Objectives

At this stage of your venture into data analysis with SQL, you are probably wondering why data can be placed in several tables simultaneously. It can seem peculiar to break data down into all these separate tables and then spend time joining them together again when you want to query the data.

Well, there are several reasons for taking this approach. First, one of the main objectives of relational databases (which are often the source of data used in Databricks) is to avoid data duplication. If an element of data (an address) appears in two or more tables, it must be modified in several places. This is every time it needed to be updated, complicated, and a big potential source for errors. One classic consequence is that you end up with multiple addresses and no way of knowing the right one. Relational databases try to prevent this by storing independent but homogenous chunks of data in separate tables.

Another advantage of this approach is that avoiding duplication makes the data less voluminous. So, the data storage cost is reduced during explosive data growth.

Another reason to create multiple tables is to centralize reference data. This could, for instance, imply the creation of a table of countries to hold country data. Certain data elements (such as country names) will likely be reused frequently in multiple tables. Storing the country name and other commonly used information in lookup tables makes sense in situations like this. You can then use a short code or even a number to refer to repetitive data in another table. The reference data (such as the country name) will always appear the same in all your analytical reports because it appears only once in the database. This is specifically the case in data warehouses where dimension tables contain reference data that link to large, centralized fact tables.

Due to these architectures, database designers often need to add fields that allow tables to be linked, as you will see throughout this chapter. These fields are called key fields and may contain numbers or alphanumeric codes. These keys allow data to be mapped across tables so that information can be reconstituted harmoniously and coherently from several tables.

Another reason for storing data in separate tables is that the data has come from disparate sources for analysis. So, you must meld the data together by linking (or joining) the data from different tables.

To get used to the concept of using multiple tables, this chapter will show you how to:

- Join two or more tables.
- Select data from multiple tables.
- Remove duplicates from the output.

Now it is time to move on to the practice of the real-world SQL that you will need to master. This chapter teaches you how to use the links between tables to write more complex and powerful queries. This is an essential step in enabling you to deliver coherent source data analysis.

This chapter and those that follow will use a different set of tables, not just the **Allsales** table you have used in this book. Consequently, as *Appendix A* explains, you must ensure you have loaded all the source tables.

In this chapter, you will be required to forget the **AllSales** table you have used until now in this book. Instead, you will be using multiple smaller relational tables as the source of your queries.

Joining tables

As an initial step on your path to analyzing the data for Prestige Cars Ltd., you want to produce a complete list of every vehicle purchased and the amount paid to purchase it. After looking at the tables in the **PrestigeCars** database, you have found the stock table containing every car's price. However, it does not contain the model but only an internal ID number that means nothing to you. However, you have also found a table called model, and this table contains the list of all the types of models that the company sells, as well as what appears to be the same ID number used in the stock table. You can see this represented graphically in *Figure 10.1*:

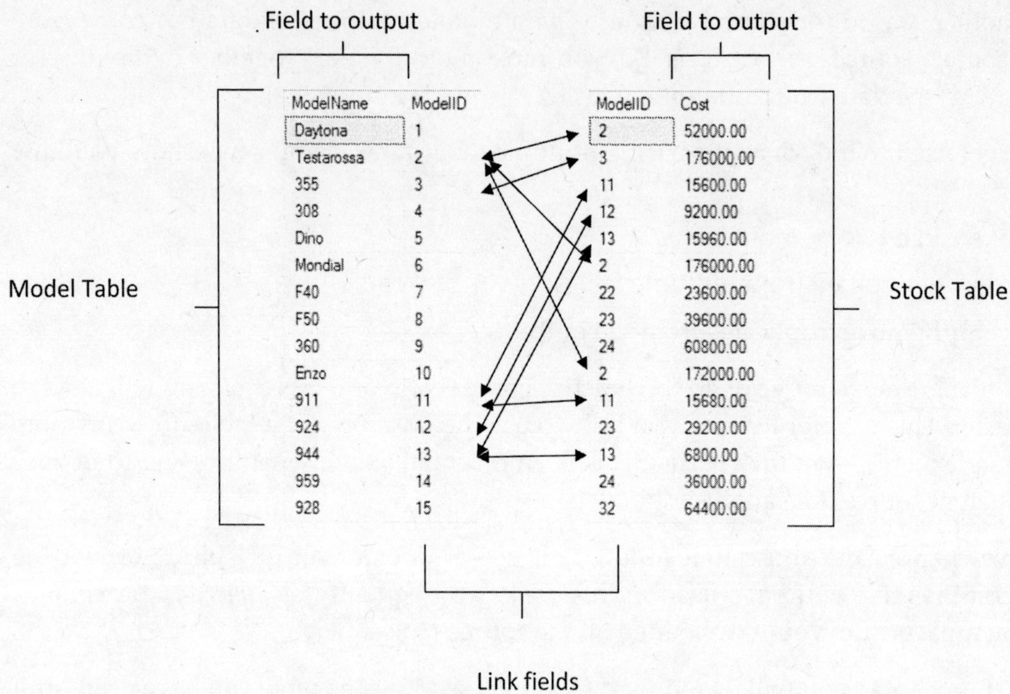

***Figure 10.1:** Linking tables*

So, now you need to collate data from both tables to see information from both in a single query. This will let you see both the model and the cost. The following is the SQL code that will do exactly this for you:

```
SELECT      ModelName, Cost

FROM        Model

INNER JOIN Stock

           ON Model.ModelID = Stock.ModelID

ORDER BY    ModelName;
```

Running this query gives the results shown in *Figure 10.2* (assuming you have scrolled further down the output list):

	ModelName	Cost
109	Arnage	68520
110	Arnage	79960
111	Arnage	45440
112	Boxster	18000
113	Brooklands	151600
114	Brooklands	79600

Figure 10.2: *Using a join to output data from two tables*

How does it work

The code you just wrote to join two tables is a little dry, to say the least. It is probably easier to understand what you have done if it is presented more visually. *Figure 10.3* illustrates what joining tables look like:

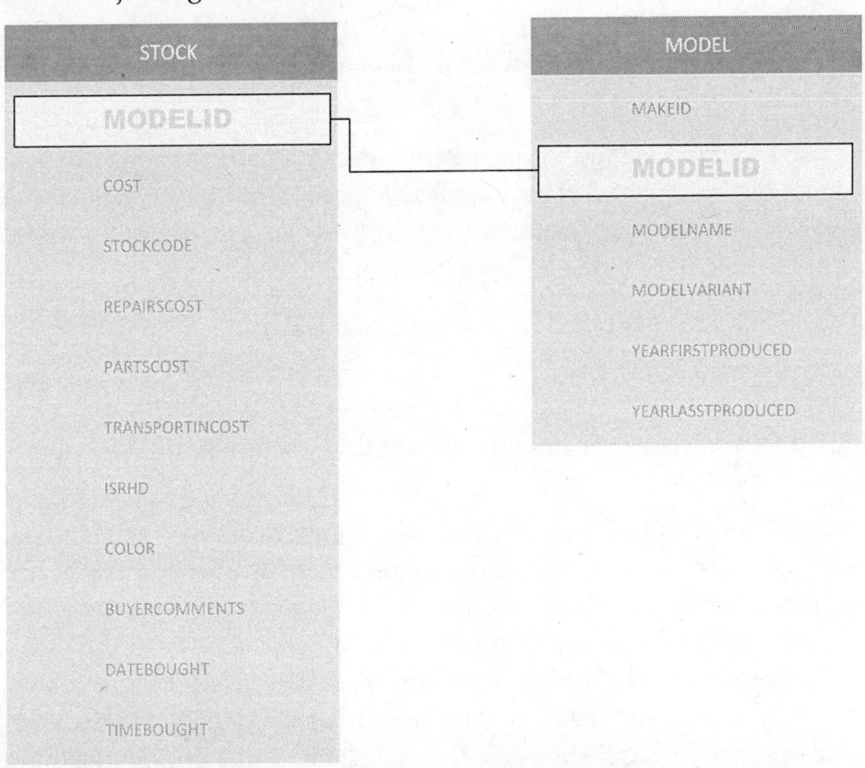

Figure 10.3: *Representing table joins visually*

Conceptually, joining pairs of tables means knowing which fields can be used to create the link between the two tables. This could mean talking to the people who designed the database or delving into any documentation you may have been given. Sometimes you can easily guess which fields can be used as joins, such as when the two fields have the same name or when the data is clearly the same in both tables. Sometimes it can be difficult to guess the join fields just by looking at the tables. For the moment, we will learn how the sample tables are joined each time to avoid you having to guess.

This code snippet takes three keywords you already know well (**SELECT**, **FROM**, and **ORDER BY**) and extends the **FROM** clause with two new keywords: **INNER JOIN** and **ON**. These keywords allow you to create links between tables to simultaneously display fields from both tables. Linking (or joining) two tables in SQL consists of the following steps:

1. Enter the name of the first table to join after the **FROM** keyword.
2. Add the **INNER JOIN** keyword after the table name.
3. Enter the name of the second table to join.
4. Add the **ON** keyword.
5. Enter the names of the two fields that link the tables, separated by the equal (=) sign.

Each field used to link the tables must be preceded by the table name that contains the field followed by a period. This enables Databricks to identify which field can be found in which table when creating the link. You can see this in the **INNER JOIN** statement of the SQL used in the following example:

```
INNER JOIN Stock ON Model.ModelID = Stock.ModelID
```

Tricks and traps

As joining tables is a core concept, you should note the following key points from the start:

- The fields you use to join the two tables may not have the same name. If the two fields' names differ, you can enter them as is, separated by an equal sign, without adding the table name. However, if the two fields have the same name, then you need to precede each field name with the table name and a period. This is because Databricks gets confused if there is no way of uniquely identifying the field name, almost as if it does not know which one to take to finish the join. Adding the table name and a period like this allows SQL to trace the field name back to its source table and consequently identify the correct field to use.

- In practice, it is often best to identify uniquely the fields that establish the join by preceding each field with the name of the table it comes from and a period, even if the field names are different in the two tables. Once again, this is a little like identifying a person by their last name and first name. In the world of SQL, it avoids confusion by making names uniquely identifiable. In more complex SQL, it allows you to see instantly which field in which table is being linked to which another field in another table. This will help you understand complex queries more easily. Ideally, then, the code for this example could have been written as follows:

  ```
  SELECT     Model.ModelName, Stock.Cost
  ```
- While taking this table-field approach is not strictly necessary, we will apply it as a best practice in the SQL examples in this chapter.
- The order in which you enter the tables in the **FROM** clause is unimportant. You could write the **FROM** clause in this example as follows without altering the result:

  ```
  FROM Stock INNER JOIN Model
  ```
- Equally, the order of the fields in the **ON** clause is irrelevant; they do not have to be in the same order as the tables in the query.
- The data in the tables you join is probably not stored in the same order. However, this is irrelevant to SQL. What matters is using—and referring to—the correct tables.

Other join syntax

Over time database developers have created several ways of using SQL to join tables.

One traditional technique to join tables uses the **WHERE** keyword to define table joins. Using this approach, the initial table join that you saw in this chapter would look like the following:

```
SELECT      ModelName, Cost

FROM        Model, Stock

WHERE       Model.Modelid = Stock.Modelid
```

This technique lists all the tables to join in the **FROM** clause and then uses a **WHERE** clause to define the fields that join the tables.

While nothing is wrong with this approach, it can lead to extremely complex **WHERE** clauses. We prefer using the **ON** syntax to define table joins for these reasons.

Joining multiple tables

The CEO firmly believes that effective cost control is vital for the company's survival. So, she wants a list of all the cars ever bought since Prestige Cars started trading and a list of the purchase costs for every make and model held in stock.

This query reflects the fact that most databases consist of many tables. In certain queries, you will have to join not just two tables as you did in the previous section but several tables at once. SQL lets you extend the technique you saw in the previous example to join multiple tables. For example, suppose you want to list the cost of every make and model of car sold. However, a quick look at the database makes it clear that while the cost is in the stock table, this table contains only the ID for the model and does not contain the make at all. Equally, the **`Model`** table contains only an ID for the make and not the full name of the make. The full name of the **`Make`** in the **`Make`** table. So, you need to *chain* all three tables (**`Stock`** to **`Model`** to **`Make`**) to return the data that you want to see.

This is probably easier to understand visually. *Figure 10.4* shows an image of three tables joined together using a different bridge field between each pair of tables. This approach allows you to select fields from any or all of the tables.

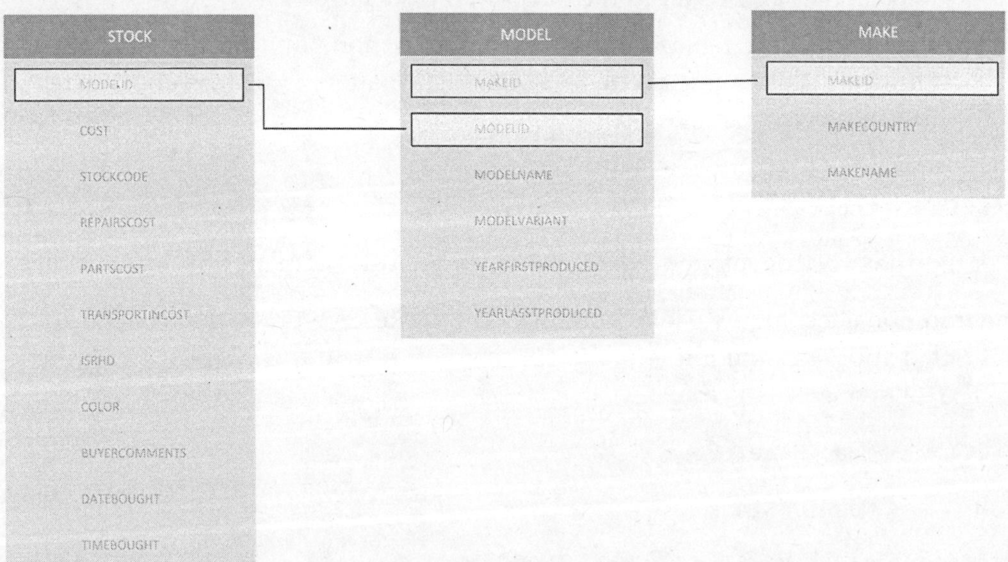

***Figure 10.4:** Chaining tables*

The following piece of SQL shows you how this can be done:

```
SELECT     Make.MakeName, Model.ModelName, Stock.Cost

FROM       Stock
```

```
INNER JOIN Model
        ON Model.ModelID = Stock.ModelID
INNER JOIN Make
        ON Make.MakeID = Model.MakeID;
```

Running the preceding query gives the results as shown in *Figure 10.5*:

	MakeName	ModelName	Cost
1	Ferrari	Testarossa	52000
2	Ferrari	355	176000
3	Porsche	911	15600
4	Porsche	924	9200
5	Porsche	944	15960
6	Ferrari	Testarossa	176000

Figure 10.5: *Data output from three tables*

How does it work

The real work done by this code is in the **`FROM`** clause. It works like the following:

- **First**: The **`Stock`** table is joined to the **`Model`** table (using the shared **`ModelID`** field in the **`ON`** clause to link the two tables).
- **Second**: The **`Make`** table is then added—with a second **`INNER JOIN`** keyword—and linked to the **`Model`** table using the **`ON`** keyword and the shared **`MakeID`** field.
- **Finally**: Any fields that you want to output are added to the **`SELECT`** clause.

The real point of this example is to demonstrate that you can chain together a sequence of virtually any number of tables to analyze data. What is essential is that any two tables share a field (or even several fields) common to both and that the fields have been designed to be used to join the tables. Each time you want to add another table to the query, you introduce it with the **`INNER JOIN`** keyword and then specify which field links it to which field in another table using the **`ON`** keyword to link the tables.

Tricks and traps

Linking multiple tables this way will take a little practice before it becomes second nature. To help you when using your SQL skills, the following are a few practical considerations that you might want to bear in mind:

- You can begin by adding the fields to the **SELECT** clause before you complete the **FROM** clause. Still, it is often easier, conceptually, to concentrate on working out which tables need to be joined (and to join them) before adding the fields that you want to see in the output.
- You can specify which tables you will join before you say which fields will be used in the joins. In other words, you can write all the **INNER JOIN** clauses before you write the **ON** clauses, as shown in the following code snippet:

```
SELECT     Make.MakeName, Model.ModelName, Stock.Cost
FROM       Stock
INNER JOIN Model
INNER JOIN  Make
           ON Make.MakeID = Model.ModelID
           AND Model.ModelID = Stock.ModelID
```

If, however, you prefer this approach, please note that you have to use the **AND** keyword to introduce all joins except the first one.

You do not always have to indicate the table from a field drawn before the field name, as we have done here in specifying **Make.MakeName**. However, you can only use the field name alone (without the table name to precede it) if the field name exists only once in all the selected tables. If there are several fields with the same name in the multiple tables you are joining, Databricks will not know which field to use and will send back an error message rather than the result that you were expecting.

As an example of this, you could try running the following SQL snippet:

```
SELECT     ModelName, Cost, ModelID
FROM       Model
INNER JOIN Stock
           ON Model.ModelID = Stock.ModelID
ORDER BY   ModelName;
```

All you will see returned is an error message similar to the one shown in *Figure 10.6*:

```
Error in SQL statement: AnalysisException: [AMBIGUOUS_REFERENCE] Reference `ModelID` is ambiguous, could be: [`spark_catalog`.`default`.`
model`.`ModelID`, `spark_catalog`.`default`.`stock`.`ModelID`].; line 1 pos 28
```

Figure 10.6: *Data output from three tables*

In this example, we select a single field from the three tables you have joined. You can select any fields from the joined tables or all the fields from all the tables. So, once again, preceding each field name with the table name and a period is the best practice when writing SQL.

You can simply use the keyword **`JOIN`** instead of using **`INNER JOIN`** if you prefer. The result will be the same. The code snippet used in this example could be written as follows:

```
SELECT     Make.MakeName, Model.ModelName, Stock.Cost

FROM       Stock

JOIN Model

           ON Model.ModelID = Stock.ModelID

JOIN Make

           ON Make.MakeID = Model.MakeID;
```

We will continue to use the complete **`INNER JOIN`** keyword to differentiate basic joins from the other join types you will encounter throughout this book.

Join fields

When you start writing the simplest queries, knowing which fields to use to join tables will rapidly become vital. Sometimes you will only need to join one field in a table to one other field in another table, and occasionally you will need to use two or more fields in each table you are joining. Hopefully, the database designers or other users can explain the required fields before you write queries.

In the **`PrestigeCars`** dataset, all the tables joined are made using a single field. Sometimes these fields contain meaningful data (such as the **`Countryiso3`** field in the country table). However, other tables use a value such as a number that has no intrinsic meaning to the user, for example, the **`ModelID`** field in the model table. You can even see meaningless strings of characters used to join tables, and the **`SalesID`** field in the sales table is an example.

The point is that the fields you use to join tables can be letters or numbers, which can be understandable to humans. This does not matter in the least. All that matters (to data analysts querying databases) is that you know which fields to join and that the dataset has been correctly designed so that the joins will work.

You could find that Databricks use numbers as the data type for join fields. While this may seem strange—or even perverse—at first sight, it is often a highly efficient way of joining tables and retrieving data. You can see this in the use of the **MakeID** and **ModelID** fields that are used to join tables in the **CarSales** database.

Join subtleties

A quick look at the database reveals a customer table containing a country field but only the ISO two-character code for the client's country. At first sight, this is an issue because you want to display the full name for each country. Then, you spot the country table containing not only the two-character ISO code but also the country's full name. So, you are hoping that if you can join these two tables, you should be able to obtain the relevant data.

Fortunately, you are right. The following is the SQL that will produce the list you require:

```
SELECT DISTINCT  CountryName

FROM             Customer

INNER JOIN       Country

                 ON Customer.Country = Country.CountryISO2;
```

This query returns the results as shown in *Figure 10.7*:

	CountryName
1	Germany
2	France
3	Belgium
4	United States
5	Italy
6	Spain

***Figure 10.7:** Joining tables and returning data from one of the tables*

How does it work

This query joins the **Customer** table to the country table. It maps the **Country** field in the **Customer** table to the **CountryISO2** field in the country table. As we mentioned earlier, it helps to know which fields you can use to join tables in practice. Once the two tables are joined, you can select fields from either. As all you want to display is the country for a customer, the **CountryName** field is all you need. SQL, in effect, goes through the **Customer** table and looks up the country name for each customer. Then, it applies the **DISTINCT** keyword to remove duplicates from the list of countries.

Before looking more deeply into the actual code, we must make a fundamental point about what this query is doing. A join like this returns data only when a common element exists in both tables. In other words, the country reference (the **Country** field in the **Customer** table and the **CountryISO2** field in the **Country** table) must exist for data to be returned from either table. If no corresponding element exists in the two tables, then no data is returned.

If you need to verify this, look at the **Country** table's contents. You will see that it contains two countries (**India** and **China**) that have no corresponding cross-reference in the **Customer** table. Consequently, these countries do not appear in the query output.

Another original aspect of this example is the **DISTINCT** keyword. This keyword is incredibly useful because it removes all duplicates from the query output before seeing the query results. To make this clearer, try running the same query without the **DISTINCT** keyword using SQL like the followin:

```
SELECT      CountryName
FROM        Customer
INNER JOIN  Country
            ON Customer.Country = Country.CountryISO2;
```

This time you will see the result as shown in *Figure 10.8*:

	CountryName
1	United Kingdom
2	United Kingdom
3	United Kingdom
4	Germany
5	France
6	Switzerland

***Figure 10.8:** Returning data from a joined table without the DISTINCT keyword*

As you can see from *Figure 10.5*, the names of many countries appear several times. Without the **DISTINCT** keyword, several country names are repeated, as many customers are in the same country. SQL would show the country for each customer, even if you did not ask for the customer to be displayed.

This happens because joining tables will cause SQL to return all the records that it can from both tables. This will happen whatever the fields in the **SELECT** clause, irrespective of which table they come from.

In the query without the **DISTINCT** keyword, Databricks returns all the records from the **Customer** table (some **87**), even if no field from the **Customer** table was requested in the output. This duplicates many of the country names because, for each customer, the query looks up the full country name and displays it in the query result.

Tricks and traps

With a little practice, joining tables is not difficult. Nonetheless, it can have far-reaching consequences. So, you need to be mindful of the following:

- You may be wondering why you did not use the **Country** table directly to produce this list. The reason is that the **Country** table is essentially a lookup table. It contains a list of country names, but you do not know if it contains all the countries in the world—or only those corresponding to countries where you have customers. So, it is best to use the **Customer** table as the basis for your query and the **Country** table to look up the country name corresponding to the actual customers' country code.
- You could, theoretically, not add the table names before the fields in the **ON** clause. That is, the **ON** clause could look like the following:

```
ON Country = CountryISO2
```

- This will work because the field names are unique across the tables used. That is, they are not identical in both tables. However, this is far from usual in real-world data analysis. So, as we have pointed out in the previous example, we prefer to add the table name to the field in the **ON** clause as a matter of good practice. This will leave you better prepared to deal with your own data sets.
- It can sometimes be hard to find out which fields you need to use to join tables in corporate databases. In practice, nothing will save you as much time as acquiring documentation on the database you use for your analysis.

Using table aliases

The analysis is often all about detail. So, it does not come as a surprise when the CEO comes to your desk and requests a list of all vehicles sold, the selling price, and any discounts that have been applied. To keep the CEO happy, you need to know that the **PrestigeCars** database contains two essential tables called Sales and **SalesDetails**. These correspond roughly to an invoice header and the individual line items that make up a sale. These two tables contain all the information needed to look at itemized sales. Suppose you need to analyze the discounts applied to make the sales and see how they vary per car sold.

As an example, look at the following code snippet:

```
SELECT     S.InvoiceNumber, D.LineItemNumber, D.SalePrice

           ,D.LineItemDiscount

FROM       Sales AS S

INNER JOIN SalesDetails AS D

           ON S.SalesID = D.SalesID

ORDER BY   S.InvoiceNumber, D.LineItemNumber;
```

Execute the preceding query; you should see the output in *Figure 10.8*. However, *Figure 10.9* shows only the first few records, and you will have to scroll to see all the records returned by this query:

	InvoiceNumber	LineItemNumber	SalePrice	LineItemDiscount
1	EURBE074	1	125000	1500
2	EURBE125	1	12500	750
3	EURBE132	1	86500	1250
4	EURBE171	1	3950	750
5	EURBE171	2	29500	750
6	EURBE171	3	12500	null

***Figure 10.9:** Using aliases when joining tables*

How does it work

This query joins the **Sales** and **SalesDetails** tables on the shared **SalesID** field. Then, it outputs required fields and sorts them by invoice number, followed by line number (this can be useful in cases where an invoice has more than one line item).

In the previous examples in this chapter, you saw that we added the table name to some field names when we built the simplest query. Although this is not difficult, it can soon become extremely laborious because it can mean repeating the table name several times in different parts of the query. Fortunately, there is a way to make your coding easier, even if it does not affect the result.

The following is the trick to use aliases for tables: a bit like when you aliased field names in previous chapters:

- **First**: Add a space after the table name.
- **Then**: Add the **AS** keyword.
- **Finally**: Enter a short acronym that you will use instead of the table name elsewhere in the query.

Aliases are applied in the **FROM** clause and used everywhere else in the query where you would use the schema and table name.

Adding an alias to a table is used not to display the alias but to make the code more understandable. This is achieved by rendering the SQL less voluminous and easier to understand.

In this example, the **Sales** table was given the alias **S**, and the **SalesDetails** table was given the alias **D**. Once you have aliased the tables, you use the alias instead of the table name everywhere in the code where you would otherwise have used the full table name.

The alias is used in the same way as the table name would be used. So, when you have duplicate field names in separate tables, you should use the alias to distinguish them rather than having to write out the full name of the table. This is particularly effective in the **ON** clause, which is much shorter and easier to read.

Tricks and traps

Aliases also have their quirks, so you need to be aware of the following:

- Once you add an alias, use it instead of the table name. You cannot use the table name elsewhere in the query in the **SELECT** or **ON** clauses. Once you have created an alias, at least you are stuck with it in the current query. You cannot, therefore, write SQL like the following, where both aliases and table names are used in the **SELECT** or **ORDER BY** statements

```
SELECT      Sales.InvoiceNumber, D.LineItemNumber, SalesDetails.
SalePrice
            ,D.LineItemDiscount
```

```
FROM        Sales AS S
INNER JOIN  SalesDetails AS D
            ON S.SalesID = D.SalesID
ORDER BY    S.InvoiceNumber, SalesDetails.LineItemNumber;
```

- Tools such as Databricks notebooks will recognize aliases when they suggest field names to help you write a query. So, this is another reason to begin writing queries with the `FROM` clause, at least when you are joining tables.
- An alias can be as short as you like. A single character will suffice, as you can see in the SQL used in this example.
- An alias can be if you like (well, 122 characters anyway). However, the main aim of an alias is to make your life easier, so it is suggested to make aliases as short as possible while trying to balance this with the need for them to be comprehensible.
- It can help to try to make aliases memorable. This will help you understand which alias refers to which table when you write SQL queries and when you revisit them many months later. As you can see in this example, we have tried to use short aliases that remind you of the table name.
- Conversely, although it is easier to alias tables using codes such as `T1`, `T2`, and so on, this can make the SQL much harder to understand. To appreciate this, look at the following, where it is much harder to understand the tables to which the aliases refer:

```
SELECT      T1.CountryName
            ,T2.MakeName
            ,T3.ModelName
            ,T4.Cost
            ,T4.RepairsCost
            ,T4.PartsCost
            ,T4.TransportInCost
            ,T4.Color
            ,T5.SalePrice
            ,T5.LineItemDiscount
            ,T6.InvoiceNumber
            ,T6.SaleDate
            ,T7.CustomerName
```

```
FROM       Stock T4
INNER JOIN Model T3
           ON T4.ModelID = T3.ModelID
INNER JOIN Make T2
           ON T3.MakeID = T2.MakeID
INNER JOIN SalesDetails T5
           ON T4.StockCode = T5.StockID
INNER JOIN Sales T6
           ON T5.SalesID = T6.SalesID
INNER JOIN Customer T7
           ON T6.CustomerID = T7.CustomerID
INNER JOIN Country T1
           ON T7.Country = T1.CountryISO2
ORDER BY    T1.CountryName
           ,T2.MakeName
           ,T3.ModelName;
```

- The **AS** keyword is optional when aliasing tables. You can simply add the table alias after the table name and a space to separate the two if you prefer. You can see this in the following code snippet:

```
FROM sales S
JOIN salesdetails D
```

- If you need to visualize the joins between the tables, you can always jump to *Figure 10.10*.

Joining many tables

Ideally, you are getting to know the **PrestigeCars** dataset better. To test your abilities, suppose you want to create a single query to look at all the important fields from the following tables:

- **Stock**
- **Model**
- **Make**
- **SalesDetails**

Specifically, let us imagine you want to produce a list of cars sold that includes all vehicle data and all the essential customer data. This means joining virtually all the core tables in a single query. This SQL is quite voluminous compared to the code snippets you have been writing so far, but it is a practical example of the sort of code you could produce when analyzing your data:

```
SELECT       CY.CountryName
            ,MK.MakeName
            ,MD.ModelName
            ,ST.Cost
            ,ST.RepairsCost
            ,ST.PartsCost
            ,ST.TransportInCost
            ,ST.Color
            ,SD.SalePrice
            ,SD.LineItemDiscount
            ,SA.InvoiceNumber
            ,SA.SaleDate
            ,CS.CustomerName
FROM        Stock ST
INNER JOIN Model MD
            ON ST.ModelID = MD.ModelID
INNER JOIN Make MK
            ON MD.MakeID = MK.MakeID
INNER JOIN SalesDetails SD
            ON ST.StockCode = SD.StockID
INNER JOIN Sales SA
            ON SD.SalesID = SA.SalesID
```

```
INNER JOIN Customer CS
          ON SA.CustomerID = CS.CustomerID
INNER JOIN Country CY
          ON CS.Country = CY.CountryISO2
ORDER BY    CY.CountryName
          ,MK.MakeName
          ,MD.ModelName;
```

If you run this query, you should see the output in *Figure 10.10* (you will see all of it in the output in your notebook if you scroll down; in this screenshot, the output has been truncated):

***Figure 10.10:** Outputting all the key data from the database*

How does it work

This query joins the **`Stock`**, **`Model`**, **`Make`**, **`SalesDetails`**, **`Customer`**, and **`Country`** tables. These tables make up the core Prestige Cars relational data set. Then, a list of fields from all the tables is added to the **`SELECT`** clause to return a list of detailed sales data from all the selected tables. It aliases each table to avoid repeating table names and sorts the data by country, make, and model (in that order of precedence).

Tricks and traps

Writing complex table joins comes with its own set of rules and constraints. They include the following:

- The order in which the tables are added to the **`FROM`** clause is unimportant. The only thing that matters is that each time a new table is added, you join it to a table that is already present in the list and correctly joined in the **`ON`** clause.
- The way we have written the fields in the **`SELECT`** clause is purely a formatting choice, and this makes the fields easier to handle in voluminous queries. You could run all the field names together on a single line if you prefer.
- We chose not to output the key fields (those that are used to link tables together) as they are largely meaningless from an analytical perspective

because they are largely codes for internal use only that have been created by the database designer to allow tables to be joined. You could extend the query to add them if you want.

- There are virtually no limits to the number of columns in queries like this. However, we suspect that you will not need more than a dozen fields in the output. This is another way of saying that there are few practical limits to the number of fields that you can return from a query.

Visualizing databases

Even after years of practice, it is extremely difficult to visualize a database based on a piece of SQL. In databases, as in so many areas, a picture is worth a thousand words. Consequently, database designers have become proficient at creating drawings of how database tables can be combined to make up a database model.

These images of databases are called entity-relationship diagrams (or ERDs in geek-speak). They outline in a lucid and visual way. The following are the two key elements that make up a database:

1. The tables that contain the data (known as entities)
2. The joins that link these tables (known as relationships)

This is, inevitably, only a high-level definition of an ERD. Indeed, a complete ERD can contain much more information about a database than this. However, this definition is enough to get you started for the moment.

Now that you have the theory, it is time for a practical application. So, in *Figure 10.11*, you can see the ERD for the **PrestigeCars** relational data tables:

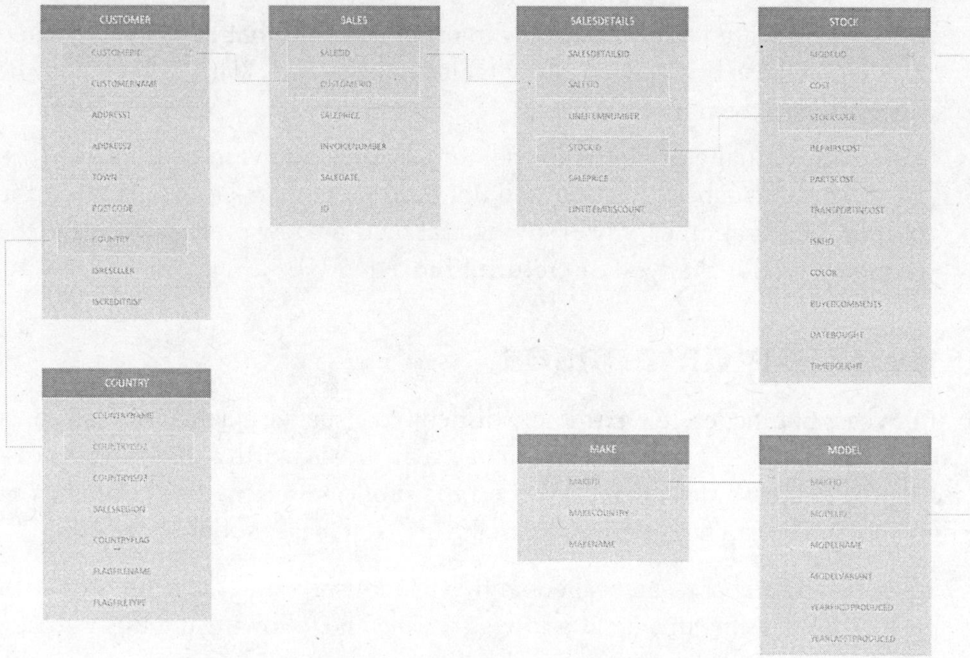

Figure 10.11: *The ERD for the PrestigeCars database*

If you are unsure of how the tables used in the SQL samples in this chapter join together, you can flip back to this diagram to better understand how the tables relate to one another. You can also use this image to visually represent the code you saw in the previous section to join all the core relational tables in the **PrestigeCars** dataset.

Querying across databases

So far in this chapter, you have always used the data from a single database: the default database. Nonetheless, it is worth knowing that Databricks allows you to query data across multiple databases. This can, of course, only be done if you have the required permissions.

As a theoretical example, suppose that you have also created a database named test that also contains a table named make. You can query data from tables in two separate databases using SQL code like the following:

```
SELECT     ModelName, MakeName
FROM       default.Model
INNER JOIN test.Make
WHERE      Model.MakeID = Make.MakeID;
```

All you have done in this snippet of code is add the required database name and a period before any table names. The SQL will run and combine data from tables in two separate databases.

Tricks and traps

Writing table joins across databases needs you to be aware of the following:

- A table name that is preceded by a database name is known as a fully qualified table name.
- A fully qualified table name can be aliased like any other. So the previous code snippet could be written as follows:

```
SELECT     MD.ModelName, MK.MakeName
FROM       default.Model AS MD
INNER JOIN test.Make AS MK
WHERE      MD.MakeID = MK.MakeID;
```

Conclusion

This chapter explained how you can use the multiple tables you will probably find in most databases as the basis for your analytics.

You saw how to join tables using a shared field to look at data in one or both tables you queried. Then, you saw how to extend this approach to join several tables and pick out any fields that interested you in the tables you joined. You also learned how to remove duplicates from a result set and join tables on a range of values and on a specific element.

Although this chapter introduced you to table joins, it has not explained everything you will ever need to know to join tables in Databricks. There is still more to learn on this subject, and you will see more in the upcoming chapters.

Core knowledge learned in this chapter

The following are the key elements you learned in this chapter:

Concept	Description
Joins	This technique is used to link tables so you can return data from multiple tables coherently.
Intermediate tables	These tables are used in joins but do not return data to the query.
`INNER JOIN`	This keyword lets you add another table to a query.
`ON`	This keyword allows you to tell SQL how two tables are to be joined and, more specifically, which fields provide the link between the two tables.
`AS`	Just as you can alias fields, you can alias tables with the AS keyword.
`DISTINCT`	This keyword removes duplicate records from a result set.

CHAPTER 11
Using Advanced Table Joins

Introduction

Joining tables to produce the data you want to see is key to creating the analyses that drive your business. In this chapter, you will build on the knowledge you acquired in the previous chapter and further develop your SQL skills so that you can create more complex and powerful queries. This means learning further variations of the `JOIN` clause to help you shape the data, which is the output from the SQL queries you write.

Structure

In this chapter, we will cover the following topics:

- Filtering data using inner joins
- Filtering data using multiple tables join
- Semi joins
- Filtering data output using intermediate tables
- Using left joins to return all the data in one table but not from the other table
- Right joins to return all the data in one table but not from the other

- Full joins to return all the data from both tables in a join
- Intermediate table joins
- Using multiple fields in joins
- Joining a table to itself
- Joining tables on ranges of values
- Cross joins
- Join concepts

Objectives

This chapter will introduce most of the join types that are available in Spark SQL. These include the following:

- Outer joins let you return all the data from one table and only some of the data in a second table that you join to it.
- Full joins that let you display all the data from both tables in a join.
- Intermediate joins are where you join multiple tables in a query, but not all the tables are used as data sources.
- Self-joins are where you join a table to itself to display hierarchical data.
- Joins on data ranges when you need to map a value in one table to a range of values in another table.
- Joins on multiple fields.
- Semi-joins show data from one table but filter using another table.
- Cross-joins allow you to return all the data from both tables in a join.

We realize that these concepts may seem more than a little abstract when you read about them for the first time. But do not worry; you will see how all these ideas have thoroughly practical applications to SQL queries and how they can be used in your day-to-day data analysis. Indeed, applying these more advanced techniques is often the only way to obtain clear and accurate results from SQL.

Filtering data using inner joins

Let us begin with an extremely important point to make about joins in the context of filtering data.

You need to remember that an inner join acts as a filter. An inner join guarantees that only the data in the records containing matching values in the fields that are used to join tables will be returned in the query result. This provides an initial filter on the underlying data. This means you can filter data in certain cases without needing a `WHERE` clause.

It might be that table joins have already filtered your data and provided the result that you are looking for. However, if this is not the case, then you can extend the filter effect of joins with a myriad of other options that are explained throughout the course of this book.

Filtering data using multiple tables join

Selling classy cars may be great fun, but sooner or later, the finance director will need to know which makes and models the company has bought and stocked. The following query lets you show him a list displaying all the makes and models ever held in stock:

```
SELECT DISTINCT     MK.MakeName, MD.ModelName
FROM                Stock ST
INNER JOIN          Model MD
                    ON MD.ModelID = ST.ModelID
INNER JOIN          Make MK
                    ON MK.MakeID = MD.MakeID
ORDER BY            MK.MakeName, MD.ModelName;
```

Execute this query, and you should see the data in *Figure 11.1:*

	MakeName	ModelName
1	Alfa Romeo	1750
2	Alfa Romeo	Giulia
3	Alfa Romeo	Giulietta
4	Alfa Romeo	Spider
5	Aston Martin	DB2
6	Aston Martin	DB4

Figure 11.1: *Table joins acting as filters*

How does it work

This query joins the **Make**, **Model**, and **Stock** tables so that you can look up the make and model names of the vehicles in the **Stock** table. Indeed, this query is similar to a query you saw in the previous chapter. However, this is not the really important thing about this query. This example emphasizes a really fundamental aspect of SQL—that joining tables actually filters data:

- **First**: This query applies two filters—one for each join clause. This restricts the data to the elements that are common to the join fields.
- **Then**: It applies the **DISTINCT** keyword to filter out any duplicate records (that is, any makes and models that appear more than once in the output).

So, even a simple query like this one is filtering data *out-of-the-box*, even though you have not applied any specific criteria.

To appreciate the filter effect produced by a join, you need to know that the **Make** table contains an exhaustive list of makes of classic cars. However, not all of these have ever been bought by Prestige Cars Ltd.—no Cadillacs have been bought so far, for instance. So if you scroll down the list of makes and models returned by this query, you will not see any Cadillacs. Yet the make Cadillac appears in the **Make** table. Equally, the **Model** table contains a couple of models that do not appear in the results from this query (the Lagonda 3 liter is an example). This is because the query is filtering the output so that only data that is in all the tables that are joined in a query is displayed. All other records in the tables that are used are excluded from the result.

To make this concept easier to grasp, take a look at the simple Venn diagram in *Figure 11.2:*

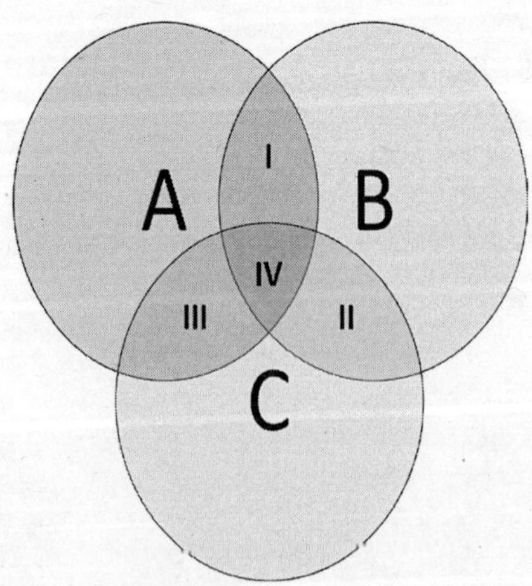

Figure 11.2: *Table filtering explained*

If you join tables A and B, you get the data outlined in I.

If you join tables B and C, you get the data outlined in II.

If you join tables A and C, you get the data outlined in III.

However, if you join tables A, B, and C, you get the data outlined in IV.

This aspect of database querying is so important that it needs to be repeated. When you join tables, only the data that can be linked across all the tables will appear in the result. If you take the principle explained in *Figure 11.2* (the Venn diagram) and show this as a set of tables, you can see what really happens when you join tables.

To get a clearer idea of how this works, take a look at *Figure 11.3*. This image shows how only a common subset of data is returned from multiple tables. This is because the common elements that make up each table join to filter the query results.

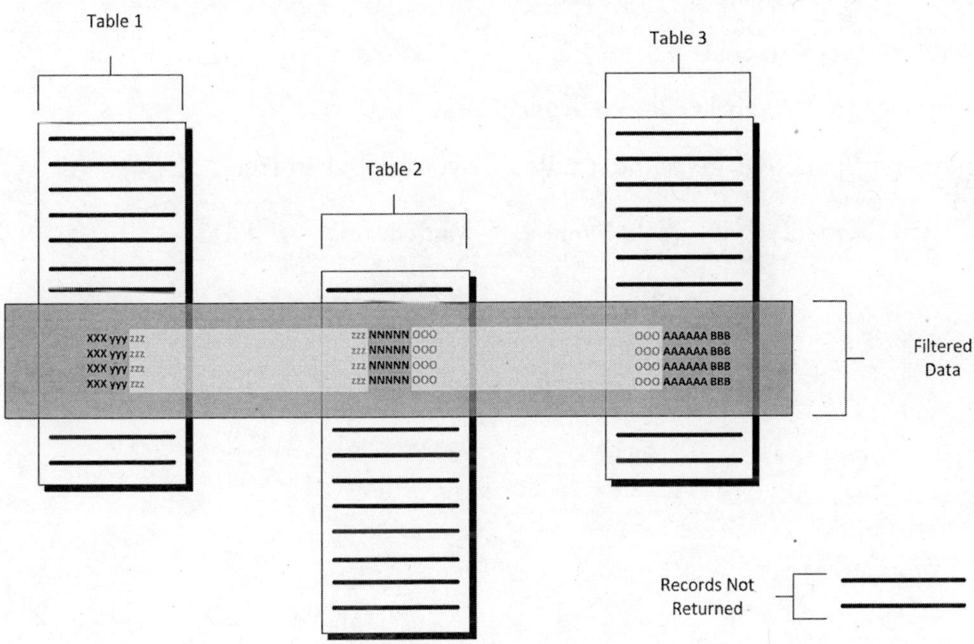

Figure 11.3: *Filtering data using table joins*

Semi joins

Occasionally you may wish to use a table join only to filter data. That is, you do not wish to return any columns from a table but wish the table to be used to filter the output.

As an example, suppose that you wish to isolate from the Stock table all vehicles that have been sold (and so are not sitting, unsold, on the forecourt). As all vehicles that have been sold appear in the **SalesDetails** table, you can use a semi-join to filter out the actual sales.

The following snippet of SQL shows this.

```
SELECT       ST.ModelID, MK.MakeName, MD.ModelName, ST.Cost

FROM         stock AS ST

INNER JOIN   model AS MD

             ON MD.modelID = ST. ModelID

INNER JOIN   make AS MK

             ON MK.MakeID = MD.MakeID

SEMI JOIN    salesdetails AS SD

             ON ST.StockCode = SD.StockID;
```

Running this Spark SQL gives the results that you can see in *Figure 11.4:*

	ModelID	MakeName	ModelName	Cost
1	2	Ferrari	Testarossa	52000
2	3	Ferrari	355	176000
3	11	Porsche	911	15600
4	12	Porsche	924	9200
5	13	Porsche	944	15960
6	22	Aston Martin	DB4	23600
7	23	Aston Martin	DB5	39600

Figure 11.4: *Using a semi-join to filter output*

How does it work

This query joins the **Make**, **Model**, and **Stock** tables so that you can look up the make and model names of the vehicles in the **Stock** table. Then, the query adds a **SEMI JOIN** to link to the **SalesDetails** table.

The **SEMI JOIN** essentially serves only as a filter. It cannot return any columns from the table at the *right* of the semi-join. This is the **SalesDetails** table in this example. However, it is filtering the data so that only columns from the **SalesDetails** with a **StockID** (because they have actually been sold) are returned.

Filtering data output using intermediate tables

Any business needs to see which products to sell. So, it is quite natural that the CEO should want to produce a list of all the models that Prestige Cars has ever sold and when they were sold.

The following SQL produces this list so that you can keep the CEO aware of the data that matters to her:

```
SELECT      MD.ModelName, SA.SaleDate, SA.InvoiceNumber

FROM        Model AS MD

INNER JOIN Stock ST

            ON ST.ModelID = MD.ModelID

INNER JOIN SalesDetails SD

            ON ST.StockCode = SD.StockID

INNER JOIN Sales SA

            ON SA.SalesID = SD.SalesID

ORDER BY    MD.ModelName;
```

Running this query gives the output shown in *Figure 11.5:*

	ModelName	SaleDate	InvoiceNumber
1	135	15/09/2018	EURFR300
2	145	05/04/2017	EURES140
3	145	15/09/2018	GBPGB301
4	175	15/09/2018	EURIT302
5	1750	15/04/2018	EURFR241
6	1750	03/06/2018	GBPCH263

Figure 11.5: *Table joins acting as filters as well as simple joins*

How does it work

This short query joins the **Model**, **Stock**, **SalesDetails**, and **Sales** tables so that you can then select a detailed list of all the models that have been sold.

The following are the reasons you need the aforementioned four tables:

- **SalesDetails**: It contains the stock number (the **StockID** field) of every car ever sold. However, it contains no details about the vehicle itself. To get these details, you need to join it to the **Stock** table.
- **Stock**: It contains all vehicles that are in stock—or have ever been in stock. It does not indicate whether they have been sold. Also, it contains only a code for the model and not the model name, which is what you need. To get the full name of the model, you need to join it to the **Model** table.
- **Model**: It contains the **Model** name.
- **Sales**: It contains the date of sale and the invoice number. You can join this to the **SalesDetails** table on the **SalesID** field.

Once these four tables have been joined, you can display the model name (and other sales details) for every vehicle that is in the **SalesDetails** table—in other words, every car ever sold. It is important to note that even if you are *not* extracting data from the **Stock** table, you need to include it in the query so that you can join the **Model** table to the **SalesDetails** table. As the **SalesDetails** and **Model** tables have no direct connection, the only way to write the query is to join them using the **Stock** table as an intermediate join table.

This query also applies filters to the data. This concept is vital to understanding how this particular query operates. In this query, the filters are applied like the following:

- **First**: The **Model** table contains one or two models that Prestige Cars has never had in stock. However, even if you are selecting the list of models from the **Model** table, as you are doing here, you will not see all the models that are in the **Model** table because only models that are in the **Stock** table will appear in the output. This is because any table join will act as a filter and limit the data that is returned to data that is in both tables.
- **Second**: The **Stock** table contains all vehicles that have ever been in stock. Yet this query only displays models that have been sold (if you want confirmation of this, you can see a **Ferrari Testarossa** in the **Stock** table that has not yet been sold—so it does not appear in the output from this query). Once again, the table join will act as a filter and limit the data that is returned to data that is in both tables.

However, no data is excluded when the **Sales** table is joined to the **SalesDetails** table. This is because the **Sales** table (which contains the data used to print the invoice header) contains a link to every item in the **SalesDetails** table. Equally, the **SalesDetails** table contains no **SalesIDs** that are not in the **Sales** table. So, in this case, you are looking at a simple join that returns data from two tables without filtering data. This is because these two tables are in a hierarchical—or parent-to-child—relationship.

As you can see from *Figure 11.1,* the names of many models appear several times. This is because the filter effect of a table join will nonetheless return all the records from both tables (after any selective filtering has been applied) based on the fields that are in the **SELECT** clause, irrespective of which table the fields come from. In this case, Databricks returns the 348 records from the **SalesDetails** table—because the **Model** table does not contain any models that are absent from the **Stock** table, and the **Stock** table does not contain any vehicles that are not in the **SalesDetails** table. This is fortunate because Prestige Cars would sell vehicles it does not own.

Using left joins to return all the data in one table but not from the other table

The IT director is convinced that the **PrestigeCars** dataset needs some polishing. IT director is certain that there are makes of vehicles stored in the **Make** table for which there are no corresponding models. Rather than manually looking through all the **MakeIDs** in the **Make** table and comparing them with the **MakeIDs** in the **Model** table, you write the following piece of code to use Databricks to find the missing values:

```
SELECT DISTINCT     MK.MakeName, MD.ModelName
FROM                Make MK
LEFT OUTER JOIN     Model MD
                    ON MK.MakeID = MD.MakeID;
```

Running this query gives the result shown in *Figure 11.6.* You will need to scroll down the output to see all the data.

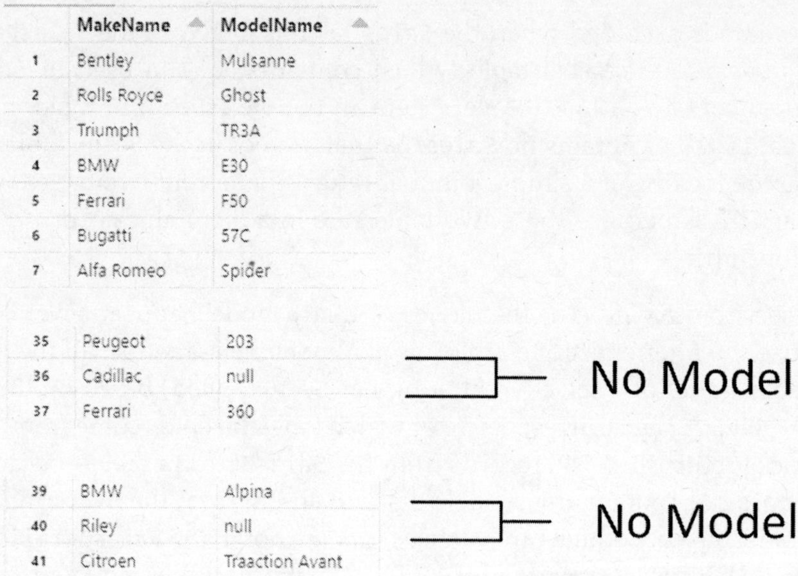

	MakeName	ModelName
1	Bentley	Mulsanne
2	Rolls Royce	Ghost
3	Triumph	TR3A
4	BMW	E30
5	Ferrari	F50
6	Bugatti	57C
7	Alfa Romeo	Spider
35	Peugeot	203
36	Cadillac	null
37	Ferrari	360
39	BMW	Alpina
40	Riley	null
41	Citroen	Traaction Avant

***Figure 11.6**: The results of a query using an OUTER JOIN*

How does it work

This piece of SQL solves what, at first sight, appears to be a conundrum. How do you join two tables and show missing data, given that joins only show data that is present in both tables?

The answer is to use a different type of join. This query did not use the **`INNER JOIN`** keyword that you learned to apply in the previous chapter. Instead, you used the **`LEFT OUTER JOIN`** keyword to join the tables. This keyword will return all the records from one of the tables (the first or left table in the join) but only match records from the second or right table. This lets you visualize any missing information across the two tables.

More precisely, the query is constructed like the following:

- **First**: Create a **`SELECT`** clause that returns the **`MakeName`** and **`ModelName`** fields. To make the results easier to read, you add the **`DISTINCT`** keyword to remove duplicates from the query result.
- **Second**: Add a **`FROM`** clause and enter the table name from which you want to return all the data, the **`Make`** table in this example.
- **Third**: You use the **`LEFT OUTER JOIN`** keyword. This tells Data-bricks that you want to return all the data in the selected columns from the first table (the **`Make`** table, the one to the left of the **`join`** keyword).

- **Fourth**: You add the second table from which you want to return information. This table will no longer only return records where the join field contains identical values in the two tables.
- **Finally**: You add an **ON** clause and specify which fields are used to *link* the two tables.

This query still joins the two tables on a specified field. However, all the contents from the **Make** table are returned, whether or not there are corresponding **MakeIDs** in the **Model** table.

To appreciate exactly what has happened here, you need to remind yourself that the **INNER JOIN** queries that you learned to use in the previous chapter returned data from tables that you joined only if there were corresponding values in the fields that were used in the **ON** clause of the query in both tables. If this was not the case, then no records were returned from either table.

You need to be aware that only a *subset* of data from one of the tables in an outer join will be returned (more precisely, this affects the data in the table on the right of the join in a left outer join and the data in the table on the left of the join in a right outer join). So, these two join types also filter data, if only partially.

If you want to reassure yourself that this query returns different results with an **INNER JOIN**, then try running the following code snippet:

```
SELECT DISTINCT    MK.MakeName, MD.ModelName

FROM               Make MK

INNER JOIN         Model MD

                   ON MK.MakeID = MD.MakeID;
```

The results will not be shown here, but if you run the query and scroll down through the output, you will see that two makes are now *missing* from the result. These are Cadillac and Riley. This means that there are no **NULL** model names in this query output.

As this is a new and fairly powerful concept, let us imagine it in a more schematic way. *Figure 11.7* shows you how a **LEFT OUTER JOIN** works:

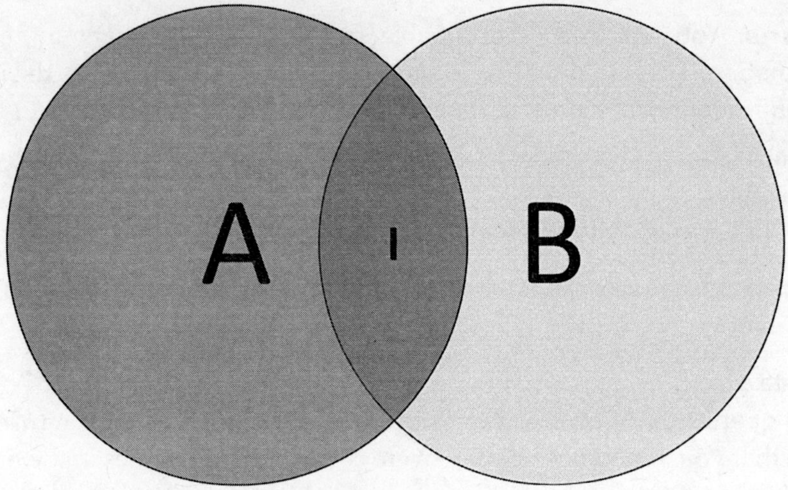

Figure 11.7: *The concept of a LEFT OUTER JOIN*

In the preceding image:

- Circle **A** represents the table on the left of the `LEFT OUTER JOIN` keyword (the `Make` table in the code used previously). All data in this table (unless it is restricted in other ways that you will learn later in this book) is returned by the query.
- Circle **B** represents the table on the right of the `LEFT OUTER JOIN` keyword (the `Model` table in the code used previously). Only records that share values in the join fields provided in the `ON` clause will be returned.
- I represent the data from table on the right of the join that can be returned.
- The result of using a `LEFT OUTER JOIN` is that all the data from table **A** is returned in the query output, but only the matching records from table **B** (shown as I in the image) are returned. Any records from table **B** with no corresponding data in the `JOIN` field are not present in the query result.

Tricks and traps

The following are a few comments to make about outer joins (and specifically about left outer joins).

- We used table aliases when writing this SQL because this approach makes the code easier to understand. This is not strictly necessary but does help you to write shorter code than if you had used full table names.
- You can write `LEFT JOIN` instead of `LEFT OUTER JOIN` if you prefer. Indeed, you may see this in code that you inherit or in examples from other sources.

The result is strictly the same. However, generally prefer to use the **complete** keyword here because this makes the point that you are using an outer join as opposed to an inner join. In other words, you are choosing not to restrict data in the output rather than aiming for a smaller result set. In other words, the original query could read as follows:

```
SELECT DISTINCT     MK.MakeName, MD.ModelName
FROM                Make MK
LEFT JOIN     Model MD
                    ON MK.MakeID = MD.MakeID;
```

- When actually writing **LEFT OUTER JOIN**s, you may choose to adopt a style that places the first table above the second table (much as is the case with many of the query examples in this book). However, this still means that the first table (the one preceded by the **FROM** clause) is considered the left-hand table in the join. So the following SQL is considered identical to the original join in the query:

```
LEFT OUTER JOIN     Model MD ON MK.MakeID = MD.MakeID;
```

- If there is no data in the table on the right of a left outer join, the data from the left-hand table will still be returned, even if nothing is returned from the right-hand table.
- If you are unsure whether applying an inner join or a left outer join will affect the result, then I suggest you run each type of query in turn and look at the number of records produced in each case.

Right joins to return all the data in one table but not from the other

There are several types of **OUTER JOIN** in SQL. Fortunately, they all follow a similar principle. That is, the **OUTER** keyword tells you that all the data from one or more tables will be returned by a query.

To show this, try running the following piece of SQL:

```
SELECT DISTINCT     MK.MakeName, MD.ModelName
FROM                Model MD
RIGHT OUTER JOIN    Make MK
                    ON MK.MakeID = MD.MakeID;
```

Results will not be given here for this query here because they are identical to those returned by the previous query. So, you can see the output in *Figure 11.1*. However, the result is only the same because the order of the tables in this query has changed in the query. As you can see, the **`Make`** table is now on the right of the **`Model`** table.

How does it work

This query uses the **`Model`** table in the **`FROM`** clause, and the **`Make`** table in the **`RIGHT OUTER JOIN`**. This means that the table order is now reversed compared to the previous query. However, using a right outer join tells Databricks to take all the data from the table on the right of the **`JOIN`** clause and only use the data from the tables on the left of the **`JOIN`** where there are matching values in both tables for the field used on the **`ON`** clause.

A right outer join is a mirror image of the left outer join that you saw previously. This applies the same principles to a join, ensuring that all the records on one *side* of a **`JOIN`** keyword (the right table) are returned by the query but only matching records from the table on the *left* of the join.

To get a more visual idea of this, take a look at *Figure 11.8:*

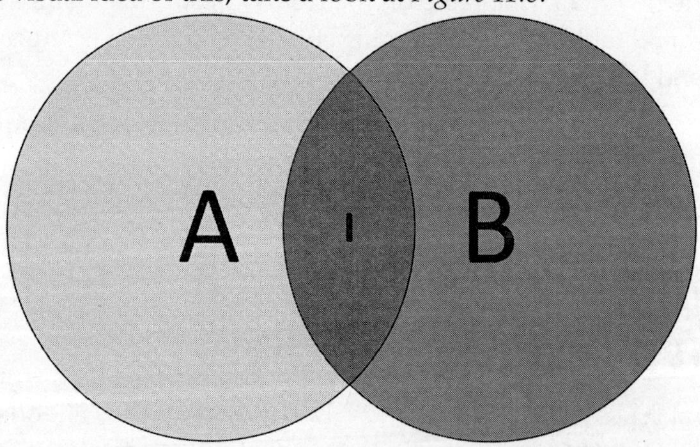

***Figure 11.8**: The concept of a RIGHT OUTER JOIN*

This figure illustrates how a **`RIGHT OUTER JOIN`** takes all the data from the right-hand table and only records that share values in the **`link`** field from the left-hand table.

In the preceding image:

- Circle **A** represents the table on the left of the **`RIGHT OUTER JOIN`** keyword (the **`Model`** table in the code used previously). Only records that share values in the join fields provided in the **`ON`** clause will be returned.

- Circle **B** represents the table on the right of the **RIGHT OUTER JOIN** keyword (the Make table in the code used previously). All data in this table (unless it is restricted in other ways that you will learn later in this book) is returned by the query.
- I represent the data returned from table **B**.

Finally, the choice between a **RIGHT OUTER JOIN**, and a **LEFT OUTER JOIN** simply depends on the order in which you place the tables in the SQL you write. So the two following SQL snippets will give the same output:

```
FROM                Model MD

RIGHT OUTER JOIN    Make MK

                    ON MK.MakeID = MD.MakeID;

FROM                Make MK

LEFT OUTER JOIN     Model MD

                    ON MK.MakeID = MD.MakeID;
```

Tricks and traps

The following are only a few comments to make about the right outer joins.

- A **RIGHT OUTER JOIN** is a mirror image of a left outer join. Essentially, it depends on which table you place before the **OUTER JOIN** keywords and which table you place after these keywords.
- You can write the SQL to place each table in a join on the same lines as the **JOIN** keywords or on separate lines; it is all the same as SQL.
- You can simply use the keyword **RIGHT JOIN** if you prefer to achieve the same result. You can see this in the following SQL snippet:

```
FROM          Model MD

RIGHT JOIN    Make MK
```

Full joins to return all the data from both tables in a join

The sales director wants to get an idea of all the customers who have ever bought a car from Prestige Cars and all those countries that the company either has sold to or might sell to one day. After a little thought, you come up with the following query:

```
SELECT            CT.CountryName, CT.SalesRegion, CS.*
FROM              Country CT
FULL OUTER JOIN   Customer CS
                  ON CS.Country = CT.CountryISO2
ORDER BY          CT.SalesRegion;
```

Executing this piece of SQL gives the result shown in *Figure 11.9:*

	CountryName	SalesRegion	CustomerID	CustomerName	Address1	Address2	Town	PostCode	Country	IsReseller	IsCreditRisk
1	China	Asia	null	null	null	null	null	null	null	null	null
2	India	Asia	null	null	null	null	null	null	null	null	null
3	Belgium	EMEA	34	Diplomatic Cars	Rue Des Coteaux, 39	null	Brussels	null	BE	1	0
4	Belgium	EMEA	49	Stefan Van Helsing	Nieuwstraat 5	null	Brussels	null	BE	0	0
5	Belgium	EMEA	67	Flash Voitures	Place Anspach 65	null	Brussels	null	BE	1	0
6	Switzerland	EMEA	6	Le Luxe en Motion	Avenue des Indes, 26	null	Geneva	CH-1201	CH	1	1
7	Switzerland	EMEA	24	Matterhorn Motors	1, Rue de la Colline	null	Lausanne	null	CH	1	0

***Figure 11.9:** Applying a FULL OUTER JOIN to a query*

How does it work

This query displays all the records from both tables. The following points show how it works:

- **First**: The `SELECT` clause specifies the two columns from the `Country` table and all the columns from the `Customer` table. The table aliases are used to specify which fields are returned from which table. Indeed, to avoid spelling out all the field names from the `Customer` table, the alias `CS` is used followed by the `*`. This will return all the fields from the `Customer` table.
- **Second**: The `FROM` clause is used, followed by the first table in the join (the `Country` table) followed by an alias.
- **Third**: The `FULL OUTER JOIN` keyword is added.
- **Fourth**: The second table is specified (the `Customer` table). This table is aliased as `CS`.
- **Finally**: An `ORDER BY` clause is added.

You can see this in the data that is returned because there are two countries (`India` and `China`) where Prestige Cars do not yet have any customers. Nonetheless, the two country records from the `Country` table appear in the output. However, these two records do not contain any customer data because none is available. Equally, all the records from the `Customer` table are returned.

To continue with the conceptual illustration of how joins return data, take a look at *Figure 11.10*:

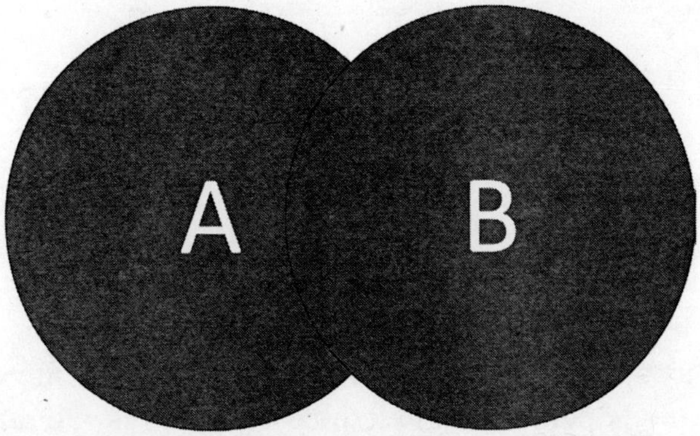

Figure 11.10: A conceptual view of the data returned from a FULL OUTER JOIN

This image makes the point that all the records from both tables will appear in the query result if you use a **FULL OUTER JOIN**. This also illustrates that, independently of the join type, you can select either one or more columns—or even all the columns—from any table in a join. More particularly, this query shows you that you can return a single column from one table (the **CountryName** field from the **Country** table) alongside all the fields from the **Customer** table in the **SELECT** statement by following the table name or alias with the * operator.

Tricks and traps

The following are few comments to make about full outer joins.

- You can enter **FULL JOIN** rather than **FULL OUTER JOIN** if you prefer. The previous query will work in the same way if you write SQL like the following:

```
FROM                Country CT
FULL JOIN           Customer CS
                    ON CS.Country = CT.CountryISO2
```

- However, nonetheless prefer to use the three-word definition as it reminds you—the query developer—that this is an outer join, and so will not automatically limit the data that is returned.
- If you used the * operator *without* a table name or alias, the query would return all the fields from *both* tables. So the following SQL will return the data you can see in *Figure 11.11:*

```
SELECT              *
FROM                Country CT
FULL OUTER JOIN     Customer CS
                    ON CS.Country = CT.CountryISO2
```

	CountryName	CountryISO2	CountryISO3	SalesRegion	CountryFlag	FlagFileName	FlagFileType	CustomerID	CustomerName	Address1	Address2	Town	PostCode	Country
1	China	CN	CHN	Asia	null	null	null	null	null	null	null	null	null	null
2	India	IN	IND	Asia	null	null	null	null	null	null	null	null	null	null
3	Belgium	BE	BEL	EMEA	null	null	null	34	Diplomatic Cars	Rue Des Coteaux, 39	null	Brussels	null	BE
4	Belgium	BE	BEL	EMEA	null	null	null	49	Stefan Van Helsing	Nieuwstraat 5	null	Brussels	null	BE
5	Belgium	BE	BEL	EMEA	null	null	null	67	Flash Voitures	Place Arspach 85	null	Brussels	null	BE
6	Switzerland	CH	CHF	EMEA	null	null	null	6	Le Luxe en Motion	Avenue des Indes, 25	null	Geneva	CH-1201	CH
7	Switzerland	CH	CHF	EMEA	null	null	null	24	Matterhorn Motors	1, Rue de la Colline	null	Lausanne	null	CH
8	Switzerland	CH	CHF	EMEA	null	null	null	58	Raimondo Delattre	9, Place de Chatelet	null	Geneva	CH-1211	CH
9	Switzerland	CH	CHF	EMEA	null	null	null	84	Francoise LeBrun	56, Rue Verte	null	Lausanne	null	CH
10	Germany	DE	DEU	EMEA	null	null	null	4	WunderKar	AlexanderPlatz 205	null	Berlin	null	DE

*Figure 11.11: Using the * operator to return all the columns from all the tables in a join*

- If you use any specific field names in a query that uses more than one table, you can use the * operator without table aliases. This will return all the fields from all the tables in the query.
- Be aware that using **`FULL OUTER JOINs`** on large tables can mean very long-running queries and many columns and rows in the output.

Intermediate table joins

When you are analyzing data, there will almost certainly be times when you will need to join tables but not use any data from them. As an example, perhaps you want to look at the sales made in each separate country. Looking at the tables in the **`PrestigeCars`** database, you have discovered that the sales figures are in the Sales table, and the country names are in the **`Country`** table. However, these two tables have no common fields and so cannot be joined one to the other. However, these two tables both connect to the **`Customer`** table. If this seems a little strange, then take a look at *Figure 11.12:*

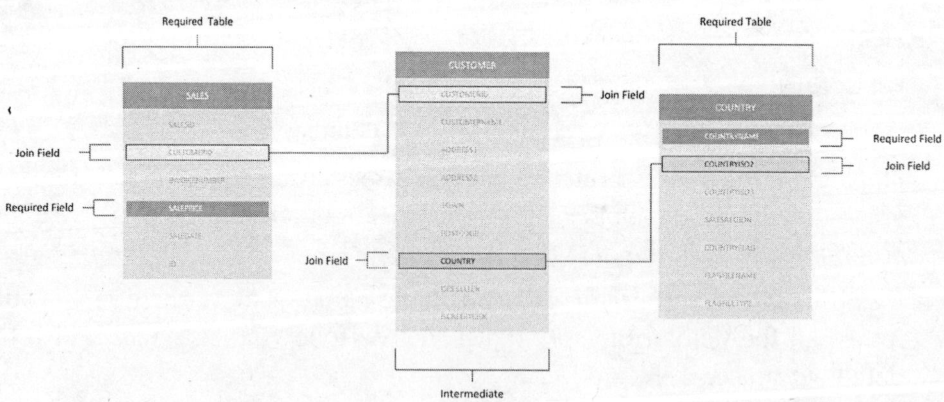

Figure 11.12: Joining tables using an intermediate table

So, you can join the **`Sales`** and **`Country`** tables if you add the **`Customer`** table as an intermediate (or link) table. The following SQL allows you to join these three tables:

```
SELECT      CO.CountryName, SA.TotalSalePrice

FROM        Sales SA

INNER JOIN Customer CS

            ON SA.CustomerID = CS.CustomerID

INNER JOIN Country CO

            ON CS.Country = CO.CountryISO2;
```

If you run this query, you should see the output in *Figure 11.13:*

	CountryName	TotalSalePrice
1	United Kingdom	65000
2	United Kingdom	220000.1
3	United Kingdom	19500
4	Germany	11500
5	France	19900
6	United Kingdom	29500

Figure 11.13: *The output when using intermediate (or bridging) tables to return data*

How does it work

This query returns the country from the table on the right (the **`Country`** table) and the sales figure from the table on the left (the **`Sales`** table) but nothing at all from the middle table (the **`Customer`** table). Yet without the **`Customer`** table to provide the *bridge* between the two tables, it would not have been possible to link the two tables, which would have made it impossible to produce this data.

You can see that in the case of the **`Country`** table, the key field is *text*, not a numeric field, unlike the previous examples. This is perfectly normal in many databases. All that matters is that the database design allows you to specify the columns that join the tables.

NOTE: This query shows the full detail of each sale. You may want to see the aggregate result of all sales per country. This kind of query is explained in *Chapter 7: Formatting Text in Query Output.*

Using multiple fields in joins

Not all tables can be successfully joined using a single field. Sometimes you may find that you need to use two or more fields to join two tables.

As an example of this, let us suppose that the marketing director of Prestige Cars has just spent a large amount of money on some external data about clients. You need to join the new table containing the data (called **MarketingInformation**) to the existing **Customer** table. However, this new table does not have a customer ID; it only consists of the customer's name and country. Fortunately, there are also customer name and country fields in the **Customer** table and SQL can join tables on multiple fields, as the following SQL snippet shows:

```
SELECT      CS.CustomerName, MI.SpendCapacity
FROM        Customer CS
INNER JOIN  MarketingInformation MI
            ON CS.CustomerName = MI.Cust
            AND CS.Country = MI.Country;
```

If you run this code, you will see the output shown in *Figure 11.14:*

	CustomerName	SpendCapacity
1	Magic Motors	Lots
2	Snazzy Roadsters	Some
3	Birmingham Executive Prestige Vehicles	None
4	WunderKar	Lots
5	Casseroles Chromes	Lots
6	Le Luxe en Motion	Lots

Figure 11.14: *Output from a multiple field join*

How does it work

In this example, you created a table join just as you did previously. However, once you have specified the first field you will be using to join the two tables, you extend the join by doing the following:

- **First**: You added the **AND** keyword.
- **Second**: You specified the second field from one of the tables that you need in the join.
- **Third**: You entered the equal (=) sign again.
- **Finally**: You specified the second field from the other table that you need in the join.

You can imagine this kind of join more easily, perhaps, if you see it displayed graphically. *Figure 11.15* illustrates a join using multiple fields:

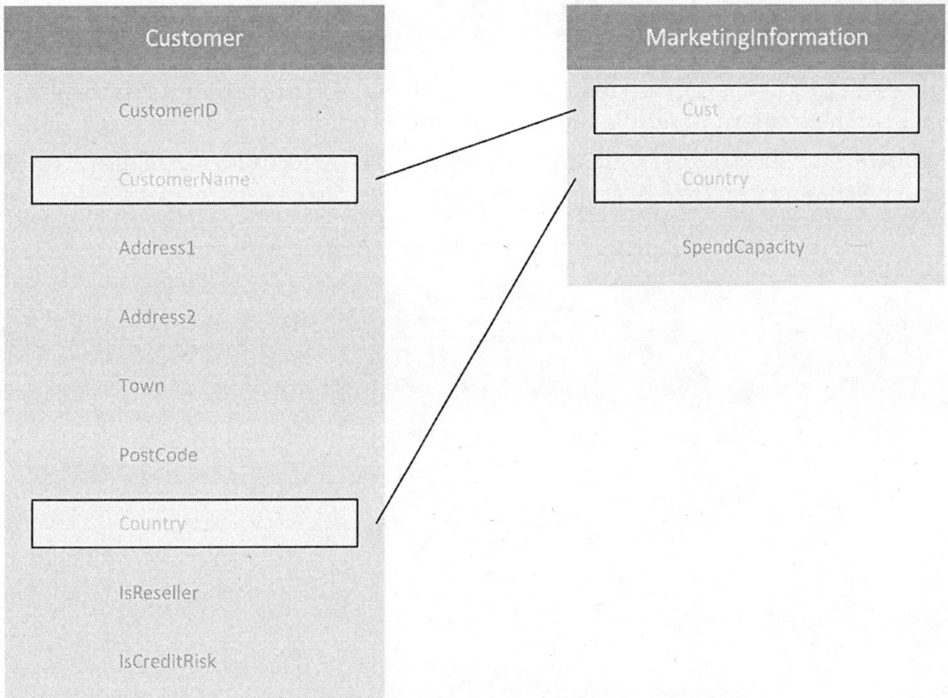

Figure 11.15: *A table join using multiple fields*

The reason for using multiple fields to join tables is that, sometimes, the data in a single column might not be sufficient to identify a record uniquely. Imagine that you are selling cars to a client with multiple sites in several countries. If each site has the same company name, the firm could exist several times in the table (the **`MarketingInformation`** table in this example). So, you need a further piece of information in the data that lets you uniquely identify each record. In this example, it is the **`Country`** field. The end result is that the combination of the elements in the fields used in the join defines a record without any risk of duplicate records being found.

Tricks and traps

The following are a couple of comments to make here.

- You can extend this principle to join on three or more fields simply by introducing each pair of join fields with the **`AND`** keyword in the **`FROM`** clause of the SQL.
- When more than one field is required to identify a record uniquely, these fields make up what is called a composite key.

Joining a table to itself

The CEO has requested a quick list of staff so that she can produce an organizational chart for the next board meeting. She has even reminded you that there is a table in the database (the **Staff** table) that contains all the staff and their managers. You can see this in *Figure 11.16:*

StaffID	StaffName	ManagerID	Department
1	Amelia	null	null
2	Gerard	1	Finance
3	Chloe	1	Marketing
4	Susan	1	Sales
5	Andy	4	Sales
6	Steve	4	Sales
7	Stan	4	Sales
8	Nathan	4	Sales
9	Maggie	4	Sales
10	Jenny	2	Finance
11	Chris	2	Finance
12	Megan	3	Marketing
13	Sandy	11	Finance

Figure 11.16: *The staff table*

Using this table (whose existence you had forgotten about), you produce the following SQL to show which staff member reports to which manager:

```
SELECT        ST1.StaffName, ST1.Department, ST2.StaffName AS ManagerName

FROM          Staff ST1

INNER JOIN    Staff ST2

              ON ST1.ManagerID = ST2.StaffID
```

Running this short piece of code gives the result shown in *Figure 11.17:*

	StaffName	Department	ManagerName
1	Gerard	Finance	Amelia
2	Chloe	Marketing	Amelia
3	Susan	Sales	Amelia
4	Andy	Sales	Susan
5	Steve	Sales	Susan
6	Stan	Sales	Susan
7	Nathan	Sales	Susan
8	Maggie	Sales	Susan
9	Jenny	Finance	Gerard
10	Chris	Finance	Gerard
11	Megan	Marketing	Chloe
12	Sandy	Finance	Chris

***Figure 11.17:** Joining the staff table to itself to display manager names*

How does it work

The `Staff` table contains a field that contains the manager for each staff member. Unfortunately, however, this reference is in the form of the staff ID number of the manager and not the manager's actual name. So, you can use the data in the table twice (once to get the staff member's name and once to return their manager's name). However, this means using the table *twice* in the `FROM` clause of the SQL.

Then, the SQL joins the table to itself. This is what allows the manager ID to be used to refer to the manager name using the second application of the table. It works like the following:

- **First**: You select the staff member's name from the `Staff` table. This is the standard and perfectly usual way of querying a table like this.
- **Second**: You add the `staff` table a second time to the query with an `INNER JOIN`. Each of the references to the `Staff` table uses a different alias (`ST1` and `ST2`) so the SQL can differentiate between the two table references.
- **Third**: You add an `ON` clause that tells the SQL that the `StaffID` field from the reference to the `Staff` table (`ST1`) is linked to the `ManagerID` field in the second reference to the `Staff` table (`ST2`).
- **Finally**: You use the table alias in the `SELECT` clause for every field reference. This allows the SQL to know whether you are referring to staff details (those

in the first table reference to **ST1**) or to the manager details (those in the second table reference to **ST2**). You also alias any fields that are used more than once.

This kind of table join is also called a **self-join**. You can see this more graphically in *Figure 11.18:*

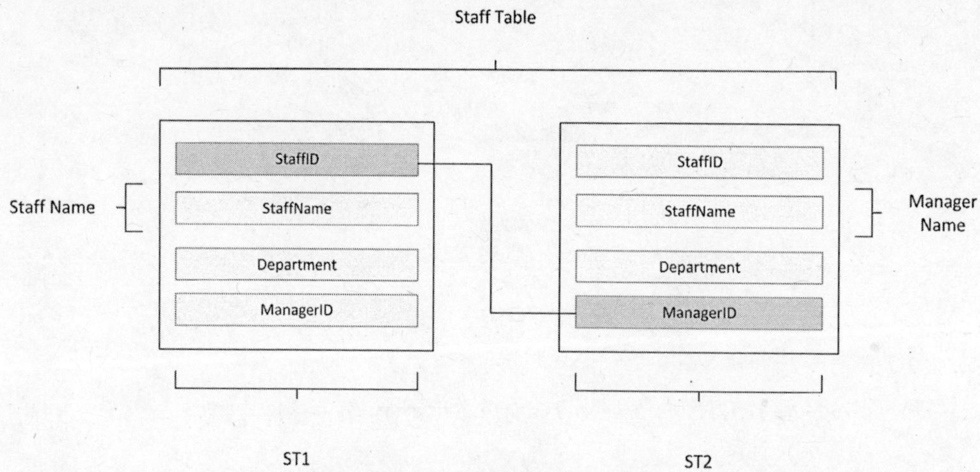

Figure 11.18: Anatomy of a self-join

Tricks and traps

You need to be aware of the following key points when joining a table to itself:

- Be sure that you alias the two table references in the **FROM** clause using different aliases. This way, you understand that you are using the information in the table **twice** to display different elements from the table. This means using a different alias each time that the same table is used in the join. In this code example, the aliases are **ST1** and **ST2**.

  It is vital to alias the fields that you use in the output that are used *twice*, such as the **StaffName** field in this example. Otherwise, you will not know which piece of information is which.
- This approach is also known as a **Hierarchical Join**.

Joining tables on ranges of values

There are infinite number of ways to store data, and you will probably encounter the need to analyze data in multiple tables where you cannot simply join one field in one table to another field in another table. An example of this is the **SalesCategory** table in the **PrestigeCars** dataset. This small table contains a company-specific set of reference information that allows the sales manager to categorize each car sold according to the sale price.

Now, the sales manager wants you to use the data in the **SalesCategory** table to define the specific sales category of each vehicle sold. So, to begin with, you take a look at the table. You can see the data it contains in *Figure 11.19:*

	LowerThreshold	UpperThreshold	CategoryDescription
1	10000	25000	Very Low
2	25001	50000	Low
3	50001	75000	Medium
4	75001	100000	High
5	100001	150000	Very High
6	150001	250000	Exceptional

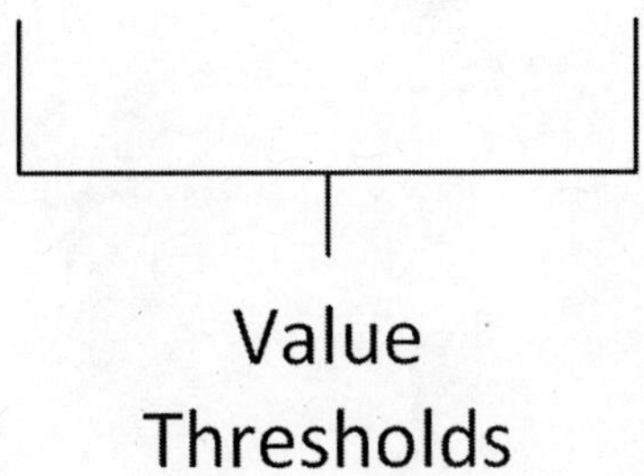

Figure 11.19: *The SalesCategory table*

The first thing you notice is that this table does not contain a unique value in a single column that you can link to a single value (the sale price) in another table. So, you need to find a way to map the range of values that are stored in the **SalesCategory** table to the **SalePrice** field in the **SalesDetails** table.

The following SQL shows you how this can be done:

```
SELECT
 MK.MakeName
,MD.ModelName
,SD.SalePrice
,CAT.CategoryDescription
FROM       Stock ST
INNER JOIN Model MD
           ON ST.ModelID = MD.ModelID
```

```
INNER JOIN  Make MK
            ON MD.MakeID = MK.MakeID
INNER JOIN  SalesDetails SD
            ON ST.StockCode = SD.StockID
INNER JOIN  SalesCategory CAT
            ON SD.SalePrice BETWEEN
                          CAT.LowerThreshold AND CAT.UpperThreshold;
```

Running this piece of SQL gives the result shown in *Figure 11.20*:

	MakeName	ModelName	SalePrice	CategoryDescription
1	Ferrari	Testarossa	65000	Medium
2	Ferrari	355	220000	Exceptional
3	Porsche	911	19500	Very Low
4	Porsche	924	11500	Very Low
5	Porsche	944	19950	Very Low
6	Aston Martin	DB4	29500	Low
7	Aston Martin	DB5	49500	Low
8	Aston Martin	DB6	76000	High
9	Porsche	911	19600	Very Low
10	Aston Martin	DB5	36500	Low

Figure 11.20: *Joining tables on a range of values*

How does it work

This query starts by joining the **`SalesDetails`**, **`Stock`**, **`Make`**, and **`Model`** tables using the techniques you have explored so far in this chapter. You need to link these four tables so that you can return the following information:

- **Make name**: From the **`Make`** table.
- **Model name**: From the **`Model`** table.
- **Sale price**: From the **`SalesDetails`** table.

You are not actually returning any data from the **`Stock`** table. However, you need this table to act as a **`link`** table so that you can join the **`Model`** table to the **`SalesDetails`** table.

Once you have this core query in place, you can extend it by looking up the **CategoryDescription** value from the **SalesCategory** table. This is where you need to use the **SalePrice** field in the **SalesDetails** table and see into which category of the **SalesCategory** table each car falls.

This operation is carried out in the final three lines of SQL in the query (shown in bold). This join says, *Use the* **SalePrice** *field and compare it to the two fields (***UpperThreshold** *and* **LowerThreshold***) in the* **SalesCategory** *table*. If the **SalePrice** field is between the upper threshold value and the lower threshold value, then join the tables.

This *range join* introduces a new keyword combination. This is the **BETWEEN...AND** operator. This keyword combination can be used to look up a value between a lower threshold and an upper threshold:

- **First**: Add the table to the **FROM** clause of the SQL query.
- **Second**: Add the **ON** keyword to introduce the fields that will be used to link the tables.
- **Third**: Add the **BETWEEN** keyword and the field name from the linked table that contains the lower threshold value.
- **Finally**: Add the **AND** keyword and the field name from the linked table that contains the upper threshold value.

This allows you to look up the category description from the **SalesCategory** table for each sale price value.

Tricks and traps

Joining tables on ranges of data is, admittedly, a fairly rare occurrence in practice. However, should you ever have to do this, it helps to be aware of the following points:

- Joining tables on a range of values is nearly always used—as was the case in this example—to look up data from a **reference** table. This kind of operation presumes that the ranges in the **lookup** table have been defined coherently and do not overlap.

Cross joins

The CEO wants a list of all countries Prestige Cars sells to, with a list of all the makes the company has ever stocked. However, when you ask for more details, she says that she wants to see every make appear for every country because this allows her to galvanize the sales teams to sell every make in every country. After a little thought, you produce the following piece of SQL:

```
SELECT        CountryName, MakeName
FROM          Country
CROSS JOIN    Make
ORDER BY      CountryName, MakeName;
```

Running this SQL produces the result shown in *Figure 11.21.* This query produces some 260 records, so I am not displaying the entire output. However, if you scroll through the output, you can see that the makes of the car are repeated for each country:

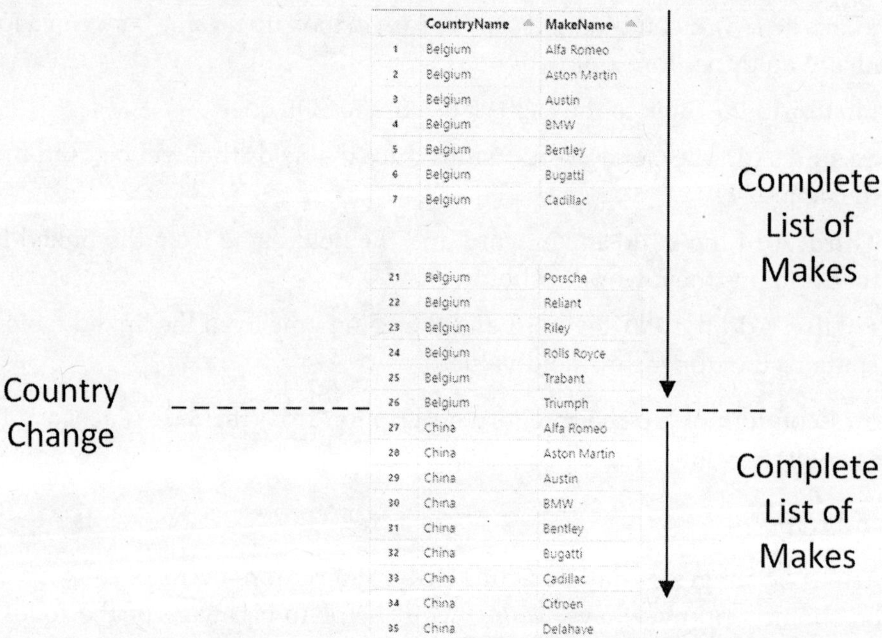

Figure 11.21: The output from a CROSS JOIN

How does it work

This query consists of the following four elements:

- **First**: The **SELECT** clause, where you list the fields that you want returned from the two tables.
- **Second**: The first table that you want to return all the data from.
- **Third**: The **CROSS JOIN** keyword.
- **Finally**: The second table that you want to return all the data from—and do not indicate which fields the two tables will be joined on.

It really is that simple. A cross-join query like this will return a collection of records where each record from each of the two tables will be paired up with each record in the other table.

Tricks and traps

There is one vital point to be aware of if you ever start using cross joins in your queries—and a few minor points of interest—listed as follows:

- Cross-joins can produce huge result sets. This is because they multiply all the rows in one table by the number of rows in the second table in the join. So, you should use them only when you need the specific kind of output that they deliver.
- A Cross-join does not have an **ON** clause because there is no link between any fields in the two tables.
- This kind of join is also known as a Cartesian join.

Join concepts

Learning about the various join types in Databricks can seem a little daunting at first sight. To make your learning curve smoother, take a look at *Figure 11.22*, where the main types of joins are explained graphically:

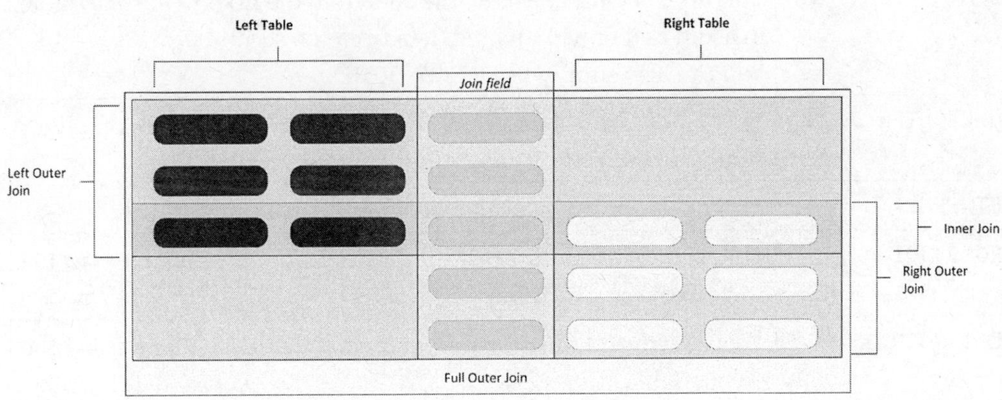

Figure 11.22: Join concepts

Conclusion

This chapter has extended the knowledge that you acquired in the previous chapter and has taken you further toward understanding some of the many techniques that you can apply when joining tables in Databricks.

You have seen the difference between inner and outer joins and how using the **LEFT** and **RIGHT** keywords in a join can completely change the data that is returned by a query. While looking at types of joins, you saw how an **OUTER** join could be used to return all the data from both tables in a join as well as how a **CROSS JOIN** can return a complete cross-mapping of every field in the two tables. You have also learned how to use multiple fields in a table join and how to join tables on a range of data and not just on a single value. As a final flourish, you even saw how to join a table to itself when querying hierarchies of data.

However, for the moment, it is appropriate to move on to another subject. So, in the upcoming chapter, you will begin learning about some of the techniques you can apply in SQL queries to filter your data.

Core knowledge learned in this chapter

The following are the keywords and concepts you learned in this chapter:

Concept	Description
`LEFT OUTER JOIN`	This type of join returns all the data from the first (*left-hand*) table in a join and only matches data from the second (*right-hand*) table. You can also simply use `LEFT JOIN`.
`RIGHT OUTER JOIN`	This type of join returns all the data from the first (*right-hand*) table in a join and only matching data from the second (*left-hand*) table. You can also simply use `RIGHT JOIN`.
`FULL OUTER JOIN`	This kind of join returns all the data from both tables on either side of a join. You can also simply use `FULL JOIN`.
`BETWEEN…AND`	This operator can be used to join tables on a range of values.
`CROSS JOIN`	This keyword multiplies all the rows in the first table by all the rows in the second table.
`SEMI JOIN`	This keyword returns data from the first table yet filters using the second table.

Chapter 12
Subqueries

Introduction

In the previous eleven chapters of this book, you have learned the basics of SQL. From this chapter onwards, we will understand resolving some more complex analytical challenges. The first step on this path is to learn how to use independent SQL queries inside other queries. This technique is called using subqueries. It is particularly useful in data analysis as it allows you to include (among other things) aggregated data in detailed row sets or to compare a whole dataset with subsets of data.

Structure

In this chapter, we will cover the following topics:

- Adding aggregated fields to detailed datasets
- Displaying a value as the percentage of a total
- Using a subquery to filter data
- Using a subquery as part of a calculation to filter data
- Filtering on an aggregated range of data using multiple subqueries
- Filtering on aggregated output using a second aggregation

- Using multiple results from a subquery to filter data
- Complex aggregated subqueries
- Nested subqueries
- Using subqueries to exclude data
- Filtering across queries and subqueries
- Applying separate filters to the subquery and the main query

Objectives

Subqueries are more of a new technique than a new set of SQL keywords. In fact, you can write subqueries easily with the help of the SQL knowledge you acquired in the previous chapters. Nonetheless, learning to use subqueries to resolve data challenges is a key part of your SQL apprenticeship. Once you master the art of the subquery, you can produce clear, concise, and in-depth analytics quickly and efficiently.

This chapter will help you to see how subqueries are not an abstract database concept but an analytical skill that helps in digging deep into data and unearthing the insights that keep the user ahead of the competition. In this chapter, you learn how to:

- Compare categories of data to the whole dataset and calculate percentages.
- Isolate top and bottom elements in a dataset and use them as a basis for filtering records.
- Filter data by comparing records to averages and overall thresholds.

These—and many more analytical solutions—are made possible through the application of subqueries in SQL. Let us now move on to some real-world examples that illustrate how subqueries can turn raw data into meaningful information.

Adding aggregated fields to detailed datasets

Data analysis often means comparing individual elements to either all or a part of a dataset. Suppose that you want to calculate the number of cars sold per country and also want to see the total car sales for all vehicles, regardless of the country, in the same query. The following is the SQL that lets you to do this:

```
SELECT      CO.CountryName
           ,COUNT(SD.StockID) AS CarsSold
           ,(SELECT COUNT(SalesDetailsID)
             FROM SalesDetails) AS SalesTotal
FROM       SalesDetails SD
INNER JOIN Sales AS SA ON SA.SalesID = SD.SalesID
INNER JOIN Customer CU ON SA.CustomerID = CU.CustomerID
INNER JOIN Country CO ON CU.Country = CO.CountryISO2
GROUP BY   CO.CountryName;
```

Running this query gives the results that you can see in *Figure 12.1*:

	CountryName	CarsSold	SalesTotal
1	Germany	13	351
2	France	69	351
3	Belgium	10	351
4	United States	31	351
5	Italy	18	351
6	Spain	27	351

***Figure 12.1:** Using a subquery*

How does it work

Inevitably, there are occasions when one wants to see how a part of a set of data relates to a whole dataset. This approach frequently allows the user to relativize values and put them in a wider context.

This query exists to help you add perspective to the data. At its heart, it is a simple aggregation of sales by country. Once the sales, sales details, customer, and country tables have been joined, the SQL groups the data on the country field and uses the **COUNT()** function to return the total number of sales for each country. Then—and this is where you are moving on to new territory—it adds a subquery to the **SELECT** clause to return the total number of sales without any grouping. In effect, this returns the total for all sales as a separate column alongside the number of cars sold. Moreover, the SQL is carrying out this calculation for every row in the query output so that you can see—and possibly use—the total in every row.

To get a more visual idea of how a subquery works, refer to *Figure 12.2*. The outer query *hosts* the separate inner query, yet both queries run at the same time and output their results together.

Figure 12.2: *A conceptual view of subqueries*

The code shows you how Databricks helps to mix separate queries in a single output using a technique called **subquery**. The subquery in the previous code example is as follows:

```
SELECT COUNT(SalesDetailsID)

            FROM SalesDetails
```

The principal characteristics of a subquery are as follows:

- It is included in the **SELECT**, **WHERE**, or **HAVING** clause of the *main* (outer) query, just as a normal field name would be.
- It is enclosed in parentheses.
- It is a complete, separate query with—at a minimum—its own **SELECT** and **FROM** clauses.
- If used in the **SELECT** clause, it can only return one value (that is, you cannot output more than one field and one row from the subquery).
- In the **SELECT** clause, the subquery is separated from the other fields by a comma, just like a normal field.

Tricks and traps

Examining a new concept implies a few key points that are important to remember, which are given as follows:

- You do not have to use an alias for the name of the field returned by a subquery, but it is easier to understand the results if you use aliases. You may also find that using a meaningful alias helps you understand the query better when you return to it later.
- Any subquery can be executed independently of the main/outer query. This means that you can select the text that makes up the subquery (but not including the parentheses that contain it) and run it by *Shift* + *Ctrl* + *Enter* or *Run* selected text at any time. In this example, you select the following code:
  `SELECT COUNT(SalesDetailsID) FROM SalesDetails;`
  Running this code returns a dataset like the one shown in *Figure 12.3*:

	count(SalesDetailsID)
1	351

***Figure 12.3:** Executing a subquery independently*

- Although you can only output a single value from a subquery in the **`SELECT`** clause, you can make the value that is returned the result of a calculation in the subquery if you need to, as you will discover in the next section.
- The subquery can be as simple or as complex as your requirements demand and can contain its own independent **`WHERE`** or **`GROUP BY`** clauses, for instance. Indeed, a subquery can be any valid SQL.

Displaying a value as the percentage of a total

Calculating ratios, or percentages of a whole, is a core requirement in data analysis. For example, the sales director has put in a request for a list of sales by the make of car sold that also displays the percentage of the total sales that the value for each make represents. Subqueries can help you do this easily, as the following SQL snippet shows:

```
SELECT     MK.MakeName

           ,SUM(SD.SalePrice) AS SalePrice

           ,SUM(SD.SalePrice) / (SELECT SUM(SalePrice)

                                 FROM SalesDetails) AS SalesRatio

FROM       Make AS MK

INNER JOIN Model AS MD ON MK.MakeID = MD.MakeID
```

```
INNER JOIN Stock AS ST ON ST.ModelID = MD.ModelID
INNER JOIN SalesDetails SD ON ST.StockCode = SD.StockID
GROUP BY   MK.MakeName;
```

Running this query gives the results that you can see in *Figure 12.4*:

	MakeName	SalePrice	SalesRatio
1	Peugeot	21045	0.0009545321567800358
2	Delahaye	107000	0.004853168960582743
3	Jaguar	882955	0.040047942052255474
4	Reliant	1900	0.00008617776658978702
5	Trabant	8440	0.0003828107105356855
6	Lamborghini	1727150	0.0783378576660793

Figure 12.4: *Using a subquery to calculate a ratio*

How does it work

This query works in the following way:

- **First**: It joins the tables (**Make**, **Model**, **Stock**, and **Sales Details**) that are required to return the make and the selling price for each vehicle sold.
- **Second**: It groups on the **MakeName** field and selects this field and the **SUM()** of the sale price to aggregate the selling price per make.
- **Finally**: It adds a new calculated field that divides the sum of the sale price by the total sale price of all vehicles sold. This is carried out using the following SQL:

```
,SUM(SD.SalePrice) / (SELECT SUM(SalePrice)
                      FROM SalesDetails) AS SalesRatio
```

The grand total for all sales is defined using a subquery. In effect, this field (**SalesRatio**) divides the aggregate total for each **Make** by the overall total and calculates the percentage of total sales that each sale represents.

Tricks and traps

We are pushing the concept of subqueries a bit further in this example. Note the following:

- SQL frequently forces you to repeat a calculation if you need its output more than once. In this example, you can see that you need the total of vehicles sold twice to calculate the percentage of total sales: once for each make and once to calculate the overall total. Consequently, you have to repeat the formula **SUM(SalePrice)** in both the main query and the subquery.

- This means that SQL is not like a spreadsheet where you can chain cells using cell references to produce ripple-through calculations. However, it is perfectly normal to repeat a calculation several times in a piece of SQL each time it is needed.
- Percentages are expressed as a decimal value when they are calculated, just as they are in a spreadsheet. You may prefer to multiply the result by 100 to obtain a more comprehensible result as follows:

```
SUM(SalePrice) / (SELECT SUM(SalePrice)
                        FROM SalesDetails) * 100 AS SalesRatio
```

- If you want to format the result as a percentage, you can use the following SQL in the third line of the code snippet:

```
FORMAT_NUMBER(SUM(SalePrice) / (SELECT SUM(SalePrice)
FROM SalesDetails), "0.00%") AS SalesRatio
```

Doing so gives you the kind of output that you can see in *Figure 12.5*:

	MakeName	SalePrice	SalesRatio
1	Peugeot	21045	0.10%
2	Delahaye	107000	0.49%
3	Jaguar	882955	4.00%
4	Reliant	1900	0.01%
5	Trabant	8440	0.04%
6	Lamborghini	1727150	7.83%

Figure 12.5: Formatting a percentage output

As you can see, if you are formatting the output, you do not need to multiply the result by 100.

- The main query in both these examples and the previous one is an aggregate query. In practice, the outer and inner queries can apply different levels of aggregation. This means that you can use aggregated subqueries inside simple list queries and list-style subqueries inside aggregate outer queries.

NOTE: It is vital to remember that the two queries are completely independent of each other. This is why the `SalePrice` field has an alias in the *main* query but does not need an alias in the subquery.

Using a subquery to filter data

Prestige Cars' new marketing director is convinced that some colors of cars sell better than others. She wants you to find the color(s) of the most expensive vehicles sold. The following is the SQL that can do this:

```
SELECT     ST.Color
FROM       Stock AS ST
INNER JOIN SalesDetails SD ON ST.StockCode = SD.StockID
WHERE      SD.SalePrice = (SELECT MAX(SalePrice) FROM SalesDetails);
```

Running this query gives the results you can see in *Figure 12.6*:

	Color
1	British Racing Green

***Figure 12.6:** Using a subquery in the WHERE clause of a query*

How does it work

This query is really in two parts:

A subquery: This short piece of code finds the sale price for the most expensive vehicles sold. In this example, the subquery is as follows:

```
SELECT MAX(SalePrice) FROM SalesDetails
```

The main query: It uses the figure calculated by the subquery as the criterion for returning the color (or colors) of any vehicles sold at this price from the main query

The main query itself simply selects the **`Color`** field from the **`Stock`** table and joins this table to the **`SalesDetails`** table so that the sale price can be used in the **`WHERE`** clause as a filter criterion.

This example shows that subqueries are not restricted to being used in a **`SELECT`** clause. As you can see here, you can also use them in a **`WHERE`** clause to restrict the results returned from the main/outer query.

Tricks and traps

We only have one comment to make about this kind of subquery:

Technically this piece of SQL is a single query. However, we prefer to describe it as a main query and a subquery purely because we feel that this helps you understand the code more easily.

Selecting the subquery and running it (by selecting **Run | Run Selected Text** or pressing *Ctrl + Shift + Enter*) gives you the result you can see in *Figure 12.7*:

	max(SalePrice)
1	395000

Figure 12.7: *The output from a subquery*

This is the value that is used by the main query to filter the query output.

Using a subquery as part of a calculation to filter data

As part of a company cost containment exercise, you have been asked to take a closer look at any vehicles whose repair cost is significantly over the average of all the vehicles in stock. Specifically, the finance director wants to see a list of all vehicles whose repair cost is more than three times the average repair cost. The following SQL snippet does this:

```
SELECT     MK.MakeName, MD.ModelName, ST.RepairsCost

FROM       Make AS MK

INNER JOIN Model AS MD ON MK.MakeID = MD.MakeID

INNER JOIN Stock AS ST ON ST.ModelID = MD.ModelID

WHERE      ST.RepairsCost

           > 3 * (SELECT AVG(RepairsCost) FROM Stock);
```

Running this query gives the results that you can see in *Figure 12.8*:

	MakeName	ModelName	RepairsCost
8	Ferrari	Dino	5500
9	Ferrari	F40	5500
10	Ferrari	F50	9250
11	Ferrari	F50	5500
12	Ferrari	360	5500
13	Ferrari	360	9250
14	Ferrari	Enzo	9250
15	Ferrari	Enzo	9250
16	Lamborghini	Diabolo	9250
17	Lamborghini	Diabolo	5500
18	Lamborghini	400GT	9250
19	Aston Martin	DB6	5500
20	Rolls Royce	Phantom	5500
21	Rolls Royce	Wraith	9250

Figure 12.8: *Applying a calculation and a subquery in the WHERE clause*

How does it work

This query shows how to use a subquery in a calculation to highlight certain records in a dataset. The main/outer query simply selects the cost of repairs for all makes and models of vehicles in the database using the `Make`, `Model`, and `Stock` tables. The clever part is placing a subquery in the `WHERE` clause. What this subquery (`SELECT AVG(RepairsCost) FROM Stock`) does is as follows:

- **First**: It calculates the average repair cost. This is £1533.14 for the `PrestigeCars` dataset. You can verify this by selecting and running only the SQL for the subquery.
- **Then**: It multiplies this average repair cost by a factor of three.
- **Finally**: It compares this to the repair cost for each vehicle and only displays the repair costs greater than three times the average repair cost, that is, over £4,599.42.

You may be thinking that it is a little strange to refer to the same table (the Stock table) in this example and twice in the same query. After all, it is already used in the outer query, so why is it needed in the subquery, too?

The reason is that you are looking at the data in the following two different ways:

1. **The outer query**: This looks at the data at a detailed level, where each record is processed individually.
2. **The subquery**: This looks at the whole table to calculate the average repair cost for all records in the table.

Because *each query is completely independent of the other*, both have separate `SELECT` and `FROM` clauses, no matter which tables and fields are used.

The technical term for these two ways of looking at data is **granularity**. In effect, a SQL query can look at either the detail (that is, at a granular level), groups of records (a higher level of granularity), or even the whole dataset. However, it cannot combine multiple levels of focus at the same time in the same query. So, if you need to mix the whole with the parts, you need to use more than one query, even if the queries combine their results in a single output.

To see this more clearly, take a look at *Figure 12.9*. This is a visual representation of how granularity works in datasets:

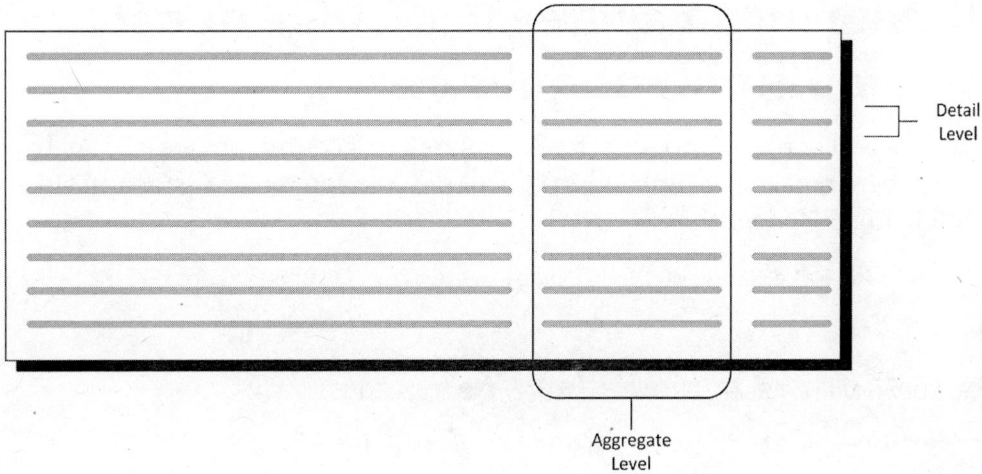

Figure 12.9: Data granularity

Using subqueries enables you to look at data at two or more separate levels of detail. Indeed, you need subqueries to return data at different levels of granularity in a single query.

Tricks and traps

The following are a couple of useful points that you may need to remember when applying this kind of query:

- If you want to check that the calculation of the average cost of repairs matches the quoted figure, select the SQL in the subquery and execute it. This means running the following short piece of code that you can see in the **WHERE** clause of the SQL at the start of this section:

  ```
  SELECT AVG(RepairsCost) FROM Stock
  ```

  You should see the result shown in *Figure 12.10*. This is the average repair cost for all vehicles in the **Stock** table.

	avg(RepairsCost)
1	1533.1472081218274

  Figure 12.10: The output from a subquery

- It is perfectly normal to query the same table or tables in both the main query and a subquery. This only proves that the two queries are strictly independent of each other.

Filtering on an aggregated range of data using multiple subqueries

A further aspect of the finance director's corporate cost control project is to analyze all sales where repair costs are within 10% of the average repair cost for all stock. The following SQL does this:

```
SELECT     MK.MakeName, MD.ModelName, ST.Cost, ST.RepairsCost

FROM       Make AS MK

INNER JOIN Model AS MD ON MK.MakeID = MD.MakeID

INNER JOIN Stock AS ST ON ST.ModelID = MD.ModelID

WHERE      RepairsCost BETWEEN

                        (SELECT AVG(RepairsCost) FROM Stock) * 0.9

                       AND

                        (SELECT AVG(RepairsCost) FROM Stock) * 1.1;
```

Running this query gives the results that you can see in *Figure 12.11*:

	MakeName	ModelName	Cost	RepairsCost
1	Porsche	959	71600	1490
2	Porsche	959	53200	1490
3	Aston Martin	DB6	66072	1490
4	Aston Martin	DB6	55600	1490
5	Aston Martin	DB9	79600	1490
6	Aston Martin	DB9	62000	1490

Figure 12.11: *Using multiple subqueries in the WHERE clause*

How does it work

You can use as many subqueries as you need in a SQL query. A practical use for this is when you need to isolate a dataset that falls between a range of values, for example, when you are using a **BETWEEN...AND** operator in the **WHERE** clause.

This query selects the make, model, cost, and repair cost for all vehicles. It then filters the data in the **WHERE** clause. However, as the **WHERE** clause uses the **BETWEEN...AND** technique to select a range of values, and this approach requires a lower and an upper limit to the range, and it needs two subclauses to calculate the average repair cost.

The range boundaries are defined using the following two separate subqueries:

- **The lower limit**: Takes the overall average repair cost and multiplies it by 0.9 to get the figure for 90% of the average value (£1,379.83). Here, the subquery is `SELECT AVG(RepairsCost) FROM Stock) * 0.9`.
- **The upper limit**: Takes the overall average repair cost and multiplies it by 1.1 to get the figure for 110% of the average value (£1,686.46). Here, the subquery is `SELECT AVG(RepairsCost) FROM Stock) * 1.1`.

These two range limits are then used by the **BETWEEN...AND** elements of the **WHERE** clause to filter the rows that are returned by the main query. This way, only vehicles whose repair cost is plus or minus 10% of the average repair cost are displayed.

So, once again, you need to write a separate and independent subquery to return a specific result. You can even include multiple subqueries to apply multiple calculations across many different data tables.

Tricks and traps

We need to make a couple of points as follows:

- In cases like these, you have to repeat the subquery and make sure that to have made both subqueries perform what is required of them in their separate contexts.
- While using the **BETWEEN...AND** technique, remember to always begin with the lower threshold (90% in this example) and end with the higher threshold (110% in this example).

Filtering on aggregated output using a second aggregation

On certain occasions, your analysis may lead you to compare an aggregate from one dataset with a completely different aggregate. This can happen, for instance, when salesmen request a list of the average sale price of all makes whose average sale price is over twice the average sale price. SQL allows you to compare data in this way, as the following SQL snippet shows:

```
SELECT     MK.MakeName, AVG(SD.SalePrice) AS AverageUpperSalePrice

FROM       Make AS MK

INNER JOIN Model AS MD ON MK.MakeID = MD.MakeID

INNER JOIN Stock AS ST ON ST.ModelID = MD.ModelID
```

```
INNER JOIN SalesDetails SD ON ST.StockCode = SD.StockID
GROUP BY   MK.MakeName
HAVING     AVG(SD.SalePrice) > 2 * (SELECT AVG(SalePrice)
                                    FROM   SalesDetails);
```

Running this query gives the results that you can see in Figure *12.12:*

Figure 12.12: *Applying a calculation and a subquery in the HAVING clause*

How does it work

You can also use a subquery in the `HAVING` clause of an SQL query. As you might remember from *Chapter 3: Applying Complex Filters to Queries*, the `HAVING` clause operates at the level of aggregation that has been applied to a dataset rather than at the level of individual records. So, when you apply a subquery to an aggregate query's `HAVING` clause, you are filtering the data on a total, an average, or any other aggregated value.

In the preceding example:

- **First**: The outer query calculates the average sale price for each make.
- **Next**: The subquery calculates the overall average sale price for all vehicles sold.
- **Then**: The subquery then multiplies this average by two and compares it to the average sale price by make for all the makes of car sold. In this example, the subquery is as follows:

  ```
  SELECT AVG(SalePrice) FROM SalesDetails
  ```

The result is that any make with an average sale price over twice the overall average sale price is then listed in the query output.

Tricks and traps

When using calculations to filter data, you need to be aware of the following:

- There are several ways of carrying out the calculation used in the query. If you prefer, you can use arithmetic like the following:
- ```
  HAVING AVG(SD.SalePrice) / 2 < (SELECT AVG(SalePrice)
                                  FROM   SalesDetails)
  ```

This code gives exactly the same result as the SQL at the start of this example. It is a simple choice between two arithmetical approaches.

Using multiple results from a subquery to filter data

The sales director has asked you to find all the sales for the top five bestselling makes. A request like this illustrates that some data analysis challenges require you to output a set of records that uses the result of a second set (a derived table) as a filter.

The (slightly more complex) SQL to solve this problem is as follows:

```
SELECT     MKX.MakeName, SDX.SalePrice

FROM       Make AS MKX

INNER JOIN Model AS MDX ON MKX.MakeID = MDX.MakeID

INNER JOIN Stock AS STX ON STX.ModelID = MDX.ModelID

INNER JOIN SalesDetails SDX ON STX.StockCode = SDX.StockID

WHERE      MakeName IN (

                        SELECT     MK.MakeName

                        FROM       Make AS MK

                        INNER JOIN Model AS MD

                                   ON MK.MakeID = MD.MakeID

                        INNER JOIN Stock AS ST

                                   ON ST.ModelID = MD.ModelID

                        INNER JOIN SalesDetails SD
```
```

```
                                ON ST.StockCode = SD.StockID
                      INNER JOIN Sales SA
                                ON SA.SalesID = SD.SalesID
                      GROUP BY   MK.MakeName
                      ORDER BY   SUM(SA.TotalSalePrice) DESC
                      LIMIT 5
                      )
ORDER BY   MKX.MakeName, SDX.SalePrice DESC;
```

Running this query gives the results as shown in *Figure 12.13*, where you can also see the output from the subquery. Although this list contains five makes (*Aston Martin, Bentley, Bugatti, Ferrari,* and *Lamborghini*), it is, nonetheless, fairly long. You have to scroll through the output to ensure that only these five makes are displayed.

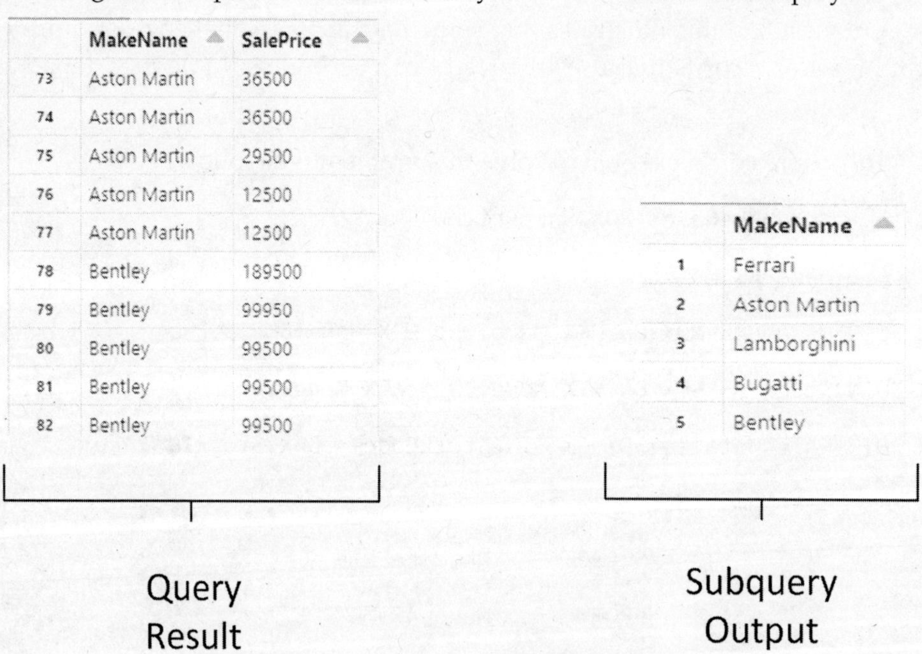

Figure 12.13: A complex derived table used to restrict data in the outer query

How does it work

Here you can see how data analysis can be a multi-step process. This example shows you how to:

- **First**: Use a subquery to find the top five bestselling makes by sale value.
- **Then**: Use this data to filter the results from a simpler outer query.

This example is another one of those times when a subquery can be a lot more complex yet powerful than the rest of the query that uses it. Once again, most of the work is done by the subquery, so it makes sense to look at this first.

- **The subquery**: Joins a series of tables so that you can return the make and sale price. It then aggregates sales by make, calculates the total sale price for each make, and finally, returns only the top five makes.
- **The main query**: Uses this result as a filter as it joins to the derived table on the `MakeName` field.

It is worth noting that the two queries (subquery and outer query) can be different types of queries. In this example, the subquery is an aggregate query, whereas the outer query is a simple *list* (or detail-level) query.

NOTE: When a subquery returns more than one record, you must use the `IN` operator in the `WHERE` clause. If you do not, you will get an error message.

Tricks and traps

Handling complex queries like the one you just saw inevitably introduces some key points to take away, which are given as follows:

- This example introduces something new but so subtly that it is easy to miss. Here the subquery returns more than one record. In fact, it returns precisely five elements, that is, the top five bestselling makes of cars.
- When solving complex analytical problems like this one, you may well find yourself beginning with the subquery and then moving on to the outer query.
- You should be able to run any subquery independently of the outer query. So, you can select the subquery and execute it at any time, just as you would execute the entire query.
- You can begin a complex query like this by writing the subquery first if you prefer. That way, you can be sure that it returns the data you need to filter the outer query correctly.
- You can create a subquery using many separate tables that are joined together, just as you would any ordinary query.
- You can see in this code that we use different aliases in the inner and outer queries, even when the same tables are used. This is not strictly necessary because the two queries are totally separate. However, we prefer to do this for the following reasons:

  - o It highlights the fact that you are dealing with two separate queries.
  - o It is less confusing to read because you can easily see which field comes from which table.
- More complex subqueries like this one can take longer to run, so do not be surprised if it takes a few seconds for the results to appear.
- Instead of an **ON** clause, you may prefer (or may sometimes see) **SEMI JOINs** being used. This approach delivers the same results as the **ON** clause.

```
SELECT     MKX.MakeName, SDX.SalePrice
FROM       Make AS MKX
INNER JOIN Model AS MDX ON MKX.MakeID = MDX.MakeID
INNER JOIN Stock AS STX ON STX.ModelID = MDX.ModelID
INNER JOIN SalesDetails SDX ON STX.StockCode = SDX.StockID
SEMI JOIN    (
              SELECT     MK.MakeName
              FROM       Make AS MK
              INNER JOIN Model AS MD
                         ON MK.MakeID = MD.MakeID
              INNER JOIN Stock AS ST
                         ON ST.ModelID = MD.ModelID
              INNER JOIN SalesDetails SD
                         ON ST.StockCode = SD.StockID
              INNER JOIN Sales SA
                         ON SA.SalesID = SD.SalesID
              GROUP BY   MK.MakeName
              ORDER BY   SUM(SA.TotalSalePrice) DESC
              LIMIT 5
              ) FiveMake
ON FiveMake.MakeName = MKX.MakeNAme
ORDER BY   MKX.MakeName, SDX.SalePrice DESC;
```

Complex aggregated subqueries

After all the work that you did for the sales director, your reputation as an analyst now hit new heights. Now, it is the CEO's turn to request some assistance. She wants to know which makes are generating the most sales and, specifically, how many cars have been sold for the top three bestselling makes. The following code snippet lets you impress her with your SQL abilities:

```
SELECT      MK.MakeName
           ,COUNT(MK.MakeName) AS VehiclesSold
           ,SUM(SD.SalePrice) AS TotalSalesPerMake
FROM       Make AS MK
INNER JOIN Model AS MD ON MK.MakeID = MD.MakeID
INNER JOIN Stock AS ST ON ST.ModelID = MD.ModelID
INNER JOIN SalesDetails SD ON ST.StockCode = SD.StockID
WHERE      MakeName IN (
                         SELECT     MK.MakeName
                         FROM       Make AS MK
                         INNER JOIN Model AS MD
                                    ON MK.MakeID = MD.MakeID
                         INNER JOIN Stock AS ST
                                    ON ST.ModelID = MD.ModelID
                         INNER JOIN SalesDetails SD
                                    ON ST.StockCode = SD.StockID
                         INNER JOIN Sales AS SA
                                    ON SA.SalesID = SD.SalesID
                         GROUP BY    MK.MakeName
                         ORDER BY   COUNT(MK.MakeName) DESC
                         LIMIT 3
                        )
GROUP BY  MK.MakeName
ORDER BY  VehiclesSold DESC;
```

Running this query gives the results that you can see in *Figure 12.14:*

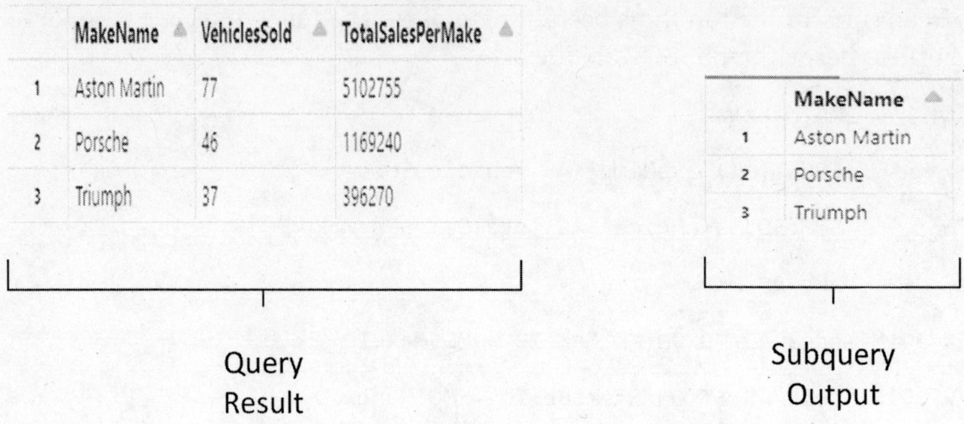

Figure 12.14: Using a complex subquery as a filter in an aggregated query

How does it work

Some queries are two queries in one. In these cases, subqueries unlock the real power of SQL to allow you to carry out complex filtering that then becomes the basis of further analysis. This example extends the code from the previous example to show that the two queries that generate the final result are and have to be totally independent of one another. Even though the subquery counts the sales per make, you cannot pass this value back to the outer query. You have to count the number of vehicles sold twice: once in the subquery to act as a filter and once in the outer query to display the result.

Otherwise, this query is very similar to the previous one. The subquery finds the top three makes sold by quantity. Then these three makes are used as the filter by the outer query.

Tricks and traps

The following are a couple of points to be noted:

- In this example, both queries (outer query and subquery) aggregate data. As you saw in the previous example, this does not necessarily need to be the case.
- This code applies the same aliases for the tables in both the outer query and the subquery. This reinforces the point that the two queries are completely separate and that the aliases in the outer query only refer to tables in the

outer query and the aliases in the inner query only refer to tables in the inner query, even if the same aliases are used in both queries.

Nested subqueries

This time the sales director wants you to find the top five vehicles sold by value in the color of the most expensive car sold. The following piece of SQL does this:

```
SELECT      MK.MakeName, MD.ModelName, SD.SalePrice

FROM        Make AS MK

INNER JOIN Model AS MD ON MK.MakeID = MD.MakeID

INNER JOIN Stock AS ST ON ST.ModelID = MD.ModelID

INNER JOIN SalesDetails SD ON ST.StockCode = SD.StockID

INNER JOIN Sales AS SA ON SA.SalesID = SD.SalesID

WHERE       Color IN (SELECT     ST.Color

                      FROM       Model AS MD

                      INNER JOIN Stock AS ST

                                 ON ST.ModelID = MD.ModelID

                      INNER JOIN SalesDetails SD

                                 ON ST.StockCode = SD.StockID

                      WHERE      SD.SalePrice =

                                       (

                                        SELECT      MAX(SD.SalePrice)

                                        FROM        SalesDetails SD

                                        INNER JOIN  Sales SA

                                        ON SA.SalesID = SD.SalesID

                                    )

                      )

ORDER BY    SD.SalePrice DESC

LIMIT 5;
```

Running this query gives the results that you can see in *Figure 12.15*:

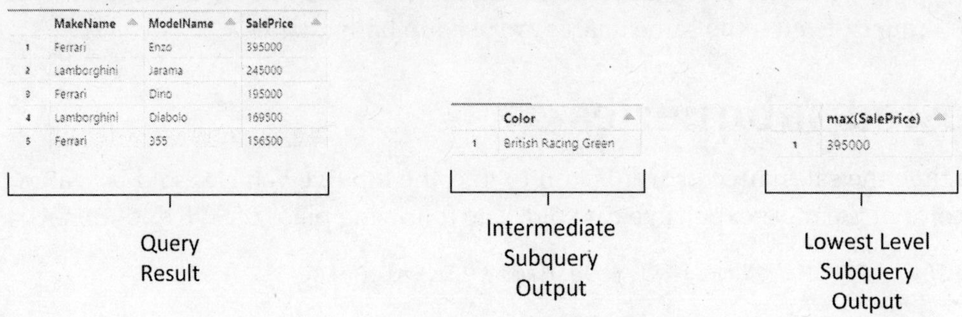

***Figure 12.15:** A query containing nested subqueries*

How does it work

Answering some questions can require more complex queries. This is where Databricks's ability to *nest* subqueries inside subqueries can help you find a solution to such issues. The query you just ran is an example of this kind of approach because it contains a subquery inside another subquery. As is often the case with subqueries, it is easiest to start on the inside with the deepest nested subquery and then work outward to explain the SQL.

The innermost query (at the lowest level)

Joins the **`Sales`** and **`Sales Details`** tables and returns the highest sale price for any vehicle sold.

The middle (or intermediate) subquery

Uses the sale price from the deepest nested subquery as a filter (in its **`WHERE`** clause) to find any vehicles that have been sold at this price. It then returns the colors of this vehicle or other vehicles.

The outer query

Lists the **`Make`**, **`Model`**, and **`Sale Price`** for all the vehicles sold in the color returned by the middle subquery. Note that the **`WHERE`** clause uses **`IN`** and not = (equals) because there is potentially more than one vehicle of this color returned by the intermediate query.

When faced with a challenge such as *Find the Top Five Vehicles Sold for the Bestselling Color by Value*, it can be hard to analyze the question and then break the solution down into separate parts that can then be answered as separate SQL queries. In these cases, our advice is to look hard at the question before starting to write any SQL. Often the code itself is easier than the analysis, and if the initial analysis is correct, then you are likely to write simpler and better SQL.

Figure 12.16 explains the concept of nested queries. Here you can see how each query uses the output from the query at a lower level to filter the data that it passes up to the query above it. Finally, the topmost query returns the required result.

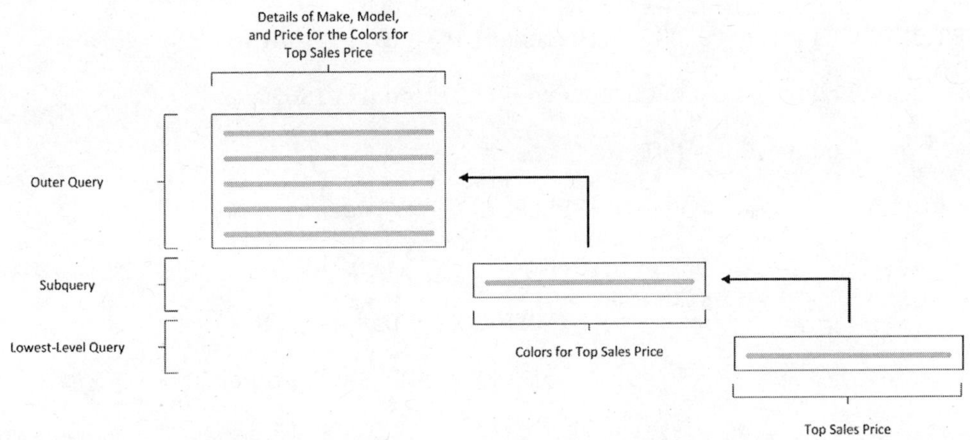

Figure 12.16: *Using subqueries to filter data progressively*

Tricks and traps

This approach is best applied when you bear the following points in mind:

- There is a theoretical limit to the number of nested subqueries that you can use in Databricks. In practice, however, it is rare when you need to use more than 3 or 4 levels, so it is unlikely that you will hit the limit.
- As you can see in the query you just ran, you can easily end up repeating table joins in nested subqueries. This is perfectly normal, considering that each query is completely independent of the others.

Using subqueries to exclude data

Some analysis requires you to examine data that lies outside a certain range or category. For instance, at Prestige Cars, the CEO wants a report that shows sales by make for all vehicles sold that are not in the sales made to the bottom four countries by value. Subqueries can often be the solution to these requirements, as the following SQL illustrates:

```
SELECT     MK.MakeName, SUM(SA.TotalSalePrice) AS TotalSales
```

```
FROM       Make AS MK INNER JOIN Model AS MD
           ON MK.MakeID = MD.MakeID
INNER JOIN Stock AS ST ON ST.ModelID = MD.ModelID
INNER JOIN SalesDetails SD ON ST.StockCode = SD.StockID
INNER JOIN Sales AS SA ON SA.SalesID = SD.SalesID
INNER JOIN Customer CU ON SA.CustomerID = CU.CustomerID
INNER JOIN Country CO ON CU.Country = CO.CountryISO2
WHERE      CountryName NOT IN (
                                 SELECT     CO.CountryName
                                 FROM       Sales AS SA
                                 INNER JOIN Customer CU
                                            ON SA.CustomerID =
                                                          CU.CustomerID
                                 INNER JOIN Country CO
                                            ON CU.Country = CO.CountryISO2
                                 GROUP BY   CountryName
                                 ORDER BY   SUM(SA.TotalSalePrice) ASC
                                 LIMIT 4
                                 )
GROUP BY   MK.MakeName;
```

Running this query gives the results that you can see in *Figure 12.17*:

	MakeName	TotalSales
1	Peugeot	12545
2	Delahaye	119500
3	Jaguar	1101395
4	Reliant	1900
5	Trabant	74140
6	Lamborghini	1167600
7	Austin	40900
8	Mercedes	703615
9	Alfa Romeo	244085
10	Rolls Royce	1372500
11	McLaren	295000
12	Noble	177400
13	BMW	60500
14	Ferrari	5630900.1
15	Porsche	1301940

Query Result

	CountryName
1	Belgium
2	Switzerland
3	Germany
4	Italy

Subquery Output

***Figure 12.17:** Excluding data from a dataset using a subquery and NOT IN*

How does it work

This query extends the concepts that you have seen so far in this chapter. It also tries to show that what appears to be complex or convoluted SQL is, in fact, simple.

If you look at the preceding SQL, you can see that it breaks down into two main elements:

- **First**: Create a subquery that uses the tables required to aggregate sales by country. This subquery then isolates the bottom four countries by sales by sorting the resulting data from lowest to highest.
- **Second**: The outer query joins a series of tables so that you can use the make, customer country, and sales price fields. Even if you are only displaying the make and sales price fields, you are using the customer country field in the `WHERE` clause to use the subquery as a filter. So, the code must make the country field accessible by joining the table that contains this data to the query.

Once you have defined these queries, it is simply a question of using the output from the subquery (the top four countries for vehicle sales) and excluding it from the result that the outer query returns. You do this by using the **`NOT IN`** operator in the **`WHERE`** clause of the outer query. So, what you have commanded is, *find me makes and sales where the sales are not made to the bottom four least-performing countries.*

So, a query that seems long and complex is, in fact, relatively simple once you break it down into its constituent parts. Here, as in most SQL, it is largely a question of ensuring that a query or subquery can access all the required fields by ensuring that all the necessary tables are joined in the **`FROM`** clause of each query and the fields used to include or exclude records in the outer query are available in both inner and outer queries.

Tricks and traps

To finish this introduction to simple subqueries, you should take note of the following:

Once again, if a subquery is returning potentially more than one element (and because we are asking for four countries, we hope that more than one element is returned), you cannot use equals or not equals (=, !=, or <>); you have to use the **`IN`** keyword. Then, you make it negative by adding **`NOT`** to the **`IN`**. This way, you are excluding from the outer query an element returned from the subquery. So the **`WHERE`** clause starts with the following:

```
WHERE       CountryName NOT IN
```

Filtering across queries and subqueries

In your analytical career, you will probably have to produce reports that do not look at a dataset in its entirety. The following SQL snippet returns each make sold in 2015, along with the total sales figure per make for 2015 and the percentage that this represents of the total sales for that year only:

```
SELECT      MK.MakeName

            ,SUM(SD.SalePrice) AS SalePrice

            ,SUM(SD.SalePrice) /

                       (SELECT     SUM(SD.SalePrice)

                        FROM       SalesDetails SD

                        INNER JOIN Sales AS SA

                                   ON SA.SalesID = SD.SalesID
```

```
                         WHERE     YEAR(SaleDate) = 2015
                        ) AS SalesRatio
FROM       Make AS MK
INNER JOIN Model AS MD ON MK.MakeID = MD.MakeID
INNER JOIN Stock AS ST ON ST.ModelID = MD.ModelID
INNER JOIN SalesDetails SD ON ST.StockCode = SD.StockID
INNER JOIN Sales AS SA ON SA.SalesID = SD.SalesID
WHERE      YEAR(SA.SaleDate) = 2015
GROUP BY   MK.MakeName;
```

Running this query gives the results that you can see in *Figure 12.18*, where you can also see the result of the subquery:

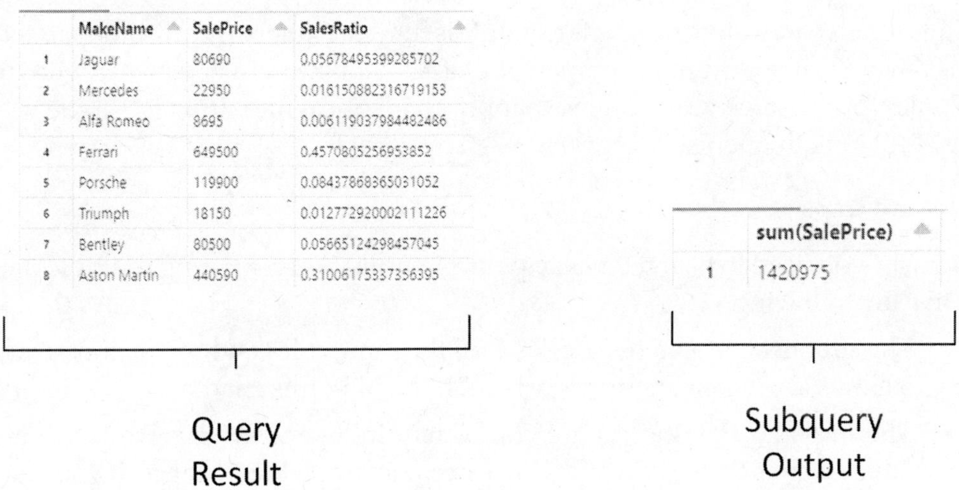

	MakeName	SalePrice	SalesRatio
1	Jaguar	80690	0.05678495399285702
2	Mercedes	22950	0.016150882316719153
3	Alfa Romeo	8695	0.006119037984482486
4	Ferrari	649500	0.4570805256953852
5	Porsche	119900	0.08437868365031052
6	Triumph	18150	0.012772920002111226
7	Bentley	80500	0.05665124298457045
8	Aston Martin	440590	0.31006175337356395

	sum(SalePrice)
1	1420975

Figure 12.18: Applying filters to subqueries

How does it work

As you saw earlier in this chapter, a classic analytical requirement is comparing the whole with its constituent parts. Sometimes, however, you need to compare a subset of data with another subset. You do this by applying separate filters to both the main/outer query and the subquery (which some people call the inner query). So even if this query does look familiar, there is a major difference. Each query has a separate **WHERE** clause.

- **The subquery**: Finds the figure for the total sales for 2015.
- **The outer query**: Finds the sales per make for 2015. It then divides this by the total sales figure for the same year to display the percentage of sales per make for the year.

First, we prefer to explain the subquery because SQL queries nearly always work from the inside to the outside and not the other way around. The subquery is calculated first, and it returns the total sales for 2015. This query merely provides the total figure with no subsetting of data at all. It joins the necessary tables (only `Sales` and `Sales Details` are needed to find the annual total) and calculates the `SUM()` of the sale price field. The outer query finds the sales for each make for the same year and then divides the sales for each make by the yearly total, giving the percentage of sales by value for each make. The outer query needs to return not only the sales total (from the `Sales Details` table) but also the year (from the `Sales` table). It also needs to return the make of cars sold. Consequently, it needs to add joins to the `Stock` and `Make` tables.

The important part to note from this example is that each query is truly independent of the other. So, if you want to compare the sales by make for a given year with the total sales for the same year, you must apply an identical filter (that is, set the year to be 2015) in both queries.

Tricks and traps

Obviously, you need to bear a few key points in mind when filtering multiple data sets like the following:

- The subquery shown here follows all the same rules and restrictions as the subqueries, which are previously mentioned in this chapter.
- The fact that the queries are completely independent can work to your advantage as they make querying extremely fluid. For instance, if you want to compare the sales per make for a given year to the total for all vehicles ever sold, all you have to do is omit the `WHERE` clause from the subquery. The subquery then calculates the value of all cars ever sold by the company, which you still use in the outer query to calculate the percentages of sales per make.
- Remember to test the subquery and ensure that it gives the result you expect before you rely blindly on the output that it sends to the outer query.
- If you are filtering inner and outer queries, you need to pay particular attention to the filters that you apply and ensure that you are using similar filters in both queries if you are attempting to analyze comparable datasets.

Applying separate filters to the Subquery and the main query

Like comparisons are a mainstay of business analysis. Like most companies that make their margin by buying and selling, *Prestige Cars* needs to see if sales are up or down compared to previous years. Specifically, the CEO wants to see the difference in the sale price for each car sold compared to the average price for the previous year. As the following SQL snippet shows, year-on-year sales comparisons are not overly difficult:

```
SELECT       MK.MakeName
            ,MD.ModelName
            ,SD.SalePrice AS ThisYearsSalePrice
            ,SD.SalePrice
              - (SELECT    AVG(SD.SalePrice)
                 FROM       Stock ST
                 INNER JOIN SalesDetails SD
                            ON ST.StockCode = SD.StockID
                 INNER JOIN Sales AS SA
                            ON SA.SalesID = SD.SalesID
                 WHERE      YEAR(SA.SaleDate) = 2015)
                                                 AS DeltaToLastYearAverage
FROM        Make AS MK INNER JOIN Model AS MD
            ON MK.MakeID = MD.MakeID
INNER JOIN Stock AS ST ON ST.ModelID = MD.ModelID
INNER JOIN SalesDetails SD ON ST.StockCode = SD.StockID
INNER JOIN Sales AS SA ON SA.SalesID = SD.SalesID
WHERE       YEAR(SA.SaleDate) = 2016;
```

Running this query gives the results that you can see in *Figure 12.19*:

	MakeName	ModelName	ThisYearsSalePrice	DeltaToLastYearAverage
1	Ferrari	Testarossa	195000	144250.89285714284
2	Ferrari	Testarossa	165000	114250.89285714286
3	Ferrari	355	205000	154250.89285714284
4	Ferrari	355	159500	108750.89285714286
5	Ferrari	355	156500	105750.89285714286
6	Ferrari	Mondial	102950	52200.892857142855
7	Ferrari	360	99500	48750.892857142855
8	Porsche	911	45950	-4799.107142857145
9	Porsche	911	68900	18150.892857142855
10	Porsche	911	20950	-29799.107142857145

Query Result
(detailed sales for 2016)

	avg(SalePrice)
1	50749.107142857145

Subquery Output
(average sales for 2015)

Figure 12.19: *Using different filters and aggregations in outer and inner queries*

How does it work

Being able to use completely independent queries together is particularly useful when you want to compare data over time. This time the subquery (or the inner query, if you prefer) calculates the average vehicle sale price for 2015. The outer query, however, filters in 2016, that is, the following year.

When the outer query returns the list of makes sold in 2016, it calculates for each make the difference between the sale price for 2016 (returned by the outer query) and the average sale price for 2015 (returned by the inner query). This way, you can compare data from two separate years.

The fact that the two queries can work together while remaining completely independent allows you to see how sales evolve over time from one year to the next.

Tricks and traps

One important point to remember when applying different filters to queries and subqueries is as follows:

- Another indication of the fact that subqueries are completely independent of the query that contains them is given by the fact that you can use different filters for each query. In the current example, for instance, the outer query filters on one year, whereas the subquery filters on another year.

Conclusion

In this chapter, you saw how you can nest queries inside queries to deliver more powerful analytics. As you have learned, a subquery is nothing more than a standard SQL query in its own right. However, the ability to return two or more independent datasets inside a single query opens up the road to a much more advanced comparative analysis of your data. You can compare data at different levels of aggregation and calculate percentages of a total with a minimum of effort. Subqueries also let you isolate data in many subtle and surprising ways and can, consequently, help you deliver deeper insights into your data.

Core knowledge learned in this chapter

The concepts that you have seen in this chapter are as follows:

- A subquery is completely independent of the outer query.
- You can refer to the subquery in the `SELECT`, `WHERE`, or `HAVING` clauses of the outer query.
- You must enclose a subquery in parentheses.
- A subquery must include a `SELECT` clause and a `FROM` clause.
- A subquery can include optional `WHERE`, `GROUP BY`, and `HAVING` clauses.
- You can include an `ORDER BY` clause only when a `TOP` clause is included.
- If a subquery returns more than one record, then you have to use the `IN` operator in the `WHERE` or `HAVING` clause of the outer query.
- You can nest subqueries inside other subqueries.

Join our book's Discord space

Join the book's Discord Workspace for Latest updates, Offers, Tech happenings around the world, New Release and Sessions with the Authors:

https://discord.bpbonline.com

CHAPTER 13
Derived Tables

Introduction

Some analytical challenges may require combining different types of queries to get the result that you are looking for. You may need to compare data at different levels of aggregation or carry out calculations that mix and match different methods of grouping data. For these problems, SQL has a clear answer which is called derived tables.

A derived table lets you focus on producing complex datasets inside a single query. You can then use this data to solve your analytical conundrum. As you will observe throughout the chapter, whenever a challenge seems to require different types of SQL queries at the same time, derived tables are extremely helpful. This is not only because they deliver a technical answer, but they also help to analyze a problem by breaking it down into smaller, separate components. This assists the user in constructing the code that can produce the desired result.

Structure

In this chapter, we will cover the following topics:

- Using a derived table to create intermediate calculations

- Grouping and ordering data using a custom classification
- Joining derived tables with other tables
- Joining multiple derived tables
- Using multiple derived tables for complex aggregations
- Using derived tables to join unconnected tables
- Compare year-on-year data using a derived table
- Synchronizing filters between a derived table and the main query

Objectives

A derived table is, in many ways, a subquery. However, it is also often the *engine room* where most of the hard work is done. After the work is complete, the derived query may pass its output to the outer query that shapes and presents the final dataset.

Indeed, trying to carry out certain calculations and aggregations without a derived table is extremely difficult, both conceptually and practically. So, in this chapter, you learn how to use derived tables to:

- Define calculated metrics that you can reuse several times without redefining the calculation each time.
- Create your own ad-hoc classifications that you can use to group data.
- Analyze ratios for subgroups of data.
- Mix different data sources that have differing levels of data aggregation, such as monthly budgets and daily sales.
- Compare values across years.
- Isolate maximum, minimum, and average values, and use them to analyze the classified data.
- Filter data based on the first or last recorded output from a derived table.

The aim of this chapter is to enhance and extend the knowledge acquired so far in the book. The chapter further aims to find ways of juggling data that not only enhance SQL skills but help to understand datasets as a way of solving analytical challenges.

Using a derived table to create intermediate calculations

There is no point in conducting business unless it is profitable, at least for the boss of *Prestige Cars*. She wants a printout of the sales, costs, gross, and net profit for every car sold. Fortunately, Databricks makes delivering this kind of output easy, as the following code shows:

```
SELECT
 MakeName
,ModelName
,SaleDate
,SalePrice
,Cost
,SalePrice - DirectCosts AS GrossProfit
,SalePrice - DirectCosts - NVL(LineItemDiscount, 0) AS NetProfit
FROM
(
  SELECT
   MK.MakeName
  ,MD.ModelName
  ,SA.SaleDate
  ,SD.SalePrice
  ,ST.Cost
  ,LineItemDiscount
  ,(NVL(ST.RepairsCost, 0) + NVL(ST.PartsCost, 0)
  + ST.TransportInCost) AS DirectCosts
  FROM       Make AS MK INNER JOIN Model
             AS MD ON MK.MakeID = MD.MakeID
             INNER JOIN Stock AS ST ON ST.ModelID = MD.ModelID
             INNER JOIN SalesDetails SD ON ST.StockCode
                                         = SD.StockID
             INNER JOIN Sales AS SA ON SA.SalesID = SD.SalesID
  ) DT
ORDER BY  MakeName, ModelName, SaleDate;
```

Running this query gives the results that you can see in *Figure 13.1*:

	MakeName	ModelName	SaleDate	SalePrice	Cost	GrossProfit	NetProfit
1	Alfa Romeo	1750	2018-04-15T12:00:00.000+0000	9950	7960	8550	8550
2	Alfa Romeo	1750	2018-06-03T12:00:00.000+0000	3575	2860	2175	1425
3	Alfa Romeo	Giulia	2015-07-12T10:00:00.000+0000	8695	6956	7395	7300
4	Alfa Romeo	Giulia	2016-01-07T12:00:00.000+0000	2550	2040	1150	1100
5	Alfa Romeo	Giulia	2016-02-17T12:00:00.000+0000	6000	4800	4600	4600
6	Alfa Romeo	Giulia	2016-04-30T11:27:00.000+0000	17500	14000	15765	15265

Figure 13.1: A derived table that creates intermediate calculations

How does it work

It sometimes gets a little laborious to write the SQL required for financial analysis. The speed at which Databricks can perform calculations on a large set of data is rarely a problem. However, as you have probably seen while practicing SQL, the coding process can get rather wearing. This is because you are required to repeat field names over and over as you create intermediate and final calculations.

Fortunately, there is a convenient way to minimize the repetitive use of field names. Start by creating a core query that carries out any basic analysis. You can then use the results of these calculations in the outer query without repeating the initial arithmetic.

In this piece of SQL, the derived table (which has the alias `DT` in the preceding code and makes up the entire `FROM` clause of the query) calculates the direct costs associated with a sale by adding up the total for the cost of repairs, parts, and transport. This inner query also ensures that any `NULL`s in the data are handled at the source to avoid `NULL`s falsifying the results. It does this by enclosing any *suspect* field names in the `NVL()` function (as you first learned in *Chapter 4: Simple Calculations*). The derived table joins all the tables that we need to output the make, model, date of sale, selling price, and vehicle cost. To see this more clearly, refer to *Figure 13.2*, which displays part of the output from the derived table.

	MakeName	ModelName	SaleDate	SalePrice	Cost	LineltemDiscoun	DirectCosts
1	Ferrari	Daytona	2018-12-31T12:00:00.000+0000	145000	116000	5000	null
2	Ferrari	Daytona	2018-03-08T12:00:00.000+0000	99500	79600	null	2750
3	Ferrari	Testarossa	2017-09-20T12:32:00.000+0000	250000	200000	null	4650
4	Ferrari	Testarossa	2016-07-25T10:00:00.000+0000	195000	156000	null	9050
5	Ferrari	Testarossa	2016-01-01T08:00:00.000+0000	165000	132000	5000	8100

Figure 13.2: The output from a derived table

As you can see, the columns that are returned are not the same in the derived table as they are in the outer query. Nonetheless, the columns in the derived table are the basis for any data that is output by the outer query.

In such cases, a derived table is a query in a query. More precisely, it is a completely independent piece of SQL that feeds its output into an outer query that wraps around the derived table. In this example, you can see that the outer query has a **FROM** clause that does not directly use a table or a set of joined tables. Instead, the outer query refers to a self-sufficient query (the derived table or inner query) to isolate a dataset. This dataset is then used as the data source for the outer query.

The outer query is a straightforward list of the fields that are in the **SELECT** clause of the derived table. These fields are then extended with a couple of simple calculations to deliver both the gross profit and the net profit.

You can achieve the final calculation of gross and net profit without using a derived table. However, in this case, the query that returns the gross and net profit looks like the following:

```
,SD.SalePrice - (NVL(ST.RepairsCost, 0)

              + NVL(ST.PartsCost, 0) + ST.TransportInCost)

                AS GrossProfit

,SD.SalePrice - (NVL(ST.RepairsCost, 0) + NVL(ST.PartsCost, 0)

              + ST.TransportInCost + LineItemDiscount) AS NetProfit;
```

Although this code is not difficult to write, it is laborious and certainly more repetitive; it is also possibly a greater source of potential errors precisely because of its repetitive nature. Defining a derived table not only removes the need to repeat fields (as well as their **NULL** handling code) but also makes any additional calculations you have to apply to these fields easier.

This technique is similar to using a spreadsheet to perform financial arithmetic. In a spreadsheet, you carry out basic arithmetic in multiple cells to get an intermediate result that is used for other calculations. The principle is similar when a derived table is used in SQL:

- **First**: You carry out any essential calculations in a derived table and give the result an alias.
- **Then**: You use the derived table as the basis for any further calculations in the outer query.

The derived table we use in this example shows the following two basic techniques used to define a derived table:

- **Enclosed in parentheses**: A derived table must be enclosed in parentheses.

If you forget the parentheses, an error message is displayed. Think of them as isolating and enclosing the derived table and making it into a separate self-contained table.

- **Must have an alias**: A derived table need not necessarily have an alias. In this example, the derived table is given the derived table, the alias DT. You can use this alias just as you would use the alias for any normal table in a SQL query.

Refer to *Figure 13.3* to see how a derived table works from a high level:

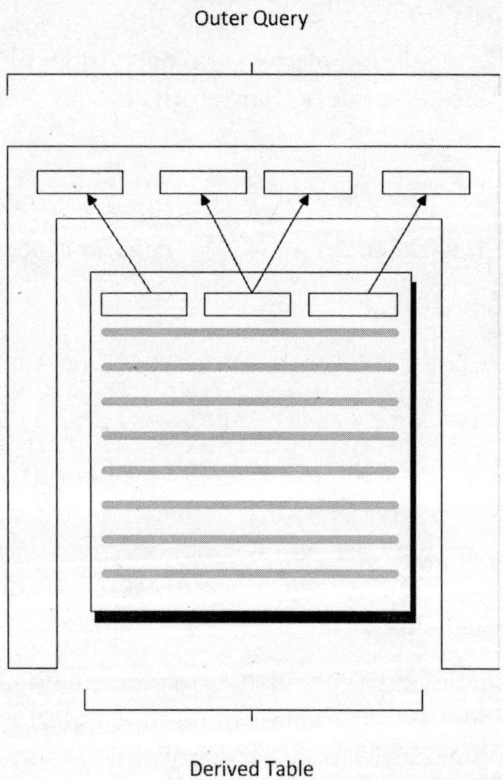

***Figure 13.3:** The concept of a derived table*

Tricks and traps

Derived tables are a fundamental concept in SQL. There are several key points to remember when they are used in data analysis, which are given as follows:

- When you use a derived table in the **FROM** clause of an outer query, you must include all the fields that you wish to return from the outer query in the **SELECT** clause of the inner derived table. This is because the derived table is the source of all the data that is accessible to the outer query. Consequently, you must ensure that every field that you want to output from the overall code is part of the inner **SELECT** clause. If you forget to include a field in the derived table and then try to select it in the main query, Databricks returns an error message. Adding the field to the derived table normally solves this problem. In this example, for instance, you could not add the **CountryName** field to the main **SELECT** clause as this field is not in the **SELECT** clause for the derived table.

- Another advantage of beginning with a derived table when calculating metrics is that you have to handle potential NULLs only once in the derived table at the heart of the query.
- Another factor that argues in favor of using a derived table to simplify calculations is that if a core calculation changes, you only make the change once in the derived table (just like in a spreadsheet). Any modifications ripple up through the rest of the query. Without a derived table, you have to make the change every time the calculation is repeated in the query.
- It is important to ensure that every field in a derived table has a name. Databricks does not add a name (such as *Column 1*) if you forget to add an alias. Indeed, the query does not work if any calculated fields (such as **SalePrice** and **GrossProfit** in this example) that are used in the outer query are not given aliases.
- The **AS** keyword that introduces the derived table alias is not strictly necessary, but it is good practice to use it, so we have kept it, even if the query would work without it.

Grouping and ordering data using a custom classification

Suppose the CEO decides that she wants you to classify all your customers by spend. You realize that what she really wants is five categories of customers (tiny, small, medium, large, and mega-rich) according to a series of thresholds of total sales per customer. Then, she wants the total spent for customers in each of these spending brackets.

As complex as it sounds, we can do it with only a few lines of SQL and the clever use of a derived table:

```
SELECT     DT.CustomerClassification

           ,COUNT(DT.CustomerSpend) AS NumberOfCustomers
```

```
FROM
         (
           SELECT      SUM(SD.SalePrice) AS CustomerSpend
           ,SA.CustomerID
           ,CASE
            WHEN SUM(SD.SalePrice) <= 100000 THEN 'Tiny'
            WHEN SUM(SD.SalePrice) BETWEEN 100001 AND 200000
                 THEN 'Small'
            WHEN SUM(SD.SalePrice) BETWEEN 200001 AND 300000
                 THEN 'Medium'
            WHEN SUM(SD.SalePrice) BETWEEN 300001 AND 400000
                 THEN 'Large'
              WHEN SUM(SD.SalePrice) > 400000 THEN 'Mega Rich'
           END AS CustomerClassification
           FROM        SalesDetails SD
                       INNER JOIN Sales AS SA
                       ON SA.SalesID = SD.SalesID
           GROUP BY    SA.CustomerID
        ) AS DT
GROUP BY    DT.CustomerClassification
ORDER BY    NumberOfCustomers DESC;
```

Running this query gives the results as shown in *Figure 13.4*:

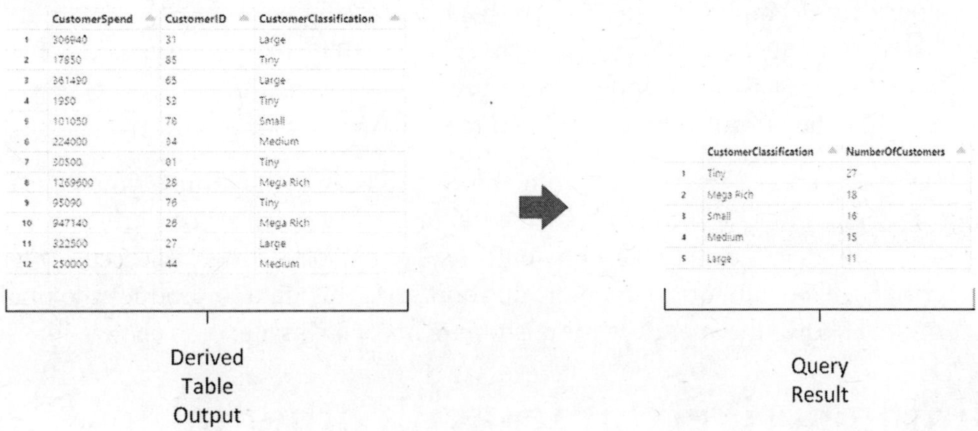

	CustomerSpend	CustomerID	CustomerClassification
1	306940	31	Large
2	17850	85	Tiny
3	361490	65	Large
4	1950	52	Tiny
5	101050	78	Small
6	224000	34	Medium
7	30500	81	Tiny
8	1269600	28	Mega Rich
9	95090	76	Tiny
10	947140	26	Mega Rich
11	322500	27	Large
12	250000	44	Medium

	CustomerClassification	NumberOfCustomers
1	Tiny	27
2	Mega Rich	18
3	Small	16
4	Medium	15
5	Large	11

Figure 13.4: *An aggregated derived table feeding into a separate outer aggregation*

How does it work

In the case of SQL queries, a problem broken down into smaller parts is often a problem that becomes easier to solve. Using derived tables is a fundamental technique for breaking down seemingly complex challenges into smaller and more comprehensible solutions. The preceding piece of SQL is an example of how a derived table can help you break down analytical tasks into component parts.

Consequently (as is the case with much SQL), the logic of this code begins at the center and works its way outward. The overall query does the following two things:

- **The inner query**: Takes the data from the **`Sales`** and **`SalesDetails`** tables and finds the total value of sales per customer. This query then uses a **`CASE`** statement to test the total value of sales for each customer and places each one in one of five custom categories (from the tiny customers to the mega-rich ones). In this kind of statistical query, we do not need to see the customer name because we are not interested in detail-level analysis. We can group on the **`CustomerID`** field from the **`SalesDetails`** table, and we do not need to refer to the Customer table for any customer data.
- **The outer query**: Aggregates the results of the derived table by counting the number of customers in each category and grouping on the category itself (the field that has been given the alias *Customer classification*). Finally, it sorts the categories in descending order of the number of customers per classification.

As you can see, the main element in this piece of code is the derived table (the inner query), where the core aggregation is carried out. Indeed, you can run the derived table separately if you wish. You can do this by selecting only the SQL inside the parentheses, from **`SELECT SUM (SA.SalePrice) to GROUP BY SA.CustomerID`**. This way, you can check that the inner query gives you the result that you expect—something like the output from the derived table shown earlier in *Figure 13.4*.

Now that you can see the output from the derived table, hopefully, you have a clearer understanding of the way that the overall query works. The derived table lets you create a classification of your entire customer base where each customer is categorized. The main query then groups and sorts this data to produce the final result set that shows the spending for customers in each classification *bucket*.

Joining derived tables with other tables

When you are buying and selling, it can help to see how an article compares to others in its category. Specifically, it is assumed that you want to look at the purchase and selling price of each vehicle that has been sold and see how this data maps to the average cost and sale price for every similar model. This is all in a day's work for SQL:

```
SELECT    ST.DateBought, MK.MakeName, MD.ModelName, ST.Color
          ,ST.Cost, SD.SalePrice, DT.AveragePurchasePrice
          ,DT.AverageSalePrice
FROM
    (
     SELECT      MK1.MakeName
                 ,MD1.ModelName
                 ,AVG(ST1.Cost) AS AveragePurchasePrice
                 ,AVG(SD1.SalePrice) AS AverageSalePrice
     FROM        Make AS MK1
                 INNER JOIN Model AS MD1 ON MK1.MakeID = MD1.MakeID
                 INNER JOIN Stock AS ST1 ON ST1.ModelID =
                                                       MD1.ModelID
                 INNER JOIN SalesDetails SD1
                 ON ST1.StockCode = SD1.StockID
```

```
     GROUP BY   MK1.MakeName, MD1.ModelName
    ) AS DT
    INNER JOIN Make AS MK
    INNER JOIN Model AS MD ON MK.MakeID = MD.MakeID
    INNER JOIN Stock AS ST ON ST.ModelID = MD.ModelID
    INNER JOIN SalesDetails SD ON ST.StockCode = SD.StockID
    AND MK.MakeName = DT.MakeName
    AND MD.ModelName = DT.ModelName
ORDER BY   ST.DateBought, MK.MakeName, MD.ModelName;
```

Running this query gives the results that you can see in *Figure 13.5*:

	DateBought	MakeName	ModelName	Color	Cost	SalePrice	AveragePurchasePrice	AverageSalePrice
1	2015-01-01 12:00:00	Ferrari	Testarossa	Red	52000	65000	139200	174000
2	2015-01-01 12:00:00	Porsche	944	Red	15960	19950	9818.461538461539	12273.076923076924
3	2015-01-10 12:00:00	Ferrari	355	Blue	176000	220000	136165.7142857143	170207.14285714287
4	2015-01-29 12:00:00	Porsche	911	British Racing Green	15600	19500	29357.14285714286	36696.42857142857
5	2015-02-14 12:00:00	Porsche	924	British Racing Green	9200	11500	12448	15560
6	2015-03-05 12:00:00	Aston Martin	DB4	Night Blue	23600	29500	32194.285714285714	40242.857142857145
7	2015-03-15 12:00:00	Aston Martin	DB5	Black	39600	49500	40045.333333333336	50056.666666666664
8	2015-03-26 12:00:00	Aston Martin	DB6	Canary Yellow	60800	76000	58234	72792.5
9	2015-04-02 12:00:00	Aston Martin	DB5	Blue	29200	36500	40045.333333333336	50056.666666666664
10	2015-04-04 12:00:00	Porsche	911	Blue	15680	19600	29357.14285714286	36696.42857142857

Figure 13.5: *A derived table that is part of a complex join clause*

How does it work

Databricks considers derived tables to be just like any *ordinary* tables that exist in a database. This means that you can collate or aggregate data from one or more tables to obtain a derived table and then join the result to another table, or tables, just as you would for any table.

This is particularly useful when you need to aggregate data and include the aggregated result in a query that contains `nonaggregate` data. This example shows how a single query can show the average selling price for that model of car for every sale. This opens up a whole spectrum of analytical possibilities that allow you to put each sale into perspective and see how it compares to other similar sales.

This example differs from those that you have seen so far in this chapter in that it does not have an inner and outer query structure. Instead, it contains a series of table joins, which are:

Standard joins: Using regular database tables to return the cost and sale price for every model of car sold. These are all the `INNER JOINS` that make up the final part of the query.

A derived table joins where a derived table is joined to existing tables in the query. This is the subquery aliased as DT in the preceding code. You can see this in the following extract from the preceding SQL:

```
AND MK.MakeName = DT.MakeName

AND MD.ModelName = DT.ModelName
```

The derived table is interesting because it operates on a different level of data granularity than the other tables. More precisely, the derived table is an aggregation that calculates the average cost and selling price of each model of car. The derived table is then joined to the `Make` and `Model` tables in the query perfectly normally.

Figure 13.6 is a visual representation of the joins, including the joins to the derived table:

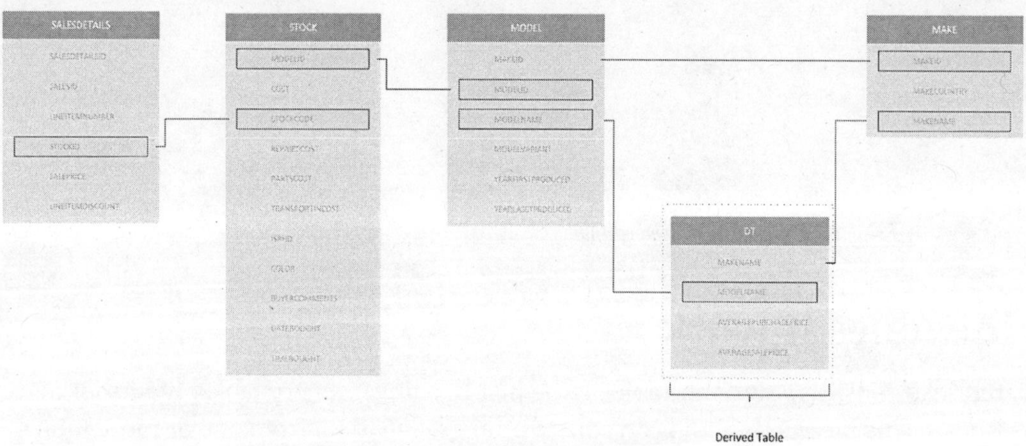

***Figure 13.6:** Visualizing a complex join using a derived table*

To help you understand derived tables, refer to *Figure 13.7*. You will notice the output from the derived table (aliased as DT in the SQL code that you used to obtain this output).

	MakeName	ModelName	AveragePurchasePrice	AverageSalePrice
1	Bentley	Mulsanne	62580	78225
2	Rolls Royce	Ghost	63780	79725
3	Triumph	TR3A	31600	39500
4	BMW	E30	26800	33500
5	Ferrari	F50	202920	253650
6	Bugatti	57C	269600	339000

***Figure 13.7:** The output from an aggregated derived table*

As the derived table isolates data by two fields in this example (make and model), it needs to join with the other tables using both these fields. Consequently, the derived table has to contain both these fields in its `SELECT` clause; otherwise, the derived cannot join the table to the outer query.

The trick, in these cases, is to establish the join as you normally would. However, when you link a table to two tables at the same time, you start with an `ON` clause, as you would normally, and then you continue adding further field joins using the `AND` keyword.

The query then outputs fields from any or all of the tables that make up the `FROM` clause. It is, in all other respects, a perfectly standard query. However, using the derived table to calculate the average cost and average sale price allows you to show these aggregated figures in the query output and make some interesting comparisons.

Tricks and traps

When joining derived tables, you need to remember the following:

- We chose to use independent table aliases in the derived query (`ST1` for the `Stock` table in the derived table and `ST` in the main query, for instance) even if it is possible to use the same aliases in the derived table subquery as those we used in the main query's `FROM` clause. This is because it is generally easier to understand and debug queries when all the component elements are identifiable separately and uniquely.

Joining multiple derived tables

Continuing with the theme of comparisons, let us suppose the most purchased car colors. You not only want to produce such an analysis but also find the percentage of cars purchased by value for each color of the vehicle. The following SQL does this for you:

```
SELECT
TOT.PurchaseYear
,AGG.Color
,(AGG.CostPerYear / TOT.TotalPurchasePrice) * 100 AS PercentPerColorPerYear
FROM
   (
   SELECT       STX.Color
                ,SUM(STX.Cost) AS CostPerYear
                ,YEAR(STX.DateBought) AS YearBought
   FROM         Stock AS STX
   INNER JOIN   Model AS MDX
                ON STX.ModelID = MDX.ModelID
   GROUP BY     STX.Color
                ,YEAR(STX.DateBought)
   ) AGG
INNER JOIN
   (
   SELECT       YEAR(DateBought) AS PurchaseYear, SUM(Cost)
                AS TotalPurchasePrice
   FROM         Stock
   GROUP BY     YEAR(DateBought)
   ) TOT
ON TOT.PurchaseYear = AGG.YearBought
ORDER BY TOT.PurchaseYear, PercentPerColorPerYear DESC;
```

Running this query gives the results that you can see in *Figure 13.8*:

	PurchaseYear	Color	PercentPerColorPerYear
1	2015	Black	24.389503541066716
2	2015	Red	16.763940055151153
3	2015	British Racing Green	12.683976796305386
4	2015	Blue	11.56636765201554
5	2015	Night Blue	10.564658715281679
6	2015	Silver	10.28910005854143

Figure 13.8: Using two separately derived tables in a query

How does it work

This query requires you to produce the following two completely different aggregations and then use them together to deliver the final result:

- **The first aggregation**: Is the total cost of vehicles purchased for each year for each color.
- **The second aggregation**: Is the total cost of purchases per year.

Using derived tables allows you to handle each aggregation as a separate derived table. Before going any further, it is probably worth taking a look at the output from each of the derived tables so that you can see what each aggregation is doing. *Figure 13.9* illustrates how multiple derived tables relate to an outer query.

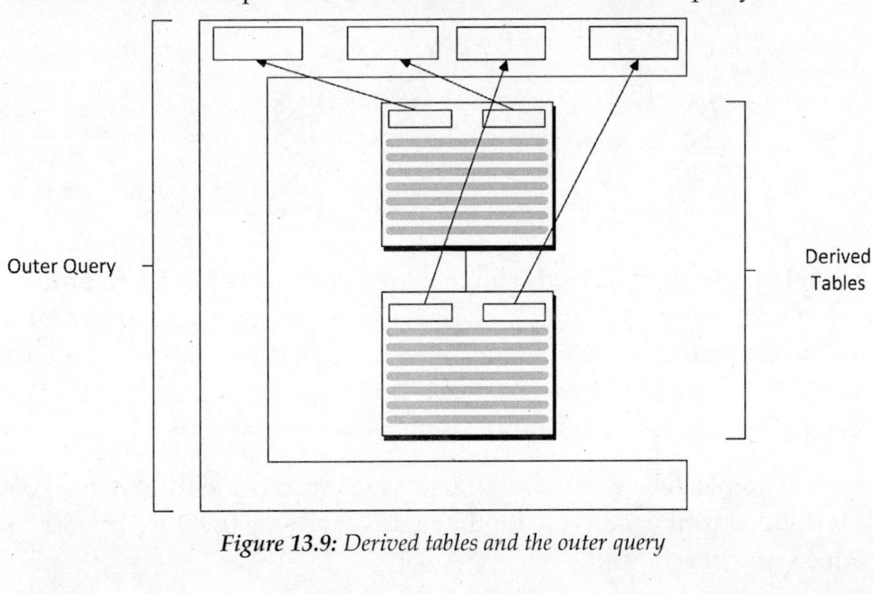

Figure 13.9: Derived tables and the outer query

The first derived table (aliased as **AGG** in this example) shows the year, color, and cost per year for each color of vehicle bought. If you select just the SQL for the first of the two derived tables, you see output similar to that in *Figure 13.10*:

	Color	CostPerYear	YearBought
1	Black	1816476	2018
2	Green	173280	2015
3	Night Blue	481864	2018
4	Canary Yellow	256456	2016
5	Dark Purple	203812	2017
6	Night Blue	192400	2016

Figure 13.10: *The output from an aggregated derived table*

This derived table needs three database tables to be joined to return the required data: **Make**, **Model**, and **Stock**. It then aggregates the result by year and color and returns the total vehicle cost for all available combinations of the two fields, **Year** and **Color**.

Running the second of the derived table queries (aliased as **TOT** in the SQL code for this section) shows you the data in *Figure 13.11*:

	PurchaseYear	TotalPurchasePrice
1	2018	6265020
2	2015	2029332
3	null	null
4	2016	4380988
5	2017	7083824

Figure 13.11: *The output from a high-level aggregated derived table*

This high-level aggregated derived table only needs the Stock table to produce the annual cost of cars that have been purchased. These two derived tables output the **Year** field. Consequently, the overall query can use this field to join the two derived tables. Once the derived tables are constructed and joined, you can treat this query like any other query and use the fields it contains to analyze your data.

In the current example, the year and color fields are output, and the cost per color for each year is divided by the total cost for the same timeframe to return the percentage cost of each color for each year.

Finishing the query with an **ORDER BY** clause allows you to list the result first by year and second in descending order of sales per color. This makes it easy to see which color tops the sales charts each year.

Once again, we use derived tables to break down the problem into component parts. The challenge is to produce two sets of data that aggregate at different *levels*. One requires the year and the color, the other only the year. We build the query to handle these requirements using the flexibility that derived tables bring for analysis with SQL.

What is interesting here is that the query uses nothing but derived tables to carry out its analysis. Once again, each derived table is a completely separate entity that works independently of the other parts of the overall query.

Tricks and traps

One point needs to be made about joining derived tables is given as follows:

- Because derived tables are always independent entities in a query, you reuse base tables in separate derived tables. Here, for instance, the Stock table is used twice, once in each derived table. Each derived table makes use of the Stock table separately and in different ways.

Using multiple derived tables for complex aggregations

Good analysis is about seeing the wood for the trees. This is where SQL can be really useful. The following code lets you create a report for the CEO that lists sales per customer by volume and value. Not only that, but also the output is broken down by country and sorted to make it clear who the best customers are in each country. All of this is possible in a single query that produces an analysis of sales ratios per customer per country, as shown in the following code:

```
SELECT

 DT2.CountryName

,DT2.CustomerName

,DT2.NumberOfCustomerSales

,DT2.TotalCustomerSales

,DT2.NumberOfCustomerSales
```

```
  / DT1.NumberOfCountrySales
      AS PercentageOfCountryCarsSold
,DT2.TotalCustomerSales / DT1.TotalCountrySales
      AS PercentageOfCountryCarsSoldByValue
FROM
(
    SELECT      CO.CountryName
               ,COUNT(*) AS NumberOfCountrySales
               ,SUM(SD.SalePrice) AS TotalCountrySales
    FROM       Stock AS ST
    INNER JOIN SalesDetails SD ON ST.StockCode = SD.StockID
    INNER JOIN Sales AS SA ON SA.SalesID = SD.SalesID
    INNER JOIN Customer CU ON SA.CustomerID = CU.CustomerID
    INNER JOIN Country CO ON CU.Country = CO.CountryISO2
    GROUP BY   CO.CountryName
) AS DT1
INNER JOIN
(
    SELECT      CO.CountryName
               ,CU.CustomerName
               ,COUNT(*) AS NumberOfCustomerSales
               ,SUM(SD.SalePrice) AS TotalCustomerSales
    FROM       Stock AS ST
    INNER JOIN SalesDetails SD ON ST.StockCode = SD.StockID
    INNER JOIN Sales AS SA ON SA.SalesID = SD.SalesID
    INNER JOIN Customer CU ON SA.CustomerID = CU.CustomerID
    INNER JOIN Country CO ON CU.Country = CO.CountryISO2
```

```
    GROUP BY   CO.CountryName, CU.CustomerName
) AS DT2
ON DT1.CountryName = DT2.CountryName
ORDER BY DT2.CountryName, NumberOfCustomerSales DESC;
```

Running this query gives the results shown in *Figure 13.12*:

	CountryName	CustomerName	NumberOfCustomerSales	TotalCustomerSales	PercentageOfCountryCarsSold	PercentageOfCountryCarsSoldByValue
1	Belgium	Stefan Van Helsing.	6	80900	0.60000000000	0.2594195927529261
2	Belgium	Diplomatic Cars	3	224000	0.30000000000	0.7162940516273849
3	Belgium	Flash Voitures	1	6950	0.10000000000	0.022286355619688954
4	France	Vive La Vitesse	13	1269600	0.18840579710	0.21591523115653914
5	France	Laurent Saint Yves	11	1343950	0.15942028986	0.22845374914369154
6	France	SuperSport S.A.R.L	9	509630	0.13043478261	0.08663036882034265

Figure 13.12: *A complex use of derived tables to apply different levels of aggregated calculation*

How does it work

Given the size of this query, it is probably easier to understand what it does if you begin by looking at the output from the two derived tables that are the core of the SQL.

The first derived table (aliased as **DT1**) shows the number of sales per country and the total value of sales per country, as shown in *Figure 13.13*:

	CountryName	NumberOfCountrySales	TotalCountrySales
1	Germany	13	873040
2	France	69	5882810
3	Belgium	10	311850
4	United States	31	1995620
5	Italy	18	1215280
6	Spain	27	1693060

Figure 13.13: *An aggregate-derived table to produce high-level totals*

The second derived table (**DT2**) goes into greater detail and shows the value and number of sales per customer for each country, as you can see (partially, at least) in *Figure 13.14*:

	CountryName	CustomerName	NumberOfCustomerSales	TotalCustomerSales
1	France	Jacques Mitterand	1	69500
2	United Kingdom	Screamin' Wheels	5	121450
3	France	Capots Reluisants S.A.	6	583115
4	Germany	Glitz	8	589490
5	United Kingdom	Stan Collywobble	6	261850
6	Belgium	Stefan Van Helsing	6	80900

Figure 13.14: *An aggregate-derived table that produces detail-level totals*

The query builds on the data that is returned from the two derived tables. It joins the derived tables on the country field so that it can then list countries, clients, the number of sales made per client, and the value of those sales. So far, then, it is just an extension of the derived table **DT2**. However, once the aggregate data at the country level is added to the query, it allows you to see the percentage of both the value of sales and the number of sales that each customer represents. This is done by dividing the sum totals for the number of sales and sale value by country in the derived table **DT1** by the number of sales and sale value for each customer in the derived table **DT2**. *Figure 13.15* represents the SQL that creates and uses an aggregated derived table.

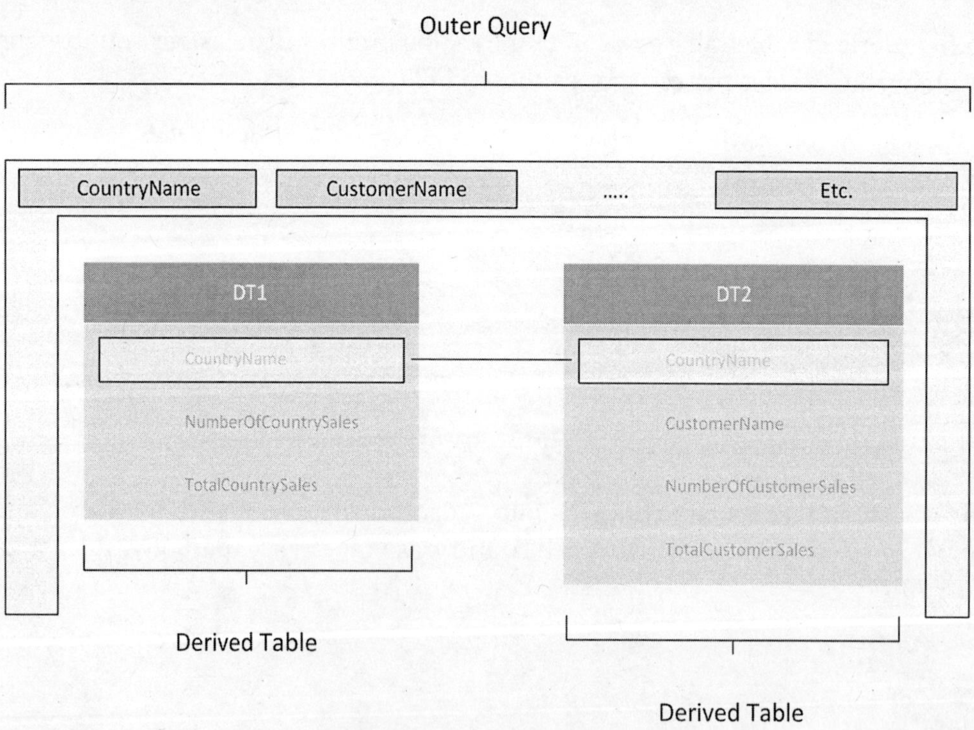

Figure 13.15: *Joining on derived tables*

Data visibility

As we have noted already, one important aspect of derived tables is that they only allow access to the data that you specify. So, if you want the outer query to access a field from the derived table, you must include the field name in the **SELECT** clause of the derived table.

So *self-contained* also means *locked away* as far as the data in a derived table is concerned. It does not matter if a table is a part of the derived table definition; none of its fields will be accessible to the rest of the query if they are not made visible in the **SELECT** clause of the derived table.

Using derived tables to join unconnected tables

A well-managed business almost certainly defines budgets and then tracks them over time. Fortunately, SQL can be very efficient for monitoring budgets, comparing, and forecasts. So, when the financial director comes to your desk requesting a report that compares sales to the budget for each country by year and month, the following SQL will help you resolve the query:

```
SELECT      CO.CountryName
           ,SUM(SD.SalePrice) AS Sales
           ,SUM(CSQ.BudgetValue) AS BudgetValue
           ,YEAR(SA.SaleDate) AS YearOfSale
           ,MONTH(SA.SaleDate) AS MonthOfSale
           ,SUM(CSQ.BudgetValue)
           - SUM(SD.SalePrice) AS DifferenceBudgetToSales
FROM      SalesDetails SD
INNER JOIN Sales AS SA ON SA.SalesID = SD.SalesID
INNER JOIN Customer CU ON SA.CustomerID = CU.CustomerID
INNER JOIN Country CO ON CU.Country = CO.CountryISO2
INNER JOIN          (
                        SELECT     BudgetValue, BudgetDetail, Year,
```

```
                       Month
                FROM   Budget
                WHERE  BudgetElement = 'Country'
            ) CSQ
    ON CSQ.BudgetDetail = CO.CountryName
    AND CSQ.Year = YEAR(SaleDate)
    AND CSQ.Month = MONTH(SaleDate)
GROUP BY CO.CountryName, YEAR(SA.SaleDate), MONTH(SA.SaleDate)
ORDER BY CO.CountryName, YEAR(SA.SaleDate), MONTH(SA.SaleDate);
```

Running this query gives the results that you can see in *Figure 13.16*:

	CountryName	Sales	BudgetValue	YearOfSale	MonthOfSale	DifferenceBudgetToSales
1	Belgium	125000	100000	2016	8	-25000
2	Belgium	12500	15500	2017	2	3000
3	Belgium	86500	100000	2017	3	13500
4	Belgium	45950	137850	2017	7	91900
5	Belgium	34000	68000	2017	11	34000
6	Belgium	950	950	2018	1	0

Figure 13.16: *A derived table used to join otherwise unconnected tables*

How does it work

Even a well-thought database model can have some tables that conventionally do not link to the core data tables that you are using. Budget data is frequently an example of this. Yet you can use the budget data stored in your database and compare it to other data. This allows you to compare sales and budget data and highlight any differences. This only works, however, if you shape the budget data in a way that allows it to be joined to other tables.

This query joins the tables that contain the essential data for make, model, stock, sales details, and sales used in the book so far. Then, it also joins data from a new table, that is, the **`Budget`** table, to the query so that you can also display data from this source.

However, the Budget table cannot be joined directly to the other tables that contain sales and stock data. This is because it contains budget data for many different elements (countries, makes of vehicles, and so on). Moreover, the data it contains is at a different level of granularity from the data for sales. That is, the budget is at a month level, whereas sales are at a day level. As a result, you have to query this table and select the required data only. In this example, you need to filter the table on the **Budget** element to limit it to budgets for country sales. If you highlight and run the **SELECT** query for the derived table, then you will see the data as shown in *Figure 13.17*:

	BudgetValue	BudgetDetail	Year	Month
1	100000	Belgium	2016	8
2	15500	Belgium	2017	2
3	100000	Belgium	2017	3
4	45950	Belgium	2017	7
5	34000	Belgium	2017	11
6	950	Belgium	2018	1

Figure 13.17: *A derived table that filters source data*

As you can see from *Figure 13.17*, the budget data is for country, year, and month. To join the derived table to the other tables in the query, you must perform a complex join using three fields country, year, and month of sale. This is why the join for the derived table uses the **YEAR()** and **MONTH()** functions to isolate these elements from the **SaleDate** field that is used to join in the **SalesDetails** table to the derived table of budget data.

Finally, the elements that are output from the outer query have to be grouped and aggregated. This is because the data from the tables used in the outer query is at a much more detailed level than the budget data used in the subquery. Mixing data at different levels of detail (or granularity, as it is also called) almost never produces coherent results. It is up to you to ensure that the data from all your tables is at the same level of granularity.

Tricks and traps

The following are the couple of points that need to be noted:

- In the outer query, you have to aggregate the budget value that is returned from the derived query (that is, the figure for each month's projected sales per country), even if the value is already at an aggregate level. This is because the outer query is an aggregate query, and so every value that is used must be used as part of an aggregate function such as **SUM()** (even if this does not alter the value since there is only one value per country per month).

- Unless you extract the year and month elements from the **SalesDate** field, the join to the derived tables cannot work correctly because it attempts to match a year (or a month) to a full date. This means that no data matches between the two tables and, consequently, no records are returned by the query.

Compare year-on-year data using a derived table

As part of a relentless focus on profitability, the CEO wants to look at all vehicle sales in 2016 and see how each sale compares to the best price achieved in 2015 for the same model of car. All this can be done with the following SQL:

```
SELECT      MK.MakeName
           ,MD.ModelName
           ,SD.SalePrice
           ,CSQ.MaxSalePrice - SD.SalePrice
               AS PriceDifferenceToMaxPrevYear
FROM       Make AS MK
INNER JOIN Model AS MD ON MK.MakeID = MD.MakeID
INNER JOIN Stock AS ST ON ST.ModelID = MD.ModelID
INNER JOIN SalesDetails SD ON ST.StockCode = SD.StockID
INNER JOIN Sales AS SA ON SA.SalesID = SD.SalesID
INNER JOIN  (
                   SELECT     MAX(SDX.SalePrice) AS MaxSalePrice
                             ,YEAR(SAX.SaleDate) AS SaleYear
                             ,MKX.MakeName
                   FROM       Make AS MKX
                   INNER JOIN Model AS MDX
                              ON MKX.MakeID – MDX.MakeID
                   INNER JOIN Stock AS STX
```

```
                        ON STX.ModelID = MDX.ModelID
            INNER JOIN SalesDetails SDX
                        ON STX.StockCode = SDX.StockID
            INNER JOIN Sales AS SAX
                        ON SAX.SalesID = SDX.SalesID
            WHERE       YEAR(SAX.SaleDate) = 2015
            GROUP BY    YEAR(SAX.SaleDate)
                        ,MKX.MakeName
       ) CSQ
    ON CSQ.MakeName = MK.MakeName
WHERE       YEAR(SA.SaleDate) = 2016;
```

Running this query gives the results that you can see in *Figure 13.18*:

	MakeName	ModelName	SalePrice	PriceDifferenceToMaxPrevYear
1	Jaguar	XJ12	35250	-12260
2	Jaguar	XJ12	3575	19415
3	Jaguar	XK120	27890	-4900
4	Jaguar	XK120	19600	3390
5	Jaguar	XK120	99500	-76510
6	Jaguar	XK120	35000	-12010

***Figure 13.18:** Applying different filters to a query and a derived table*

How does it work

In this chapter, you have seen that a derived table is a completely independent dataset relative to the rest of the query. You can use this to your advantage when comparing virtually identical datasets.

In this code, the main query is the part of the query that is not a derived table. It lists the makes and models of cars sold in 2016, along with their sale prices.

The derived table does something similar. It, too, finds makes, models, and sale price. However, only it finds the maximum sale price for each model for a different year to the outer query, which is, in fact, the previous year (2015). The output from this inner query (if you run it separately) is shown in *Figure 13.19*:

	MaxSalePrice	SaleYear	MakeName
1	123590	2015	Aston Martin
2	8695	2015	Alfa Romeo
3	22950	2015	Porsche
4	22990	2015	Jaguar
5	80500	2015	Bentley

Figure 13.19: *Output from a derived table query*

As you can see, the derived table shows the maximum sale price per model for one year, yet a close examination of the code shows that the outer query looks at the data for another year. The trick is to join the derived table to the rest of the query using the make as the join element.

You can then output not only the details for sales in 2016 but also the maximum value of each make sold in the previous year. In this example, the current sale price is subtracted from the maximum sale price for the previous year. You can then analyze the difference to compare sales growth from year to year, as you can see in the **`PriceDifferenceToMaxPrevYear`** column of the SQL for this section.

Tricks and traps

While using derived tables for data comparison, the following must be kept in mind:

This type of query is extremely extensible and can become a basis for varied types of comparative analysis. For instance, you cannot ever use a year in the **`WHERE`** clause of the derived table and compare the current sale price to the maximum sale price. The fact that the derived table and the outer query are completely independent makes derived queries ideal for comparing certain types of data over time.

Synchronizing filters between a derived table and the main query

Clever buying strategies can make or break a business. Because of this, the finance director wants to ensure that *Prestige Cars* is not spending too much when buying stock. The following piece of SQL compares the purchase price of every car bought in 2015 with the minimum price of cars of the same color bought in 2016:

```
SELECT      ST.Color, ST.DateBought, ST.Cost, CSQ.MinPurchaseCost
FROM        Stock ST
INNER JOIN
            (
            SELECT      Color, MIN(Cost) AS MinPurchaseCost
                        ,YEAR(DateBought) AS PurchaseYear
            FROM        Stock
            WHERE       YEAR(DateBought) = 2016
            GROUP BY    Color, YEAR(DateBought)
            ) CSQ
            ON ST.Color = CSQ.Color
            AND YEAR(ST.DateBought) = CSQ.PurchaseYear - 1;
```

Running the preceding query gives the results shown in *Figure 13.20*. You can also see the output from the derived table:

	Color	DateBought	Cost	MinPurchaseCost
1	Red	2015-01-01 12:00:00	32000	10000
2	Blue	2015-01-10 12:00:00	176000	10200
3	British Racing Green	2015-01-29 12:00:00	15600	10000
4	British Racing Green	2015-02-14 12:00:00	9200	10000
5	Red	2015-01-01 12:00:00	15960	10000
6	Black	2015-03-03 12:00:00	176000	10000
7	Night Blue	2015-03-05 12:00:00	23600	10120
8	Black	2015-03-15 12:00:00	39600	10000
9	Canary Yellow	2015-03-26 12:00:00	60800	26800
10	Red	2015-04-04 12:00:00	172000	10000
11	Blue	2015-04-04 12:00:00	15680	10200
12	Blue	2015-04-02 12:00:00	29200	10200
13	Blue	2015-04-15 12:00:00	6800	10200
14	Night Blue	2015-04-30 12:00:00	26000	10120
15	British Racing Green	2015-05-01 12:00:00	64400	10000

Query Result

	Color	MinPurchaseCost	PurchaseYear
1	Black	10000	2016
2	Blue	10200	2016
3	British Racing Green	10000	2016
4	Canary Yellow	26800	2016
5	Dark Purple	10000	2016
6	Green	100000	2016
7	Night Blue	10120	2016
8	Pink	18000	2016
9	Red	10000	2016
10	Silver	11672	2016

Derived Table Output

Figure 13.20: *Extending the JOIN clause for a derived table*

How does it work

The SQL in the current example is essentially two pieces of code given as follows:

- **A derived table**: That calculates the minimum price for each color of the car bought for 2016.
- **An outer query**: That displays the key stock information for all the cars bought in 2015.

An interesting tweak is the way that the outer query and the inner derived table are joined. As the grouping for the derived table is by color and year, these are the fields that must be used in the **JOIN** clause. However, as the derived table contains data for all years, you can tweak the **JOIN** clause so that the data from the derived table is mapped not to a year that is specified in the **WHERE** clause of the outer query but to a year that is defined in the **ON** clause that joins the outer query to the derived table. This is done simply by specifying the following code:

```
AND YEAR(ST.DateBought) = CSQ.PurchaseYear - 1
```

This filters the data returned from the outer query so that only data for the previous year is returned.

Of course, you could have specified the year to filter on in the outer query, but this approach is more fluid and extensible because it automatically finds data from the previous year in the outer query, regardless of the year defined in the **WHERE** clause of the derived table.

Tricks and traps

To end your introduction to derived tables, you should remember the following points:

- This particular technique can be used in **JOIN** clauses whenever the fields used in a join are numeric.
- It is particularly useful when comparing data across years. It also makes the point that the fields used in a **JOIN** can themselves be calculated, if necessary.

Conclusion

In this chapter, methods of combining data that help to answer some tough analytical questions were introduced. We did all of this using derived tables, a technique that assembles complex datasets *on the fly* inside other queries.

These virtual tables let you aggregate, filter, and slice data in-depth and use the results to carry out all sorts of queries. Moreover, derived tables help you think in terms of sets of data and, consequently, learn to adapt your way of tackling data-based problems, which is helpful in handling more complex data analysis. Derived tables also let you aggregate and filter data so that you can join otherwise incompatible datasets.

Core knowledge learned in this chapter

The concepts that you have seen in this chapter are as follows:

Concept	Description
Derived tables	When creating complex joins, you can define any or all of the component tables to be derived tables—that is, SQL that returns a table of data.
Multiple join fields	You can join derived tables to other tables using several fields if you need to.

CHAPTER 14
Common Table Expressions

Introduction

The previous two chapters have shown you that SQL is all about creating the datasets that allow you to deliver the desirable analysis. As you have probably surmised while reading this book, SQL imposes a particular way of thinking *on its practitioners*. More specifically, it is a language that wants you to adapt its worldview and think in terms of sets of data that become the building blocks of the analysis. *Thinking in datasets* can, nonetheless, be a skill that takes a while to acquire. Moreover, the way that some SQL solutions nest queries inside other queries can make for complex code that seems to hide—rather than expose—the true simplicity of the approach. The time has come to demonstrate a powerful way to simplify working with complex *datasets.*

Structure

In the chapter, we will cover the following topics:

- Simplifying complex queries with CTEs
- A basic common table expression
- Calculating averages across multiple values using a CTE

- Reusing CTEs in a query
- Using a CTE in a derived table to deliver two different levels of aggregation
- Using a CTE to isolate data from a separate dataset at a different level of detail
- Multiple common table expressions in a single query
- Nested CTEs
- Using multiple CTEs to compare disparate datasets

Objectives

As you have probably surmised while reading this book, SQL imposes a particular way of thinking `on its practitioners`. More specifically, it is a language that wants you to adopt its worldview and to think in terms of sets of data that become the building blocks of your analysis. *"Thinking in datasets"* can, nonetheless, be a skill that takes a while to acquire. Moreover, the way that some SQL solutions nest queries inside other queries can make for complex code that seems to hide—rather than expose—the true simplicity of the approach. The time has come to demonstrate a powerful way to simplify working with complex datasets.

Simplifying complex queries with CTEs

Once again, Databricks can come to the rescue if an analytical challenge seems too daunting at first sight. This is because SQL helps not only to create the code that delivers the analysis but also in defining the analytical approach and focusing on how one structures the datasets based on the underlying tables. This can be accomplished using a technique known as **Common Table Expressions** (**CTEs**).

CTEs can help in the following:

- Creating datasets outside the core of a query to help in thinking through a problem.
- Create separate datasets to isolate part of the SQL.
- Reusing datasets to avoid rewriting or copying SQL code several times.
- Creating CTEs that use the output from other CTEs. This allows breakdown of an analytical challenge into a sequence of coherent steps, where the results created by one CTE ripple through other CTEs in a query to deliver the final output.

Let us now see how CTEs can help in taming some of the most complex SQL queries.

A basic common table expression

In sales and marketing, it is essential that you understand the customer's needs. The first step to knowing this can be analyzing what the customers have bought in the past. The following code snippet lets you prepare a report for the CEO of *Prestige Cars* that displays the make, model, and color combinations of every vehicle sold in 2015:

```
WITH Sales2015_CTE

AS

(

SELECT     MK.MakeName, MD.ModelName, ST.Color

FROM       Make AS MK

INNER JOIN Model AS MD ON MK.MakeID = MD.MakeID

INNER JOIN Stock AS ST ON ST.ModelID = MD.ModelID

INNER JOIN SalesDetails SD ON ST.StockCode = SD.StockID

INNER JOIN Sales AS SA ON SA.SalesID = SD.SalesID

WHERE      YEAR(SA.SaleDate) = 2015

)

SELECT     MakeName, ModelName, Color

FROM       Sales2015_CTE

GROUP BY   MakeName, ModelName, Color

ORDER BY   MakeName, ModelName, Color;
```

Running this query gives the results that you can see in *Figure 14.1:*

	MakeName	ModelName	Color
1	Alfa Romeo	Giulia	Red
2	Aston Martin	DB4	Night Blue
3	Aston Martin	DB5	Black
4	Aston Martin	DB5	Blue
5	Aston Martin	DB6	Canary Yellow
6	Aston Martin	DB6	Silver

Figure 14.1: *A simple CTE*

How does it work

The preceding code snippet takes a two-phased approach to find all the existing make, model, and color combinations of cars sold in 2015.

- **First:** An independent initial query, that is, a CTE, joins the **`Make`**, **`Model`**, **`Stock`**, **`SalesDetails`**, and **`Sales`** tables. It then selects the **`MakeName`**, **`ModelName`**, and **`Color`** fields from these tables. As the query contains joins to the two tables (**`Sales`** and **`SalesDetails`**) that contain data for actual sales, the output only shows details of cars that have been sold. It also filters on the **`SaleDate`** field.
- **Then:** The output from this CTE is used as the data source in the **`FROM`** clause of the subsequent SQL statement.

A CTE is a kind of derived table, like the ones in the previous chapter. It is a perfectly normal **`SELECT`** query that you can build to isolate a subset of data. As you can see from this example, a CTE is composed of the following:

- **A CTE name**: A CTE must have a name. In this example, it is called **`Sales2015_CTE`**. The name can be a single character or something more complex that explains more clearly what the CTE does.
- **A WITH clause**: Begins the CTE.
- **A query**: This is the core of the CTE. It must be a valid SQL **`SELECT`** query. It can be as complex as your needs require. The query must be enclosed in parentheses.
- **Use for the CTE**: By this, I mean that you must do something using the CTE—such as using the **`SELECT`** data from it as we do in this example.

You can see how a CTE can be imagined in *Figure 14.2*:

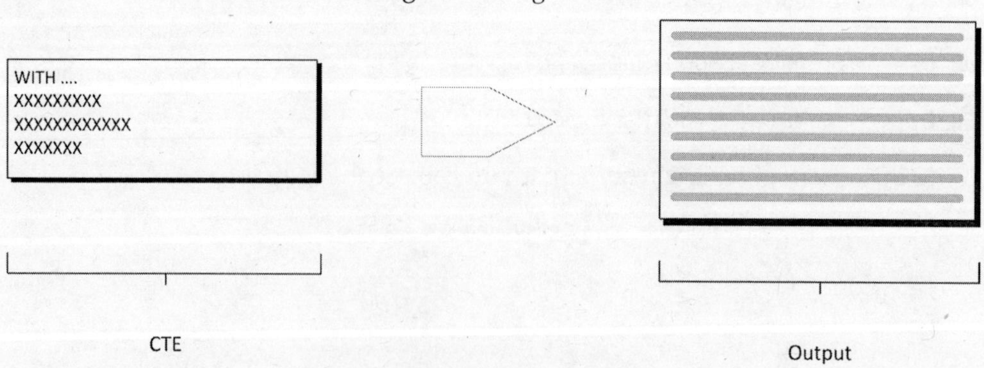

Figure 14.2: Conceptualizing a CTE

The CTE that we apply here is not strictly necessary. You could have written the SQL like the following:

```
SELECT     MakeName, ModelName, Color
FROM
(
SELECT     MK.MakeName, MD.ModelName, ST.Color
FROM       Make AS MK
INNER JOIN Model AS MD ON MK.MakeID = MD.MakeID
INNER JOIN Stock AS ST ON ST.ModelID = MD.ModelID
INNER JOIN SalesDetails SD ON ST.StockCode = SD.StockID
INNER JOIN Sales AS SA ON SA.SalesID = SD.SalesID
WHERE      YEAR(SA.SaleDate) = 2015
)
GROUP BY   MakeName, ModelName, Color
ORDER BY   MakeName, ModelName, Color;
```

However, as you will see in this chapter, CTEs can be extremely useful in many different ways. We begin with a simpler example. However, there is more to using CTEs than just resolving coding challenges. A CTE helps you break down a problem into its component parts. In this specific example, this means:

- **First**: Defining the list of data that you want to aggregate (this is the query inside the CTE).
- **Finally**: Grouping the data subset from the CTE to achieve the desired result.

So, using CTEs is more than merely a variation on a theme; it can also help you think through a problem and enable you to separate the building blocks that SQL uses to provide a solution in a clear and sequential way.

Tricks and traps

The following are some key points to remember:

- You do not have to include the acronym CTE in a Common Table Expression name; however, the book adopts this approach so that readers can identify CTEs more easily among all the other SQL objects that we use.
- The name of a CTE in Databricks can be up to 122 characters.

- If you decide to use a CTE to isolate a subset of data, then you have to apply the CTE in some way. In other words, you cannot *declare* a CTE and then not use it. Indeed, if you do not use a CTE that you have created, then your code will not work.
- It is best to avoid spaces and special characters in the names of CTEs.
- The query that makes up a CTE is completely independent of the rest of the query. This means you can always test the CTE by first selecting the SQL inside the parentheses that constitute the CTE and then executing it (by pressing *Ctrl* + *Shift* + *Enter,* for instance). *Figure 14.3* shows the results for the code in the CTE in this example:

	MakeName	ModelName	Color
1	Ferrari	Testarossa	Green
2	Ferrari	Testarossa	Red
3	Ferrari	355	Black
4	Ferrari	355	Blue
5	Porsche	911	Black
6	Porsche	911	Blue

***Figure 14.3:** The independent query constituting a CTE*

Calculating averages across multiple values using a CTE

One simple metric can inform numerous businesses of their profitability. This is the average profit for each type of product. A CTE helps in producing the given analysis for the CEO of *Prestige Cars*:

```
WITH Sales_CTE
AS
(
SELECT    MK.MakeName
          ,SalePrice - (
                         ST.Cost
```

```
                    + ST.RepairsCost
                    + NVL(ST.PartsCost, 0)
                    + ST.TransportInCost
                   ) AS Profit
FROM       Make AS MK
INNER JOIN Model AS MD ON MK.MakeID = MD.MakeID
INNER JOIN Stock AS ST ON ST.ModelID = MD.ModelID
INNER JOIN SalesDetails SD ON ST.StockCode = SD.StockID
)
SELECT     MakeName, AVG(Profit) AS AverageProfit
FROM       Sales_CTE
GROUP BY   MakeName;
```

If you run this query, you will see the results shown in *Figure 14.4*:

	MakeName	AverageProfit
1	Peugeot	-979.1
2	Delahaye	3473.25
3	Jaguar	4997.36
4	Reliant	-1210
5	Trabant	-957.4
6	Lamborghini	27957

***Figure 14.4:** Calculating averages across multiple values using a CTE*

How does it work

Calculating averages is fundamental to many data analyses, and SQL does it well. The preceding piece of SQL uses multiple fields to calculate the profit for each car sold and returns the average profit per make. One might wonder why a CTE is required to carry out this calculation.

Indeed, it can be done manually; however, adding and subtracting overall averages is not the same thing as calculating the average profit. To get this information, it is essential to calculate the profit per car and then work out the average of this figure. This is a prime example of how a CTE can prove invaluable. It allows you to:

- **First**: To calculate the profit figure for each car in the `Stock` table. This is the essence of the `SELECT` clause of the CTE. This metric is worked out at the most detailed level possible, that of each car in the source data table. Moreover, using CTEs lets you handle NULLs at the most granular level possible, as you can see from using the `NVL()` function inside the CTE. This means that `NULL`s are handled once and for all in this entire query.
- **Finally**: To return the average of the profit figure, aggregated by `Make` in the main query that refers to the CTE.

CTE or derived table?

One might notice that CTE works similarly to the derived tables described in a previous chapter.

They are largely identical as both are independent of the query that they are used by; both must specify the fields that can be read by the *outer* query and must have an alias.

CTEs, however, can help when developing an SQL solution. This is possible as they help in isolating sections of a data challenge. Indeed, they can help considerably when conceptualizing a solution as they guide you toward separating data subsets as CTEs. This approach can also make SQL queries easier to extend and maintain.

CTEs can also alias the field names in the CTE header if required. You can see this in the SQL snippet in the next section. So, if a challenging query lends itself to using a derived table or a CTE, users may choose the suitable approach as per their discretion.

Reusing CTEs in a query

When you are trying to control costs, it can help to compare various metrics to a multiple of an average value to focus on higher-than-expected values. Let us assume the same is required by the finance director. In fact, he has asked for a report that finds all makes and models sold where the discount was more than twice the average discount for any vehicle sold in that year. The following piece of SQL is an example of this type of analysis:

```
WITH Discount2015_CTE (Make, Model, Color, SalePrice, LineItemDiscount)
```

```
AS
(
SELECT     MK.MakeName, MD.ModelName, ST.Color
           ,SD.SalePrice, SD.LineItemDiscount
FROM       Make AS MK
INNER JOIN Model AS MD ON MK.MakeID = MD.MakeID
INNER JOIN Stock AS ST ON ST.ModelID = MD.ModelID
INNER JOIN SalesDetails SD ON ST.StockCode = SD.StockID
INNER JOIN Sales AS SA ON SA.SalesID = SD.SalesID
WHERE      YEAR(SaleDate) = 2015
)
SELECT     Make, Model, Color, LineItemDiscount, SalePrice
           ,(SELECT AVG(LineItemDiscount) * 2 FROM Discount2015_CTE)
           AS AverageDiscount
FROM       Discount2015_CTE
WHERE      LineItemDiscount > (SELECT AVG(LineItemDiscount) * 2
                                         FROM Discount2015_CTE);
```

Running this query gives the results shown in *Figure 14.5*:

	Make	Model	Color	LineItemDiscount	SalePrice	AverageDiscount
1	Ferrari	355	Blue	60000	220000	9655.29411764706

Figure 14.5: *Reusing a CTE in a query*

How does it work

This piece of analytical SQL uses a CTE to produce a list of the makes and models of cars sold in 2015. It also displays the **color**, **sale price**, and sales discount (a column named **LineItemDiscount**) for each model.

Once the CTE has defined the data subset that will be used by the main query, the following take place:

- **First**: The rest of the query selects the fields passed into it by the CTE.
- **Then**: A `WHERE` clause in the main query reuses the CTE to calculate the average sales discount for 2015. This is then doubled and used as a filter so that only sales where a discount greater than twice the average sales discount for the year has been applied appear in the final output.
- **Finally**: The average sales discount for 2015 is recalculated and added to the `SELECT` clause as a subquery.

The key point here is that a CTE can be reused several times in the main query. This approach is based on the following two fundamental ideas:

1. You only have to write the SQL that defines a subset of data once because you can reuse it over and over again. In this example, the main advantage of this approach is that the filter (the `WHERE` clause that limits the data to the sales for a specific year) is only applied once in the CTE.
2. Whenever the CTE is reused to calculate or display the average value, the filter that it contains is applied every time.

The following are clear advantages to this way of working:

- **Less complexity**: Subqueries can sometimes be fairly complex, so having to rewrite the same piece of SQL (or adapt it without making any errors) to use in a subquery can become laborious. Reusing a CTE means that you only write the core query once to get a reusable dataset.
- **Avoid repetition**: This means you are less likely to make a SQL syntax error or enter a wrong value in one of the multiple `WHERE` clauses that would otherwise be necessary when you rewrite or copy and paste multiple query elements.
- **Forgetting is harder**: You do not have to remember to add or update a `WHERE` clause in multiple subqueries.
- **Modification is easier**: If you want to filter the data on a different year, you must change the `WHERE` clause in the CTE. This change cascades to the main query everywhere the CTE is used, so you only have to change filter values in one place. Equally, any other modifications (such as calculations) that you make to a CTE are subsequently available wherever the CTE is used in the main query.

Tricks and traps

A set of key points are worth noting, which are given as follows:

- As was the case with derived tables, the `SELECT` clause of the CTE must include all the fields that you want to use in the main query. If you do not select a field in the CTE, then it is completely invisible downstream in the main query that returns the final recordset based on the CTE. So, in this example, the fields used in the main query (`Make`, `Model`, `Color`, `LineItemDiscount`, and `SalePrice`) must appear in the `SELECT` clause of the CTE.
- Although you absolutely must use a CTE if you have added one to your code, you are not obligated to use all the fields that you have selected in the CTE elsewhere in your query. In practice, however, it is probably best only to select the fields that you need when creating a CTE.
- You can make sure a CTE makes clear the names of the fields that it returns (as the CTE in this example does) by placing a list of fields in parentheses after the CTE name. However, this is not compulsory. Doing so is nothing more than a way of giving aliases to the fields that the CTE outputs. This can be useful for making the column names in underlying tables easier to understand for users.

Using a CTE in a derived table to deliver two different levels of aggregation

The sales director for *Prestige Cars* wants a slightly subtler analysis of who the most valuable customers are. In this case, she wants a list of customers who bought the most expensive model of car for each make in 2015. The following piece of SQL lets you deliver this information:

```
WITH ExpensiveCar_CTE (

                        MakeName, ModelName, SalePrice

                       ,Color, TransportInCost, SaleDate

                       ,InvoiceNumber, CustomerName

)

AS

(

SELECT     MK.MakeName, MD.ModelName, SD.SalePrice, ST.Color
```

```
            ,ST.TransportInCost, SA.SaleDate, SA.InvoiceNumber
            ,CU.CustomerName
FROM        Make AS MK
INNER JOIN Model AS MD ON MK.MakeID = MD.MakeID
INNER JOIN Stock AS ST ON ST.ModelID = MD.ModelID
INNER JOIN SalesDetails SD ON ST.StockCode = SD.StockID
INNER JOIN Sales AS SA ON SA.SalesID = SD.SalesID
INNER JOIN Customer CU ON SA.CustomerID = CU.CustomerID
WHERE       YEAR(SaleDate) = 2015
)
SELECT      SLS.MakeName, SLS.ModelName, SLS.Color, CustomerName
            ,SLS.TransportInCost, SLS.SaleDate, SLS.InvoiceNumber
FROM        ExpensiveCar_CTE SLS
            INNER JOIN (
                        SELECT    MakeName
                                 ,MAX(SalePrice) AS MaxSalePrice
                        FROM     ExpensiveCar_CTE
                        GROUP BY MakeName
                       ) MX
            ON SLS.MakeName = MX.MakeName
            AND SLS.SalePrice = MX.MaxSalePrice;
```

Running this query gives the results shown in *Figure 14.6*:

	MakeName	ModelName	Color	CustomerName	TransportInCost	SaleDate	InvoiceNumber
1	Mercedes	280SL	Red	La Bagnole de Luxe	150	2015-06-04T04:37:00.000+0000	EURFR015
2	Ferrari	355	Blue	Snazzy Roadsters	1950	2015-01-25T12:00:00.000+0000	GBPGB002
3	Jaguar	XK150	Night Blue	Alexei Tolstoi	150	2015-07-15T12:00:00.000+0000	GBPGB017
4	Bentley	Flying Spur	British Racing Green	Wonderland Wheels	750	2015-04-30T12:00:00.000+0000	GBPGB011
5	Triumph	TR5	Green	Peter McLuckie	150	2015-09-05T12:00:00.000+0000	GBPGB020
6	Alfa Romeo	Giulia	Red	Convertible Dreams	150	2015-07-12T10:00:00.000+0000	GBPGB016

***Figure 14.6:** Using a CTE in a derived table to deliver two different levels of aggregation*

How does it work

The challenge here is to isolate the highest-value car sold for each make and return all the important details for each sale. Fortunately, a CTE is helpful here in the following ways:

- **First**: You define a CTE that contains all the key sales information (customer, sale price, make, model, and so on).
- **Second**: You select all the important data from this CTE.
- **Third**: You use the CTE a second time in a derived table that groups and aggregates the data from the CTE by make and maximum sale price.
- **Finally**: You join the derived table to the main query on the `MakeName` and `SalePrice` fields (or rather, join the maximum sale price field from the derived table to the sale price field from the main query).

This way, the derived table (aliased as `MX`) filters out all cars from the main query where the sale price is not equal to the greatest sale price, in effect isolating the most expensive car sold for each make.

Once again, you have reused a CTE. Rather than rewrite complex joins in a derived table, the CTE used the CTE as the basis for a simple aggregation. This allowed you to concentrate on getting the initial query (the one used in the CTE) correct and then focus separately on how to use this data twice:

- Once, to find the most expensive car for each make.
- Another is to list the details of that particular sale.

To understand this more easily, refer to *Figure 14.7*, which provides a visual breakdown of the query used in this example:

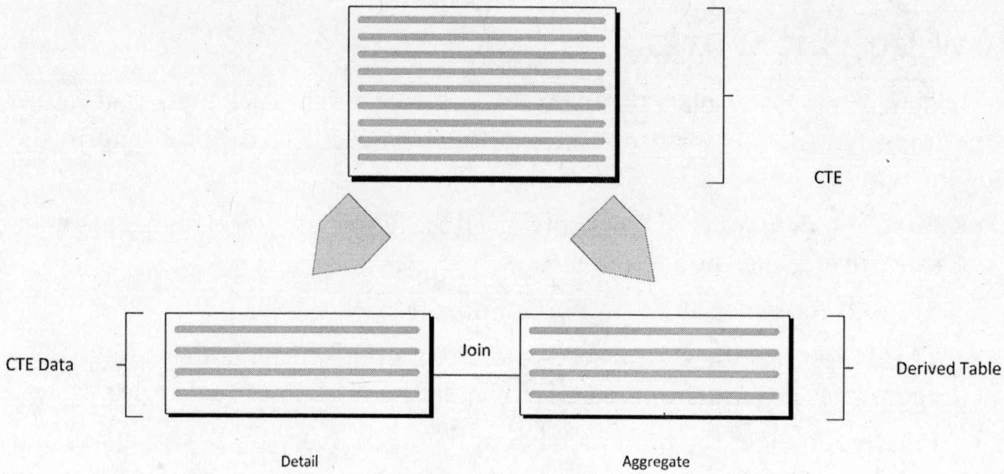

Figure 14.7: Analyzing a complex CTE

Tricks and traps

When creating more complex CTEs, you need to remember the following:

- If you have created a CTE that outputs many fields, then you need to pay attention to the list of column names that you add inside the parentheses that follow the name of the CTE. This involves doing the following:
    - You should make sure to have the same number of fields as those in the **SELECT** clause of the CTE.
    - The order of the fields can be easily mixed up and consequentially produce unrequired output. Therefore, you ensure that all the fields are in the same order, both in the **SELECT** clause and inside the parentheses.

Using a CTE to isolate data from a separate dataset at a different level of detail

The sales director has asked you to produce a regular report that ensures that the salesmen are meeting their targets. To do so, you need to compare sales figures to budget projections. The SQL that follows is one way of doing this:

```
WITH SalesBudget_CTE
AS
(
SELECT     BudgetValue, BudgetDetail, Year, Month
```

```
FROM        Budget
WHERE       BudgetElement = 'Country'
)
SELECT      CO.CountryName, YEAR(SA.SaleDate) AS YearOfSale
            ,MONTH(SA.SaleDate) AS MonthOfSale
            ,SUM(SD.SalePrice) AS SalePrice
            ,SUM(CTE.BudgetValue) AS BudgetValue
            ,SUM(CTE.BudgetValue)
            - SUM(SD.SalePrice) AS DifferenceBudgetToSales
FROM        Make AS MK
INNER JOIN Model AS MD ON MK.MakeID = MD.MakeID
INNER JOIN Stock AS ST ON ST.ModelID = MD.ModelID
INNER JOIN SalesDetails SD ON ST.StockCode = SD.StockID
INNER JOIN Sales AS SA ON SA.SalesID = SD.SalesID
INNER JOIN Customer CU ON SA.CustomerID = CU.CustomerID
INNER JOIN Country CO ON CU.Country = CO.CountryISO2
INNER JOIN SalesBudget_CTE CTE
            ON CTE.BudgetDetail = CO.CountryName
            AND CTE.Year = YEAR(SA.SaleDate)
            AND CTE.Month = MONTH(SA.SaleDate)
GROUP BY    CO.CountryName, YEAR(SA.SaleDate), MONTH(SaleDate);
```

Running this query gives the results shown in *Figure 14.8*:

	CountryName	YearOfSale	MonthOfSale	SalePrice	BudgetValue	DifferenceBudgetToSales
1	United States	2015	10	123590	123590	0
2	United Kingdom	2015	7	31685	63370	31685
3	United Kingdom	2018	8	258550	1034200	775650
4	France	2016	2	39500	39500	0
5	Germany	2017	5	45000	45000	0
6	France	2016	9	51065	153195	102130

Figure 14.8*: Using a CTE to isolate data from a separate dataset at a different level of detail*

How does it work

One might notice the preceding example uses CTE as a derived table. More precisely, we are using the CTE to isolate the budget data from the Budget table so that it can be joined to a query in a way that allows us to compare actual and budget data. Now, the budget data does not fit into the tightly structured *relational* model of the main tables of the *Prestige Cars* database. However, it is possible to produce budget data that returns a list of makes along with the predicted sales for each month and year. The **SELECT** query that makes up the CTE does this. To get a clearer idea of how this works, refer to *Figure 14.9*, which shows you the output from the CTE if you select the SQL and run it independently:

	BudgetValue	BudgetDetail	Year	Month
1	100000	Belgium	2016	8
2	15500	Belgium	2017	2
3	100000	Belgium	2017	3
4	45950	Belgium	2017	7
5	34000	Belgium	2017	11
6	950	Belgium	2018	1

***Figure 14.9:** The records returned by a CTE that filters data*

As you can see, this is nothing more than a *virtual table* of selected budget data. However, you can now join this data to sales data in the following three fields:

1. **CountryName**: This maps to the **BudgetDetail** field in the **Budget** table (once the **BudgetDetail** table is filtered to show the makes).
2. **Year of Sale**: This requires you to use the **YEAR()** function to extract the year from the **SaleDate** field.
3. **Month of Sale**: This requires you to use the **MONTH()** function to extract the month from the **SaleDate** field.

The main query in this code snippet then joins the CTE to the other tables treating it like a normal table. The main query can then select any necessary fields and carry out any required calculations.

Tricks and traps

When using a CTE to join data from separate data areas at different levels of granularity, be sure to remember that:

- In the main query, all the numeric values have to be aggregated (using **SUM()** functions in this example), and the text fields have to appear in a **GROUP BY** clause. This is because you are comparing budget data that is pre-aggregated by country, year, and month with data that is at a more detailed level. So, to make the figures meaningful, the detailed sales data has to be aggregated into country, year, and month also, or it cannot be joined to the CTE.

Multiple common table expressions in a single query

It may be near the end of the day, but the sales director has appeared at your desk with an urgent request. She wants to see how her budget predictions for sales by color stack up against actual sales for 2016. Fortunately, you can answer this request in a few minutes with the kind of SQL that you can see as follows:

```
WITH

ColorSales_CTE

AS

(

SELECT      ST.Color

            ,SUM(SD.SalePrice) AS TotalSalesValue

FROM        Stock ST

INNER JOIN SalesDetails SD

            ON ST.StockCode = SD.StockID

INNER JOIN Sales SA

            ON SD.SalesID = SA.SalesID

WHERE       YEAR(SA.SaleDate) = 2016

GROUP BY    Color

)
```

```
,
ColorBudget_CTE
AS
(
SELECT  BudgetDetail AS Color, BudgetValue
FROM    Budget
WHERE   BudgetElement = 'Color'
            AND YEAR = 2016
)
SELECT      BDG.Color, SLS.TotalSalesValue, BDG.BudgetValue
            ,(SLS.TotalSalesValue - BDG.BudgetValue) AS BudgetDelta
FROM        ColorSales_CTE SLS
INNER JOIN  ColorBudget_CTE BDG
            ON SLS.Color = BDG.Color;
```

Running the preceding code gives you the result, as shown in *Figure 14.10*. In this figure, you can also see the output of the two separate CTEs:

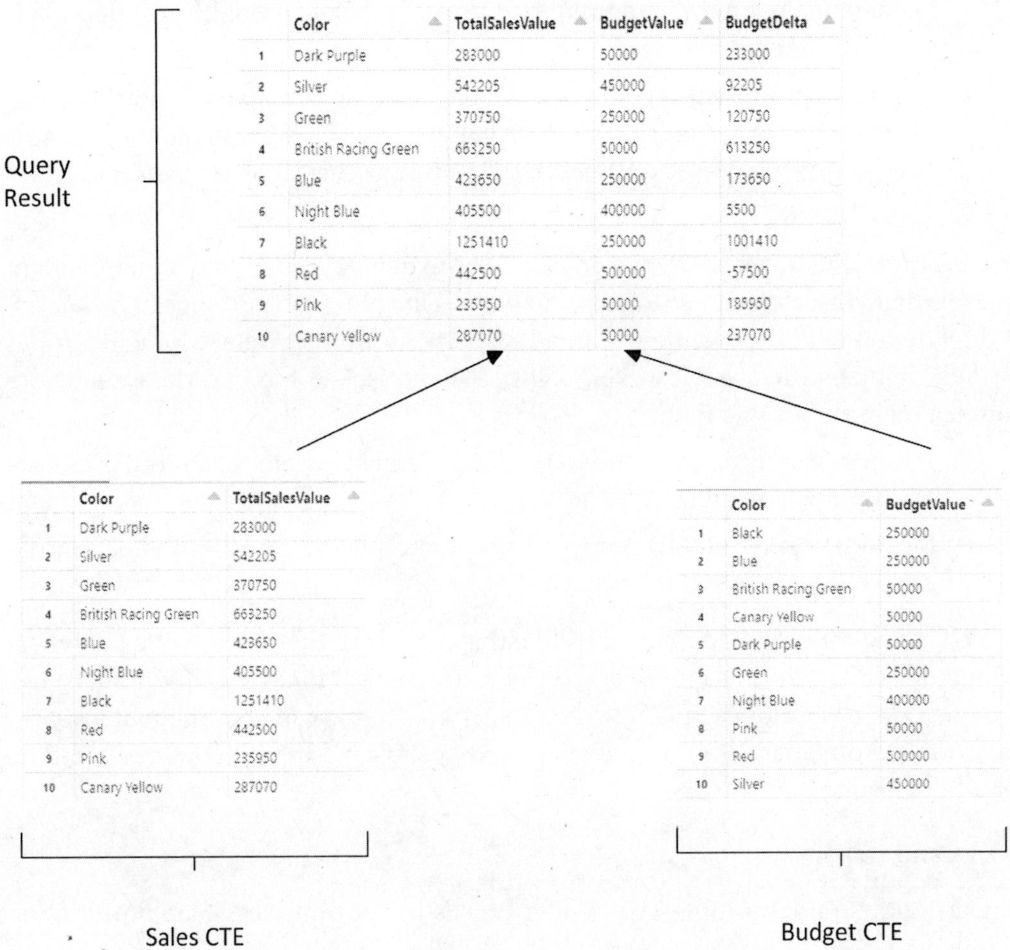

	Color	TotalSalesValue	BudgetValue	BudgetDelta
1	Dark Purple	283000	50000	233000
2	Silver	542205	450000	92205
3	Green	370750	250000	120750
4	British Racing Green	663250	50000	613250
5	Blue	423650	250000	173650
6	Night Blue	405500	400000	5500
7	Black	1251410	250000	1001410
8	Red	442500	500000	-57500
9	Pink	235950	50000	185950
10	Canary Yellow	287070	50000	237070

	Color	TotalSalesValue
1	Dark Purple	283000
2	Silver	542205
3	Green	370750
4	British Racing Green	663250
5	Blue	423650
6	Night Blue	405500
7	Black	1251410
8	Red	442500
9	Pink	235950
10	Canary Yellow	287070

	Color	BudgetValue
1	Black	250000
2	Blue	250000
3	British Racing Green	50000
4	Canary Yellow	50000
5	Dark Purple	50000
6	Green	250000
7	Night Blue	400000
8	Pink	50000
9	Red	500000
10	Silver	450000

***Figure 14.10**: Using multiple CTEs in a query*

How does it work

This query uses the following two separate CTEs to isolate two different datasets that are then joined in the final *output* query.

- **The first CTE:** Joins the **`Sales`**, **`Stock`**, and **`SalesDetails`** tables to return all the required sales values per color of vehicle sold for 2016. This CTE is called **`ColorSales_CTE`**.
- **The second CTE**: Isolates the budget data for colors for 2016 from the **`Budget`** table. As mentioned previously, the **`budget`** table contains data for many budget elements. Therefore, it needs to be filtered on both the budget

element (color, in this example) and the year that you want to get data. This CTE is called **`ColorBudget_CTE`**.

- **The output query**: Joins the two source CTEs on the shared color field and returns both the sales and budget values for all the available colors. As a final flourish, it uses the values to calculate any sales that are over (or under) budget values.

This example illustrates how you can use CTEs to generate completely independent datasets that you can then use together to deliver insight. In the *Prestige Cars* dataset, budget data is held independently, in all respects, from sales data. Moreover, it has its own unique structure. However, using CTEs to isolate the two datasets before you join them shows you that:

- **First**: You can isolate separate data elements from each other before attempting to combine them.
- **Second**: The two CTEs are totally separate—neither has any effect on the other.

Indeed, using multiple separate CTEs like this can prove to be a valuable analytical technique. This is because you can concentrate on each dataset individually (and even test the output of each CTE in isolation). Often this can be a valuable way to break down your analysis into smaller, more digestible pieces that you then combine for a final result.

Tricks and traps

If you decide to use multiple independent CTEs in your queries, keep in mind the following:

- You can use multiple independent CTEs as a way of testing various approaches to solving data analysis challenges.
- You only need to introduce CTEs with a single **`WITH`** keyword. After that, you can separate each CTE from the others with a comma.

Nested CTEs

As part of your analytical quest to deliver the insight that will lead to increased sales and profits, you want to look at the cars that sell more than a minimum quantity. More specifically, you want to display all the makes of cars sold each year where more than two cars are sold per make. After all, perhaps these are the ones that the company should be pitching to potential buyers. The following SQL shows this process:

```
WITH Outer2015Sales_CTE
AS
(
SELECT     MK.MakeName
FROM       Make AS MK
INNER JOIN Model AS MD ON MK.MakeID = MD.MakeID
INNER JOIN Stock AS ST ON ST.ModelID = MD.ModelID
INNER JOIN SalesDetails SD ON ST.StockCode = SD.StockID
INNER JOIN Sales AS SA ON SA.SalesID = SD.SalesID
WHERE      YEAR(SA.SaleDate) = 2015
)
,
CoreSales_CTE (MakeName, NumberOfSales)
AS
(
SELECT     MakeName
           ,COUNT(*)
FROM       Outer2015Sales_CTE
GROUP BY   MakeName
HAVING     COUNT(*) >= 2
)
SELECT      CTE.MakeName, MK2.MakeCountry AS CountryCode
           ,CTE.NumberOfSales
FROM       CoreSales_CTE CTE
INNER JOIN Make MK2
           ON CTE.MakeName = MK2.MakeName;
```

Running this query gives the results shown in *Figure 14.11*:

	MakeName	CountryCode	NumberOfSales
1	Jaguar	GBR	4
2	Ferrari	ITA	4
3	Porsche	GER	8
4	Triumph	GBR	2
5	Aston Martin	GBR	7

***Figure 14.11:** Nested CTE output*

How does it work

This query demonstrates how to create a short sequence of two CTEs where the second uses the output from the first as its source of data. This way, CTEs can be used as a way of breaking down the initial requirement into a series of successive steps that lead to the solution. What the query does is take the following three-phased approach:

1. **First**: The initial CTE joins all the tables that are required to produce a list of all makes of vehicles sold in 2015. Even though only two fields are used by this query (`MakeName` and `Sale-Date`), these fields are in the `Sales` and `Make` tables. Therefore, several intermediate tables must be part of the `FROM` clause to link the source data tables correctly.
2. **Then**: The second CTE (`CoreSales_CTE`) is built using the first CTE (`Outer2015Sales_CTE`) as its data source. This query is an aggregate query that only returns makes of cars where more than two have been sold. The sales for 2015 are analyzed as this CTE is based on the first CTE.
3. **Finally**: A regular query lists the makes of the vehicle returned by the second CTE. It joins this result to the Make table to add further columns to the output.

Figure 14.12 explains nested CTEs:

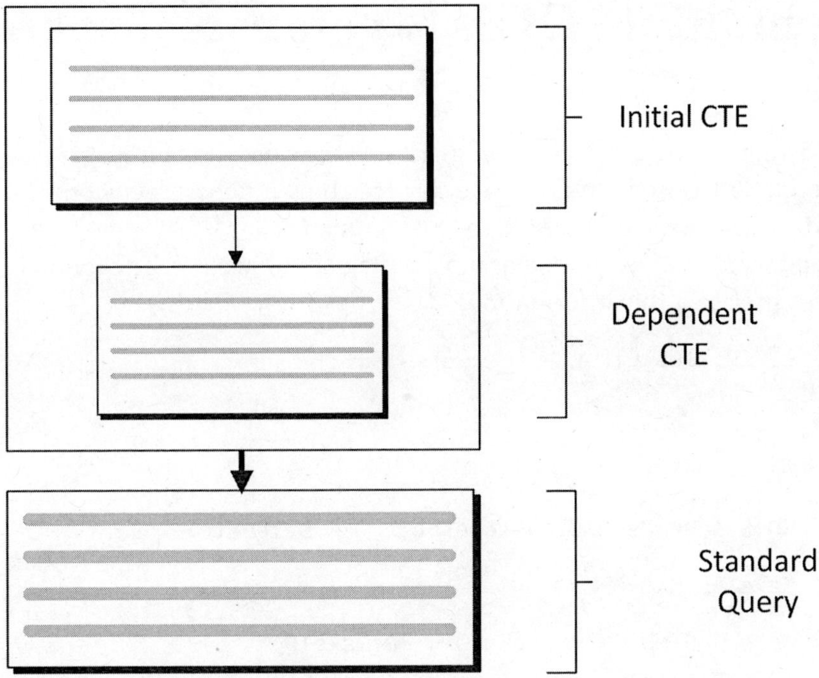

Figure 14.12: *The data flow in nested CTEs*

Although you could probably arrive at the same result using different approaches, this example shows you that CTEs can be *linked* in a way that lets SQL reflect on the given analytical challenge. It has the advantage of being more sequential than some other approaches as it lets you see the following steps, which are required to produce the final output, more clearly:

- **First**: Filter the data.
- **Second**: Aggregate the data.
- **Finally**: Extend the data selection.

Tricks and traps

The following are a couple of points to take away:

- When you are writing SQL that uses multiple CTEs, the core principles of using any CTE continue to apply. You must begin with a semicolon (`;`) if there is any other code before the CTE, and you must use all of the CTEs that you write. This means you still need an SQL query after the final CTE to output the data.
- When writing dependent CTEs like this, you only need to use a single `WITH` keyword. This serves to introduce any number of CTEs. The CTEs can be independent of one another or derived from one another.

Using multiple CTEs to compare disparate datasets

When an existing customer contacts *Prestige Cars*, the sales director wants to know if they are profitable. Consequently, she wants to see how much each customer spent in 2017 and how this relates to *Prestige Cars'* total annual sales. What is more, she wants to see sales per customer expressed as a percentage of total sales. The following SQL snippet gives precisely this information:

```
WITH Initial2017Sales_CTE
AS
(
SELECT     SD.SalePrice, CU.CustomerName, SA.SaleDate
FROM       Make AS MK
INNER JOIN Model AS MD ON MK.MakeID = MD.MakeID
INNER JOIN Stock AS ST ON ST.ModelID = MD.ModelID
INNER JOIN SalesDetails SD ON ST.StockCode = SD.StockID
INNER JOIN Sales AS SA ON SA.SalesID = SD.SalesID
INNER JOIN Customer CU ON SA.CustomerID = CU.CustomerID
WHERE      YEAR(SA.SaleDate) = 2017
)
,
AggregateSales_CTE (CustomerName, SalesForCustomer)
AS
(
SELECT     CustomerName, SUM(SalePrice)
FROM       Initial2017Sales_CTE
GROUP BY   CustomerName
)
,
```

```
TotalSales_CTE (TotalSalePrice)
AS
(
SELECT     SUM(SalePrice)
FROM       Initial2017Sales_CTE
)
SELECT
 IT.CustomerName
,IT.SalePrice
, IT.SaleDate
,FORMAT_NUMBER(IT.SalePrice / AG.SalesForCustomer, '0.00%')
           AS SaleAsPercentageForCustomer
,FORMAT_NUMBER(IT.SalePrice / (SELECT TotalSalePrice FROM TotalSales_
CTE), '0.00%') AS SalePercentOverall
FROM       Initial2017Sales_CTE IT
           INNER JOIN AggregateSales_CTE AG
           ON IT.CustomerName = AG.CustomerName
ORDER BY  IT.SaleDate, IT.CustomerName;
```

Running this query gives the results shown in *Figure 14.13:*

	CustomerName	SalePrice	SaleDate	SaleAsPercentageForCustomer	SalePercentOverall
1	Vive La Vitesse	22500	2017-01-01T11:12:00.000+0000	2.47%	0.29%
2	Peter Smith	125000	2017-01-05T11:55:00.000+0000	43.48%	1.59%
3	Eat My Exhaust Ltd	85000	2017-01-10T03:56:00.000+0000	60.71%	1.08%
4	Le Luxe en Motion	22500	2017-01-11T05:52:00.000+0000	7.61%	0.29%
5	Magic Motors	125950	2017-01-12T06:57:00.000+0000	28.01%	1.60%
6	Le Luxe en Motion	8850	2017-01-13T07:58:00.000+0000	2.99%	0.11%
7	Posh Vehicles Ltd	9950	2017-01-14T09:58:00.000+0000	18.11%	0.13%
8	La Bagnole de Luxe	1250	2017-01-21T01:56:00.000+0000	100.00%	0.02%
9	Vive La Vitesse	56500	2017-01-30T10:59:00.000+0000	6.21%	0.72%
10	Screamin' Wheels	55000	2017-01-31T09:59:00.000+0000	32.63%	0.70%

Figure 14.13: *Using multiple CTEs to compare disparate datasets*

How does it work

The preceding piece can appear complex at first glance. After all, this example uses no less than three CTEs to deliver the required analysis. Furthermore, the second CTE is based on the first CTE. However, before looking at the code, let us see exactly what we are trying to deliver. In essence, the request asks for the following information:

- **Individual Customer Sales**: We need the detail of each sale for each customer for the given period (2017).
- **Total Customer Sales**: We want the total sales figure for each customer for the given period.
- **Total Sales**: We also require the total overall sales for the sales period.

Each of the three CTEs, used in this query corresponds to one of the preceding analytical requirements:

- **`Initial2017Sales_CTE`**: Provides the sales data at a detailed level. It joins all the necessary tables needed to output the date of each sale, the customer, and the amount of the sale. This CTE also filters the data to restrict it to a specified year.
- **`AggregateSales_CTE`**: Takes the data supplied by the initial CTE (**`Initial2017Sales_CTE`**) and aggregates it by customer. This is helpful in obtaining the total sales per customer.
- **`TotalSales_CTE`**: Also takes the data supplied by **`Initial2017Sales_CTE`** and aggregates it; only this time, the total figure for the dataset is returned without any grouping.

Once the CTEs have been defined (or *declared*), the final query can then assemble the data from all of them. It is done in the following two ways:

- **First**: **`Initial2017Sales_CTE`** (the detailed list of sales) is joined to **`AggregateSales_CTE`** (the total sales per customer). As both contain the **`CustomerName`** field, they are joined on this field. This join allows the user to return the total sales per customer and the detail of each sale for every sale. Dividing the total sales per customer by the value of each sale gives you the percentage of total customer sales that each individual sale represents.
- **Second**: The total overall sales figure is added to the query. This is done using a subquery. However, this time the subquery uses a CTE. This adds the total sales figure to each row that is output. The calculated total can be used to provide the percentage of total sales that each individual sale represents.

This example illustrates how versatile CTEs can be. As you can see, the initial detailed CTE (**`Initial2017Sales_CTE`**) is used not only in the final query but also in the other two CTEs. This makes the code much simpler by avoiding the repetition of the series of table joins several times. Instead, you define a source dataset once that is then reuse*d* on multiple occasions to deliver different levels of aggregation. Moreover, if you need to change the filter that underlies the analysis (the year, in this case), you only need to alter it once in the top CTE for the filter to be cascaded down through the subsequent, dependent CTEs.

Tricks and traps

Despite its apparent complexity, this CTE needs only one principal comment, which is given as follows:

- In the given SQL, we have formatted the percentage output using the **`FORMAT()`** function. This makes the output more readable. If the same data is entered for another application, you may want to remove this function from the code because it can cause the percentages to be interpreted as text by some programs.

Conclusion

This chapter demonstrated how to harness the power of SQL to rise to the most daunting data analysis challenges. It was done using CTEs, a technique that allows breakdown of data analysis problems into smaller, more manageable parts that can be joined together to obtain the desired results.

CTEs not only solve technical problems but also help in the step-by-step handling of data analysis. This combination makes them one of the most useful SQL techniques available and, almost certainly, a valuable tool for developers.

Core knowledge learned in this chapter

The concepts and keywords that you have seen in this chapter are

Concept	Description
Common Table Expressions (CTEs)	A CTE is a separate derived table that allows you to define a dataset outside the main query for use—and reuse—in the body of the query. Multiple CTEs can be used in the same query; CTEs can be chained so that one CTE depends on the output of another CTE, and CTEs can be independent of each other.
`WITH`	This keyword introduces one or more CTEs in a query.

Join our book's Discord space

Join the book's Discord Workspace for Latest updates, Offers, Tech happenings around the world, New Release and Sessions with the Authors:

https://discord.bpbonline.com

CHAPTER 15
Correlated Subqueries

Introduction

The title of the chapter may appear complex at first glance. However, it is a commonly used term throughout the industry. It implies that certain kinds of subquery can be used to filter the data in the outer query in a particular way. This is done by applying a specific method to join the subquery to the outer query, creating a mutual interdependency between the queries. Using correlated subqueries can often enable you to deliver some uniquely powerful data analysis.

Structure

In this chapters, we will cover the following topics:

- Simple correlated subqueries
- Correlated subqueries to display percentages of a specific total
- Comparing datasets using a correlated subquery
- Duplicating the output of a correlated subquery in the query results
- Using correlated subqueries to filter data on an aggregate value
- Using correlated subqueries to detect if records exist

Objectives

The concept of correlated subqueries is easier to understand when seen in action. In this chapter, you see how to:

- Calculate ratios and percentages of parts relative to a whole.
- Filter data in a table only if corresponding data exists in another table.
- Filter data based on a calculation that relates to a specific aspect of the data.
- Isolate data according to certain characteristics of another linked dataset.

The chapter further elaborates on a few correlated subqueries that will enhance the knowledge of SQL. This will help in pushing the readers' analytical abilities to a higher level to help in solving numerous challenging requests.

Simple correlated subqueries

Most of the clients of *Prestige Cars* only buy one vehicle at a time. However, some do buy two or more at once. To this end, the sales director wants a list of all invoice items and the total for the invoice for further analysis. The following SQL provides the following:

```
SELECT

SD.SalesDetailsID

,SalePrice

,(SELECT SUM(TotalSalePrice) FROM sales

        WHERE       SalesId = SD.SalesId) AS TotalSales

FROM        SalesDetails SD

ORDER BY    SalesDetailsID;
```

Running the preceding SQL returns the data shown in *Figure 15.1*. Although the sale price is equal to the total sales in most cases, on occasion (such as in lines 11 and 12), two lines make up a single invoice, and the combined sale prices make up the total sales:

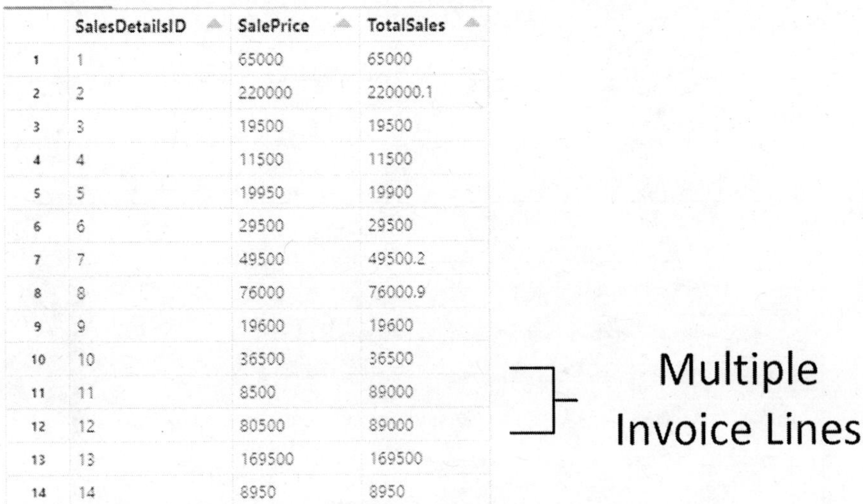

	SalesDetailsID	SalePrice	TotalSales
1	1	65000	65000
2	2	220000	220000.1
3	3	19500	19500
4	4	11500	11500
5	5	19950	19900
6	6	29500	29500
7	7	49500	49500.2
8	8	76000	76000.9
9	9	19600	19600
10	10	36500	36500
11	11	8500	89000
12	12	80500	89000
13	13	169500	169500
14	14	8950	8950

Figure 15.1: *A simple correlated subquery*

How does it work

This query is created from an outer query and an inner query, like many of the examples illustrated in the previous three chapters. Nonetheless, the given example has one important difference. The two queries are not independent of each other; they are linked. More specifically, they both contain the **`SalesID`** field, and this field is used in the **`WHERE`** clause of the subquery to connect the inner and outer queries. The following SQL handles this:

```
WHERE SalesId = SD.SalesId
```

Once the subquery is *connected* to the outer query (or once it becomes a correlated subquery), the working of the whole query alters radically. The outer query now depends on the inner query, and the inner query is run once for each record in the outer query, which is shown in *Figure 15.2*:

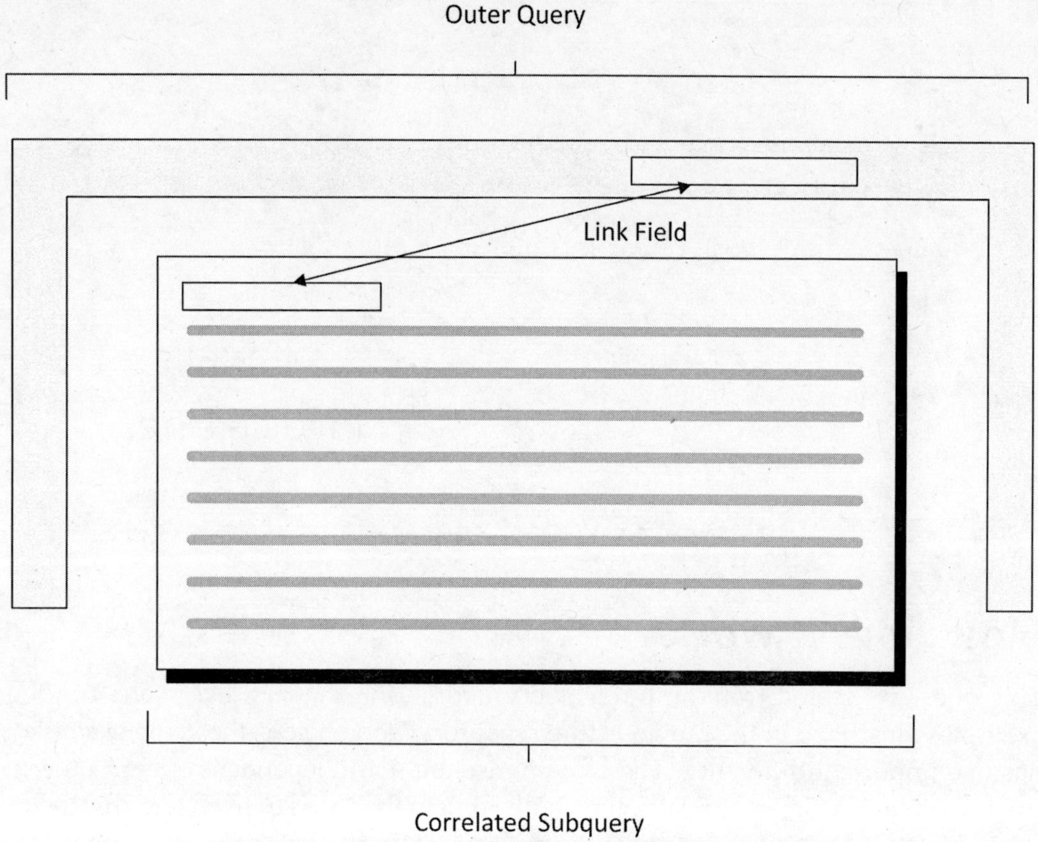

Figure 15.2: The concept of a correlated subquery

Figure 15.2 illustrates how the inner and outer queries relate to one another.

- **The outer query**: Returns the first record that it finds from the **`SalesDetails`** table (which is the list of line items in every invoice) and passes a link field (**`SalesID`**) to the correlated subquery (the inner query).
- **The inner query**: Reads the **`Sales`** table (the invoice header table) and returns the total sales price only for records containing the **`SalesID`** passed in from the outer query.

This is a simple example of the use of correlated queries. This chapter explains the application of correlated subqueries to deliver the kinds of analysis that necessitates this kind of SQL.

Tricks and traps

The following are some fundamental points to keep in mind when creating correlated subqueries:

- You cannot execute the correlated subquery independent of the outer query because the correlated subquery depends on the outer query in its **WHERE** clause. You can, however, remove the **WHERE** clause from the correlated subquery and then execute the SQL for the inner query.
- Any values returned from a correlated subquery *must* be aggregated to return only a single value for each correlated record. This is why the **TotalSalePrice** column is wrapped in a **SUM()** function in the correlated subquery.

Correlated subqueries to display percentages of a specific total

When negotiating each sale, the sales director wants to see a history of all previous sales for every client and the percentage of the total value of vehicles sold to the client that each individual sale represents. According to her, this will be helpful in developing a discount strategy. The following piece of SQL uses a correlated subquery to deliver this insight:

```
SELECT
 CS.CustomerName
,SA.INVOICENUMBER
,SD.SalePrice
,SD.SalePrice
/
(
SELECT     SUM(SDC.SalePrice)
FROM       SalesDetails SDC
INNER JOIN Sales SAC
           ON SDC.SalesID = SAC.SalesID
INNER JOIN  Customer CSC
           ON SAC.CustomerID = CSC.CustomerID
WHERE      SAC.CustomerID = CS.CustomerID
) * 100 AS PercentSalesPerCustomer
```

```
FROM        SalesDetails SD

INNER JOIN  Sales SA

            ON SD.SalesID = SA.SalesID

INNER JOIN  Customer CS

            ON SA.CustomerID = CS.CustomerID

ORDER BY    CS.CustomerName;
```

Running this piece of SQL displays the percentage of each sale for each client relative to the total sales for the client, as shown in *Figure 15.3*. If you add up the percentage sales records for each client, you will see that they equate to 100% per client:

	CustomerName	INVOICENUMBER	SalePrice	PercentSalesPerCustomer
1	Alex McWhirter	GBPGB308	17850	100
2	Alexei Tolstoi	GBPGB017	22990	4.40852173579550 9
3	Alexei Tolstoi	GBPGB023	22600	4.3337360256189
4	Alexei Tolstoi	GBPGB026	69500	13.327197069934227
5	Alexei Tolstoi	GBPGB046	39500	7.57445013327197
6	Alexei Tolstoi	GBPGB046	9950	1.907994400659648

***Figure 15.3:** Using a correlated subquery to calculate percentages of a subset*

How does it work

This query extends the correlated subquery principle in the previous example to more complex datasets. More specifically, the code consists of the following:

- **An outer query**: It joins the **`Sales`**, **`SalesDetails`**, and **`Customer`** tables to return the details (the customer name and sale amount) for every sale made by the company.
- **A correlated subquery**: It calculates the total sales per customer. This uses the same tables as the outer query (**`Sales`**, **`SalesDetails`**, and **`Customer`**); however, it groups the data by the customer to give the total sales for each customer. You can see this in the following part of the SQL for this section:

  ```
  WHERE SAC.CustomerID = CS.CustomerID
  ```

The correlated subquery is joined to the outer query by the **`CustomerID`** field, so the total returned is only for the customer from the outer list and not for the whole **`SalesDetails`** table.

The overall query essentially works as a whole. When each record of the outer query is returned, the correlated subquery calculates the individual sales only for the relevant customer. This figure is then used in the percentage calculation of the sales ratio for this particular sale.

Tricks and traps

There is one point to note as follows:

- Because the correlated subquery is linked to the outer query, you cannot just select the SQL for the subquery and run it. Should you wish to test the subquery, it is advised to copy the correlated subquery into a new query window and replace the reference to the outer query (**`CS.CustomerID`** in this example) with a real customer ID. Indeed, it might be helpful to develop and test a correlated subquery in this way before adding it to the outer query. In this example, a test case could be to use a real customer ID in the correlated subquery, like the following:

  ```
  WHERE SAC.CustomerID = 90
  ```

Comparing datasets using a correlated subquery

Once again, the finance director is determined to reduce the cost of repairs. This time he has asked you to produce a list of vehicle repair costs that are 50% higher than the average for each make. The following code lets you deliver the following:

```
SELECT     MKX.MakeName, STX.RepairsCost, STX.StockCode

FROM       Make AS MKX INNER JOIN Model AS MDX

           ON MKX.MakeID = MDX.MakeID

INNER JOIN Stock AS STX ON STX.ModelID = MDX.ModelID

INNER JOIN SalesDetails SDX ON STX.StockCode = SDX.StockID

WHERE      STX.RepairsCost >

               (

                SELECT     AVG(ST.RepairsCost) AS AvgRepairCost

                FROM       Make AS MK

                INNER JOIN Model AS MD

                           ON MK.MakeID = MD.MakeID
```

```
                INNER JOIN Stock AS ST
                           ON ST.ModelID = MD.ModelID
                WHERE     MK.MakeName = MKX.MakeName
                ) * 1.5;
```

Running the preceding query gives the results shown in *Figure 15.4*:

	MakeName	RepairsCost	StockCode
1	Ferrari	9250	15108517-AD0C-4FF2-A7D4-57679C374A68
2	Ferrari	9250	98299E86-0B98-42D8-A549-37D89435B4E3
3	Ferrari	9250	66C9034C-23A3-44F1-B946-2DDA65E684D8
4	Ferrari	9250	A326183E-7D45-4CF2-A353-7177A3EAB71F
5	Ferrari	9250	20041639-9549-415A-AEC2-7159352E8CB7
6	Ferrari	9250	5D11974B-326C-44C5-BA1D-57968CAB0DEE

Figure 15.4: *A correlated query used for comparison*

How does it work

Finding exceptions, especially cost exceptions, is a core requirement in data analysis. Correlated subqueries are especially useful to compare values to an aggregated value, such as an average for a particular category of items. This query begins by calculating the average repair cost for all vehicles in stock and then multiplying this figure by 150%(defined in the SQL as a value of 1.5). However, since it is a correlated subquery where the inner and outer queries are linked using the **MakeName** field, this average is calculated for every record in the outer query. You can see this in the following single line of SQL that connects the inner and outer queries:

```
WHERE MK.MakeName = MKX.MakeName
```

As a result, the repair cost is evaluated not for all vehicles in stock but as the average for each make of vehicle in stock. This changes the calculation completely. Now, for each record in the outer query, the average repair cost is only calculated relative to that particular make of car. If the repair cost for a car is over 1.5 times the average repair cost for that make, then the query output shows the repair cost for the car.

Tricks and traps

Exception reporting can prove complex in practice. Keep the following points in mind for better results:

- The filter effect of a correlated subquery is not limited to finding records that are (or are not) in a dataset, as was the case with the three previous examples. You can use a correlated subquery to compare values using all the traditional comparison operators like greater than (>), less than (<), greater than or equal to (>=), less than or equal to (<=), or not equal to (<>). The given example only shows how to compare using less than, but all the others are available if required for analysis.
- You are also not limited to comparing results to an average. You can easily access the **`MAX()`** or **`MIN()`** functions to find records that are close to the upper and lower limits of a dataset for a specific element.
- In this example, the two queries (inner and outer) use very similar datasets. This is not always the case with correlated subqueries. It can, however, be a frequent occurrence.
- In a correlated subquery, it is vital to create individual aliases for any tables that are used in both the inner and outer tables of the query. We distinguished the tables by adding an **`X`** for each outer query table alias because many of the same tables are used in both the outer query and the correlated subquery.
- Using the same aliases for the inner and outer queries will cause the whole query to fail.

Avoid correlated subqueries in certain cases

Correlated subqueries can be an incredibly useful tool for mixing data from two or more datasets. However, it is an often-overused technique and can complicate otherwise simple SQL solutions.

Before you conclude that a correlated subquery is the only answer to a particular problem, it is advised to decipher if simple table joins or derived tables can help you achieve your objectives. If your requirement boils down one way or another to a classic **`WHERE`** query, then it can be easier to avoid a subquery.

Equally, if the challenge does not require different levels of aggregation between the outer query and the correlated subquery, then you can apply a series of table joins and a WHERE clause.

This is not to say that any code that works is to be avoided. However, a more *classic* SQL approach can often help in both the analysis of needs and faster, easier delivery of a solution.

Duplicating the output of a correlated subquery in the query results

The finance director was pleased with the data received; however, he now wants the average repair cost per make to appear in the resulting data while keeping the filter on the average repair cost per vehicle you set up previously.

If you want to ensure the functioning of the query, the best way to find out is to display the average repair cost per make in the output. This means you need to duplicate the correlated subquery that you use in the **WHERE** clause in the actual **SELECT** clause of the query. If you do this, the code looks like the following:

```
SELECT     MKX.MakeName, STX.RepairsCost, STX.StockCode
,(
    SELECT     AVG(ST.RepairsCost) AS AvgRepairCost
    FROM       Make AS MK
    INNER JOIN Model AS MD
               ON MK.MakeID = MD.MakeID
    INNER JOIN Stock AS ST
               ON ST.ModelID = MD.ModelID
    WHERE     MK.MakeName = MKX.MakeName
 ) AS MakeAvgRepairCost
FROM       Make AS MKX
INNER JOIN Model AS MDX
           ON MKX.MakeID = MDX.MakeID
INNER JOIN Stock AS STX ON STX.ModelID = MDX.ModelID
INNER JOIN SalesDetails SDX ON STX.StockCode = SDX.StockID
WHERE      STX.RepairsCost >
                (
                 SELECT     AVG(ST.RepairsCost) AS AvgRepairCost
                 FROM       Make AS MK
```

```
INNER JOIN Model AS MD
           ON MK.MakeID = MD.MakeID
INNER JOIN Stock AS ST
           ON ST.ModelID = MD.ModelID
 WHERE     MK.MakeName = MKX.MakeName
) * 1.5;
```

The output looks as shown in *Figure 15.5*:

	MakeName	RepairsCost	StockCode	MakeAvgRepairCost
1	Ferrari	9250	15108517-AD0C-4FF2-A7D4-57679C374A68	4645
2	Ferrari	9250	98299E86-0B98-42D8-A549-37D89435B4E3	4645
3	Ferrari	9250	66C9034C-23A3-44F1-B946-2DDA65E684D8	4645
4	Ferrari	9250	A326183E-7D45-4CF2-A353-7177A3EAB71F	4645
5	Ferrari	9250	20041639-9549-415A-AEC2-7159352E8CB7	4645
6	Ferrari	9250	5D11974B-326C-44C5-BA1D-57968CAB0DEE	4645

Figure 15.5: *Using a correlated query in two parts of a query*

How does it work

This query extends the SQL from the previous section by repeating the entire content of the subquery in the main query's **`SELECT`** clause. The identical correlated subqueries are linked to the outer query using the **`MakeName`** field.

Using correlated subqueries to filter data on an aggregate value

No firm wants to spend extensive money when buying goods. This implies that you must analyze purchases that exceed certain calculated thresholds. As the finance director is homing in on purchasing costs as a part of his drive to control spending, he wants you to create a report that shows all models of cars where the maximum purchase cost is more than one and a half times the average purchase price for that model. The following SQL is an example of how to do this:

```
SELECT     MKX.MakeName, MDX.ModelName
FROM       Make AS MKX
           INNER JOIN Model AS MDX ON MKX.MakeID = MDX.MakeID
```

```
          INNER JOIN Stock AS STX ON STX.ModelID = MDX.ModelID
GROUP BY  MKX.MakeName, MDX.ModelName
HAVING    MAX(STX.Cost) >=
                (
                 SELECT       AVG(ST.Cost) * 1.5 AS AvgCostPerModel
                 FROM         Make AS MK
                 INNER JOIN Model AS MD
                              ON MK.MakeID = MD.MakeID
                 INNER JOIN Stock AS ST
                              ON ST.ModelID = MD.ModelID
                 WHERE        MD.ModelName = MDX.ModelName
                              AND MK.MakeName = MKX. MakeName
                 );
```

Running the preceding query gives the results shown in *Figure 15.6*:

	MakeName	ModelName
1	Aston Martin	DB6
2	Aston Martin	DB2
3	Jaguar	Mark X
4	Porsche	911
5	Jaguar	XK150
6	Aston Martin	DB9

***Figure 15.6:** Using a correlated subquery in the HAVING clause of the outer query*

How does it work

Let us begin by looking at the outer query in this example.

The outer query generates a list of vehicle makes and models based on the **`Make`**, **`Model`**, and **`Stock`** tables. It uses a **`GROUP BY`** to make this into an aggregate list where the make and model names only appear once. This can be seen in the following part of the query:

```
SELECT     MKX.MakeName, MDX.ModelName

FROM       Make AS MKX

           INNER JOIN Model AS MDX ON MKX.MakeID = MDX.MakeID

           INNER JOIN Stock AS STX ON STX.ModelID = MDX.ModelID

GROUP BY   MKX.MakeName, MDX.ModelName
```

Then, the outer query gets interesting. As it is an aggregate query, it can have a **HAVING** clause (which filters data at the level of the aggregation, not at the level of individual records). It applies a **HAVING** clause to say *only if the maximum cost for any make and model is greater than or equal to 150% of the average cost for this make and model.* The subquery in the **HAVING** clause is a correlated subquery.

It is the correlated subquery that calculates 150% of the average cost. Yet again, because this is a correlated subquery, it is filtered on data passed in from the outer query (the make and model). The following part of the query handles this:

```
WHERE      MD.ModelName = MDX.ModelName

           AND MK.MakeName = MKX. MakeName
```

The subquery calculates the average cost for a specific make and model, then multiplies it by 1.5. This result is, in turn, passed back up to the outer query so it can be compared to the greatest vehicle cost for each make and model combination. Finally, the comparison operator (>=, or greater than or equal to) allows only those records that meet the filter criterion to pass through into the final output. That is, only makes and models are shown if any car of this type costs more than one and a half times the average for that particular car.

Tricks and traps

The following are a few points to take away from this section:

- Correlated subqueries are, at the core, a filtering mechanism, so you need to analyze the kind of filter required. If you are filtering data row by row, then you will probably use the correlated subquery in the **WHERE** clause. If, however, you are filtering records to compare a value with an aggregate result (such as the maximum cost for a vehicle model here), then you will almost inevitably want to apply the correlated subquery to the **HAVING** clause of the outer query.

- If the outer query is an aggregation query, then you can use any of the classic aggregation functions—**SUM()**, **AVG()**, **MIN()**, or **MAX()**, for instance, in the **HAVING** clause. This allows you to compare a result from the subquery to the total, the average, the highest, or the lowest aggregate value for a specific data group.
- Correlated queries can be joined to the outer query on several fields—as you can see in this example.

What makes a query correlated

A correlated query is not one query but two interdependent queries. The inner query is filtered on a field that it shares or can link to in the outer query. The outer query filters its results based on the calculation carried out by the inner query.

Each query uses something shared with the other query as a filter. Each record in the outer query will pass a value into the subquery (often for filtering). The outer query will only return rows that match the results of the inner query.

This mutual interdependence can appear complicated at first. In practice, however, it opens up whole vistas of analysis that would be difficult any other way.

Using correlated subqueries to detect if records exist

Know your customer is the mantra that resounds throughout businesses worldwide. For many firms, however, the refrain could just as well be *known who your customer is*. The following SQL shows you how to create a list of all the active clients of Prestige Cars in 2017:

```
SELECT DISTINCT    CU.CustomerName
FROM               Customer CU
WHERE              EXISTS
                   (
                    SELECT    *
                    FROM      Sales SA
                    WHERE     SA.CustomerID = CU.CustomerID
                              AND YEAR(SA.SaleDate) = 2017
```

```
                )
ORDER BY        CU.CustomerName;
```

The list in *Figure 15.7* shows only the customers that have bought a vehicle from *Prestige Cars* in a specific year (2017) in this example. Any potential customer in the **Customer** table who did not buy a car in 2017 is not displayed:

	CustomerName
1	Alicia Almodovar
2	Antonio Maura
3	Autos Sportivos
4	Birmingham Executive Prestige Vehicles
5	Capots Reluisants S.A.
6	Casseroles Chromes

Figure 15.7: A simple correlated subquery using EXISTS

How does it work

Correlated subqueries are not just for calculations. They can also be very useful in determining whether data should be included in a result set. In practice, it implies that you need to apply the **EXISTS** keyword to the query. When you use this new keyword, the outer query checks to see if any records exist for this specific **CustomerID**. If it does, then the output is the customer's name. The flip side to this is that if no records exist, then data for this customer is not displayed.

This means that *if* the correlated subquery contains any records for this particular **CustomerID**, then the customer's name is returned by the outer query. This is because the filter in the outer query says *where a record exists in the inner query*. If there is no corresponding record in the correlated subquery, then no customer name is output. This way, the query as a whole only returns data from one dataset when a criterion applied to a second set of data is met.

Tricks and traps

When using correlated subqueries, one must be aware of the following points:

- Correlated subqueries depend on a link existing between the inner and outer queries, so if you can use a JOIN to link tables in a query, then you can use the same tables in a correlated subquery.
- When you use the **EXISTS** keyword, you are looking simply for the existence of a record in the subquery. This means that you can make the **SELECT** clause of the correlated subquery simple without specifying any particular column names. In this case, no aggregation is required either. After all, column names in the subquery will not be used in this type of correlated subquery since you are only confirming the existence of the records.
- You have already seen queries in the previous two chapters that compare data in tables. However, the use of correlated subqueries is specifically tailored to tables that can be joined.

Using a correlated subquery to exclude data

.The company finance director wants to know which vehicles have not yet been sold and are paralyzing valuable cash in the parking lot as no business wants to carry excess stock. The following SQL code shows you how to produce this list:

```
SELECT     MakeName || ', ' || ModelName AS VehicleInStock, ST.STOCKCODE
FROM       Make AS MK
INNER JOIN Model AS MD ON MK.MakeID = MD.MakeID
INNER JOIN Stock AS ST ON ST.ModelID = MD.ModelID
WHERE      NOT EXISTS
                (SELECT *
                 FROM    SalesDetails SD
                 WHERE   ST.StockCode = SD.StockID);
```

Running the preceding query gives the results shown in *Figure 15.8*. You can see all the results if you scroll down this list:

	VehicleInStock	STOCKCODE
1	Ferrari, Testarossa	8BD326B3-8DE8-4DC9-9F96-FD132C5E1BF2
2	Ferrari, Testarossa	DE3096AD-76F9-4AAF-B2E1-49FA8E2C377F
3	Ferrari, 355	C82D133F-3442-464B-A16A-D5419A9E1CDF
4	Ferrari, 308	FBF39066-2C13-469D-B913-EBCF22CCFD63
5	Ferrari, Dino	F187F74F-3909-4291-A15B-F793AB88DE3B
6	Ferrari, 360	579AD98F-B7A5-456A-8F17-5B77A5479767

Figure 15.8: *A correlated subquery using NOT EXISTS*

How does it work

Just as you may need to know when data exists (like in the previous example), there could be cases when you need to find out when data is not present in related tables. In the *Prestige Cars* data model, the **`Stock`** table contains all the vehicles ever bought. The **`SalesDetails`** table contains all the vehicles ever sold. A correlated subquery can compare the data in one table with the data in the other.

When you want to run this kind of analysis, it is probably easier to use the table that contains the most data as the outer query and the table that contains a limited set of data as the correlated (or inner) subquery. The preceding code does exactly the same:

- **The outer query**: Joins the **`Make`**, **`Model`**, and **`Stock`** tables so that the required fields can be output—as well as ensuring access to a field that can be shared with the subquery (the **`StockCode`** field in this example).
- **The inner query**: Selects all the data from the **`SalesDetails`** table, but as this is a correlated subquery, it only finds records where the **`StockID`** matches the **`StockCode`** of the outer query.

Once again, the subquery is rerun for every record that the outer query finds. If there is a match on the **`StockCode`**/**`StockID`** fields, then the **`WHERE`** clause of the outer query comes into play. This filter says *tell me if there is not a match* which is the colloquial way of saying **`WHERE NOT EXISTS`**. If the two tables do not match a record in the outer query, this record is returned by the query.

Tricks and traps

Practice is required to successfully use the **`NOT EXISTS`** function. When you are applying this concept to your queries, be sure to remember the following key points:

- A correlated subquery that uses **`NOT EXISTS`** is also only looking for the existence of data in the subquery; the actual fields selected by the subquery are irrelevant.
- A correlated subquery like this can run much more slowly than a simpler query does. It is precisely because the inner query has to run once for every record in the outer query. However, you need to be aware that a query like this can take quite a while to run for a large dataset.

Conclusion

This chapter introduced you to a new tool to extend your SQL skillset, correlated subqueries. Correlated subqueries allow the linking of subqueries to main queries and filter the data in the outer query by checking every record that it contains against the result of a subquery.

Core knowledge learned in this chapter

The keywords and concepts that you have seen in this chapter are as follows:

Concept	Description
Correlated subqueries	Correlated subqueries let you link subqueries to main queries and filter the data in the outer query by checking every record that it contains against the result of a subquery.
`EXISTS`	This keyword tests for the existence of a record in a subquery that is linked to the outer query.
`NOT EXISTS`	This keyword tests for the absence of a record in a subquery that is linked to the outer query.

Join our book's Discord space

Join the book's Discord Workspace for Latest updates, Offers, Tech happenings around the world, New Release and Sessions with the Authors:

https://discord.bpbonline.com

CHAPTER 16
Dataset Manipulation

Introduction

Sometimes the data you use may not be in a single table but spread across a series of tables with identical structures. Moreover, as *m*ost data analysis is comparative, you may want to compare one specific set of data with another, possibly a separate dataset, and isolate any differences. You can accomplish this by seeing if two sets of data overlap, for instance. Yet another potential requirement could be isolating the data that exists in one dataset but not in another. These challenges involve dataset manipulation.

Structure

In this chapter, we will cover the following topics:

- Read data from multiple identical tables using the **UNION** operator
- Isolate identical data in multiple tables using the **INTERSECT** operator
- Isolating nonidentical records using the **EXCEPT** operator
- Joining multiple identical tables in a subquery

Objectives

The chapter dives deeper into the domain of comparative analysis of data using Databricks. It builds on the techniques mentioned in the previous chapters and teaches you how to mix and match datasets in order to delve deep into the information they contain.

More specifically, this chapter elaborates on how to:

- Read data from several identically structured tables simultaneously.
- Create separate subsets of data to be used for comparison purposes.
- Compare the data in two tables and only display data that is common to both tables.
- Compare the data in two tables and only display data that is in one table but not the other.

Read data from multiple identical tables using the UNION operator

Data comes in a multitude of shapes and forms and is not always available as a relational set of tables that can be joined. Sometimes you may have to query data from two or more tables that have identical structures, meaning each table contains a slice of a total dataset. For instance, imagine you have been asked to look at three tables of sales information, one for sales in each of the years 2015, 2016, and 2017. All three tables contain the same columns of data in the same order.

The SQL to query the three tables at once looks like the following:

```
SELECT  MakeName, ModelName, CustomerName, CountryName
        ,Cost, RepairsCost, PartsCost, TransportInCost
        ,SalePrice, SaleDate
FROM    Sales2015
UNION
SELECT  MakeName, ModelName, CustomerName, CountryName
        ,Cost, RepairsCost, PartsCost, TransportInCost
        ,SalePrice, SaleDate
FROM    Sales2016
```

```
UNION

SELECT  MakeName, ModelName, CustomerName, CountryName
        ,Cost, RepairsCost, PartsCost, TransportInCost
        ,SalePrice, SaleDate

FROM    Sales2017;
```

Running the preceding query gives the results as shown in *Figure 16.1*. As you can see, the data is returned for any of the required three years, whereas each source table only contains data for a single year:

	MakeName	ModelName	CustomerName	CountryName	Cost	RepairsCost	PartsCost	TransportInCost	SalePrice	SaleDate
21	Aston Martin	DB5	Birmingham Executive Prestige Vehicles	United Kingdom	39600	2500	1500	550	49500	2015-03-24T12:00:00.000+0000
22	Aston Martin	DB6	Alexei Tolstoi	United Kingdom	55600	1490	1500	750	69500	2015-12-01T12:00:00.000+0000
23	Ferrari	Testarossa	Magic Motors	United Kingdom	52000	2175	1500	750	65000	2015-01-02T12:00:00.000+0000
24	Porsche	924	Posh Vehicles Ltd	United Kingdom	7160	360	750	150	8950	2015-09-15T12:00:00.000+0000
25	Porsche	911	Birmingham Executive Prestige Vehicles	United Kingdom	15600	660	500	150	19500	2015-02-03T12:00:00.000+0000
26	Porsche	911	Convertible Dreams	United Kingdom	18360	500	750	150	22950	2015-11-10T12:00:00.000+0000
27	Ferrari	355	Snazzy Roadsters	United Kingdom	176000	5500	2200	1950	220000	2015-01-25T12:00:00.000+0000
28	Triumph	TR4	Theo Kowalski	United States	4400	500	750	150	5500	2015-06-02T12:00:00.000+0000
29	Triumph	TR6	Prestissimo!	Italy	7960	500	750	150	9950	2016-06-26T12:00:00.000+0000
30	Porsche	924	King Leer Cars	United Kingdom	7960	500	750	150	9950	2016-09-18T12:00:00.000+0000
31	Aston Martin	Virage	Convertible Dreams	United Kingdom	36720	500	500	550	45900	2016-08-22T12:00:00.000+0000
32	Triumph	TR7	Honest Pete Motors	United Kingdom	7600	500	750	150	9500	2016-12-02T12:00:00.000+0000

Figure 16.1: *Joining data from multiple identically structured queries using the UNION operator*

How does it work

SQL lets users read data from multiple tables at once if the structure of the queries is identical. This operation takes place by writing a **`SELECT`** query for each table and then by amalgamating the queries using the **`UNION`** operator.

Clearly, using **`UNION`** to merge the data from several tables is only useful if you have a database that contains identically structured tables. This technique is extremely useful in practice because this is often the case for data analysis and reporting (where the original, relational data is kept separate) or when dealing with data sent from outside suppliers.

In the given example, you joined the three tables sequentially (or *vertically*) rather than *horizontally*, as done for many queries so far in the book. In other words, you have added the contents of one table to the contents of another. *Figure 16.2* conceptually illustrates the process:

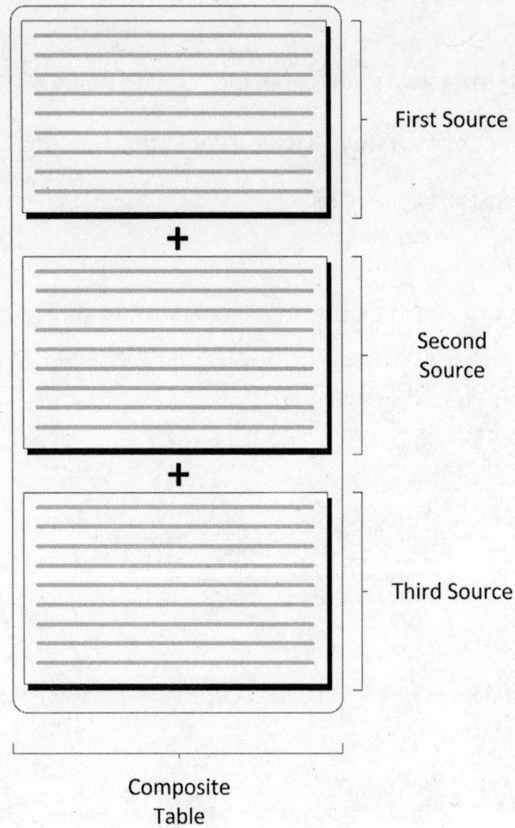

Figure 16.2: Compiling a dataset from multiple identical tables

Tricks and traps

The **UNION** operator requires you to remember the following points:

- You can use aliases to rename the columns in a **UNION** query just as you can in an SQL query; however, you only need to add aliases to the first query in the series, that is, the query for 2015 sales, in this example. The other queries use the aliases that you applied to the topmost query. After all, a column can only have one name, so the name is taken from the topmost query.
- In a **UNION** query, it is vital that you select the columns from each of the separate queries *in the same order*.

If the underlying tables do not contain identical columns in the same order, you can replace the name of any columns that are missing from a table with **NULL** in the **SELECT** statement. For instance, if the table **Sales2016** does not contain a **TransportInCost** field, you can write the following SQL, and the query over the three tables will still work:

```
SELECT MakeName, ModelName, CustomerName, CountryName, Cost, RepairsCost,
PartsCost, NULL, SalePrice, SaleDate

FROM    Sales2015

UNION

SELECT MakeName, ModelName, CustomerName, CountryName ,Cost, RepairsCost,
PartsCost, TransportInCost, SalePrice, SaleDate

FROM    Sales2016

UNION

SELECT MakeName, ModelName, CustomerName, CountryName, Cost, RepairsCost,
PartsCost, TransportInCost, SalePrice, SaleDate

FROM    Sales2017;
```

Isolate identical data in multiple tables using the INTERSECT operator

The sales director needs to compare elements that are similar across separate time periods. Her exact requirement is to find all the makes bought this year that were also bought the previous year. The following query does this using the separate tables of yearly sales that you saw in the previous section:

```
SELECT     MK.MakeName

FROM       Make AS MK

INNER JOIN Model AS MD ON MK.MakeID = MD.MakeID

INNER JOIN Stock AS ST ON ST.ModelID = MD.ModelID

WHERE      YEAR(ST.DateBought) = 2015

INTERSECT

SELECT     MK.MakeName

FROM       Make AS MK

INNER JOIN Model AS MD ON MK.MakeID = MD.MakeID

INNER JOIN Stock AS ST ON ST.ModelID = MD.ModelID

WHERE      YEAR(ST.DateBought) = 2016;
```

Running the preceding query gives the results as shown in *Figure 16.3*.

	MakeName
1	Jaguar
2	Alfa Romeo
3	Ferrari
4	Porsche
5	Triumph
6	Bentley
7	Aston Martin

***Figure 16.3:** Using the INTERSECT operator*

How does it work

In this query, you have two separate queries, which are given as follows:

- **The first**: Joins the **`Stock`**, **`Make`**, and **`Model`** tables and adds only the **`MakeName`** field to the **`SELECT`** clause. This query then filters the results so that only vehicles bought in 2015 are returned.
- **The second**: Duplicates the first query, but it sets the year to 2016.

Combining these two queries with the **`INTERSECT`** operator runs both queries and identifies the results common to both. Only these shared results are finally output. The Venn diagram in *Figure 16.4* illustrates how an **`INTERSECT`** query works:

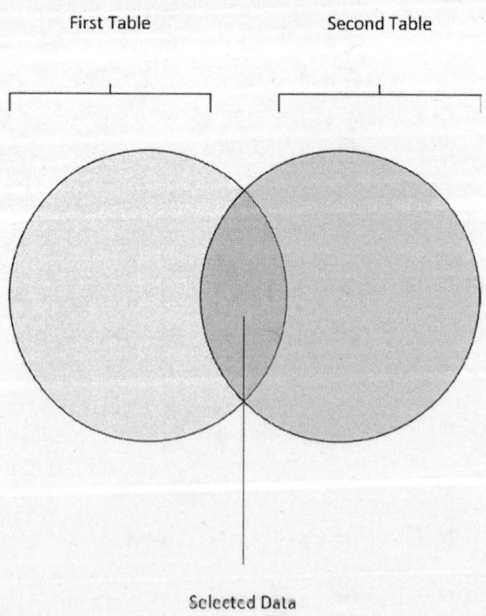

***Figure 16.4:** How an INTERSECT query works*

Tricks and traps

The following are several key points to note with an operator as powerful as **INTERSECT**:

- The two queries in this example are not, technically, subqueries because they are both on the same *level*. Consequently, they do not have to be placed inside parentheses. However, they are completely separate datasets, like subqueries.
- You can see that an **INTERSECT** query automatically removes any duplicates in the final result. If you run each query separately, you see that many examples of each make are sold in either of the two years, as shown in *Figure 16.5*. However, the final result removes all duplicates from the output.

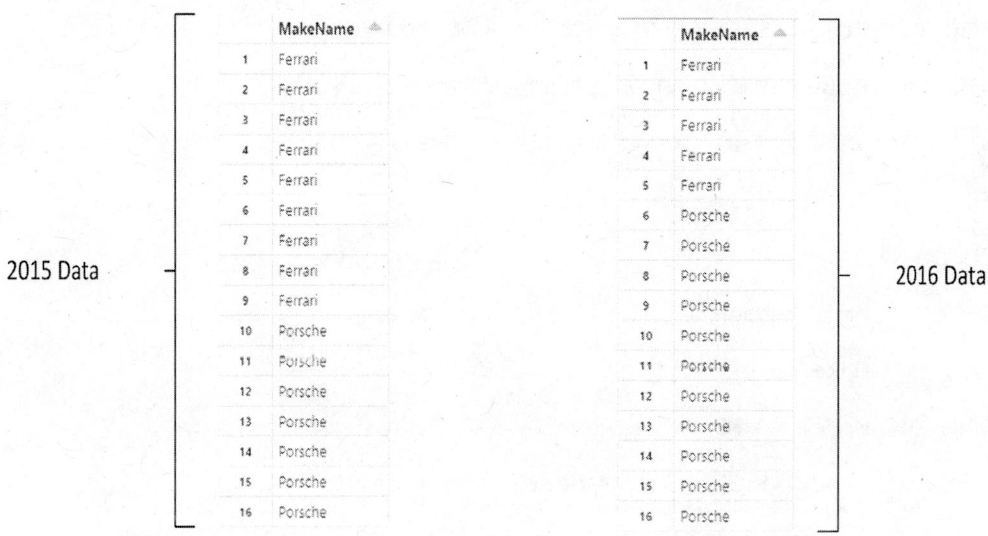

Figure 16.5: Duplicate data before it is removed using the INTERSECT operator

- An **INTERSECT** query must have the same fields in the same order in the **SELECT** clause. If this is not the case, it does not return the correct result or, (in most cases) any result at all. In all other respects, queries can be completely different, as long as they return the datasets that you want to compare.
- You are not limited to just two queries in an **INTERSECT** query. You can add multiple queries, all linked with the **INTERSECT** keyword if needed.
- You do not have to select all the fields in each table to isolate data; however, any fields that you do select must be identical in all the source tables if the record is to be returned.

Isolating nonidentical records using the EXCEPT operator

Sometimes, it is not the overlap of data that is significant but the data that is not shared between two datasets. A practical example of this is when the CEO requests a list of all the vehicle models sold this year but not in the previous year. The following SQL shows you how to isolate such a result:

```
SELECT     MK.MakeName || ' ' || MD.ModelName AS MakeModel
FROM       Make AS MK
INNER JOIN Model AS MD ON MK.MakeID = MD.MakeID
INNER JOIN Stock AS ST ON ST.ModelID = MD.ModelID
INNER JOIN SalesDetails SD ON ST.StockCode = SD.StockID
INNER JOIN Sales AS SA ON SA.SalesID = SD.SalesID
WHERE      YEAR(SA.SaleDate) = 2015
EXCEPT
SELECT     MK.MakeName || ' ' || MD.ModelName
FROM       Make AS MK
INNER JOIN Model AS MD ON MK.MakeID = MD.MakeID
INNER JOIN Stock AS ST ON ST.ModelID = MD.ModelID
INNER JOIN SalesDetails SD ON ST.StockCode = SD.StockID
INNER JOIN Sales AS SA ON SA.SalesID = SD.SalesID
WHERE      YEAR(SA.SaleDate) = 2016;
```

Running the preceding query gives the results as shown in *Figure 16.6*.

	MakeModel
1	Mercedes 280SL

Figure 16.6: *Using the EXCEPT operator to isolate data*

How does it work

In certain respects, this query is similar to the queries in the two previous examples. Once again, you have multiple queries that output identical field sets in the same order. This time, however, the **EXCEPT** operator is used to link the datasets returned by the individual queries.

This operator finds all the elements (the make and model of vehicles sold in a specific year) and then compares these rows with the make and model of vehicles sold the following year. Any models of cars that are present in both datasets *are* left out of the final result. This way, you can see which cars were sold in 2015 but not in 2016.

Figure 16.7 conceptually illustrates the working of this approach:

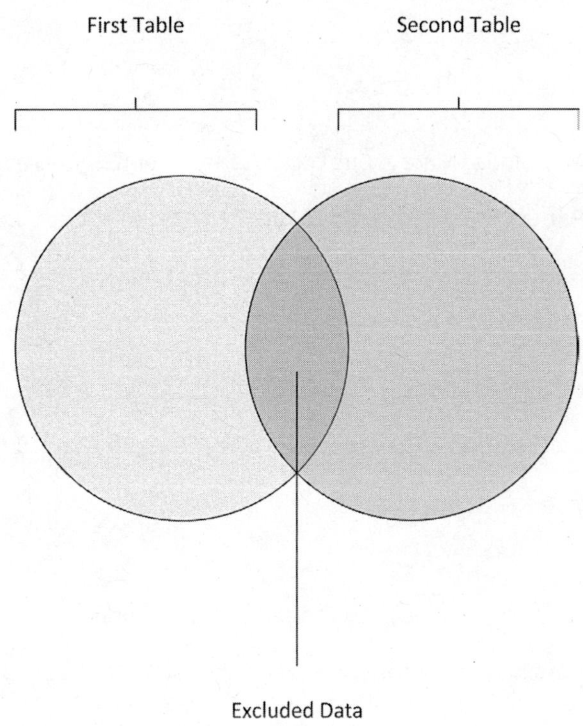

***Figure 16.7:** Excluding the shared items from two sets of data*

Tricks and traps

Keep in mind the following point:

- The two queries used in this example are, once again, entirely separate. Indeed, they must be different for the query to work properly. Consequently, each query has its own **WHERE** clause, and this is what allows you to specify completely different datasets, even if the two queries are otherwise identical.

Joining multiple identical tables in a subquery

The CEO has returned to the sales data that you joined together in the first section of this chapter and is now requesting that you produce a simple list of makes and models from all three tables sold to German clients.

After a little thought, you adapt the query used previously to satisfy her request. The SQL looks like the following:

```
SELECT  MakeName, ModelName
FROM
(
   SELECT  MakeName, ModelName, CustomerName, CountryName, Cost
   ,RepairsCost, PartsCost, TransportInCost, SalePrice, SaleDate
   FROM    Sales2015
   UNION
   SELECT  MakeName, ModelName, CustomerName, CountryName, Cost
   ,RepairsCost, PartsCost, TransportInCost, SalePrice, SaleDate
   FROM    Sales2016
   UNION
   SELECT  MakeName, ModelName, CustomerName, CountryName, Cost
   ,RepairsCost, PartsCost, TransportInCost, SalePrice, SaleDate
   FROM    Sales2017
) SQ
WHERE   CountryName = 'Germany';
```

Running the preceding code produces the output as shown in *Figure 16.8*:

	MakeName	ModelName
1	Porsche	924
2	Alfa Romeo	Giulia
3	Bentley	Flying Spur
4	Aston Martin	Rapide
5	Ferrari	360
6	Lamborghini	Diabolo

Figure 16.8: *Using a derived query with tables joined using the UNION operator*

How does it work

The ability of SQL to deliver the output from multiple identical tables is certainly useful on many occasions; however, you need a way to make the resulting data easy to filter. Moreover, undoubtedly, there will be times when you want to select only some of the columns that each table contains.

This is the perfect opportunity for wrapping the **`UNION`** query inside an outer query and treating the **`UNION`** query as a derived table. The derived table is enclosed in parentheses and aliased as **`SQ`** in this example. This simple technique allows you to select only the required fields. Then, filter the data using a single **`WHERE`** clause and even group the data if you so choose.

Tricks and traps

You should keep a note of the following points:

- It is perfectly possible to apply the same **`SELECT`** and **`WHERE`** clauses to each query that is used in a **`UNION`** query. However, this can be both more laborious and more prone to error than making the **`UNION`** query into a derived table and filtering on the combined data.
- Extending a query to include a derived table is a great example of code reuse, where just a small tweak can make SQL the previously created even more applicable. Therefore, developers must save the code snippets in case they turn out to be important later.

Conclusion

The chapter helps readers to better understand how data analysis in Databricks depends on using datasets correctly. Furthermore, filtering separate datasets individually to effect comparisons over time as well as combining multiple tables to create a single result set, is explained.

The chapter concludes with the extraction of overlapping data from two tables. Furthermore, readers discover how to do the opposite and return data that is present in one table but not in another.

Core knowledge learned in this chapter

The concepts that you have seen in this chapter are as follows:

Concept	Description
`UNION`	This operator lets you pull data from multiple tables or views that are identical in structure and removes duplicates.
`UNION ALL`	This operator lets you pull data from multiple tables or views that are identical in structure and preserves duplicates.
`INTERSECT`	This operator returns a subset of data that is common to two tables or views.
`EXCEPT`	This operator returns a subset of data that is present in one table or view but not in another.

CHAPTER 17
Using SQL for More Advanced Calculations

Introduction

In *Chapter 4: Simple Calculations*, you saw how to perform elementary math on the data in Databricks data. Although SQL is not a language that is designed for advanced mathematical calculations, it can go much further than the simple addition, subtraction, division, and multiplication done previously. However, these highly advanced calculations require one to understand how SQL handles numbers more completely.

Structure

In this chapter, we will cover the following topics:

- Calculating the percentage represented by each record in a dataset
- Replacing multiple subqueries
- Remove decimals in calculations
- Numeric datatypes
- Converting between numeric datatypes
- Avoiding divide-by-zero errors

- Finding the remainder in a division using the modulo function
- Creating financial calculations
- Using a tally table to produce a sequential list of numbers
- Generating completely random sample output from a dataset
- Handling source data where figures are stored as text

Objectives

The chapter aims to enhance developers' essential mathematical skills with Databricks. It takes a more real-world approach and shows how Databricks deals with numbers internally. Initially, this means learning to ensure that SQL accepts data as being numeric. This may be necessary because what appears as a number to humans may not be interpreted as a numeric value by SQL. Making sure that numbers are correctly handled will help in writing robust SQL that can handle potentially unpleasant surprises and deliver the expected results. After this, you begin learning to use SQL to write more complex formulas for data analysis.

In this chapter, you will learn how to:

- Ensure that you are using the appropriate datatypes in certain types of calculation.
- Understand numeric datatypes.
- Remove currency symbols from source data so that you can calculate columns that are not *pure* numbers.
- Handle divide-by-zero errors.
- Use calculated columns several times in a SQL snippet without having to copy the calculation.
- Test for errors in SQL calculations and resolve them so that queries do not fail but perform the appropriate calculation while handling errors.
- Convert figures stored as text into usable numbers where possible.

This chapter is focused on enhancing the results of the analysis with some more complex calculation techniques. It establishes a firm base for developers to deliver sound and accurate metrics to improve analysis with SQL.

Calculating the percentage represented by each record in a dataset

All businesses like consistent customers. Therefore, the CEO of *Prestige Cars* wants to know what percentage of individual sales can be attributed to each client. After reviewing the approaches applied in the previous chapters, you delivered the required output to the CEO using the following SQL:

```
SELECT        CustomerName
             ,FORMAT_NUMBER(
                      COUNT(CustomerName)
                      / (SELECT COUNT(*)
                         FROM allsales)
                      , "0.00 %")
              AS PercentageSalesPerCustomer
FROM         allsales
GROUP BY     CustomerName
ORDER BY     CustomerName;
```

Running the preceding query gives the results as shown in *Figure 17.1*. If you scroll down the list, you will see all the customers and the percentage of individual sales for each one. Moreover, if you add up all the percentage sales per customer, you will find that the total is 100%.

	CustomerName	PercentageSalesPerCustomer
1	Alex McWhirter	0.29 %
2	Alexei Tolstoi	2.59 %
3	Alicia Almodovar	2.01 %
4	Andrea Tarbuck	0.57 %
5	Andy Cheshire	0.57 %
6	Antonio Maura	2.59 %
7	Autos Sportivos	0.29 %

Figure 17.1: *Formatting output as a percentage*

How does it work

In the `AllSales` tables, you group on the `CustomerName` field to see a record for each customer. Then, you select the following:

- **First**: The customer's name.
- **Second**: The number of records for each customer. This is done using the `COUNT()` function.
- **Then**: You create a subquery to calculate the total number of records in the joined table set. This subquery is as follows:
- `(SELECT COUNT(*) FROM allsales), "0.00 %")`
- **Finally**: You divide the number of sales (or records representing an individual sale) by the total number of sales to give the percentage of individual sales per customer. To make the result more instantly comprehensible, this is formatted as a percentage.

Tricks and traps

The following is one core of points to remember when calculating percentages:

- You can multiply the result of the division in the calculation by 100 if required; however, this does not alter the fact that the figures are integers. Consequently, the result still does not display any decimals.

Replacing multiple subqueries

The sales director wants to see a list of all vehicles sold in 2017, with the percentage of sales each sale represents for the year and the variation to the average sales figure. You know that this will require adding a couple of subqueries. Moreover, SQL allows you to use a single subquery in cases like these. The developer produces the code that follows:

```
SELECT       MakeName, ModelName, SalePrice
             ,(SalePrice / CRX.TotalSales) * 100 AS PercentOfSales
             ,SalePrice - CRX.AverageSales AS DifferenceToAverage
FROM         SalesByCountry
CROSS JOIN   (SELECT SUM(SalePrice) AS TotalSales
                     ,AVG(SalePrice) AS AverageSales
              FROM   SalesByCountry
```

```
            WHERE   YEAR(SaleDate) = 2017) AS CRX
WHERE          YEAR(SaleDate) = 2017;
```

Running the preceding code produces the output shown in *Figure 17.2*:

	MakeName	ModelName	SalePrice	PercentOfSales	DifferenceToAverage
1	Aston Martin	DB6	45000	0.5719315080245169	-34475.505050505046
2	Porsche	911	49500	0.6291246588269686	-29975.505050505046
3	Aston Martin	DB6	225000	2.859657540122584	145524.49494949495
4	Triumph	TR6	12500	0.15886986334014355	-66975.50505050505
5	Porsche	Boxster	22500	0.28596575401225843	-56975.505050505046
6	Aston Martin	Virage	125000	1.5886986334014357	45524.494949494954

Figure 17.2: *Replacing multiple subqueries by a JOIN*

How does it work

Some calculations require multiple subqueries. This, potentially, means writing almost similar subqueries several times. You might need one subquery to return a total, another to get an average, yet another to find a standard deviation, and so on. Fortunately, you can apply a workaround to make the SQL more comprehensible and easier to maintain.

The trick is to write a subquery that calculates all the aggregate values that you need in a single query and then uses the **`CROSS JOIN`** operator to apply the output from the subquery for every single record returned from the main query.

The overall query works like the following:

- **First**: It begins with a subquery (once again, it is the subquery at the heart of the solution). The subquery simply calculates the total sales and average sales for 2017. It uses the **`SalesByCountry`** view as the source of this data. This subquery uses the following SQL:

  ```
  (SELECT SUM(SalePrice) AS TotalSales
                ,AVG(SalePrice) AS AverageSales
          FROM   SalesByCountry
          WHERE  YEAR(SaleDate) = 2017) AS CRX
  ```

- **Then**: The main query extracts the make name, model name, and sale price from the same data source (the **`SalesByCountry`** view) for the same year (2017).

The next step is to join the main query to the subquery using the JOIN function. This ensures that every record can use the output from the subquery in the main query and that the join does not filter the data in any way.

- **Finally**: The **SELECT** clause of the main query is extended to use the output from the cross-joined subquery. In this example, we are dividing the sale price of each vehicle sold by the total sales for the year to calculate the percentage of total sales that this figure represents. As a final flourish, we subtract the average selling price from the sale price of each car to find out how much each sale differs from the average sale price for the year.

If you want to verify that the calculations are accurate, you can always select the SQL for the subquery and run it. You will see the output shown in *Figure 17.3*:

	TotalSales	AverageSales
1	7868075	79475.50505050505

Figure 17.3: *The output from the subquery*

Tricks and traps

Using a **CROSS JOIN** (with no join field) can simplify certain calculations. Nonetheless, you need to be aware of the following points:

- The subquery is a perfectly standard subquery. This means that it is completely independent of the main query, so any filters that you apply to restrict the output from the subquery may have to be applied to the main query as well, assuming you want to use them both to examine similar ranges of data.
- A **CROSS JOIN** does not require an **ON** clause because it is not attempting to link the tables or queries in any way. Indeed, it specifically wants to use *all* the fields from both tables and/or queries together.
- As the subquery is aliased, you need to use the subquery alias (**CRX** in this example) when referring to the fields that are output from the subquery in the calculations in the main query's **SELECT** clause.

Remove decimals in calculations

If you are trading high-value products, you might not need to show pennies (or cents or centimes) in your results. Indeed, the financial director wants a list of vehicles sold that shows core costs without pennies to avoid rounding errors. An easy way to deliver on this requirement is shown in the following SQL:

```
SELECT      MakeName
           ,ModelName
           ,INT(Cost) AS Cost
           ,INT(RepairsCost) AS RepairsCost
           ,INT(PartsCost) AS PartsCost
           ,INT(SalePrice) AS SalePrice
FROM       SalesByCountry;
```

Running the preceding query gives the results shown in *Figure 17.4*:

	MakeName	ModelName	Cost	RepairsCost	PartsCost	SalePrice
1	Ferrari	Testarossa	52000	2175	1500	65000
2	Ferrari	355	176000	5500	2200	220000
3	Porsche	911	15600	660	0	19500
4	Porsche	924	9200	500	750	11500
5	Porsche	944	15960	1360	500	19950
6	Aston Martin	DB4	23600	500	750	29500

Figure 17.4: *Using the INT() function for a specific numeric data type conversion*

How does it work

The **INT()** function can be extremely useful for numbers. In this example, you take the **SalesByCountry** table (to avoid having to join seven tables) and select five key fields. However, in this view, the fields that contain numeric values may allow decimals. One way to remove any decimals and present only whole numbers is to convert these fields to integers.

This is done by applying the **INT()** function to the numeric fields and specifying that each is converted as an integer. The result is that the values are now integers, whereas the decimals have disappeared.

Numeric datatypes

Now is probably a good moment to explain the multifarious ways in which Databricks can store and manipulate numbers. In other words, it is time to look at all the numeric datatypes offered by Databricks. Each has its uses and limitations. They are given in *Table 17.1*:

Data type	Comments
`Tinyint`	1-byte integer value without any decimals
`SmallInt`	2-byte integer value without any decimals
`Int`	4-byte integer value without any decimals
`Bigint`	8-byte integer value without any decimals
`Decimal`	Specify the precision and scale (total allowable numbers and numbers after the decimal)
`Float`	4-byte single-precision floating point numbers, that is, potentially large numbers, but not stored precisely
`Double`	8-byte double-precision floating point numbers, that is, potentially huge numbers, but not stored precisely

Table 17.1: *Numeric datatypes*

There are so many numeric datatypes, especially for integers, to address the issue of the space that data can take up on disk and in memory. If a field uses a data type that can contain the maximum value that will ever be stored in that field, it will take up less space. It will also make fetching data from disk into memory faster.

This further implies that database designers nearly always try and use appropriate numeric datatypes so that databases run faster, with low-cost maintenance.

Originally, this was because the disk storage and main memory were extremely expensive. Now, despite lower hardware costs, the exponential growth of data means that it is still important to choose appropriate numeric datatypes when designing and building databases, particularly when dealing with very large datasets.

Converting between numeric datatypes

You can force Databricks to convert a numeric datatype to another numeric datatype using a series of numeric conversion functions. As an example, refer to the following short SQL snippet:

```
SELECT       DOUBLE(RepairsCost) AS Repairs
FROM         allsales
```

How does it work

The **`DOUBLE()`** function (like all numeric conversion functions) takes on y one parameter. This is the field to convert.

Table 17.2 describes the Databricks functions used to convert between numeric datatypes (or to convert from text datatype if the number can actually be converted):

Function	Description
`INT()`	Converts a text (wherever possible) or a numeric value to an integer.
`SMALLINT()`	Converts a text (wherever possible) or a numeric value to a small integer.
`TINYINT()`	Converts a text (wherever possible) or a numeric value to a tiny integer.
`BIGINT()`	Converts a text (wherever possible) or a numeric value to a big integer.
`FLOAT()`	Converts a text (wherever possible) or a numeric value to a floating-point value.
`DOUBLE()`	Converts a text (wherever possible) or a numeric value to a double floating-point value.

Table 17.2: *Converting numeric Datatypes*

Tricks and traps

Handling numeric datatypes requires practice. The following are a few essential points to remember:

- When casting numeric data to an integer data type, you must always use an integer type that can hold the largest value that you are converting to an integer. So, for example, if the field that you want to cast contains values in the millions, you cannot use the **`SmallInt`** data type because it only goes up to 32,767. This data type physically cannot store a larger value. Indeed, if you try a data type conversion on a field that contains values that are simply too large for the destination data type to hold, then Databricks refuses to display any output and only shows an error message.
- You should only convert to the Float or Real data type if your calculations do not require total accuracy. These datatypes can handle extremely large values, but they do not necessarily restitute the number that they contain accurately, so it is not advisable to use them for business or financial calculations. These datatypes were specifically designed for scientific data analysis where precision can be less important.
- Alternatively, you can apply the **`CAST()`** function shown as follows:

```
SELECT        CAST(RepairsCost AS DOUBLE) AS Repairs
FROM          allsales
```

- The **`CAST()`** function requires the following three elements:
  1. **First**: The name of the numeric field you wish to convert to a different numeric data type.
  2. **Then**: The **`AS`** keyword.
  3. **Finally**: The datatype you wish to convert to. This can be any one of the numeric datatypes that are shown in *Table 17.1*.
- The **`CAST()`** function is very powerful, but it can be rather picky about the data that it converts. If a field that you are trying to convert using **`CAST()`** contains a number that cannot be converted, then a **`NULL`** will be returned for the record in question.
- When converting numbers (or texts that can be converted to numbers, as you discover in the following section) to the numeric or decimal datatypes, you should specify the total allowable numbers (including decimals) as well as the number of decimal places.

  So, for instance, the following code:

  ```
  CAST(COST AS NUMERIC(10,2))
  ```

  Converts the contents of the **`COST`** field to the numeric data type. It allows a maximum value of 99999999.99, ten figures in all, and two decimal places.

Avoiding divide-by-zero errors

The people in the finance department want to see what the multiple of the cost of parts is when compared to the cost of each vehicle in stock. The following SQL will help in achieving this:

```
SELECT      ModelName
            ,Cost
            ,CASE
                WHEN PartsCost != 0 THEN Cost / PartsCost
                ELSE 0
            END AS PartsCostMultiple
FROM        allsales;
```

Running the preceding query gives the results shown in *Figure 17.5*:

	ModelName	Cost	PartsCostMultiple
1	Testarossa	52000	34.666666666666664
2	355	176000	80
3	911	15600	0
4	924	9200	12.266666666666667
5	944	15960	31.92
6	DB4	23600	31.466666666666665

Figure 17.5: *Using CASE statements to handle divide-by-zero errors*

How does it work

The query joins the **`Stock`** and **`Make`** tables so that you can access the **`Make`** name and vehicle cost elements. Then, it divides the **`Cost`** field by the **`PartsCost`** field.

However, at least one record has a zero as the parts cost. This, unfortunately, is a problem for Databricks, as it prevents any data from being returned and instead causes the NULLs to appear in any records where a divide by zero error occurs, as you can see in record 3 in *Figure 17.6:*

	ModelName	Cost	PartsCostMultiple
1	Testarossa	52000	34.666666666666664
2	355	176000	80
3	911	15600	null
4	924	9200	12.266666666666667
5	944	15960	31.92
6	DB4	23600	31.466666666666665

Figure 17.6: *NULLS returned when dividing by zero divide-by-zero errors*

This might be inconvenient. However, it can be handled using a CASE statement. What this does is as follows:

- **First**: Test the contents of the **`PartsCost`** field. If the field contains anything other than a zero, it divides the **`Cost`** field by the **`PartsCost`** field.
- **Otherwise**: It returns a zero and does not calculate anything because this would be a division by zero, which must be avoided.

Refer to the third record in *Figure 17.6*; this shows zero for the parts cost multiple. This is the record that has a zero in the **`PartsCost`** field or is one of them, at least. In any case, the calculation now works perfectly, and the results are ready to be shared.

Tricks and traps

You can apply many techniques to avoid divide-by-zero errors. You may also want to note the following point:

- You can also use the **`IFF()`** function to handle divide-by-zero errors. For this example, the code will be as follows:

  ```
  IFF(PartsCost != 0,  Cost / PartsCost, 0 ) AS PartsCostMultiple
  ```

Finding the remainder in a division using the modulo function

The marketing director wants you to generate a list of clients who will receive a letter saying that they have won a special customer discount on the next purchase of a classic sports car. She insists that this process must produce a list of around one-third of the client base. The following code helps you process this request:

```
SELECT    CustomerID

FROM

     (

     SELECT      CustomerID

                 ,CustomerID % 3 AS ModuloOutput

                 ,CASE

                       WHEN CustomerID % 3 = 1 THEN 'Winner'

                           ELSE NULL

                   END AS LuckyWinner

     FROM        Customer

     ) Rnd

WHERE       LuckyWinner IS NOT NULL;
```

Running the preceding query gives the results shown in *Figure 17.7*:

	CustomerID
1	1
2	4
3	7
4	10
5	13
6	16

Figure 17.7: *Using the modulo function to return the remainder in a calculation*

How does it work

SQL can calculate the remainder after dividing one number by another. This is called a **`modulo`** operation, and Databricks calls the function that carries out this calculation the **`modulo`** operator.

What happens is as follows:

- **First**: A field is defined that contains a numeric value. In this example, it is the **`CustomerID`** field.
- **Then**: The **`modulo`** operator (**`%`**) is added after the field name.
- **Finally**: The value that you are dividing the field by is added.

So, the key part of this code is as follows:

```
CustomerID % 3
```

However, as merely finding the remainder is of little practical interest, a small amount of logic is added to the calculation. What this logic does is it flags the record if the remainder is 1. The logical selection is then used as a subquery so that only winning records are returned in the final output.

To make this clearer, refer to *Figure 17.8,* where you can see the output from the subquery. It illustrates how the modulo function displays the remainder of a calculation and also shows the output from the **`CASE`** statement for every record.

	CustomerID	ModuloOutput	LuckyWinner
1	1	1	Winner
2	2	2	null
3	3	0	null
4	4	1	Winner
5	5	2	null
6	6	0	null

Figure 17.8: *The modulo function applied to all records*

Tricks and traps

A couple of interesting aspects of this example are as follows:

- The figure that is used by a modulo operator does not have to be a number, provided that the text value can be converted internally by Databricks to a number.
- You do not have to display the modulo output in a calculation. We did it here to make the use of this operator clearer.

Creating financial calculations

The finance director devoted countless hours to develop spreadsheets that count the cost of unsold stock in the showroom. Now, he wants you to adapt his basic compound interest calculation to SQL so that your reports can show the amount that *dead metal* (unsold stock) costs the company.

To help you in your work, the finance director has added the following points:

- You have to use a standard compound interest calculation.
- The interest is to be compounded monthly.
- The rate that he wants to apply is 0.75% per month.
- You are only to calculate interest when a vehicle has been in stock for over two months.
- You only need to analyze vehicles that have been sold.

As a further hint, he has kindly e-mailed you the exact calculation that he wants you to apply, as shown in *Figure 17.9*:

$$CI = K * \left(1 + \frac{P}{100}\right)^{t}$$

Figure 17.9: *A compound interest calculation*

In this formula:

- *CI* is the compound interest (including the original capital value)
- *K* is the initial value
- *P* is the interest rate
- *t* is the number of periods

You come up with the following SQL that shows not only the interest charge but also the number of months in stock as well as the cost price and the total cost, including interest for all cars sold.

```
SELECT
 InitialCost
,MonthsSincePurchase
,(InitialCost * POWER(1 + (0.75 / 100), MonthsSincePurchase))
- InitialCost AS InterestCharge
,InitialCost * POWER(1 + (0.75 / 100), MonthsSincePurchase)
 AS TotalWithInterest
FROM
(
   SELECT
    DATEDIFF(MONTH, DateBought, SaleDate) AS MonthsSincePurchase
   ,(Cost + NVL(PartsCost, 0) + RepairsCost)
                AS InitialCost
   FROM         allsales
```

```
    WHERE       DATEDIFF(MONTH, DateBought, SaleDate) > 2
) SRC;
```

Running the preceding code snippet gives the result as shown in *Figure 17.10*:

	InitialCost	MonthsSincePurchase	InterestCharge	TotalWithInterest
1	38000	23	7125.274557736615	45125.274557736615
2	7930	9	551.6174546729198	8481.61745467292
3	130550	12	12246.490490946948	142796.49049094695
4	45075	28	10489.482021894852	55564.48202189485
5	40600	15	4815.26532583333	45415.26532583333

***Figure 17.10:** Calculating compound interest*

How does it work

Creating complex calculations in SQL is a vast subject. Given that this challenge could be complex, it is bifurcated into the following parts:

- **An inner query**: That calculates the total cost of a vehicle by adding up the purchase cost, cost of spares, and any repair costs. This query then also determines the number of months between the purchase date and the sale date.

  This query uses the **`Stock`**, **`SalesDetails`**, and **`Sales`** tables to source the required information. Once the joins are in place, it adds a **`WHERE`** clause to restrict the output to vehicles where the time between purchase and sale is more than two months. The inner join between the **`Stock`** and **`SalesDetails`** tables ensures that only vehicles that have been sold are taken into consideration.

- **An outer query**: That displays the two fields isolated by the inner query (**`InitialCost`** and **`MonthsSincePurchase`**). The outer query then uses these two fields as core elements in calculating the compound interest.

What is both interesting and new in this query is the compound interest calculation, discussed in detail:

Essentially, you have applied a two-step process to calculating compound interest, which is given as follows:

- **First**: Take the arithmetical formula and adapt it so that it can be read on a single line.
- **Second**: Convert the single-line formula to SQL.

Converting the formula from *Figure 17.10* to a single line gives you the following:

```
CI = K * (1 + P/100)t
```

The SQL that delivers the **CI** takes **k** to be the purchase cost, cost of spares, and any repair costs. It then *hard-codes* the interest rate as 0.75 and divides it by 100 to express it as a percentage. Finally, it uses the **POWER()** function to apply the **t** as the exponent for the formula. The number of periods is, in fact, the number of months between purchase and sale.

The **POWER()** function takes the following two parameters:

- **First**: The base value you wish to raise to the power of the exponent (one plus the percentage interest rate in this example)
- **Second**: The exponent to apply (the number of months in this example)

The SQL for the compound interest formula is, therefore, given as follows:

```
InitialCost * POWER(1 + (0.75 / 100)
```

As a final tweak, this calculation is applied a second time. Only on this occasion the initial cost is subtracted from the compound interest to leave the actual interest amount. This way, you can see the total cost as well as the interest.

This is, of course, only a simple example. Financial calculations can get more complicated than this one.

Tricks and traps

The following is one idea that you can take away from this example:

- It is possible to write a query like this one without using a subquery. However, the improved simplification and increased clarity that a subquery brings to both the analysis and the coding can make a subquery worth any extra effort.

Using a tally table to produce a sequential list of numbers

The CFO has come with a request for you. He wants to calculate the straight-line depreciation for any vehicle in stock. You come up with the following code:

```
SELECT                    RowNo AS PeriodNumber

                          ,Cost

                          ,Cost / 5 AS StraightLineDepreciation
```

```
                        ,Cost - ((Cost / 5) * RowNo) AS RemainingValue
FROM                    allsales
CROSS JOIN
(
    SELECT 1 AS RowNo
    UNION ALL
    SELECT 2
    UNION ALL
    SELECT 3
    UNION ALL
    SELECT 4
    UNION ALL
    SELECT 5
) Tally
WHERE  StockCode = 'A2C3B95E-3005-4840-8CE3-A7BC5F9CFB5F';
```

Running the preceding piece of code gives the result shown in *Figure 17.11*:

	PeriodNumber	Cost	StraightLineDepreciation	RemainingValue
1	1	176000	35200	140800
2	2	176000	35200	105600
3	3	176000	35200	70400
4	4	176000	35200	35200
5	5	176000	35200	0

Figure 17.11: *Using a tally table to calculate straight-line depreciation*

How does it work

Producing a depreciation table requires a sequence of durations against which the series of amortization amounts can be calculated. However, it is not possible to enter a series of numbers to represent the time periods in Databricks, like spreadsheets. The concept of a tally table solves this query. This is a record set (it could be a table but does not have to be) that contains a series of numbers, generally starting from 1, that increment regularly and have no gaps in the series. This suite of numbers can then be used to create sets of records.

In the case of a depreciation table, the first thing that you need is a record set that contains the number of records corresponding to the number of years over which the vehicle will be amortized. In this example, I presume that this is a five-year period, so a record set containing five rows is created using a set of **`UNION`** queries. You can see this in the **`JOIN`** clause of the SQL. Running the code inside the **`CROSS JOIN`** clause produces the result shown in *Figure 17.12*:

	RowNo
1	1
2	2
3	3
4	4
5	5

Figure 17.12: *The output from a tally table*

Once you have the tally table, you can calculate the depreciation and the residual value of a specific car. Calculating the depreciation each year is as simple as dividing the cost of the vehicle by the number of years. Calculating the residual value means subtracting the accumulated depreciation each year from the cost. So, to work out the accumulated amortization amount, you multiply the depreciation amount by the number of years. This number is provided by the tally table; in effect, it takes the single record for the car cost and makes it into a table of five records by using a **`CROSS APPLY`** clause to multiply the number of records in the **`SELECT`** clause (one) by the number of records in the **`CROSS APPLY`** clause (all five of them). As a final and necessary flourish, the row number of the tally table is used as the multiplier to calculate the accumulated depreciation.

Tricks and traps

A few points need to be kept in mind are given as follows:

- If you need to include a salvage cost in the calculation for the depreciation, you can subtract the salvage cost from the cost of the vehicle every time the **`Cost`** field is used.

- You will discover other ways to create a tally table in a later chapter.
- You can use tally tables in many situations to resolve otherwise seemingly intricate SQL issues. Although they may not be something that you use daily, they can be a valuable resource in certain circumstances.
- You can simply write `JOIN` instead of `CROSS JOIN` if you prefer.

Generating completely random sample output from a dataset

The CEO wants to call up a handful of clients at random and ask them about the service that they have received from *Prestige Cars*. She asks you to produce a totally arbitrary list of sales with the relevant customers. The following piece of SQL helps to satisfy her request:

```
SELECT        *

FROM          allsales TABLESAMPLE (5 PERCENT);
```

Running the preceding code delivers the results that you can see in *Figure 17.13*. The row counter at the bottom of the workbook cell indicates the number of returned records:

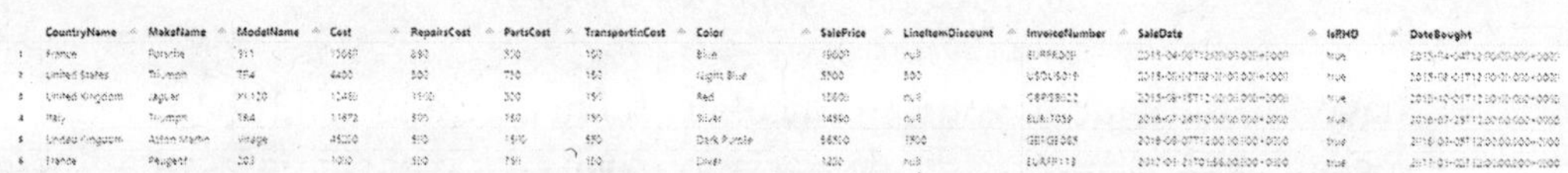

Figure 17.13: Generating random output from a table using TABLESAMPLE

How does it work

SQL has a function called `TABLESAMPLE` that reduces the output to a completely random sample of the original table or tables defined in the query. To define this sample dataset, you extend the `FROM` clause like the following:

- **First**: Enter the `FROM` keyword.
- **Second**: Add the `TABLESAMPLE` keyword.
- **Third**: In parentheses, add the percentage sample you require, followed by the `PERCENTAGE` keyword.

Tricks and traps

The following are some important points to remember about this technique:

- You can apply **TABLESAMPLE** to any table used in a **FROM** clause, even if there are multiple tables using various join types. You can see an example of this in the following SQL snippet:

```
SELECT        *
FROM          sales TABLESAMPLE (5 PERCENT)
JOIN          customer
ON            sales.CustomerID = customer.CustomerID;
```

  You can use **TABLESAMPLE** to return a completely random number of rows if required. You can see this in the following SQL snippet:

```
SELECT        *
FROM          sales TABLESAMPLE (5 ROWS)
JOIN          customer
ON            sales.CustomerID = customer.CustomerID;
```

Handling source data where figures are stored as text

The sales director has been using a spreadsheet to juggle some data and has then had it loaded into Databricks by the *Prestige Cars* IT department. You now have to query that data. However, all the figures have been saved as strings of unorganized text. This can make handling the data trickier than it usually is. The following SQL helps you work around this kind of issue by converting texts to numbers wherever possible:

```
SELECT      CountryName
           ,MakeName
           ,TRY_CAST(SalePrice AS NUMERIC(20,4)) AS SalePriceConverted
FROM       SalesText;
```

Running the preceding query gives the results that you can see in *Figure 17.14*:

	CountryName	MakeName	SalePriceConverted
1	United Kingdom	Ferrari	null
2	United Kingdom	Ferrari	220000.0000
3	United Kingdom	Porsche	null
4	Germany	Porsche	11500.0000
5	France	Porsche	19950.0000
6	United Kingdom	Aston Martin	null
7	United Kingdom	Aston Martin	49500.0000

Figure 17.14: *Using the TRY_CAST() function to convert text to numeric values*

How does it work

This example uses a new table of data. This is the **`SalesText`** table introduced to emphasize that not all the data will be perfect. In this example, the original data in the table **`SalesText`** is similar to the output shown in *Figure 17.15*:

	CountryName	MakeName	ModelName	SalePrice
1	United Kingdom	Ferrari	Testarossa	�65,000
2	United Kingdom	Ferrari	355	220000
3	United Kingdom	Porsche	911	19 500
4	Germany	Porsche	924	11500
5	France	Porsche	944	19950
6	United Kingdom	Aston Martin	DB4	29500 .00
7	United Kingdom	Aston Martin	DB5	49500

Figure 17.15: *Invalid numeric data that cannot be converted* **as is** *to a numeric value*

As you can see, the **`Cost`** field contains spaces and currency units. These make it impossible for Databricks to convert the underlying values to numbers.

Nonetheless, Databricks can help you deal with situations like this. In these cases, you can use the **`TRY_CAST()`** function to convert strings that are composed of numbers into numeric values where this is possible.

Tricks and traps

Developers must remember the following points:

- Converting invalid source data is a vast subject outside the scope of a book such as this one. **TRY_CAST()** helps the query function; it does not solve the underlying issues with the data. When faced with complex data that causes SQL to choke, it is best advised to have the data converted by IT professionals.

Conclusion

This chapter explained some of the techniques that may be required when carrying out more advanced calculations in SQL. These include handling data type conversions, managing divide-by-zero errors, and avoiding other circumstances where SQL can potentially prevent some calculations from working properly. The chapter explained more about numeric datatypes and the conversion of numbers to numeric values when they are stored as text. Finally, you saw a few examples of how you can use SQL to carry out complex calculations.

Core knowledge learned in this chapter

The keywords that you have seen in this chapter are as follows:

Concept	Description
`INT()`	The `INT()` function is used to convert datatypes, where possible. It can convert a numeric data type to a different numeric data type or convert a string that is, in effect, a number to a numeric data type.
`TINYINT()`	Converts a string or number to a `tinyint` data type.
`SMALLINT()`	Converts a string or number to a `smallint` data type.
`BIGINT()`	Converts a string or number to a `bigint` data type.
`FLOAT()`	Converts a string or number to a `float` data type.
`DOUBLE()`	Converts a string or number to a `double` data type.
`% (modulo)`	The `%` function called the `modulo` function returns the remainder after dividing one value by another.
`POWER()`	`POWER()` is a math function used to raise one value to the power of another.
`TABLESAMPLE`	This function returns a random sample of records from the source table(s).
`TRY_CAST()`	This function attempts to convert one datatype to another specified datatype.

Chapter 18
Segmenting and Classifying Data

Introduction

Selecting and filtering information can certainly help you gain a deeper insight into your data, yet there are times when you have to prioritize and classify lists of data to better analyze the elements of importance. In this chapter, you see how applying a few analytical functions can help you deliver real insight from your data. You will learn a range of techniques that can help you isolate the valuable information hidden inside your data. This can help both you and your organization stay one step ahead of the competition.

Structure

In this chapter, we will cover the following topics:

- Organizing data by rank
- Creating multiple groups of rankings
- Creating multiple ranked groups and subgroups
- Filtering data by ranked items
- Classifying data by strict order of rank
- Segment data into deciles

- Plot values for a percentile
- Extract data from a specific quintile
- Display median values

Objectives

Databricks offer a useful set of functions that can be helpful when it comes to segmenting datasets. Specifically, it can:

- Rank data according to a given criterion.
- Break down record sets into multiple segments.
- Isolate the top or bottom elements in multiple data segments.
- Return the top percentage of a record set.
- Determine median values.

Analyzing data in this way is the first step on the path to in-depth statistical analysis. With this chapter, you will grasp the knowledge of how to slice and dice data with an increased appreciation of the power of SQL in data analysis.

Organizing data by rank

The analysis is all about turning data into information. To tailor the offering for your clients, you need to assess the comparison of individual sales. For instance, the sales director wants a list that shows sales for 2018 with an indicator of their relative value. The following SQL can help you deliver this:

```
SELECT      CustomerName
           ,MakeName || ', ' || ModelName AS MakeAndModel
           ,SalePrice
           ,RANK() OVER (ORDER BY SalePrice DESC)
                  AS SalesImportance
FROM       allsales
WHERE      YEAR(SaleDate) = 2018
ORDER BY   SalesImportance;
```

Running the preceding query gives the results as shown in *Figure 18.1*. The figure that indicates the relative position of each sale shows the rank for each record.

	CustomerName	MakeAndModel	SalePrice	SalesImportance
1	La Bagnole de Luxe	Bugatti, 57C	365000	1
2	Andrea Tarbuck	Bugatti, 57C	355000	2
3	Bling Bling S.A.	Bugatti, 57C	345000	3
4	Capots Reluisants S.A.	Ferrari, F50	310000	4
5	Laurent Saint Yves	Ferrari, F40	269500	5
6	Kieran O'Harris	Lamborghini, Diabolo	255000	6

***Figure 18.1:** The RANK() function*

How does it work

This query starts by using the **allSales** table to save you from the task of joining multiple source tables. Once a **WHERE** clause has been added to filter on a specific year for sales, these fields are added to the **SELECT** clause. Finally, the customers are clearly ranked by order of importance using a new function called **RANK()**.

As the name implies, **RANK()** indicates where a row stands in a list of elements. We also used the **RANK()** function to sort the records to specify the relative importance of each row. In this example, we used the alias applied to the **RANK()**function—**SalesImportance**—in the **ORDER BY** clause to sort the data by rank without repeating the complete calculation like the following:

```
ORDER BY    SalesImportance
```

However, the **RANK()** function must be informed on how to classify the data that it will convert into an ordered hierarchy. Therefore, to set up a ranked dataset, you at least need the following elements:

- **RANK()**: This function informs Databricks that you want to classify a dataset.
- **OVER**: This keyword is compulsory and follows the **RANK()** keyword.
- **ORDER BY**: This statement is added inside parentheses after the **OVER** keyword. Then, add the field that will be used to grade the results.

In this example, the vehicle sale price is used as the basis for ranking the output. The final result is a list of sales ordered, ranked by value.

Tricks and traps

The **RANK()** function can be an extremely powerful addition to a developer's SQL toolkit; however, you need to be aware of the following points while using it:

- The **RANK()** function is one of a group of SQL functions called the windowing functions. You will see many of these in this chapter and the upcoming chapter. The windowing functions essentially group data into subsets of rows.

- The **ORDER BY** clause in a windowing function works just like a standard SQL **ORDER BY** clause. However, it only affects the data inside the windowing function. You can use multiple fields separated by a comma or add the **ASC** (for ascending) or **DESC** (for descending) keywords to inform Databricks how to sort the data inside the windowing function. So the **RANK()** function could also be written as follows:
- `RANK() OVER (ORDER BY SalePrice ASC)`
- It is not strictly necessary to add an alias for the column that displays the result of the **RANK()** function, but it helps make the output clearer. An added benefit of this approach is that it avoids the repetition of the entire **RANK()** function code inside the **ORDER BY** clause.
- Adding a **RANK()** function automatically sorts the output data.

Creating multiple groups of rankings

Classifying product sales can be essential for an accurate understanding of which products sell best. Keeping this in mind, CEO said when she requested a report showing sales for 2017 ranked in order of importance by make. The following short piece of SQL shows you how to look at the relative sales value of each model for each make of car:

```
SELECT      MakeName || ', ' || ModelName AS MakeAndModel
            , SalePrice
            , RANK() OVER (PARTITION BY MakeName
                           ORDER BY SalePrice DESC) AS SalesImportance
FROM        allsales
WHERE       YEAR(SaleDate) = 2017
ORDER BY    MakeName, SalesImportance;
```

Running the preceding query gives the results that you can see in *Figure 18.2*:

	MakeAndModel	SalePrice	SalesImportance
1	Alfa Romeo, Giulia	25000	1
2	Alfa Romeo, Giulietta	21500	2
3	Alfa Romeo, Spider	12500	3
4	Alfa Romeo, Spider	11500	4
5	Alfa Romeo, Giulia	10500	5
6	Alfa Romeo, Giulietta	6500	6
7	Alfa Romeo, Spider	5650	7
8	Aston Martin, DB6	225000	1
9	Aston Martin, Virage	125000	2
10	Aston Martin, DB9	99500	3
11	Aston Martin, Rapide	99500	3
12	Aston Martin, Rapide	86500	5
13	Aston Martin, DB9	77500	6
14	Aston Martin, Vantage	66500	7
15	Aston Martin, DB2	61500	8
16	Aston Martin, Vanquish	56950	9

***Figure 18.2:** Applying the PARTITION BY clause to a RANK() function*

How does it work

The core of this code snippet is, once again, the **`RANK()`** function. As was the case in the previous example, you need the **`RANK()`** keyword, the **`OVER`** clause, and an **`ORDER BY`** statement with the field that you are using to prioritize the field used as a basis for the ranking.

This time you want to classify the output in a subtler way. Specifically, you want to grade each model of car, not compared to all the sales for the year, but relative to all models of the same make rather than relative to all sales for the year.

This is done by adding the **`PARTITION BY`** clause and a field name inside the parentheses that follow the **`OVER`** keyword. In this way, you are, in effect, telling SQL to break the data down into subgroups by make of car. The **`PARTITION BY`** clause creates subgroups by the make of the vehicle. The **`ORDER BY`** clause then grades the records for each subgroup on the **`SalePrice`** field.

Tricks and traps

When partitioning or grouping datasets, you need to remain aware of the following key points:

- Databricks can handle situations where there is a tie that occurs when data is ranked. In such a case, it gives any tied rows the same ranking, and then it makes the next-lowest record two or more places lower. *Figure 18.3* shows you an example of this from further down the list:

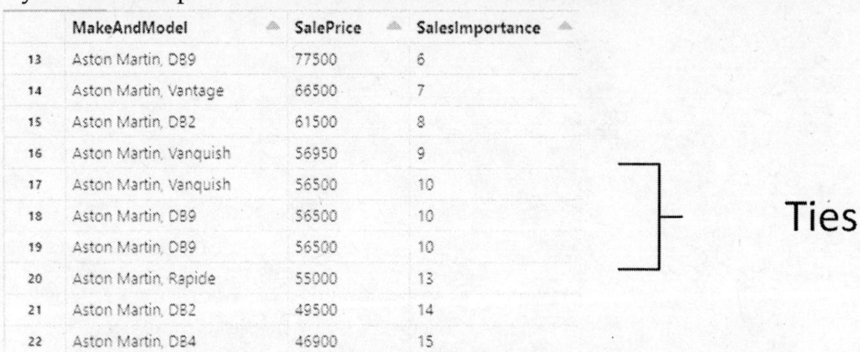

	MakeAndModel	SalePrice	SalesImportance
13	Aston Martin, DB9	77500	6
14	Aston Martin, Vantage	66500	7
15	Aston Martin, DB2	61500	8
16	Aston Martin, Vanquish	56950	9
17	Aston Martin, Vanquish	56500	10
18	Aston Martin, DB9	56500	10
19	Aston Martin, DB9	56500	10
20	Aston Martin, Rapide	55000	13
21	Aston Martin, DB2	49500	14
22	Aston Martin, DB4	46900	15

Figure 18.3: *The effect of tied records when using the RANK() function*

- Most times, you are likely to find yourself ranking data on a numeric field. You will nearly always partition data using a text field. This is not, however, inevitable, but likely. You can just as easily partition on a numeric field and order on an alphabetical field.

Creating multiple ranked groups and subgroups

The finance director has requested an immediate report that shows the profit per vehicle sold ranked in order of importance by make per customer. After a little thought, you conclude that he wants a list of customers where you can see which makes of the vehicle each client bought with the data ranked by the customer, make, and profit. The following SQL query uses a windowing function and a **Common Table Expression** (CTE) to deliver this essential piece of analysis:

```
WITH

AllSalesProfit_CTE  (CustomerName,  MakeName,  ModelName,  SalePrice,
ProfitPerModel)
```

```
AS
(
SELECT      CustomerName, MakeName, ModelName
            ,SalePrice
            ,((SalePrice -
                (Cost + NVL(RepairsCost,0)
                 + PartsCost + TransportInCost))
               / SalePrice) * 100
FROM        SalesByCountry
)

SELECT      CustomerName, MakeName, ModelName, ProfitPerModel, SalePrice
            , RANK() OVER
                     (PARTITION BY CustomerName, MakeName
                      ORDER BY ProfitPerModel DESC) AS SalesImportance
FROM        AllSalesProfit_CTE
ORDER BY    CustomerName, MakeName, SalesImportance;
```

Running the preceding query gives the results that you can see in *Figure 18.4*:

	CustomerName	MakeName	ModelName	ProfitPerModel	SalePrice	SalesImportance
1	Alex McWhirter	Jaguar	XJ12	9.523809523809524	17850	1
2	Alexei Tolstoi	Aston Martin	Virage	15.682926829268293	102500	1
3	Alexei Tolstoi	Aston Martin	DB6	14.618705035971221	69500	2
4	Alexei Tolstoi	Ferrari	355	14.170731707317072	205000	1
5	Alexei Tolstoi	Jaguar	XK150	16.998695084819488	22990	1
6	Alexei Tolstoi	Jaguar	XJS	13.097345132743362	22600	2
7	Alexei Tolstoi	Jaguar	E-Type	11.645569620253164	39500	3

Figure 18.4: *Combining a CTE with a RANK() function to create multiple ranked groups and subgroups*

How does it work

This piece of code is in the following two parts:

- **First**: A CTE that calculates the net profit for every car sold.
- **Finally**: A query that uses the data from the CTE to classify the output.

A CTE can in defining the key data that is required by the overall query. Although not absolutely necessary, it can help to isolate the core data that is then categorized and hierarchized. This example uses a CTE to define the essential data that is required. Once the essential data has been isolated using the `SalesByCountry` view as the data source, the relevant fields (`CustomerName`, `MakeName`, `ModelName`, and `Profit`) are output, and a `RANK()` function is added to the final query that delivers the categorized output based on the record set defined by the CTE.

Thinking back to *Chapter 14: Common Table Expressions*, you will remember that a CTE can be executed separately from the rest of the query. So, if you select the SQL that is contained inside the CTE and execute it, you obtain the output as shown in *Figure 18.5* (remember that the final column is aliased in the CTE header).

	CustomerName	MakeName	ModelName	SalePrice	(((SalePrice - (((Cost + nvl(RepairsCost, 0)) + PartsCost) + TransportInCost)) / SalePrice) *
1	Magic Motors	Ferrari	Testarossa	65000	18.192307692307692
2	Snazzy Roadsters	Ferrari	355	220000	15.613636363636363
3	Birmingham Executive Prestige Vehicles	Porsche	911	19500	15.846153846153847
4	WunderKar	Porsche	924	11500	7.82608695652174
5	Casseroles Chromes	Porsche	944	19950	9.924812030075188
6	Magic Motors	Aston Martin	DB4	29500	15.254237288135593

***Figure 18.5:** CTE output to be used in a ranking query*

This dataset calculates sales figures and profit per sale, so it can be used in the final query to group and rank the records by customer and make. A few aspects of this query make it a little subtler than the previous two you have seen.

- **First**: The output is ranked by the customer and make. As you can see, the `PARTITION BY` clause (like an `ORDER BY` clause) can specify multiple fields. All fields you use in the `PARTITION BY` clause must be comma-separated.
- **Second**: You can override the sort order provided by the `RANK()` function by adding a standard `ORDER BY` clause in the final query. In this example, the `ORDER BY` clause is applied to guarantee that the final output is both clear and comprehensible.

Tricks and traps

We have a couple of remarks about using CTEs when ranking datasets, which are given as follows:

- You could just as easily use a derived table instead of a CTE. The two techniques are essentially interchangeable. Moreover, the chosen approach is largely a matter of personal preference.
- If the query inside the CTE does not have column names, then you must add names to the output fields inside parentheses at the top of the CTE after the CTE name. Any elements added inside parentheses after the CTE name are called the *CTE header*.

Filtering data by ranked items

To better understand *Prestige Cars'* clients, the sales director has decided that she wants to find the bestselling make for each color of vehicle sold. The following short SQL snippet gives you this information:

```
SELECT      Color, MakeName
FROM
            (
            SELECT      DISTINCT MakeName, Color
                        ,RANK() OVER (PARTITION BY MakeName
                                      ORDER BY SalePrice DESC)
                                         AS ColorRank
            FROM        allsales
            ) SQ
WHERE       ColorRank = 1
ORDER BY MakeName;
```

Running the preceding query gives the results shown in *Figure 18.6*:

	Color	MakeName
1	Black	Alfa Romeo
2	Black	Aston Martin
3	Night Blue	Austin
4	Black	BMW
5	Blue	Bentley
6	Red	Bugatti

***Figure 18.6:** Filtering on the results of a RANK() function in a subquery*

How does it work

This query works by breaking down the problem into the following two constituent parts:

- **First**: A derived table (aliased `SQ` in the preceding code snippet) joins all the required tables to produce a list of sales that displays only the make, color, sale price, and the hierarchy of each color sold per make using the `RANK()` function. The `OVER` clause specifies that the data is partitioned (or grouped) by the make of the car, and the value used to rank the data is the `SalePrice` field.
- **Finally**: The outer query returns the make, color, and sale price of each car if it is ranked first for each make. The outer query does this by applying a `WHERE` clause to the output from the derived table so that only records where the rank equals to 1 are allowed through to the final data set.

Figure 18.7 shows a few of the records from the data returned by the derived table to the outer query:

	MakeName	Color	ColorRank
1	Alfa Romeo	Black	1
2	Alfa Romeo	Dark Purple	2
3	Alfa Romeo	Blue	3
4	Alfa Romeo	Night Blue	4
5	Alfa Romeo	Green	5
6	Alfa Romeo	Black	6

***Figure 18.7:** Grouping and classifying data using the RANK() function*

This output shows that the derived table has effectively classified sales by color for each make. Then the outer query simply discards most of the data that the derived table has returned so that only the top-ranked records for each make are displayed.

Tricks and traps

The following are a couple of points worth noting at this juncture:

- Remember that you have to add an alias to all columns that are used in a derived table. This is required by SQL and not just because you are using the output of the `RANK()` function to filter data. If you forget to add an alias to a column, you get an error message.
- You could have just as easily used a CTE instead of a derived table to perform the initial ranking of the data. The methods used are entirely your choice.

Classifying data by strict order of rank

SQL mainly focuses on segmenting data to deliver real insight. Management now wants you to perform a more complex analysis of the *Prestige Cars'* sales data by finding the ten highest-selling sales values, but only when these cars belong to the category of the five bestselling colors by quantity sold. The SQL that does this is slightly longer than the code snippets seen so far; however, it is definitely worth a closer look that SQL is given as follows:

```
SELECT      Color, MakeAndModel, SalesImportance

FROM

(
```

```
SELECT      ST.Color, MakeName || ', ' || ModelName AS MakeAndModel
            , SalePrice
            , DENSE_RANK() OVER (ORDER BY SalePrice DESC)
                           AS SalesImportance
FROM        allsales ST
INNER JOIN
           (
            SELECT          Color, COUNT(*) AS NumberOfSales
            FROM            allsales
            GROUP BY        Color
            ORDER BY        NumberOfSales
            LIMIT 5
            ) CL
            ON CL.Color = ST.Color
) RK
WHERE       SalesImportance <= 10
ORDER BY    SalesImportance;
```

Running the preceding query gives the results as shown in *Figure 18.8*:

	Color	MakeAndModel	SalesImportance
1	Green	Lamborghini, Jarama	1
2	Dark Purple	Ferrari, F40	2
3	Green	Ferrari, Testarossa	3
4	Green	Ferrari, F50	3
5	Green	Rolls Royce, Phantom	4
6	Night Blue	Ferrari, Testarossa	5

***Figure 18.8:** Using the DENSE_RANK() function to classify items*

How does it work

Sometimes an analytical request can seem more complicated than it is. However, if you break the problem down into its components, it can prove to be easier. This query is a case in point. Let us look more closely at what is required and then see how SQL can provide the information that you want to extract from the source data. This is as follows:

- **Top five by color**: First, you must isolate the five bestselling colors by quantity. This has to be done first, as it restricts the data only to those vehicles whose color is one of the five bestselling colors.
- **Top ten bestselling**: Then you need to find the bestselling cars that make up the ten best sales by value if the vehicle color is one of the five bestselling colors.

Getting this query right requires a nested derived table inside a derived table. Let us begin at the lowest level of the query, that is, the inner derived table that deduces the five bestselling colors by quantity.

The inner derived table finds the five bestselling colors by joining the `Stock` and `SalesDetails` tables and then counting the number of sales per color. Next, it selects only the top five records, giving the list of the five bestselling colors. If you select the query that makes up the inner derived table (the one that is aliased as `CL`), you see something like the data in *Figure 18.9*:

	Color	NumberOfSales
1	Pink	11
2	Canary Yellow	14
3	Dark Purple	16
4	Green	24
5	Night Blue	32

***Figure 18.9:** Using a derived table to filter a subset of elements that are passed up to an outer query*

Once you have the list of colors that make up the five bestselling colors, you can build the *core* query that returns the make and model of the car sold along with its color, the sale price, and the ranking of the sale relative to the selling prices of all vehicles sold. The inner-derived table is used in the outer-derived table's `JOIN` clause to filter the colors so that only the five records returned by the inner query are used in the outer query. If you select this query (which includes the inner derived table, aliased as **RK**), you see something like the data in *Figure 18.10*:

	Color	MakeAndModel	SalePrice	SalesImportance
1	Green	Lamborghini, Jarama	305000	1
2	Dark Purple	Ferrari, F40	269500	2
3	Green	Ferrari, Testarossa	195000	3
4	Green	Ferrari, F50	195000	3
5	Green	Rolls Royce, Phantom	182500	4
6	Night Blue	Ferrari, Testarossa	165000	5

***Figure 18.10:** A derived table that filters data based on an inner-derived table*

Once you have a list of all the sales of cars in a ranked dataset, it is easy to add the final step. It consists of using the derived table obtained as the data source for the outermost query, where you select only those cars whose rank is 10 or less. This is done in the **WHERE** clause that says **WHERE SalesImportance <= 10**. An **ORDER BY** clause is added as a final tweak to present that data in an order that visually enhances the result by sorting the output in ascending sequence of sales importance.

Notice that this SQL uses the **DENSE_RANK()** function rather than the **RANK()** function. The two are virtually identical but have one vital difference. You saw in previous examples that the **RANK()** function skips numbers if there is a tie. The **DENSE_RANK()** function does not do this and continues the numbering sequentially. This way, you are sure to get the top ten sales values, even if there are duplicate values for some sales. This is why the final output shows thirteen records when you only asked for the top ten. This is because there are only ten distinct top-selling prices, but these represent thirteen different sales since there can always be more than one sale at the same price.

Tricks and traps

A query as complex as this one inevitably means that there will be a few key points to take away, which are given as follows:

- This query could also be solved by nesting the inner derived table inside a CTE and then using the output from the CTE for the final query. Once again, how you solve it is simply a question of personal preference.
- The inner derived table can be used by the outer derived table either in a **JOIN** with the outer query (as is the case here) or in a **WHERE** clause. Either of these approaches gives the same result.

- You might be tempted to use a **LIMIT** 10 clause in the outer derived table to get the top ten sales. However, this might not give you the exact top 10 values. This is because **LIMIT** merely returns a specified number of rows. In the case of this query, it is perfectly possible that the top ten largest values could represent eleven or more sales. Only showing the top 10 would not exactly answer the question since it might not display a full 10 *values*, just 10 *records*.

Segment data into deciles

In line with the exploration of the area of data classification, suppose that the sales director wants to group sales by sale price into deciles, that is, buckets of equal size, where each group of data contains one-tenth of the records in the total dataset. The top decile will contain the most expensive cars, the second decile the next most expensive cars, and so on. The following SQL does this for you:

```
SELECT       Color, MakeName || ', ' || ModelName AS MakeAndModel
             ,SalePrice
             ,NTILE(10) OVER (ORDER BY SalePrice DESC) AS SalesDecile
FROM         allsales
ORDER BY     SalesDecile, Color, MakeAndModel;
```

Running the preceding query gives the results shown in *Figure 18.11*. You have to scroll down the result to see how the **SalesDecile** field changes every 35 records or so:

	Color	MakeAndModel	SalePrice	SalesD
29	Red	Bugatti, 57C	345000	1
30	Red	Bugatti, Veyron	220500	1
31	Red	Rolls Royce, Wraith	162500	1
32	Silver	Bugatti, 57C	335000	1
33	Silver	Ferrari, 355	159500	1
34	Silver	Ferrari, F50	310000	1
35	Silver	McLaren, P1	295000	1
36	Black	Aston Martin, Vantage	102500	2
37	Black	Aston Martin, Virage	123590	2
38	Black	Aston Martin, Virage	123500	2
39	Black	Bentley, Arnage	99950	2

End of First Decile

Start of Second Decile

Figure 18.11: *Using the NTILE() function to group data into segments*

How does it work

You can see from the output that this query added a field that indicates the decile (or segment/bucket) that each record belongs to. You can then use this segmentation to pursue your analysis.

This query delivers an easy solution to a potentially complex question to the credit of the **NTILE()** function. This windowing function segments the dataset into as many separate subgroups as specified when the function was applied. Quite simply, the figure that you place inside the function defines the number of data *buckets* that you want to create. Whatever the number of records in the dataset, the **NTILE()** function subdivides them into the number of groups that you specify as a parameter of the function.

This query, at the core, is a simple **SELECT** query, where you join the necessary tables and select the required fields. Then you added a final field using the **NTILE()** function.

Just like the **RANK()** and **DENSE_RANK()** functions, the **NTILE()** function requires you to add the **OVER** keyword and an **ORDER BY** clause inside parentheses in addition to a value that is used for classifying the data. The **NTILE()** function requires another element, the number of *buckets* that you want to appear in the output. This is defined by adding a number inside the parentheses just after the **NTILE()** function. The number is added to the number of groups into which the dataset will be divided.

Tricks and traps

We have only one comment to make is as follows:

- **NTILE()** can also contain a **PARTITION BY** clause to add a further level of segmentation if required. It works like it does for the **RANK()** function mentioned in the previous sections.

Plot values for a percentile

SQL can be particularly useful when it comes to inferring meaning from statistics. As a result, the sales director wants you to provide her with a dataset that contains the total cost for vehicles for each cost percentile and the corresponding repair cost. The sales director wants to use this to create a chart that displays any potential correlation between the cost of a car and its repair cost, the SQL for this is given as follows:

```
WITH PercentileList_CTE
AS
(
SELECT     RepairsCost
          , Cost
          , NTILE(100) OVER (ORDER BY Cost DESC) AS Percentile
FROM      Stock
)
SELECT Percentile
          , SUM(Cost) AS TotalCostPerPercentile
          , SUM(RepairsCost) AS RepairsCostPerPercentile
              , SUM(RepairsCost) / SUM(Cost) AS RepairCostRatio
FROM      PercentileList_CTE
GROUP BY  Percentile
ORDER BY  RepairCostRatio DESC;
```

Execute the preceding code snippet, and you will obtain the results shown in *Figure 18.12*:

	Percentile	TotalCostPerPercentile	RepairsCostPerPercentile	RepairCostRatio
1	100	3000	1500	0.5
2	15	9680	2000	0.2066115702479339
3	68	25996	2860	0.11001692568087398
4	82	48360	5220	0.10794044665012408
5	4	20240	2000	0.09881422924901186
6	14	23560	2000	0.08488964346349745

***Figure 18.12:** Purchase cost versus repairs cost per percentile*

How does it work

This piece of SQL is essentially in the following two stages:

- **A CTE**: That attributes each sale to a percentile of sales. It also gives the repair cost for each sale. This CTE uses the **`NTILE()`** function and specifies that the function is to distribute the results over 100 groups, in effect segmenting the sales into percentiles.
- **A query**: That aggregates the output from the CTE to obtain the total for each percentile.

The CTE produces the output that you can see in *Figure 18.13*:

	RepairsCost	Cost	Percentile
1	NULL	NULL	1
2	2175	98872	1
3	2000	98800	1
4	2175	98800	1
5	2000	98800	2
6	2175	96000	2
7	500	9592	2

***Figure 18.13:** Attributing each sale to a percentile*

Once you have the percentile that each sale belongs to, it is simple to aggregate the output so that you are grouping the result on each percentile and using the **`SUM()`** function to return the total for sales and repair costs per percentile.

Tricks and traps

It is well worth noting the following points:

- Databricks can export the data in a format that can be opened by a spreadsheet. Alternatively, you can connect many applications directly to a Databricks database. Indeed, you can use Databricks notebooks to hone your queries and then copy the query into the application that you are using to display and/or analyze the data.

- Be careful when exporting large result sets from Databricks into other applications. It is easy to forget that they can run to millions of records and prove too much for either the destination workstation or the capacity of a spreadsheet.

Extracting data from a specific quintile

Prestige Cars caters to a wide range of clients, and the sales director does not want to forget about the 80% of customers that are outside the top 20% that the company focuses on. She wants you to take a closer look at the second quintile of customers, those making up the second 20% of sales. Her exact request is this *find the sales details for the top three selling makes in the second 20% of sales*. The following is the SQL to do this:

```
WITH Top20PercentSales_CTE

AS

(

SELECT      SalesDetailsID, MakeName, ModelName, SalePrice

            ,NTILE(5) OVER (ORDER BY SalePrice DESC)

                AS SalesQuintile

FROM        allsales

)

SELECT      MakeName, ModelName, SalePrice

FROM        Top20PercentSales_CTE CTE

WHERE       MakeName IN (

                        SELECT   MakeName

                        FROM     Top20PercentSales_CTE

                        WHERE    SalesQuintile = 2

                        GROUP BY MakeName
```

```
                        ORDER BY SUM(SalePrice) DESC
                        LIMIT 3
                        )
ORDER BY   SalePrice DESC;
```

Running the preceding query gives the results shown in *Figure 18.14*:

	MakeName	ModelName	SalePrice
1	Aston Martin	DB6	225000
2	Bentley	Brooklands	189500
3	Rolls Royce	Phantom	182500
4	Rolls Royce	Wraith	165000
5	Rolls Royce	Wraith	162500
6	Rolls Royce	Silver Seraph	139500

Figure 18.14: *Using the NTILE() function to isolate a segment of data*

How does it work

The ability to segment and classify your customers can make or break a business. This query illustrates the process of isolating a segment of sales data to produce useful information. The SQL in this example uses a CTE as the core of the query. The CTE uses the **`NTILE()`** function to list makes, models, and sale prices for all cars sold. Then it calculates the quintile for each sale.

Once the quintile has been defined, the subsequent query carries out the following two operations:

- **First**: It uses a subquery to isolate the top three makes belonging to the second quintile.
- **Then**: Once these makes have been found, the outer query outputs all sales for these makes from the CTE.

Tricks and traps

Segmenting data can be an interesting challenge. Be sure to remember the following point when dealing with such queries:

- It is interesting to note that CTE is used twice. The key technique is to first define the quintile and then select a specific quintile from the dataset.

However, because the CTE also joins the tables required to list the make, model, and sale price, it can be reused in the main query so you can avoid rewriting all the SQL needed to produce this specific output.

You can, of course, isolate deciles, percentiles, or any segment of data. For this, you must enter the appropriate figure inside the parentheses, which is a part of the **NTILE()** function. For a decile, you would have entered the following SQL in the preceding example:

```
NTILE(10) OVER (ORDER BY SalePrice DESC) AS SalesDecile
```

Display median values

The CEO has asked for a report that shows the difference between the median discount and the actual discount for all sales per customer. SQL can also isolate a median value from a dataset, as the following piece of SQL shows:

```
SELECT      DISTINCT  CustomerName
            ,TotalSalePrice
            ,TotalSalePrice - PERCENTILE_CONT(0.5)
            WITHIN GROUP(ORDER BY TotalSalePrice)
                        OVER(PARTITION BY CustomerName)
                AS SaleToMedianDelta
FROM        allsales;
```

Running the preceding query gives the results shown in *Figure 18.15*:

	CustomerName	TotalSalePrice	SaleToMedianDelta
1	Alex McWhirter	17850	0
2	Alexei Tolstoi	22990	-26460
3	Alexei Tolstoi	22600	-26850
4	Alexei Tolstoi	69500	20050
5	Alexei Tolstoi	49450	0
6	Alexei Tolstoi	205000	155550

Figure 18.15: *Displaying median values with the PERCENTILE_CONT() function*

How does it work

Finding a median (rather than an average) value and comparing this to sales prices is one example of obtaining purely statistical results from a query. However, SQL does not have a median function in the same way that it has an **`AVG()`** function. Nonetheless, you can calculate a median using the built-in **`PERCENTILE_CONT()`** function. Finding a median value requires you to use the following SQL elements:

- **`PERCENTILE_CONT(0.5)`**: The **`PERCENTILE_CONT()`** function finds a percentile in a dataset. Because you are looking for the median value, you need to indicate this by entering **`0.5`** inside the parentheses.
- **`WITHIN GROUP`**: This lets you specify the numeric field that you want to extract the median value from. Also, you have to include the **`ORDER BY`** clause.
- **`OVER (PARTITION BY)`**: As with the other windowing functions mentioned in the chapter, **`PERCENTILE_CONT()`** allows you to segment the dataset into subgroups to find the median value for each of the fields (or combinations of fields) that you specify after the **`PARTITION BY`** clause.

In this example, the query joins the **`Sales`** and **`Customer`** tables since they contain the required fields. Once the **`CustomerName`** and **`SalePrice`** fields have been selected, you add the clause required to extract the median value per customer and then subtract this from the sale price for each vehicle sold. In this case, it means specifying the **`SalePrice`** field for the **`WITHIN GROUP`** argument and partitioning by the **`CustomerName`** in the **`OVER`** clause.

Tricks and traps

We have one important comment to make is as follows:

- The result of the **`PERCENTILE_CONT()`** function is a calculated value and not a data element.

Conclusion

This chapter introduced some ways you can use SQL to segment and classify. You saw how to deliver hierarchies of data that can also segment the output according to the specified criteria. Furthermore, it illustrated how to subset data into deciles and quintiles that you can extract for further analysis.

Core knowledge learned in this chapter

The keywords that you have seen in this chapter are as follows:

Concept	Description
`RANK()`	The `RANK()` function hierarchizes data according to the user-defined criterion.
`OVER`	The `OVER` keyword is used by the `RANK()` function to introduce the ranking criteria.
`PARTITION BY`	The `PARTITION BY` keyword is used by the `RANK()` function to separate the data into multiple hierarchies.
`DENSE_RANK()`	The `DENSE_RANK()` function hierarchizes data without any gaps in the ranking.
`NTILE()`	The `NTILE()` function distributes the rows in an ordered partition into a specified number of groups.
`PERCENTILE_CONT()`	The `PERCENTILE_CONT()` function is used (among other things) to calculate a median value.
`WITHIN GROUP`	The `WITHIN GROUP` keyword is used by the `PERCENTILE_CONT()` function to return a median value.

Join our book's Discord space

CHAPTER 19
Rolling Analysis

Introduction

Few metrics exist in isolation. Most of the time, you want not only to compare these metrics with other figures but also to see how they evolve over time. It lets you discern trends, track growth, and establish a solid factual base to use for making predictions.

Databricks provide a range of functions that can help you present how data evolves over time or over any sequence or progression in general. These functions are easy to use. They help in delivering a range of running calculations, including the following:

- Running totals
- Running averages
- Running counts

Structure

In this chapter, we will cover the following topics:

- Adding a running total
- Using windowing functions in an aggregated query

- Grouping running totals
- Applying windowing functions to a subquery
- Adding unique ids on the fly using **ROW_NUMBER()**
- Displaying records for missing data
- Displaying a complete range of dates and relevant data
- Comparing data with the data from a previous record
- Comparing data over time using the **FIRST_VALUE()** and **LAST_VALUE()** functions
- Displaying rolling averages over a specified number of records
- Show the first sale and last four sales per client
- Calculating cumulative distribution
- Classifying data using the **PERCENT_RANK()** function
- Using the **LAG()** function with alphabetical data

Objectives

Fortunately, Databricks does not require the knowledge of any new functions to deliver such rolling analysis. It simply extends the use of a handful of already-known functions, such as **SUM()**, **AVG()**, and **COUNT()**. Once these extensions are mastered, you can also use this new approach with a few new functions to isolate:

- Comparative values across a range of records
- The first or last element in a series
- The relative standing of a record in a record set
- The most recent element in a series for comparison

Indeed, the most remarkable part of these calculations is that they all work in an extremely similar manner. Once you have mastered the fundamentals of the working of these functions, you can apply them to your queries to give new power and depth to the analysis.

This set of functions is also Databricks windowing functions. They group datasets into *windows* of data behind the scenes. They also allow you to specify what elements are calculated and how they are grouped. This implies that you can ask Databricks to restart the running total at specific breakpoints.

Consequently, you can restart a running calculation with every new year, month, or day if needed, and, in so doing, you can track the evolution of the metrics over time.

Adding a running total

This time the sales director has requested a list of sales for 2017 that includes running totals of both sales to date and average sales. Fortunately, windowing functions can help, as the following code snippet displays:

```
SELECT        InvoiceNumber
             ,DATE_FORMAT(SaleDate, "dd-MM-yy") AS DateOfSale
             ,SalePrice
             ,SUM(SalePrice)
             OVER (ORDER BY SaleDate ASC) AS AccumulatedSales
             ,AVG(SalePrice)
             OVER (ORDER BY SaleDate ASC)
                 AS AverageSalesValueToDate
FROM         allsales
WHERE        YEAR(SaleDate) = 2017
ORDER BY     SaleDate;
```

Running the preceding query gives the results shown in *Figure 19.1*:

	InvoiceNumber	DateOfSale	SalePrice	AccumulatedSales	AverageSalesValueToDate
1	EURFR110	01-01-17	22500	22500	22500
2	GBPGB111	05-01-17	125000	147500	73750
3	GBPGB112	10-01-17	85000	232500	77500
4	GBPCH114	11-01-17	22500	255000	63750
5	GBPGB115	12-01-17	125950	380950	76190
6	GBPCH116	13-01-17	8850	389800	64966.666666666664

***Figure 19.1:** Generating running totals with the OVER clause*

How does it work

A classic analytical requirement is to see how values change over time. The previous piece of SQL displays not only how to list sales values but also how the running total and average sale price change with each new sale.

The core of this query is a list of sale dates and values taken from the **`AllSales`** table. The data is filtered to limit the result to sales for a given year. Finally, to give this initial list some coherence, it is sorted by sales date.

Then two windowing functions are added to enhance the output and turbocharge the level of information that the query delivers. They do this by extending the use of two functions that you have come to know well: **`SUM()`** and **`AVG()`**.

Each of these functions is extended with an **`OVER`** clause that causes the function to be applied to the field that you are calculating from the beginning of the dataset up to and including the current record. This way, both the **`SUM()`** function and the **`AVG()`** function perform their tasks (adding up the total sales and averaging the sale price, respectively) for each record, up to and including the current record, whereas the **`AVG()`** function also calculates the average sale price for each record up to and including the current record. The final result is a mixture of detailed information for each sale and the overall data up to that date. Essentially, the **`OVER`** clause ensures that the functions are only applied to a part of the dataset and not to the entire set, as the case up until now.

Along with the analysis of the evolution of data, it is important to ensure that the **`OVER`** function orders the data using a field, or fields, that sequence the records over time. In the previous piece of SQL, we are using the **`SaleDate`** field so that the **`OVER`** function essentially says, *from the start of the filtered dataset up to the current record where the dataset is ordered by sale date.*

This is a new use of the **`SUM()`** and **`AVG()`** functions. *Figure 19.2* presents how windowing functions work:

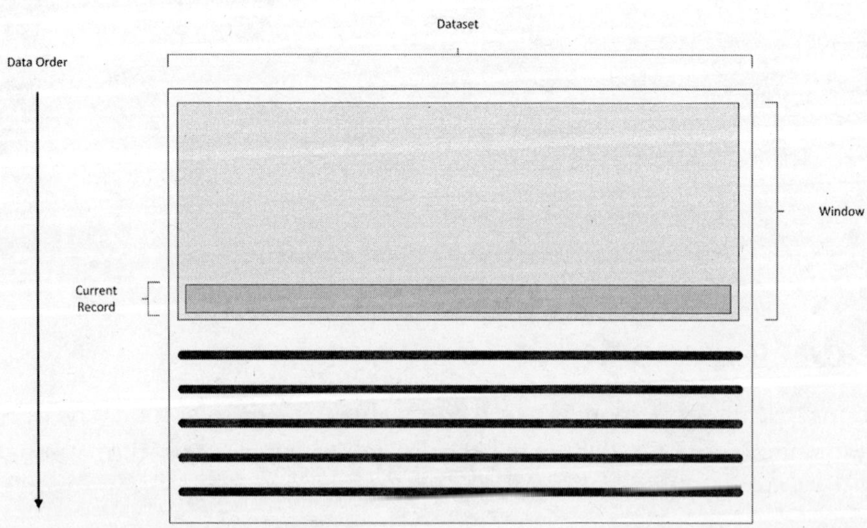

Figure 19.2: *Windowing functions used to create running totals described conceptually*

Tricks and traps

Windowing functions are extremely powerful; however, they do require you to remember the following key points to use them correctly:

- Because you are listing the individual records for each sale, it helps if you display some piece of information (such as the invoice number in this example) that lets the reader see what makes each record unique.
- In this example, we formatted the date purely for presentation purposes. You can, of course, leave the date data in its raw state while you output the query results.
- When using several running totals in a single query, it is important to make sure that they use the *same* **ORDER BY** clause in the **OVER** operator, or you could get undesirable results.
- A running total, just like any other aggregation, needs an alias if you want a column title to be displayed in the output.

Using windowing functions in an aggregated query

The CFO wants a report that displays the purchase cost per day with the cumulative cost for the year 2016, as *Prestige Cars* is perfectly capable of buying several cars on the same day. This is exactly what the following SQL code achieves:

```
SELECT      DateBought
            ,SUM(Cost) AS PurchaseCost
            ,SUM(SUM(Cost))
              OVER (ORDER BY DateBought ASC) AS CostForTheYear
FROM        Stock
WHERE       YEAR(DateBought) = 2016
GROUP BY    DateBought
ORDER BY    DateBought;
```

Running this query gives the results shown in *Figure 19.3*:

	DateBought	PurchaseCost	CostForTheYear
1	2016-01-02 12:00:00	35760	35760
2	2016-01-10 12:00:00	45560	81320
3	2016-01-31 12:00:00	44800	126120
4	2016-02-01 12:00:00	52712	178832
5	2016-02-10 12:00:00	4800	183632
6	2016-02-11 12:00:00	38280	221912

Figure 19.3: *Using windowing functions in an aggregated query*

How does it work

Sometimes, you might need to see an aggregated value, such as the cost of goods bought per day, alongside the running total over time of these same costs. This SQL delivers the required output by grouping data from the **`Stock`** table on the **`DateBought`** field and then by displaying this field alongside the **`SUM()`** of the **`Cost`** field. To avoid getting drowned in data, you made sure the output is restricted to only purchases for 2016.

After this, you commanded Databricks to provide a running total using a **`SUM()`**... **`OVER`** windowing function. However, because this function is a grouped query (or an aggregated query), it *needs to be aggregated as well*. You *have* to make the **`SUM(Cost)`** function into an aggregate function by writing it as **`SUM(SUM(Cost))`**.

Tricks and traps

We have only one important point given as follows. This example is based on a simple technique that you must bear in mind when aggregating data using windowing functions:

- It may seem peculiar, and even counterintuitive, to wrap a **`SUM()`** function inside another **`SUM()`** function. But if you write this query as follows:
  `SUM(Cost)) OVER (ORDER BY DateBought ASC)`

Then the query fails. This is because you are grouping data in a query, and consequently, you must also group data used in running totals.

Grouping running totals

You can use running totals to get an idea of the evolution of the key metrics. Sometimes, however, you want to reset a grouping element so that you can start over when some key piece of data changes, like the beginning of a new year, for instance. So, when the sales director requests a list that shows all sales to date with a running count of sales per year, you can use a windowing function to answer her query. The following SQL snippet shows you how to reset a counter or a running total:

```
SELECT      DATE_FORMAT(SaleDate, "dd-MM-yy") AS DateOfSale
            ,CustomerName, Town
            ,SalePrice
            ,COUNT(SalesDetailsID)
             OVER (PARTITION BY YEAR(SaleDate)
                   ORDER BY SaleDate ASC)
                         AS AnnualNumberOfSalesToDate
FROM        allsales
ORDER BY    SaleDate;
```

Running the preceding query gives the results shown in *Figure 19.4*:

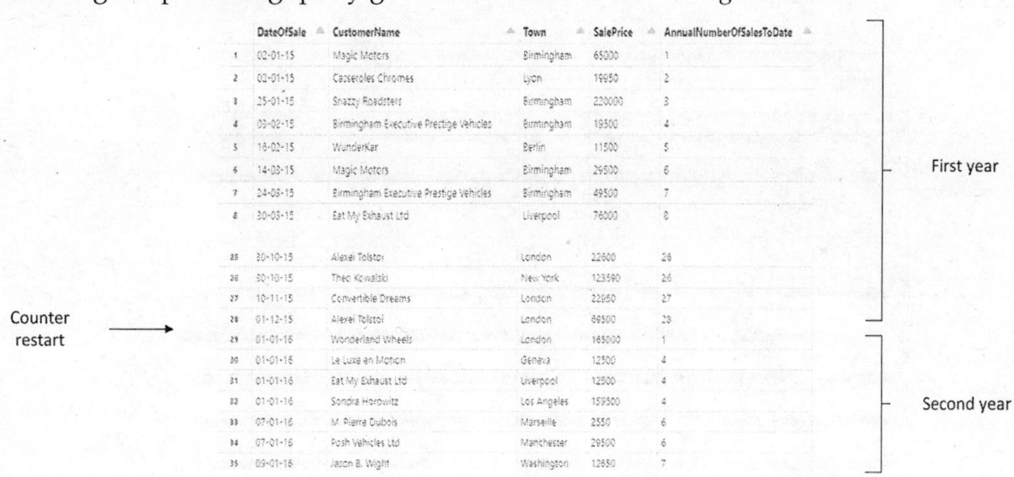

	DateOfSale	CustomerName	Town	SalePrice	AnnualNumberOfSalesToDate
1	02-01-15	Magic Motors	Birmingham	65000	1
2	02-01-15	Casseroles Chromes	Lyon	19950	2
3	25-01-15	Snazzy Roadsters	Birmingham	220000	3
4	03-02-15	Birmingham Executive Prestige Vehicles	Birmingham	19500	4
5	16-02-15	WunderKar	Berlin	11500	5
6	14-03-15	Magic Motors	Birmingham	29500	6
7	24-03-15	Birmingham Executive Prestige Vehicles	Birmingham	49500	7
8	30-03-15	Eat My Exhaust Ltd	Liverpool	76000	8
25	30-10-15	Alexei Tolstoi	London	22600	26
26	30-10-15	Theo Kowalski	New York	123590	26
27	10-11-15	Convertible Dreams	London	22950	27
28	01-12-15	Alexei Tolstoi	London	89500	28
29	01-01-16	Wonderland Wheels	London	165000	1
30	01-01-16	Le Luxe en Motion	Geneva	12500	4
31	01-01-16	Eat My Exhaust Ltd	Liverpool	12500	4
32	01-01-16	Sondra Horowitz	Los Angeles	159500	4
33	07-01-16	M. Pierre Dubois	Marseille	2550	6
34	07-01-16	Posh Vehicles Ltd	Manchester	29500	6
35	09-01-16	Jason B. Wight	Washington	12650	7

Figure 19.4: Grouped running totals using OVER and PARTITION BY

How does it work

This query begins by joining the **`Customer`**, **`Sales`**, and **`SalesDetails`** tables so that you can return sales and customer information (such as the date of sale, customer name, and sale price) for each sale. No filter is applied because you want to see all sales since *Prestige Cars* began trading. The query is sorted by date to ensure that the data appear in a clear and comprehensible way.

You can now add the running counter of sales over time. You build it like the following:

- **First**: Work out the number of sales by adding a `COUNT()` function.
- **Second**: Extended this function to make it a windowing function by adding an `OVER` clause.
- **Third**: Order the resulting counter by a unique field combination (the `SaleDate` field and the `SalesDetailsID` field) so there is no aggregation of the data, and each individual record is displayed.
- **Finally**: Add a `PARTITION BY` clause so that the counter restarts when the field specified after the `PARTITION BY` clause (the year) changes.

The result is a list of all sales over time where you can see not only the accumulated sales as the year progresses but also the total sales for the year at year-end.

Figure 19.5 shows you how a `PARTITION BY` clause works with a windowing function:

Figure 19.5: *A PARTITION BY clause with a windowing function*

Tricks and traps

When you add a `PARTITION BY` clause to a windowing function, you must remember the following key points:

- It is important to use the appropriate fields in the `ORDER BY` clause of the

OVER function to achieve the desired output. If you use the wrong fields, it probably will not return the expected result. In practice, this means you need to select a field that contains the finest level of meaningful granularity of the data. In this example, each individual sale is what matters, so you use the **SalesDetailsID** field in both the **COUNT()** function and the **ORDER BY** clause because it contains a unique value for each record. This ensures that all records are output individually and not aggregated in any way.

- If you use the **SaleDate** field instead of the **SalesDetailsID** field in this query, Databricks counts the days with sales throughout the year. Since there may be days with multiple sales (or no sales at all), the resulting record set will not give the same results.
- Generally, you want to make sure that you are repeating the field(s) that you are using to sort the data in the query (that is, the field or fields that you are using in the main **ORDER BY** clause) in the **OVER** clause. This ensures that the output is visually coherent with the actual data analysis.

Applying windowing functions to a subquery

The CEO's latest request is that you must obtain the total sales to date and then display the running total of sales by value for each year. The following code snippet shows how to do this:

```
SELECT      DATE_FORMAT(SaleDate, "dd-MM-yyyy") AS DateOfSale
            ,DailyCount AS NumberOfSales
            ,SUM(DailyCount) OVER
                   (PARTITION BY YEAR(SaleDate) ORDER BY SaleDate ASC)
                   AS AnnualNumberOfSalesToDate
            ,SUM(DailySalePrice) OVER
                   (PARTITION BY YEAR(SaleDate) ORDER BY SaleDate ASC)
                   AS AnnualSalePriceToDate
FROM        (
            SELECT      SA.SaleDate
                        ,COUNT(SalesDetailsID) AS DailyCount
```

```
                ,SUM(SalePrice) AS DailySalePrice
        FROM    SalesDetails SD
        INNER JOIN  Sales AS SA
                ON SA.SalesID = SD.SalesID
        GROUP BY    SA.SaleDate
        ) DT
ORDER BY    SaleDate;
```

Running the preceding query gives the results that you can see in *Figure 19.6*:

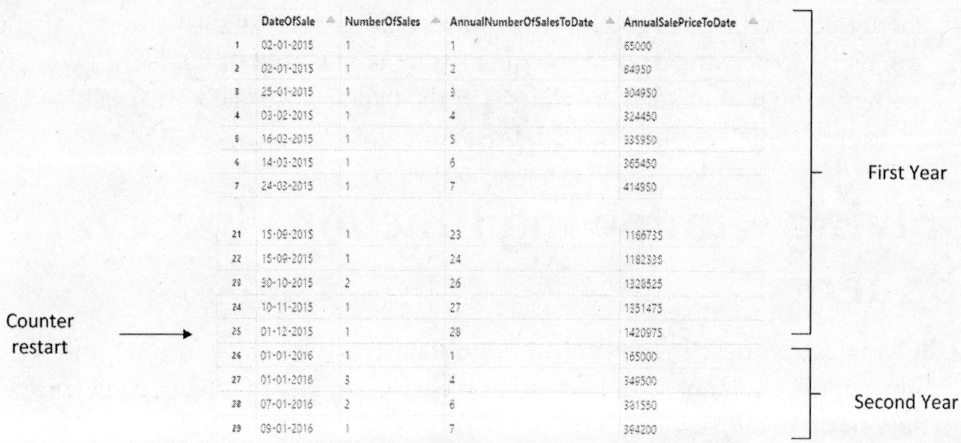

	DateOfSale	NumberOfSales	AnnualNumberOfSalesToDate	AnnualSalePriceToDate
1	02-01-2015	1	1	65000
2	02-01-2015	1	2	64950
3	25-01-2015	1	3	304950
4	03-02-2015	1	4	324450
5	16-02-2015	1	5	335950
6	14-03-2015	1	6	365450
7	24-03-2015	1	7	414950
21	15-09-2015	1	23	1166735
22	15-09-2015	1	24	1182335
23	30-10-2015	2	26	1328525
24	10-11-2015	1	27	1351475
25	01-12-2015	1	28	1420975
26	01-01-2016	1	1	165000
27	01-01-2016	3	4	349500
28	07-01-2016	2	6	381550
29	09-01-2016	1	7	394200

Figure 19.6: *Using windowing functions and a subquery*

How does it work

Possibly the easiest way to achieve the desired objectives in this query is to break the task into the following two parts:

1. **First**: Create a derived table that counts the number and value of sales per day for each individual date.
2. **Second**: Create an outer query that returns the cumulative sales for the year in addition to the running total of sales revenue from the derived table.

In this example, the subquery is an aggregate query that groups the result by date and provides a **`COUNT()`** of sales and a **`SUM()`** of sales value. We did not apply any filters so that all sales from the beginning of trading are included. To get a clearer idea of what is included, refer to *Figure 19.7*, which shows the output from the subquery:

	SaleDate	DailyCount	DailySalePrice
1	2017-03-05T02:04:00.000+0000	1743	218080688
2	2015-07-12T10:00:00.000+0000	1743	218080688
3	2017-12-12T02:41:00.000+0000	1743	218080688
4	2015-05-10T12:00:00.000+0000	1743	218080688
5	2018-08-15T12:00:00.000+0000	1743	218080688
6	2017-06-01T08:21:00.000+0000	1743	218080688

Figure 19.7: *Subquery output*

The outer query can then take the three elements that are generated by the inner query (sale date, daily sales count, and daily sales value) and use them as follows:

- **`SaleDate`**: It is displayed in the output as is and is also used to sort the query results.
- **`DailyCount`**: It is output as is to display the number of sales for each day that there are sales.
- **`DailyCount`**: It is reused in a windowing function to provide the running total of sales to date. We achieve the running total by applying the **`COUNT()`** function over the sale date. In this example, the aggregate value is also partitioned by year using the **`PARTITION BY`** clause so that the count restarts with each new year.
- **`DailySalePrice`**: It is reused (and output as **`AnnualNumberOf SalesToDate`**) in a separate windowing function that is also ordered by sale date and partitioned by the year. This allows the display of cumulative sales to date for each year.

Using a derived table to perform the initial aggregation is an effective way of preparing the initial data that is afterward used to provide the running totals. It also allows you to test the initial data simply by selecting and executing the query that underlies the derived table; this way, you can check each part of the process as you build the query.

Adding unique ids on the fly using ROW_ NUMBER()

The sales staff has asked you to create a unique numbering system to identify sales sequentially to avoid the complex identifiers that appear in the billing system. The following SQL shows how to add this distinguishing feature without changing the source data:

```
SELECT       DATE_FORMAT(SaleDate, "dd-MM-yyyy") AS DateOfSale
            ,SalePrice, CustomerName, Town, MakeName
            ,COUNT(SalesDetailsID)
              OVER (PARTITION BY YEAR(SaleDate)
              ORDER BY SaleDate ASC)
                 AS AnnualNumberOfSalesToDate
            ,ROW_NUMBER() OVER (ORDER BY SaleDate ASC)
                 AS SalesCounter
FROM        allsales
ORDER BY    SaleDate;
```

Running the preceding query gives the results as shown in *Figure 19.8*:

	DateOfSale	SalePrice	CustomerName	Town	MakeName	AnnualNumberOfSalesToDate	SalesCounter
1	02-01-2015	65000	Magic Motors	Birmingham	Ferrari	1	1
2	02-01-2015	19950	Casseroles Chromes	Lyon	Porsche	2	2
3	25-01-2015	220000	Snazzy Roadsters	Birmingham	Ferrari	3	3
4	03-02-2015	19500	Birmingham Executive Prestige Vehicles	Birmingham	Porsche	4	4
5	16-02-2015	11500	WunderKar	Berlin	Porsche	5	5
6	14-03-2015	29500	Magic Motors	Birmingham	Aston Martin	6	6
341	08-12-2018	99500	Andrea Tarbuck	Birmingham	Aston Martin	122	341
342	08-12-2018	54500	Boris Spry	Birmingham	Aston Martin	122	342
343	08-12-2018	1590	Boris Spry	Birmingham	Trabant	122	343
344	16-12-2018	11500	Antonio Maura	Madrid	Triumph	123	344
345	17-12-2018	17950	Screamin' Wheels	Los Angeles	Alfa Romeo	124	345
346	31-12-2018	5500	Laurent Saint Yves	Marseille	Citroen	127	346
347	31-12-2018	950	Mrs. Ivana Telford	Liverpool	Reliant	127	347
348	31-12-2018	145000	Andy Cheshire	Stoke	Ferrari	127	348

Figure 19.8: *Using the ROW_NUMBER() windowing function to add unique IDs to a recordset*

How does it work

Source data does not always come with all the required elements. Sometimes, you may require a way of numbering records to identify each row individually. The **`ROW_NUMBER()`** function lets you do just this with no effect on the underlying data.

This query starts with the **`AllSales`** table, which contains the fields to be output (**`SaleDate`**, **`SalePrice`**, **`CustomerName`**, **`Town`**, and **`MakeName`**). Then, it adds these fields, with the necessary formatting and aliases, to the **`SELECT`** clause.

Then, the following windowing functions are added:

- **`COUNT()`**: It displays the number of sales per day per year. This function is partitioned by year (so that the counter restarts each time the year changes) and ordered by date.
- **`ROW_NUMBER()`**: It shows an individual and progressively increasing number to identify each record that is output.

The special feature in this query is the use of the **`ROW_NUMBER()`** windowing function. This function lets you add a series of numbers to an output dataset. The series starts at 1 and increases by one for each record in the windowed dataset.

The **`ROW_NUMBER()`** also requires you to add an **`OVER`** clause containing an **`ORDER BY`** statement. To ensure that these virtual IDs are numbered sequentially in a comprehensible manner, the **`ROW_NUMBER()`** function is ordered by the sale date. As we want a continuous range of numbers defined for all the source data, we choose not to add a **`PARTITION BY`** clause to the windowing function. The result is a series of numbers consecutively increased in the query output, even if there is no numbering in the source data.

This means that the **`ROW_NUMBER()`** function in the preceding query ends up looking like the following:

```
ROW_NUMBER() OVER (ORDER BY SaleDate ASC)
```

Tricks and traps

The following are some important point to remember when applying the **`ROW_NUMBER()`** function:

- **`ROW_NUMBER()`** is not the same as **`COUNT()`**, despite the superficial similarities. If you look at the output for this query for April 30, 2015, you see two records for this date. The **`COUNT()`** windowing function shows a total of 12 sales to date for this day, and this is the same for either of the day's sales (as it should be). The **`ROW_NUMBER()`** function attributes a different number to each record, even if the **`ORDER BY`** clause for the function is the **`SaleDate`** field.
- So the **`ROW_NUMBER()`** function *always* differentiates the records that are returned. This can mean applying the numbering sequence arbitrarily to certain rows if there are ties using the sort order that is defined. You can see this in the two sales for April 30, 2015.
- Of course, if you want to specify a completely comprehensive numbering system, you can extend the sort order that is applied by the **`ROW_NUMBER()`** function. So, you could, for instance, tweak the SQL to read as follows:

```
ROW_NUMBER() OVER (ORDER BY SaleDate, Make, Model ASC) AS Sale-
sCounter
```

Displaying records for missing data

The CEO needs a weekly calendar of sales for 2016. CEO makes it clear that she wants to see a list of all the weeks in the year, whether there were any sales in that week or not. After a little effort, you produce the following SQL to deliver the sales report that she was hoping for:

```
WITH Tally_CTE
AS
(
SELECT      ROW_NUMBER() OVER (ORDER BY StockCode) AS Num
FROM        Stock
LIMIT       52
)
SELECT              CTE.Num, SLS.SalesForTheWeek
FROM                Tally_CTE CTE
LEFT OUTER JOIN
                    (
                    SELECT          SUM(TotalSalePrice) AS SalesForTheWeek
                                    ,DATE_PART("WEEK", SaleDate) AS WeekNo
                    FROM            Sales
                    WHERE           YEAR(SaleDate) = 2016
                    GROUP BY        DATE_PART("WEEK", SaleDate)
                    ) SLS
                    ON CTE.Num = SLS.WeekNo;
```

Running the preceding SQL produces the output shown in *Figure 19.9*:

	Num	SalesForTheWeek
1	1	44700
2	2	null
3	3	56950
4	4	null
5	5	null
6	6	null
7	7	183280

***Figure 19.9:** Displaying missing data using a sequence list*

How does it work

Delivering output when the data exists is rarely an issue; however, you may need to apply slightly different querying techniques if you need to show *missing* data. This is because SQL does not naturally create complete lists of dates or date elements, such as weeks, where there is no corresponding data in a database.

To understand this problem more clearly, run the SQL from the preceding snippet that returns the total sales per week for 2016, which is contained in the derived table with the alias SLS. The output from the derived table is shown in *Figure 19.10:*

	SalesForTheWeek	WeekNo
1	167350	31
2	349500	53
3	348000	34
4	15650	26
5	12500	27
6	111890	44
7	148480	22

***Figure 19.10:** The source data with missing values*

Although the figures are accurate, the data contains loopholes since there are no sales for certain weeks. Because these holes could be precisely the data to focus on, it is important to return a full list of weeks (with or without data).

Forcing Databricks to return a complete sequence (whether it is dates, weeks, or any other series of information) requires the extension of the SQL with a list that contains an unbroken and consecutive list of all the elements that you need to view. You can then use this list as the basis for a query that adds the aggregated output.

A sequence like this is often called a tally table or a numbers list. In this SQL, you:

- **First**: Create a **Common Table Expression** (**CTE**) that contains a numbers list.
- **Second**: Joined the CTE to a query (the derived subquery in this example) that calculates the sales per week.

Let us begin by looking at the numbers table. Although we call this a table, it is actually a dataset generated by a CTE. If you run the code inside the CTE named `Tally_CTE`, you see the output in *Figure 19.11*:

	Num
1	1
2	2
3	3
4	4
5	5
6	6
7	7

Figure 19.11: *A sequence list or tally table*

As you can see, this CTE simply returns a sequence of numbers. You obtain this sequence by the following:

- **First**: Choosing a table that contains more records than needed in the numbers table (the CTE output). This can be any table in the database.
- **Then**: Selecting the first n records from this table that correspond to the number of items in the required sequence. In this example, there are 52 weeks in the year, so you use `LIMIT 52` to limit the number of elements in the tally table.
- **Finally**: As you are not interested in the actual data that the source table (`Stock`) contains but only in the number of records, you define a `ROW_NUMBER()` function (ordered by any field in the table) to provide a sequence of numbers.

The CTE at the start of the SQL serves only to provide a sequential list that supplies a row for each week in the year.

Once the tally table is set, join this to the derived table that returns the actual data for each week of sales. Because you have extracted the week number from the `SaleDate` field using the `DATEPART()` function, you can join the week number for each week of sales to the corresponding record in the tally table. Defining the join as a `LEFT OUTER` join from the tally table (the CTE) to the derived query ensures that every record from the CTE is displayed, whether or not any corresponding data is in the derived query.

The result is the output from *Figure 19.9*, shown previously, which shows all the weeks in 2016 with the sales figures, even if there are no sales for a specific week.

NOTE: If you use a single table as the basis for the tally table, it must contain at least as many records as you need for the sequential list. The next section explains a technique to guarantee enough rows if it concerns you that a single source table will not contain enough records.

Displaying a complete range of dates and relevant data

CEO told the sales director to look at increasing sales and avoid days with no sales. As a result, the sales director has requested a list of daily sales for a six-month period (from January 1 to June 30, 2017, to be precise).

You come up with the following piece of SQL:

```
WITH Tally_CTE

AS

(

SELECT      ROW_NUMBER() OVER (ORDER BY ST1.StockCode) -1 AS Num

FROM        Stock ST1

JOIN        Stock ST2

LIMIT       10000

)

,DateRange_CTE
```

```
AS
(
SELECT     DATE_ADD('2017-01-01', Num) AS DateList FROM Tally_CTE
WHERE      Num <= DATEDIFF('2017-06-30', '2017-01-01')
)
SELECT              CAST(DateList AS DATE) AS SaleDate, SalesPerDay
FROM                DateRange_CTE CTE
LEFT OUTER JOIN
                    (
                    SELECT         CAST(SaleDate AS DATE) AS DateOfSale
                                  ,SUM(TotalSalePrice) AS SalesPerDay
                    FROM          Sales
                    GROUP BY      CAST(SaleDate AS DATE)
                    ) SLS
                    ON CTE.DateList = SLS.DateOfSale;
```

Running the preceding code delivers the output shown in *Figure 19.12*:

	SaleDate	SalesPerDay
1	2017-01-01	22500
2	2017-01-02	null
3	2017-01-03	null
4	2017-01-04	null
5	2017-01-05	125000
6	2017-01-06	null
7	2017-01-07	null

***Figure 19.12:** A complete range of dates including dates without any corresponding data*

How does it work

Once again, the source data used in this example does not necessarily contain records for empty values; that is, a sale is not necessarily made every day during the relevant period. Therefore, you need to ensure that you have a sequence of a range of dates where there are no missing values.

You accomplish this using the following two CTEs:

- **The first CTE**: It is a tally table (or a numbers list) that ensures a large sequence of numbers. This guarantees that you can request a range of dates over several years if necessary.
- **The second CTE**: It uses the tally table to create a sequence of dates between a start date and an end date.

As each of these, CTEs carry out a specific task. The tally table CTE works as follows:

- **First**: It specifies a large, incremented list of a range of numbers (10,000 in this case, enough for nearly 30 years of individual days) using the **`ROW_NUMBER()`** function. As the tally table begins at 1 by default, in this example, we tweaked it to start at 0 by subtracting 1 from the output of the function. This way, the **`DATEADD()`** and **`DATEDIFF()`** functions begin and end with the actual start and end dates. The SQL snippet uses (**`DATE_ADD()`**, which starts the list of dates by adding 0 days to the start date, effectively beginning at the date used in the code).
- **Second**: It uses two tables (or the same table twice with two different aliases) that are joined using the **`CROSS JOIN`** operator. This approach multiplies the number of records in the first table by the number of records in the second table producing a large set of records that become the basis for the number sequence.

The **`DateRange`** CTE works like the following:

- **First**: The **`DATE_ADD()`** function is used to increment a start date (January 1, 2017) with a sequence of days. This CTE is based on the value in the first CTE, which it, in effect, converts to a date by adding the value in the first CTE to the start date.
- **Second**: A **`WHERE`** clause filters the upper limit of the date range to June 30, 2017. It does this by using the **`DATEDIFF()`** function to calculate the number of days between the start and end dates, which are also specified in the **`DATEDIFF()`** function. The number of days becomes the upper threshold for the largest record number from the tally dataset.

If you run the following code snippet just after the two CTEs (in line 15 of the code, on the blank line before the final **SELECT** clause), you can see the range of continuous calendar dates, as shown in *Figure 19.13*. The code to run is as follows:

```
SELECT * FROM DateRange_CTE
```

	DateList
1	2017-01-01
2	2017-01-02
3	2017-01-03
4	2017-01-04
5	2017-01-05
6	2017-01-06
7	2017-01-07

Figure 19.13: *A complete range of dates based on a tally table*

Finally, the second CTE, that is, **DateRange_CTE**, is joined to the derived query that aggregates daily sales. As was the case in the previous example, it is the range of dates that is the *core* table in the query so that an unbroken range of dates is output. A **LEFT OUTER** join to the derived table ensures that a complete range of dates is output. Joining the derived table and the second CTE join on their respective date fields allows the query to return sales data where there is a sale date.

Tricks and traps

We have a couple of comments worthy of note at this point are given as follows:

- The cross-join to get a large number of records from two tables is called, technically, a Cartesian join. Such a join shows each record from one table joined to each record from the other table. Although this can be dangerous when you are carrying out precise queries, this approach is useful when you need to create a tally table.
- Unless you are sure that the date fields that you are using to join the derived table and the tally dataset are of the **DATE** data type, it is worth converting the date fields to **DATE** objects. This ensures that the join is successful.

Comparing data with the data from a previous record

The sales director of *Prestige Cars* is keen to track customer spending. The sales director wants you to track sales over time and highlight the difference between previous and current sale values per customer for each sale. The following piece of SQL helps you with the demand:

```
SELECT      CustomerName

           ,SaleDate

           ,TotalSalePrice

           ,TotalSalePrice - LAG(TotalSalePrice,1)

                               OVER (PARTITION BY CustomerName

                               ORDER BY SaleDate)

                                  AS DifferenceToPreviousSalePrice

FROM        allsales

ORDER BY    SaleDate;
```

Running the preceding query gives the results shown in *Figure 19.14*:

	CustomerName	SaleDate	TotalSalePrice	DifferenceToPreviousSalePrice
1	Magic Motors	2015-01-02T08:00:00.000+0000	65000	null
2	Casseroles Chromes	2015-01-02T10:33:00.000+0000	19900	null
3	Snazzy Roadsters	2015-01-25T12:00:00.000+0000	220000.1	null
4	Birmingham Executive Prestige Vehicles	2015-02-03T10:00:00.000+0000	19500	null
5	WunderKar	2015-02-16T08:00:00.000+0000	11500	null
6	Magic Motors	2015-03-14T12:00:00.000+0000	29500	-35500
7	Birmingham Executive Prestige Vehicles	2015-03-24T12:00:00.000+0000	49500.2	30000.199999999997

***Figure 19.14:** Comparing data between records using the LAG() function*

How does it work

Although we have seen how to compare individual pieces of data with groups of data so far, we have not compared individual records to other records. As the first example of assessing how a sequence of records varies from others, this piece of SQL shows how each sale compares to the previous one for the same customer.

In the preceding piece of code, you meet the **`LAG()`** function for the first time. This function allows you to look back over a subset of records and return data from a previous record or records.

The query works like the following:

- **First**: A perfectly normal query is constructed that returns a list of individual sales with the sale price and the customer who bought the car using the **`Sales`** and **`Customer`** tables.
- **Then**: A **`LAG()`** function is added that goes back through the record set until it finds the previous sale for the same customer as the one in the current record. It returns the previous sale price and, for this customer, subtracts this figure from the current record's sale price to give the difference between the two sale prices for the vehicles.

Just like the other windowing functions that you have seen, the **`LAG()`** function requires a few parameters to work properly. In this example, they are as follows:

- **`OVER`**: This operator introduces a windowing function.
- **`PARTITION BY`**: This operator tells Databricks how to group the data when searching for a previous record. As this example has **`PARTITION BY CustomerName`** inside the **`OVER`** clause, SQL only jumps back to records that have the same customer name as the current record and not merely the previous record in the dataset.
- **`ORDER BY`**: This clause sorts the subset of data (that is grouped by customer) in chronological order because it is the **`SaleDate`** field that provides the sort order.
- **`Field`**: This indicates the data to return from the preceding record. In this example, it is the **`SalePrice`** field.
- **`Offset Value`**: This is the number of records to jump back for this customer. The value is set to 1 in this example because we want the previous record for the same customer.

Once all these elements are in place, the **`LAG()`** function can *subset* the data into an invisible group based on the customer field. As this data subset is a list of records over time relative to the current record, the function steps back into the preceding record for the customer and returns the previous sale price. As you can see in the output, there is, by definition, no previous sale for the first sale for each customer. This is why the **`LAG()`** function returns a **`NULL`** value.

Refer to image *Figure 19.15* to see a high-level overview of how the **`LAG()`** value works:

Figure 19.15: *Conceptual overview of the LAG() function*

Tricks and traps

The **LAG()** function is extremely powerful. This means that one masters a few subtleties if applying the function constructively:

- The field that you place inside the **LAG()** function does not have to appear in the **SELECT** clause; however, it must be in one of the tables contained in the **FROM** clause of the query.
- If you do not want to see records where there is no difference with any previous sale (because this was the first sale), you can use nearly the whole query as a derived table and wrap it in an outer query. This query then selects the columns from the derived table and adds a **WHERE** clause to eliminate the **PreviousSalePriceDifference** records that contain NULLs. The code looks like the following:

```
SELECT *
FROM
(
SELECT      CustomerName
           ,SaleDate
           ,TotalSalePrice
           ,TotalSalePrice - LAG(TotalSalePrice,1)
```

```
                              OVER (PARTITION BY CustomerName
                                    ORDER BY SaleDate)
                                          AS PreviousSalePriceDifference
     FROM      allsales
     ) SQ
     WHERE PreviousSalePriceDifference IS NOT NULL
     ORDER BY   SaleDate;
```

Running the preceding query gives the output as shown in *Figure 19.16*:

	CustomerName	SaleDate	TotalSalePrice	PreviousSalePriceDifference
1	Magic Motors	2015-03-14T12:00:00.000+0000	29500	-35500
2	Birmingham Executive Prestige Vehicles	2015-03-24T12:00:00.000+0000	49500.2	30000.199999999997
3	Wonderland Wheels	2015-04-30T12:00:00.000+0000	89000	0
4	M. Pierre Dubois	2015-05-20T12:00:00.000+0000	8950	-10650
5	SuperSport S.A.R.L.	2015-07-25T12:00:00.000+0000	75500	0
6	Peter McLuckie	2015-09-15T12:00:00.000+0000	15600	2950
7	Alexei Tolstoi	2015-10-30T12:00:00.000+0000	22600	-390

Figure 19.16: *Using a subquery with a LAG() function in a derived table*

You cannot simply apply the **WHERE** clause inside the original query to filter the record set and remove any records with **NULL** values for the sale price. This is because windowing functions can only be used in **SELECT** or **ORDER BY** clauses. Consequently, you must move the **ORDER BY** clause from the derived table to the outer query.

- A **PARTITION BY** function is not required when using the **LAG()** function. However, without one, the **LAG()** function returns data from a record that precedes the current record in the overall dataset without attempting to group the comparative dataset by a specific element, such as the customer.

Comparing data over time using the FIRST_VALUE() and LAST_VALUE() functions

Prestige Cars is continuing its drive to maximize revenue per customer. This time, the sales director wants to find the initial and final sale prices for each car sold to each customer and then compare these prices with the current selling price. You create the following piece of SQL to do this:

```
SELECT      CustomerName
           ,SaleDate
```

```
        ,TotalSalePrice AS CurrentSale
        ,FIRST_VALUE(TotalSalePrice)
         OVER (PARTITION BY CustomerName
               ORDER BY SaleDate)
                   AS InitialOrder
        ,LAST_VALUE(TotalSalePrice)
         OVER (PARTITION BY CustomerName
               ORDER BY SaleDate
               ROWS BETWEEN CURRENT ROW AND UNBOUNDED FOLLOWING)
                   AS FinalOrder
FROM      allsales;
```

Running the preceding query gives the results shown in *Figure 19.17*:

	CustomerName	SaleDate	CurrentSale	InitialOrder	FinalOrder
1	Alex McWhirter	2018-10-31T12:00:00.000+0000	17850	17850	17850
2	Alexei Tolstoi	2015-07-15T12:00:00.000+0000	22990	22990	45950
3	Alexei Tolstoi	2015-10-30T12:00:00.000+0000	22600	22990	45950
4	Alexei Tolstoi	2015-12-01T08:00:00.000+0000	69500	22990	45950
5	Alexei Tolstoi	2016-05-30T12:00:00.000+0000	49450	22990	45950
6	Alexei Tolstoi	2016-05-30T12:00:00.000+0000	49450	22990	45950
7	Alexei Tolstoi	2016-07-25T12:00:00.000+0000	205000	22990	45950

Figure 19.17: *Using the FIRST_VALUE() and LAST_VALUE() functions to compare sale prices*

How does it work

A useful way to analyze how data evolves over time is to see how a record compares to the first or last record for a common element. This query starts by joining the **`Customer`** and **`Sales`** tables so that customer and sales data are accessible. Then, it outputs the **`CustomerName`**, **`SaleDate`**, and **`TotalSalePrice`** fields.

Then there comes a complication. Two output fields are added that are based, respectively, on the **`FIRST_VALUE()`** and **`LAST_VALUE()`** functions. These act like the **`LAG()`** function mentioned in the previous example. In that, for each record, they create an invisible dataset that is grouped on a shared field (**`CustomerName`** in this example). However, in this case, it is not a selected preceding record that is selected but the very first (or very last) record in this virtual subgroup.

FIRST_VALUE() and **LAST_VALUE()** require the following elements to work correctly:

- **OVER**: This clause starts the windowing function.
- **PARTITION BY**: This function tells Databricks how to subset the data when searching for the first record; in this example, this means the first value for the customer of the current record. The **PARTITION BY** function is not strictly necessary, but it is used to compare data that share a common element rather than returning the first or last value from the entire dataset.
- **ORDER BY**: This clause sorts the data subset.
- **Field**: This indicates the data to return from the preceding record. In this example, it is the **SalePrice** field.

The **FIRST_VALUE()**, **LAST_VALUE()**, and **LAG()** functions can be particularly useful for avoiding the creation of multiple, complex subqueries or derived tables to isolate values from the data. These functions traverse the data for each element that is specified in the **PARTITION BY** clause (the client in this example) and return the required record.

Figure 19.18 illustrates how these functions work:

***Figure 19.18:** The way that the FIRST_VALUE(), LAST_VALUE(), and LAG() functions operate*

Displaying rolling averages over a specified number of records

The sales director wants to see how average sale prices evolve over time for each customer in a report that shows the rolling average sale value for the last three sales per customer. Fortunately, SQL makes reports easy as the following code displays:

```
SELECT      CustomerName
           ,SaleDate
           ,TotalSalePrice
           ,AVG(TotalSalePrice)
            OVER (PARTITION BY CustomerName ORDER BY SaleDate
            ROWS BETWEEN 3 PRECEDING AND CURRENT ROW)
               AS AverageSalePrice
FROM       allsales
ORDER BY   CustomerName, SaleDate;
```

Running the preceding query gives the results shown in *Figure 19.19*:

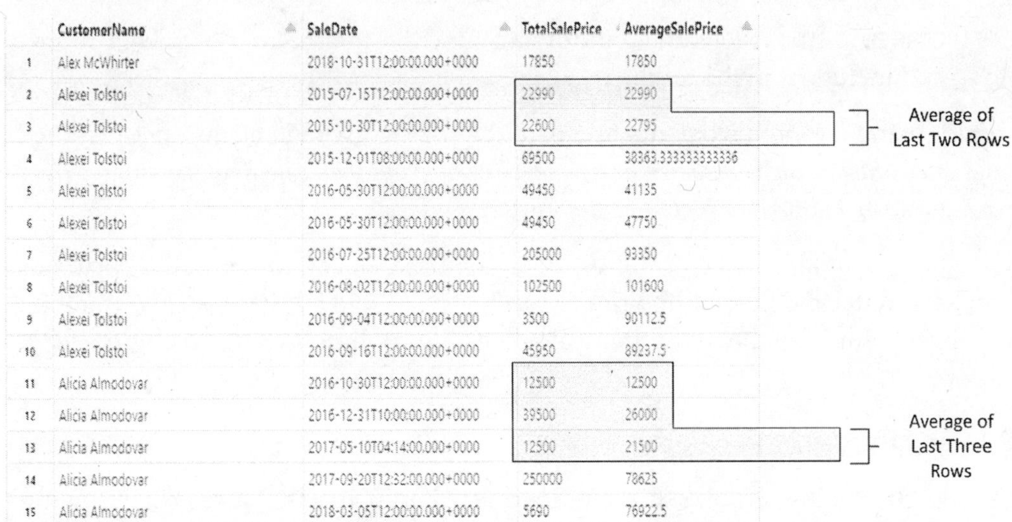

	CustomerName	SaleDate	TotalSalePrice	AverageSalePrice
1	Alex McWhirter	2018-10-31T12:00:00.000+0000	17850	17850
2	Alexei Tolstoi	2015-07-15T12:00:00.000+0000	22990	22990
3	Alexei Tolstoi	2015-10-30T12:00:00.000+0000	22600	22795
4	Alexei Tolstoi	2015-12-01T08:00:00.000+0000	69500	38363.333333333336
5	Alexei Tolstoi	2016-05-30T12:00:00.000+0000	49450	41135
6	Alexei Tolstoi	2016-05-30T12:00:00.000+0000	49450	47750
7	Alexei Tolstoi	2016-07-25T12:00:00.000+0000	205000	93350
8	Alexei Tolstoi	2016-08-02T12:00:00.000+0000	102500	101600
9	Alexei Tolstoi	2016-09-04T12:00:00.000+0000	3500	90112.5
10	Alexei Tolstoi	2016-09-16T12:00:00.000+0000	45950	89237.5
11	Alicia Almodovar	2016-10-30T12:00:00.000+0000	12500	12500
12	Alicia Almodovar	2016-12-31T10:00:00.000+0000	39500	26000
13	Alicia Almodovar	2017-05-10T04:14:00.000+0000	12500	21500
14	Alicia Almodovar	2017-09-20T12:32:00.000+0000	250000	78625
15	Alicia Almodovar	2018-03-05T12:00:00.000+0000	5690	76922.5

Figure 19.19: Using the ROWS() windowing function to display a rolling average

How does it work

A classic analytical metric is the rolling average. The rolling average requires you to isolate a certain number of records up to and including a current record and then calculate the average of a value in all the specified records. The **ROWS** windowing function helps you do this. This approach requires you to specify no fewer than the following seven different elements as part of the windowing function for it to work correctly:

- **AVG()**: It is defined as the aggregation function to apply in the query.
- **OVER**: It indicates that this is a windowing function being applied to a set of records.
- **PARTITION BY**: It specifies how records are assembled into a subgroup inside the overall record set. In this example, the **CustomerName** field is used so that a rolling average per customer can be calculated.
- **ORDER BY**: It is used inside the **OVER** operator to define how the records for the subset are sorted. This is essential to define the sequencing for the range of records used for the rolling average.
- **ROWS BETWEEN**: It indicates that this operator applies to a set of records relative to the current record.
- **PRECEDING**: It confirms how many rows back the function must go to find the starting row for the running average.
- **CURRENT ROW**: It tells the windowing function to stop at the current record and include it in the total.

In effect, using all these elements to create the rolling average claims, *create virtual groups of records for each customer, order them by date, and then calculate the average from three rows before the current row up to and including the current row.*

So, in this example, you begin by creating the basic query to show the customer name, sales date, and the selling price for each vehicle sold by *Prestige Cars*. You then add a final column to the query that calculates the running average using the **ROWS** function.

Tricks and traps

The following points are worth remembering when using the **ROWS()** windowing function:

- A rolling total can be created in almost the same way as a rolling average. The only difference is the use of the **SUM()** function instead of the **AVG()** function for the rolling total.

- Once again, we prefer to add an **ORDER BY** clause at the end of the query to guarantee that the output is in the desired way. This is because the **ORDER BY** clause inside the **OVER** function does not guarantee sorting of the final output correctly.
- You may prefer to apply an entirely different sort of order to the final output. Doing so has no effect on the way the running average is calculated. To make this clearer, try tweaking the sort order code to return a list rather like the one in *Figure 19.20* using the following code:

```
ORDER BY   SaleDate, CustomerName
```

	CustomerName	SaleDate	TotalSalePrice	AverageSalePrice
1	Magic Motors	2015-01-02T08:00:00.000+0000	65000	65000
2	Casseroles Chromes	2015-01-02T10:33:00.000+0000	19900	19900
3	Snazzy Roadsters	2015-01-25T12:00:00.000+0000	220000.1	220000.1
4	Birmingham Executive Prestige Vehicles	2015-02-03T10:00:00.000+0000	19500	19500
5	WunderKar	2015-02-16T08:00:00.000+0000	11500	11500
6	Magic Motors	2015-03-14T12:00:00.000+0000	29500	47250

***Figure 19.20:** Using a different sort order in the window function and the overall query*

As you can see, the output is based on the sale date, not on the customer name. However, the calculation for the running average has not changed. It still calculates the average from the last three records per customer, up to and including their current record for that customer; however, the output is less intuitively comprehensible and shows no clear pattern, even if it is arithmetically accurate.

- If you want to show a running average or a running total that does not include the current row, you can replace **CURRENT ROW** with 1 **PRECEDING** in the SQL. This carries out the calculation up to but not including the current row.
- You can specify any row range relative to the current row for a running total. Moreover, you can cover rows that are further down the display list (or at a later date than the current record if required). This is done by replacing **CURRENT ROW** with three following in the SQL. You can specify any number for the range of records that you want to use as a basis for your calculation.

Show the first sale and last four sales per client

The latest request is for a report that shows both the first order and the last four sales for each customer. One way of doing this is shown using the following SQL:

```
SELECT
 CustomerName
,SaleDate
,TotalSalePrice
,FIRST_VALUE(TotalSalePrice) OVER (PARTITION BY CustomerName
                                   ORDER BY SaleDate) AS FirstOrder
,LAG(TotalSalePrice, 3) OVER (PARTITION BY CustomerName
                              ORDER BY SaleDate) AS LastButThreeOrder
,LAG(TotalSalePrice, 2) OVER (PARTITION BY CustomerName
                              ORDER BY SaleDate) AS LastButTwoOrder
,LAG(TotalSalePrice, 1) OVER (PARTITION BY CustomerName
                              ORDER BY SaleDate) AS LastButOneOrder
,LAST_VALUE(TotalSalePrice) OVER (PARTITION BY CustomerName
                                  ORDER BY SaleDate) AS LatestOrder
FROM    allsales;
```

Running the preceding query gives the results shown in *Figure 19.21*:

	CustomerName	SaleDate	TotalSalePrice	FirstOrder	LastButThreeOrder	LastButTwoOrder	LastButOneOrder	LatestOrder
1	Alex McWhirter	2018-10-31T12:00:00.000+0000	17850	17850	null	null	null	17850
2	Alexei Tolstoi	2015-07-15T12:00:00.000+0000	22990	22990	null	null	null	22990
3	Alexei Tolstoi	2015-10-30T12:00:00.000+0000	22600	22990	null	null	22990	22600
4	Alexei Tolstoi	2015-12-01T08:00:00.000+0000	69500	22990	null	22990	22600	69500
5	Alexei Tolstoi	2016-05-30T12:00:00.000+0000	49450	22990	22990	22600	69500	49450
6	Alexei Tolstoi	2016-05-30T12:00:00.000+0000	49450	22990	22600	69500	49450	49450
7	Alexei Tolstoi	2016-07-25T12:00:00.000+0000	205000	22990	69500	49450	49450	205000

Figure 19.21: *Using the FIRST_VALUE(), LAST_VALUE(), and LAG() functions over time*

How does it work

To compare sales (or other metrics), you need to extract elements from several records and place them in the same row. This query helps to give the recipient an estimate of how much each client is spending and see how sales are evolving over time. The output displays as follows:

- The first sale made by a customer
- The most recent sale
- The three sales before the most recent sale

Each sale is a separate record in a SQL database. The SQL used here uses three more windowing functions to extract data from a subset of data. In this case, it is the successive sales per customer. The query selects the customer name and the date for each sale using the **Sales** and **Customer** tables. It then uses the following functions to compare the current sale with other sales for the same customer:

- **FIRST_VALUE**: Shows the sale price for the first-ever purchase made by this customer.
- **LAST_VALUE**: Shows the sale price for the latest purchase made by this customer.
- **LAG**: Shows a previous specific sale (it can be the preceding sale or any previous sale).

As you are once again dealing with windowing functions to output data from multiple records in the same row, these functions need you to apply the following keywords also:

- **OVER**: To indicate to Databricks that you are using a windowing function.
- **ORDER BY**: To specify how the records are being sorted in a subset.
- **PARTITION BY**: To group records by a criterion so that you can compare values meaningfully

In this example, you are partitioning by the client name to see the sales per client. The **ORDER** BY clause in the **OVER** function uses the **SaleDate** field so that you can compare sales over time.

The **FIRST_VALUE** and **LAST_VALUE** functions do as the names imply. They look at all the sales for a common element (defined in the **PARTITION BY** clause—in this case, the customer) and find the oldest and most recent purchases, respectively. The **LAG()** function lets you revisit a set of sales for a customer and return the item in the list that matches the figure that you used in the **LAG()** function. This way, if you write **LAG(SalePrice,1)**, you display the previous sale to a customer.

Calculating cumulative distribution

This time a salesman wants to know the relative standing of each sale by make. In other words, she expects to see a list with a column that shows what percentage of sales were made for less than the current record for each make of car. The following piece of SQL helps you with this:

```
SELECT      MakeName, ModelName, InvoiceNumber, SalePrice
           ,ROUND(CUME_DIST()
            OVER (PARTITION BY MakeName ORDER BY SalePrice),2)
            AS RelativeStanding
FROM        allsales
ORDER BY    MakeName, SalePrice, RelativeStanding;
```

Running the preceding query gives the results as shown in *Figure 19.22*. We have scrolled down the data that is returned to give you a better idea of what the output looks like for a couple of makes of car:

	MakeName	ModelName	InvoiceNumber	SalePrice	RelativeStanding
1	Alfa Romeo	Giulia	EURFR031	2550	0.05
2	Alfa Romeo	1750	GBPCH263	3575	0.09
3	Alfa Romeo	Spider	GBPGB169	5650	0.14
4	Alfa Romeo	Giulietta	EURES232	5690	0.18
5	Alfa Romeo	Spider	GBPGB220	5950	0.23
6	Alfa Romeo	Giulia	EURDE036	6000	0.27
7	Alfa Romeo	Giulietta	EURIT153	6500	0.32

Figure 19.22: *Displaying cumulative distribution with the CUME_DIST() function*

How does it work

Data analysis helps to put things in perspective. In this windowing function, you used the **`CUME_DIST()`** function to see how each sale is situated relative to all other sales for the same make of car. Only this time, you do not see a strict ranking, but the percentage of cars sold for a lower price. This means that the bestselling car for a specific make will display 1 (100%), with all other cars showing a smaller percentage figure.

This query initially requires joining all the tables that you need to select the required fields. In this case, the tables are **`Make`**, **`Model`**, **`Sales`**, **`SalesDetails`**, and **`Stock`**.

Then, you can add the **`CUME_DIST()`** function to the **`SELECT`** clause. As is the case with the other windowing functions mentioned in this chapter, you need to specify an **`ORDER BY`** element (the sale price in this example). Then, you extend the windowing function with a **PARTITION BY** clause that uses the make of the vehicle to group the records into multiple subsets. This lets you isolate the sale price for each record relative to cars of the same make.

The end result is that for each make of car, you can see the most expensive sale and the percentage of cars sold for each sale per make.

Tricks and traps

Creating a cumulative distribution with the **CUME_DIST()** function does require some attention to the following key points:

- The **PARTITION BY** clause is optional with this function. If you want, you can remove it and instead display the percentage of vehicles that sell for less than the current car for all sales, irrespective of make.
- The field that you use in the **ORDER BY** function of the **OVER** clause to establish the relative standing must be numeric.
- We have added the **ROUND()** function to the **CUME_DIST()** function to prevent the display of the 15 decimal places that otherwise appear by default. You can, of course, leave this function out of the query if required.
- You may prefer to sort a dataset such as this by the sale price in descending order so that you can see the most expensive sale per make first. In any case, the sort order that is applied to the overall query is independent of the **ORDER BY** clause that is applied to the **CUME_DIST()** function.

Classifying data using the PERCENT_RANK() function

To conclude her analyses of vehicle sales, the sales director not only wants to see vehicle sales for each country by value but also wants to get an estimate of the percentile in the sale hierarchy for each vehicle sold. The following piece of SQL delivers what she is looking for:

```
SELECT       CountryName, SaleDate, InvoiceNumber
            ,FORMAT_NUMBER(PERCENT_RANK()
             OVER (PARTITION BY CountryName
             ORDER BY TotalSalePrice), "0.00 %") AS PercentageRanking
FROM        allsales
ORDER BY    CountryName, TotalSalePrice DESC;
```

Running the preceding query gives the results shown in *Figure 19.23*:

	CountryName	SaleDate	InvoiceNumber	PercentageRanking
1	Belgium	2016-08-23T12:00:0	EURBE074	100.00 %
2	Belgium	2017-03-12T05:06:0	EURBE132	88.89 %
3	Belgium	2017-07-01T10:25:0	EURBE171	55.56 %
4	Belgium	2017-07-01T10:25:0	EURBE171	55.56 %
5	Belgium	2017-07-01T10:25:0	EURBE171	55.56 %
6	Belgium	2017-11-06T09:36:0	EURBE193	33.33 %

Figure 19.23: *Using the PERCENT_RANK() function to classify groups of data*

How does it work

One useful analytical technique is to indicate the relative rank of a row inside a group of rows. This query starts when you select the necessary tables (**Sales**, **Customer**, and **Country**). Then, you may add any desired fields to display and use the **ORDER BY** clause so that the data that is returned is more comprehensible.

Finally, you add the **PERCENT_RANK()** function to the **SELECT** clause. It requires the **OVER** clause and an **ORDER BY** function that takes a numeric value as the field to sort on (**SalePrice**). In this example (although this is optional), you added a **PARTITION BY** clause to the windowing function to subset the relative sale position by country.

The end result is an ordered list of sales per country. Starting with the highest-value sale, the list displays each vehicle sale in descending order by value and where each record stands in relation to all the other sales for the country. This *ranking* is expressed as a percentage of the number of records that appear below the current record. This means that the top record shows 100%, and the bottom record shows 0%.

Tricks and traps

When using **PERCENT_RANK()**, be sure to note the following

- The field that you use in the **ORDER BY** function of the **OVER** clause to establish the relative standing must be numeric.
- You do not need to add the field used as the basis for the **PERCENT_RANK()** function to the **SELECT** clause; however, adding it can make the output easier to understand.
- You do not need to format the output for the **PERCENT_RANK()** function as a percentage; however, it does make the output easier to comprehend.

Using the LAG() function with alphabetical data

The marketing director wants a list of all the company's customers in alphabetical order. However, she also wants a phone-book-style presentation with all customers grouped by the first letter of their name. The following code helps to achieve this:

```
SELECT       CASE
                 WHEN LEFT(CustomerName, 1) =
                      LAG (LEFT(CustomerName, 1))
                      OVER (ORDER BY CustomerName) THEN NULL
                ELSE LEFT(CustomerName, 1)
              END AS IndexLetter
             ,CustomerName
FROM         SalesByCountry
GROUP BY     CustomerName
ORDER BY     CustomerName;
```

Running the preceding code gives the output shown in *Figure 19.24*:

	IndexLetter	CustomerName
1	A	Alex McWhirter
2	null	Alexei Tolstoi
3	null	Alicia Almodovar
4	null	Andrea Tarbuck
5	null	Andy Cheshire
6	null	Antonio Maura
7	null	Autos Sportivos
8	B	Beltway Prestige Driving
9	null	Birmingham Executive Prestige Vehicles
10	null	Bling Bling S.A.
11	null	Bling Motors
12	null	Boris Spry
13	null	Bravissima!
14	C	Capots Reluisants S.A.
15	null	Casseroles Chromes

Figure 19.24: *Using the LAG() function to produce an alphabetical index*

How does it work

It is relatively easier to isolate the first letter of the name of every client. Applying the **`LEFT()`** function (and specifying 1 as the number of characters to extract) to the **`CustomerName`** field in the **`SalesByCountry`** View does this. However, tweaking this function so that it only shows the index letter when a new letter of the alphabet occurs requires a little more effort.

The answer is to use the **`LAG()`** function. As you have seen, this function shows the contents of a field in the previous record in the output. What this code snippet did are as follows:

- **First**: Apply the **`LAG()`** function to the **`LEFT()`** function that is applied to the customer name and specify 1 as the number of rows to go backwards. In effect, this selects the first letter of the customer name in the previous record. The **`LAG()`** function is ordered by the **`CustomerName`** field to ensure that the customer records are handled in alphabetical order when it is comparing records.
- **Then**: A **`CASE`** statement compares the first letter of the customer name for the current record with the first letter of the customer name for the previous record. If the two are the same, then nothing (or rather **`NULL`**) is output. However, if the two are different (which means that the customer name of the current record begins with a different letter than the customer name of the previous record), then the first letter is output.

The end result is a list of customers with a structure rather than the index of a book.

Conclusion

This chapter allowed you to focus on running totals and relative weighting when analyzing your data. You saw how to create running totals, running averages, and running counts using SQL. You then learned how to segment the output so that the *rolling* result restarted when a specified element changed.

Finally, the chapter explained how to extend these techniques to show the first or last element in a series, how to display the first or last element in a series, and ways to illustrate the relative weighting of a value in a list.

Core knowledge learned in this chapter

The functions that you have seen in this chapter are as follows:

Concept	Description
`ROW_NUMBER()`	This function adds a system-generated sequential number to each record in the dataset.
`LAG()`	This function lets you reach back over the previous records in a record set or subgroup of records to calculate metrics over a defined series of rows relative to the current record.
`FIRST_VALUE()`	This function returns the starting value in a field in a record set or subgroup of records.
`LAST_VALUE()`	This function returns the final value in a field in a record set or subgroup of records.
`ROWS BETWEEN`	It is used with a windowing function. This operator lets you define the range of records used in a running calculation.
`PRECEDING`	It is used with a windowing function. This operator also lets you define the range of records used in a running calculation.
`CURRENT ROW`	It is used with a windowing function. This operator helps you specify a range of records, including the current row.
`CUME_DIST()`	This function returns a cumulative distribution that is the relative position of a value compared to other values.
`PERCENT_RANK()`	This function returns a figure indicating what percentage of a subgroup of records can be found with smaller values than a defined column in a record set or subgroup of records.

Join our book's Discord space

Join the book's Discord Workspace for Latest updates, Offers, Tech happenings around the world, New Release and Sessions with the Authors:

https://discord.bpbonline.com

CHAPTER 20
Analyzing Data Over Time

Introduction

This chapter is all about enhancing your analytical abilities so that you can compare and contrast data over time. Here, we build on the core date and time filtering approaches that you have seen in *Chapter 6: Working with Dates in Databricks* and extend your knowledge to make you completely at ease when slicing and dicing data that contains a time element. Of course, when we talk about dealing with time, we mean looking at both date and time elements in Databricks. Mastering these techniques helps you track the evolution of sales, profits, or any metric over any time period—from years to days to hours and seconds.

Structure

In this chapter, we will cover the following topics:

- Aggregating values for the year to date
- Isolating data for the previous month
- Using a derived table to compare data with values from a previous year
- Finding the total amount for sales each weekday over a year
- Count the number of weekend days between two dates

- Aggregate data for the last day of the month
- Aggregate data for the last Friday of the month
- Analyzing timespans as years, months, and days
- Isolate time periods from date and time data
- Listing data by time of day
- Aggregating data by hourly bandings
- Aggregate data by a quarter of an hour
- Reading dates and times stored as strings

Objectives

Analyzing data over time is a potentially vast subject. The kinds of time analysis that you learn in this chapter include the following:

- Month-to-date, quarter-to-date, and year-to-date calculations
- Comparing metrics with those from previous time periods
- Parallel period calculations, that is, comparing figures for the same month in the previous year
- Comparing values for a current month-to-date with the same month-to-date from the previous year
- Displaying timespans as years, months, and days
- Calculating weekdays and weekend days
- Displaying time differences in hours and minutes
- Grouping data by time slots

Once you have mastered the essentials of adding a time factor to your SQL queries, it will be a pleasant surprise to discover the new analytical horizons to apply to your queries. Admittedly, you need to pay close attention to some of the techniques demonstrated in this chapter if you want to deliver the required output.

Aggregating values for the year to date

The sales manager keeps one eye firmly on the accumulated sales by make for the year so that she can quickly take any corrective actions that may prove necessary. SQL makes it easy to give her the data that she wants, as the following code shows (for sales in 2017):

```
SELECT     MakeName, SUM(SalePrice) AS CumulativeSalesYTD
```

```
FROM        allsales
WHERE       SaleDate BETWEEN
                DATE_TRUNC('YEAR', CURDATE())
                AND CURDATE()
GROUP BY    MakeName
ORDER BY    MakeName ASC;
```

Figure 20.1 shows the results returned by the preceding query (for a query run on the 31st of October 2017):

	MakeName	CumulativeSalesYTD
1	Alfa Romeo	46150
2	Aston Martin	1341400
3	Austin	8750
4	BMW	39000
5	Bugatti	850500
6	Citroen	69230
7	Delahaye	29500
8	Delorean	99500

Figure 20.1: *Calculating aggregate values for the year to date*

How does it work

Collating the sales for the year to date is a regular requirement in many organizations. In this sort of query, all the effort goes (once again) into the **WHERE** clause. This is because you set a range of dates in a **BETWEEN...AND** operator in order to specify a precise date range in this clause. The timespan is defined by the following:

- **A lower boundary**: The first of January for the current year that you passed into the query as **DATE_TRUNC('YEAR', CURDATE())**. This is another way of saying January 1, 2017 (assuming you run the query anytime in 2017).
- **An upper boundary**: The date that the query was run, defined here by the **CURDATE()** function. As the **CURDATE()** function only returns the date, you do not need to strip out a time part from this date.

The key here is finding the current year because the query needs to be dynamic (that is, you want to be able to run it at any time to get the sales for the year to date). It follows that you do not want to enter a fixed year, so you are using the **YEAR** function to extract the current year from the **CURDATE()** function. The **CURDATE()** function, after all, returns the current date from Databricks.

The **`DATE_TRUNC()`** function gives the *start date* for a specified time period. In this example, the time period is the year, so the **`DATE_TRUNC()`** function gives the start of the year. So, the date returned (in 2017 at least) is the 1st of January 2017.

The **`DATE_TRUNC()`** function can give the start date or time for the date and time elements shown in *Table 20.1*:

Interval	Comments
`YEAR`	It gives the start date for the year. You can also use YYYY or YY to specify the date element.
`QUARTER`	It gives the start date for the quarter.
`MONTH`	It gives the first of the month. You can also use MON or MM to specify the date element.
`WEEK`	It gives the start date for the week.
`DAY`	It removes any time part from the date and time.
`HOUR`	It removes minutes and seconds.
`MINUTE`	It removes seconds.
`SECOND`	It removes fractions of a second.
`MILLISECOND`	It zeroes out the microseconds.
`MICROSECOND`	Everything remains.

***Table 20.1:** Interval types used with DATE_TRUNC()*

Tricks and traps

Working with dates can involve using several different SQL functions all at the same time. Be sure to remember the following points:

- The actual results vary depending on the date that you run the query. This example was run in November 2017.
- You can write the following code to return on January 1 for the current year if you prefer:

  ```
  SELECT CONCAT(YEAR(CURDATE()), "-01-01")
  ```
- This code snippet extracts the year part from the current date and converts it to a string of four characters. It then adds -01-01 (to represent the month and day, which is January 1) to the year to give the date in the format YYYY-MM-DD for the current year using the **`CONCAT()`** function.
- If you are using the **`BETWEEN...AND`** keywords to set a range, you must always place the lower boundary after **`BETWEEN`** and the upper boundary after **`AND`**.

This query would not have worked if you reversed the dates used. So you cannot write the following code:

```
WHERE        SaleDate BETWEEN CURDATE() AND DATE_TRUNC('YEAR',
CURDATE())
```

- Isolating parts of dates is an essential technique for defining date ranges in SQL. It might get a little laborious at times, separating the year from the month from the day elements that constitute a date. The upside, however, is that this approach gives you unprecedented control and precision when it comes to setting date ranges.
- Instead of using the **BETWEEN...AND** operator you can use **>=** and **<=** if needed- like the following:

```
WHERE      SaleDate >= DATE_TRUNC('YEAR', CURDATE()) AND SaleDate
<= CURDATE()
```

- As an alternative to the **DATE_TRUNC()** function, you can use the **TRUNC()** function. This function would mean writing SQL like the following:

```
TRUNC(CURDATE(), 'YEAR')
```

- The **TRUNC()** function only allows the use of **YEAR**, **QUARTER**, **MONTH**, and **WEEK** as the date elements that you can specify.

Isolating data for the previous month

In his push for increased profits, the CFO always wants to know how this month's purchases compare to last month's figures. As a result, he wants to see purchases by make for the previous calendar month. SQL can help you produce data like this easily, as the following code shows:

```
SELECT     MakeName, SUM(Cost) AS TotalCost

FROM       make AS MK JOIN model AS MD

           ON MK.MakeID = MD.MakeID

JOIN       stock AS ST ON ST.ModelID = MD.ModelID

WHERE      DateBought BETWEEN TRUNC(CURDATE(), 'MONTH')

           - INTERVAL 1 MONTH

           AND

           LAST_DAY(CURDATE()) - INTERVAL 1 MONTH

GROUP BY   MakeName;
```

Running the preceding code displays the data shown in *Figure 20.2* (for April 2018, it will be different if run on another date):

	MakeName	CumulativeSalesYTD
1	Alfa Romeo	46150
2	Aston Martin	1341400
3	Austin	8750
4	BMW	39000
5	Bugatti	850500
6	Citroen	69230
7	Delahaye	29500
8	Delorean	99500

***Figure 20.2:** Filtering on data for the previous month using the INTERVAL function*

How does it work

You might be called on at any time to calculate metrics for the preceding month, such as when you compile the month-end figures at the start of the following month. In this query, you use the **`TRUNC()`** function (with the **`MONTH`** parameter) to return the start of the month and the **`LAST_DAY()`** function to find the end of the month.

Once again, in this kind of time-based query, you are defining a date range. On this occasion, however, the **`WHERE`** clause uses the **`INTERVAL`** function to simplify date and time calculations.

In essence, the **`INTERVAL`** function is an alternative to the **`DATE_ADD()`** and **`DATE_SUB()`** functions. It allows you to add or subtract a number of intervals (or periods) to or from a date. Using **`INTERVAL`** generally makes the SQL easier to understand.

In this example, the objective is to isolate data for the preceding month in a query that can run at any time without having to specify the date elements. It works by using the **`WHERE`** clause to define the time period between today's date and one month previously.

What is important is how the **`INTERVAL`** function is applied to move backward in time relative to the current date. It works in a very similar way to how you used it previously in a **`DATE_SUB()`** function.

- **First**: You enter an arithmetic operator. In this case, it is the minus sign as you want to subtract a specified number of intervals from a date.

- **Second**: You add the keyword **`INTERVAL`** and a space.
- **Third**: You add the number of intervals to subtract from the initial parameter (the starting date). This could be a figure or the result of a calculation. What this says here is find the date for today's date and subtract 1 month to give me the same date a month ago.
- **Finally**: You define what the interval is from those available in Databricks. In this example, it is the month.

By using these two date calculations in the **`WHERE`** clause, you set the *entire previous month* as the date range. This works no matter how many days are in the month and going back across year boundaries.

Table 20.2 describes the date and time interval types that you can use with the **`INTERVAL`** keyword:

Interval	Comments
`YEAR`	Specifies a year interval.
`MONTH`	Specifies a month interval.
`DAY`	Specifies a day interval.
`HOUR`	Specifies an hour interval.
`MINUTE`	Specifies a minute interval.
`SECOND`	Specifies a second interval.
`MILLISECOND`	Specifies a millisecond interval.
`MICROSECOND`	Specifies a microsecond interval.

***Table 20.2:** Interval types used with INTERVAL*

Tricks and traps

The interval function can make time period comparisons simpler. However, it is worth noting the following key points:

- The **`INTERVAL`** function must be applied to a date or datetime field or an element that Databricks can interpret as a date or datetime.
- You can, of course, use either of the other techniques that you saw in previous examples to calculate the first and last days of the month, even for the previous month, and then calculate date ranges if you prefer. However, this is generally a much more complex approach.

- If you want to test the calculation of an interval, you can write SQL like the following:

```
SELECT CURDATE() + INTERVAL 1 MONTH
```

Using a derived table to compare data with values from a previous year

Seasonal variations can often be very revealing, according to the CFO thinks. He has asked you to provide some analysis of like-for-like sales, so he can see the average sales by color for the same month in both a specified year and the previous year. The following code helps you process this:

```
SELECT      SA.Color, AVG(SA.TotalSalePrice) AS AverageMonthSales
           ,MIN(SQ.AveragePreviousMonthSales) AS AveragePreviousMonthSales
FROM        allsales AS SA
LEFT OUTER JOIN
            (
             SELECT     Color, AVG(TotalSalePrice)
                        AS AveragePreviousMonthSales
             FROM       allsales
             WHERE      YEAR(SaleDate) = YEAR(TO_DATE('2018-06-01')) - 1
                       AND MONTH(SaleDate) = MONTH(TO_DATE('2018-06-01'))
             GROUP BY   Color
            ) SQ
            ON SQ.Color = SA.Color
WHERE       YEAR(SA.SaleDate) = YEAR(TO_DATE('2018-06-01'))
            AND MONTH(SA.SaleDate) = MONTH(TO_DATE('2018-06-01'))
GROUP BY    SA.Color;
```

Running the preceding query gives the results that you can see in *Figure 20.3*:

	Color	AverageMonthSales	AveragePreviousMonthSales
1	British Racing Green	24500	null
2	Night Blue	63000	null
3	Black	18537.5	22550
4	Red	6950	null

Figure 20.3: *Displaying figures for a parallel time period using a derived table*

How does it work

This query is in the following two main parts:

- **A derived table**: It calculates the sales by color for the same month in the previous year.
- **An outer query**: It calculates the sales by color for the current month and year.

Each of these elements uses the same core query. First, the **AllSales** table is used. Then, the **Color** field is added to the **SELECT** and **GROUP BY** clauses to aggregate data by color. Finally, the average sale price is calculated. The only real difference is that the derived table (the inner query) looks at the previous year's data. This is done by adjusting the **YEAR()** function for the year so that it reads as follows:

```
YEAR(TO_DATE('2018-06-01')) - 1
```

Then the two parts of the query are joined. We do this using a **LEFT JOIN** to ensure that all the colors for sales this year will be shown. If you use a simple **JOIN** (which is an **INNER JOIN**) instead, then you will not see any colors that sold this year but not last year. Remember that the **LEFT JOIN** means *all records from the first dataset, including any that match from the second dataset.*

Finally, you added the average sale price for last year's sales from the derived table to the outer query. Using derived tables in subqueries is a standard technique for comparing data over time in SQL.

Tricks and traps

To extend your SQL knowledge, you might like to note the following points:

- Any colors that were not sold in the previous months return NULLs using this approach.

- You could use **CURDATE()** instead of specifying a date using the **TO_DATE()** function if you wanted to show sales for the current and previous years. The date was specified here so that the query always returns data.
- As the results from the outer query are aggregated, you *have* to wrap the **AveragePreviousMonthSales** field that is returned from the derived table in an aggregate function. You can use **MAX()** or **MIN()** for this, as there is only one figure output from the derived table, so the maximum and minimum are the same.
- As an alternative way to having the derived table return only the data for the previous year, you can use the **DATE_SUB** and **INTERVAL** techniques mentioned in the previous sections.
- Instead of writing **LEFT JOIN**, you can write **LEFT OUTER JOIN**, as per your discretion. This is longer but has the advantage of reminding you that you are applying an outer join.

Finding the total amount for sales each weekday over a year

The sales manager is on a mission to find out if certain weekdays are better for sales than others. You have prepared the following query for her so she can analyze sales for each day of the week (but not weekends) in 2017 where there was sale:

```
SELECT     DAYOFYEAR(SaleDate) AS DayNumber
          ,SUM(SalePrice) AS SalePrice
          ,DATE_FORMAT(SaleDate, 'EEEE') AS Weekday
FROM      allsales
WHERE     YEAR(SaleDate) = 2018
          AND WEEKDAY(SaleDate) NOT IN (5,6)
GROUP BY  DAYOFYEAR(SaleDate)
          ,DATE_FORMAT(SaleDate, 'EEEE')
ORDER BY  DayNumber
```

If you run the preceding query, you will see the result shown in *Figure 20.4*:

	DayNumber	SalePrice	Weekday
1	2	284250	Tuesday
2	5	37110	Friday
3	10	125400	Wednesday
4	15	370950	Monday
5	43	182500	Monday
6	44	22500	Tuesday

Figure 20.4: *The total sales for weekdays over the year*

How does it work

This query is an example of how succinct SQL is for overtime analysis. This query simply the following:

- **Selects**: The day of the week in full and the day of the year along with the total says per day of year.
- **Filters**: On weekdays between 0 and 4 (Monday to Friday).
- **Aggregates**: By the day of the week in full and the day of the year.

Count the number of weekend days between two dates

As a prelude to delivering some more complex analysis of staff deployment, the HR department wants to know how many weekend days there are in March and April 2018. This requires some intelligent SQL, as you can see in the following code snippet:

```
WITH TallyTable_CTE

AS

(

SELECT     ROW_NUMBER() OVER (ORDER BY StockCode) AS Nm

FROM       stock

ORDER BY   Nm

LIMIT      90
```

```
)
,WeekendList_CTE
AS
(
SELECT       DATE_ADD('2018-03-01', Nm - 1) AS WeekdayDate
FROM         TallyTable_CTE
WHERE        DAYOFWEEK(DATE_ADD('2018-03-01', Nm - 1))
                 IN (5,6)
             AND Nm <= DATEDIFF('2018-04-30', '2018-03-01')
)
SELECT    COUNT(*) AS WeekendDays FROM WeekendList_CTE;
```

When you run the preceding query, you should see the output that is shown in *Figure 20.5*:

	WeekendDays
1	18

Figure 20.5: Counting the number of non-weekdays for a date range

How does it work

What this query does is create a table of all the days between two dates (March 1 and April 30, 2018, in this example). It then deduces the number of the day of the year for each date and excludes Mondays through Fridays. Finally, it counts the number of records remaining.

The code works like the following:

- **First**: A tally CTE is created to provide a sequential list of numbers starting with 1. It is limited to slightly more than the required number of records to speed up the query and avoid a full query on the (potentially huge) table used as a basis for the numbers list.
- **Then**: A second CTE uses the tally list as part of a **DATE_ADD()** function to create a list of dates. This list begins with 0 to give the starting date, by subtracting one day from the lower date threshold that is the second parameter of the

DATE_ADD() function, and then continues adding one day for each record in the tally list. The **WHERE** clause of the second CTE filters out any weekdays by:

Reusing the same **DATE_ADD()** expression and enclosing this in a **DAYOFWEEK()** function that returns the number of the weekday. The filter only allows days 5 and 6 (Saturdays and Sundays) to appear in the second CTE output.

Limiting the number of records from the tally list that are used. It does this by creating a **DATEDIFF()** function that returns the number of days between the lower and upper threshold dates. This number of days is the number of records that the subquery should return. Consequently, the maximum number of records in the weekend list is set by filtering on the maximum ID value for the second CTE output.

- **Finally**: A simple **SELECT** clause using the data from the second CTE counts the number of weekend days between the two dates.

Tricks and traps

We have a couple of points to note are given as follows:

- Once again, you may have to repeat the date thresholds several times in queries like this one. The essential thing is to be careful and consider whether you should be using the lower or upper date thresholds in each case.
- Date tally lists are often short; however, remember that you can make quite large tally lists if you need them by using the same table name two or even three times. This approach gives you code like the following:

```
SELECT     ROW_NUMBER() OVER (ORDER BY Y.StockCode) - 1 AS nm
FROM       stock Y
CROSS JOIN Stock Z
```

Aggregate data for the last day of the month

The sales manager is still convinced that some days deliver better sales than others, so now she wants to see the sales for the last day of each month in 2016. Spark SQL can handle this easily, as the following piece of SQL shows:

```
WITH TallyTable_CTE
AS
(
```

```
SELECT      ROW_NUMBER() OVER (ORDER BY StockCode) AS nm
FROM        stock
ORDER BY    nm
LIMIT       12
)
,LastDayOfMonth_CTE
AS
(
SELECT       LAST_DAY(CONCAT('2016-', nm, '-01')) AS LastDayDate
FROM         TallyTable_CTE
)
SELECT        CTE.LastDayDate
             ,SUM(SLS.SalePrice) AS TotalDailySales
FROM         salesbycountry SLS
JOIN         LastDayOfMonth_CTE CTE
             ON CTE.LastDayDate = DATE(SLS.SaleDate)
GROUP BY     CTE.LastDayDate
ORDER BY     CTE.LastDayDate;
```

If you run the preceding query, you will see the output shown in *Figure 20.6*:

	LastDayDate	TotalDailySales
1	2016-04-30	155800
2	2016-12-31	39500

Figure 20.6: Showing aggregate data for the last day of the month

How does it work

This query is composed of the following three fundamental elements:

- **A tally CTE**: It delivers a list of incremental numbers. This CTE uses the **ROW_NUMBER()** function to create the list of numbers, starting with 1. The row number field is aliased as nm. The table that the set of numbers is based on is completely irrelevant, as it only serves as a basis for the records that are created, and none of the actual data in the underlying table is required. The list is limited to 12 as we are dealing with a maximum of 12 months in the year.

- **The second CTE**: It uses the tally CTE as the source for its data. This second CTE extracts the 12 records from the tally CTE that correspond to the 12 months in the year. Then, the second CTE creates a list of the 12 months of the year (2016 in this case) by applying the **`CONCAT()`** function to the tally list. As the tally list nm field is defined as being the second parameter of the **`CONCAT()`** function (the month in other words), the second CTE generates a list of the 12 months in the year. The last day of each month is then extracted from the month date using the **`LAST_DAY()`** function. This function automatically returns the number of the last day of the month from a **`DATE`** or **`DATETIME`** field.
- **A query**: It uses the second CTE as its data source. This query joins to the **`SalesByCountry`** view on the **`SaleDate`** field so that any sales that occurred on the last day of any month are returned. Once again, the **`DATE()`** function is applied to ensure that the fields used to join the two tables are only using date elements for the join and that any time elements of the data are discarded.

This sequence of datasets is probably easier to understand if you display the output from the second CTE. You can do this by placing the following piece of code under the second CTE and deleting the final query:

```
SELECT * FROM LastDayOfMonth_CTE
```

Figure 20.7 shows the output from the second of two CTEs:

	LastDayDate
1	2016-01-31
2	2016-02-29
3	2016-03-31
4	2016-04-30
5	2016-05-31
6	2016-06-30
7	2016-07-31
8	2016-08-31
9	2016-09-30
10	2016-10-31
11	2016-11-30
12	2016-12-31

***Figure 20.7**: Displaying the last day of the month*

Because the **LastDayDate** is used as the field that joins the second CTE to the **SalesByCountry** view, only the data for the last day of the month is returned. This is because the second CTE is, in fact, acting as a filter on the source view.

Aggregate data for the last Friday of the month

The HR director has indicated that she might want you to calculate sales commissions for payment on the last Friday of every month. However, before you perform the calculation, she wants a list of the last Friday for every month of 2018. You can deliver this using the following piece of SQL:

```
WITH TallyTable_CTE
AS
(
SELECT      ROW_NUMBER() OVER (ORDER BY StockCode) AS nm
FROM        stock
ORDER BY    nm
LIMIT       12
)
,LastDayOfMonth_CTE
AS
(
SELECT          LAST_DAY(CONCAT('2023-', nm, '-01')) AS MonthEndDate
                ,WEEKDAY(LAST_DAY(CONCAT('2023-', nm, '-01'))) + 1
                AS MonthEndDay
FROM            TallyTable_CTE
)
SELECT          MonthEndDate
                ,CASE
                    WHEN MonthEndDay >= 5 THEN DATE_ADD(MonthEndDate
                          ,5 - MonthEndDay)
                    ELSE DATE_SUB(MonthEndDate
```

```
          ,2 + MonthEndDay)
          END AS LastFridayOfMonth
FROM      LastDayOfMonth_CTE;
```

Running the preceding code snippet produces the output shown in *Figure 20.8*:

	MonthEndDate	LastFridayOfMonth
1	2023-01-31	2023-01-27
2	2023-02-28	2023-02-24
3	2023-03-31	2023-03-31
4	2023-04-30	2023-04-28
5	2023-05-31	2023-05-26
6	2023-06-30	2023-06-30
7	2023-07-31	2023-07-28
8	2023-08-31	2023-08-25
9	2023-09-30	2023-09-29
10	2023-10-31	2023-10-27
11	2023-11-30	2023-11-24
12	2023-12-31	2023-12-29

Figure 20.8: *Displaying the last Fridays of 2017*

How does it work

This query (much like the last one) is based on the following:

- A tally CTE to provide a sequence of numbers.
- A second CTE uses the tally list to produce a series of dates composed of the last day of the month.
- A final query that takes the data from the second CTE and delivers the required result.

Because the first two elements (the tally list and the CTE of month-end dates) are the same as those used in the previous section.

The output query is a little different, however. It takes the date for the last day of the month and subtracts the required number of days necessary to discover the previous Friday using either a **`DATE_ADD()`** function or a **`DATE_SUB()`** function. These functions add or subtract a specified number of days from the month-end date. The key here is to remember that Friday is normally day 5 for Databricks. However, in this piece of code, it is considered as day 6 because we are adding 1 to the last day calculation in the CTE **`LastDayOfMonth_CTE`**.

This requires first testing whether the last day is a Friday, Saturday, or Sunday. If it is (and this is the first part of the **CASE** statement), then the number of days to add is calculated to go back one or two days to jump back to the preceding Friday or remain on the Friday of the date, actually a Friday.

If the last day is Monday through Thursday, then a slightly different calculation is used. In this case, the value for the month-end day is incremented by 2 (the two remaining days of the week) and then subtracted from the last day of the month to jump back to the preceding Friday.

This sequence of datasets is also easier to understand if you display the output from the second CTE. You can do this by placing the following piece of code under the second CTE and deleting the final query:

```
SELECT * FROM LastDayOfMonth_CTE
```

Adding this line of code after the second CTE and then running the SQL gives the result shown in *Figure 20.9*:

	MonthEndDate	MonthEndDay
1	2023-01-31	2
2	2023-02-28	2
3	2023-03-31	5
4	2023-04-30	7
5	2023-05-31	3
6	2023-06-30	5
7	2023-07-31	1
8	2023-08-31	4
9	2023-09-30	6
10	2023-10-31	2
11	2023-11-30	4
12	2023-12-31	7

***Figure 20.9:** Displaying the day number of the Friday of the month*

Once you have the day of the week for the last day of the month, you can apply some logic and a simple calculation. What the **CASE** statement in the final part of the query does is as follows:

- **First**: Decide if the last day of the month is a Friday, Saturday, or Sunday (weekday 4, 5, or 6). If it is, then the **DATE_ADD()** function moves the required date back to the previous Friday.

- **Then**: If the last day of the month is a weekday from 0 to 4 then **`DATE_SUB()`** is used to move the required date back to the previous Friday.

Analyzing timespans as years, months, and days

The CEO of *Prestige Cars* is adamant. *Idle stock is a waste of resources,* she maintains. To make sure no vehicles are waiting too long between being bought and sold, she has asked you to produce a report that shows the total number of years, total number of months, and total number of days each car remains in stock. This requires the following SQL:

```
SELECT       ST.StockCode
            ,ST.DateBought
            ,SLS.SaleDate
            ,TIMESTAMPDIFF(YEAR, ST.DateBought
              ,IFNULL(SLS.SaleDate, CURDATE())) AS Years
            ,TIMESTAMPDIFF(MONTH, ST.DateBought
              ,IFNULL(SLS.SaleDate, CURDATE())) AS Months
            ,TIMESTAMPDIFF(DAY, ST.DateBought
              ,IFNULL(SLS.SaleDate, CURDATE())) AS Days
FROM        stock ST
LEFT JOIN   (
            SELECT SA.SaleDate
                   ,StockID
            FROM   salesdetails SD
            JOIN   sales SA USING(SalesID)
            ) SLS
            ON ST.StockCode = SLS.StockID
WHERE       SLS.SaleDate IS NULL
ORDER BY    Years DESC, Months DESC, Days DESC;
```

Running the preceding query gives the results shown in *Figure 20.10*. Here, you can see a selection of cars that have not yet been sold:

	StockCode	DateBought	SaleDate	Years	Months	Days
1	DE3096AD-76F9-4AAF-B2E1-49FA8E2C377F	2015-03-03 12:00:00	null	7	95	2920
2	8BD326B3-8DE8-4DC9-9F96-FD132C5E1BF2	2015-04-04 12:00:00	null	7	94	2888
3	86450D0C-EAA5-4B83-A9DA-55D742E9C2D8	2015-10-29 12:00:00	null	7	88	2680
4	26A3D067-DCEA-4FF1-9A97-E7AEE0D28C14	2015-10-29 12:00:00	null	7	88	2680
5	373B7D39-B5A3-4018-883C-AC81EF3B5D8F	2016-02-11 12:00:00	null	7	84	2575
6	C82D133F-3442-464B-A16A-D5419A9E1CDF	2016-02-27 12:00:00	null	7	84	2559
7	18974E49-6B03-4C6E-BA0C-D564CFF868E0	2016-06-01 12:00:00	null	6	81	2464

***Figure 20.10:** Using TIMESTAMPDIFF() function to calculate time in years, months, and days*

How does it work

What this query does is take advantage of the possibilities the **`TIMESTAMPDIFF()`** function offers to take a timespan between two dates and calculate the following metrics:

- The total number of elapsed years.
- The total number of elapsed months.
- The total number of elapsed days.

To begin with, this query joins the tables that are required to access the purchase and sales dates. That means joining the **`Stock`** and **`SalesDetails`** tables using a **`LEFT JOIN`** to ensure that all the vehicles from the Stock table are available in the output, whether there is a sale or not. As you are not just looking for cars that have sold but also those that are sitting on the lot waiting for a buyer, this ensures that the SQL can handle vehicles without a sale date.

This piece of SQL introduces the **`TIMESTAMPDIFF()`** function. This function requires you to enter the following three parameters:

- **First**: The time element that you want to extract from the timespan between two dates.
- **Second**: The lower—or start—date.
- **Finally**: The higher—or end—date.

At this point, you can add the following three time-based calculations that deliver the information that interests you:

1. **Years elapsed**: This calculation uses the **`YEAR`** parameter to the **`TIMSTAMP-DIFF()`** function to give the number of whole years elapsed between the two dates.

2. **Months elapsed**: This calculation uses the **MONTH** parameter to the **TIMESTAMPDIFF()** function to give the number of complete months that have passed.
3. **Days elapsed**: This calculation uses the **DAY** parameter to the **TIMESTAMP-DIFF()** function to give the number of complete days that have passed.

You may not necessarily need all of these individual calculations when you are analyzing your time-related data; however, having them at hand might prove useful.

Table 20.3 gives some of the **TIMESTAMPDIFF()** parameters that you can use when calculating elapsed periods of time in Databricks.

Interval code	Description
DAY	Extracts the number of whole days between two timestamps
WEEK	Extracts the number of whole weeks between two timestamps
MONTH	Extracts the number of whole months between two timestamps
QUARTER	Extracts the number of whole quarters between two timestamps
YEAR	Extracts the number of whole years between two timestamps

Table 20.3: *Period elements used with the TIMESTAMPDIFF() function*

TIMESTAMPDIFF() can also handle hours, minutes, and seconds differences. The parameters that you can use when calculating elapsed periods of time in Databricks are shown in *Table 20.4:*

Interval code	Description
HOUR	Extracts the number of hours between two timestamps
MINUTE	Extracts the number of minutes between two timestamps
SECOND	Extracts the number of seconds between two timestamps
MILLISECOND	Extracts the number of milliseconds between two timestamps

Table 20.4: *Time period elements used with the TIMESTAMPDIFF() function*

Tricks and traps

The following are a couple of extra points to make:

- Once again, the date elements used in the **TIMESTAMPDIFF()** function must either be **DATE** or **TIMESTAMP** data types or data that Databricks can interpret as a date.

- **TIMESTAMPDIFF()** calculates complete periods between two dates.
- In the subquery, we are joining the **Sales** and **Salesdetails** tables with the **USING()** function. This is the same as writing **SD.SalesID = SA.SalesID**. The **USING()** function can only be applied when the field names in the two tables are identical.

Isolate time periods from date and time data

The sales team has been vying to sell cars faster and faster, so they want to know which cars have spent the shortest time in stock in 2017. This can sometimes prove to be only a matter of minutes or even seconds, as the following SQL illustrates:

```
SELECT          ST.DateBought
               ,SA.SaleDate
               ,CONCAT(MakeName, '-', ModelName) AS MakeAndModel
               ,TIMESTAMPDIFF(HOUR, ST.DateBought, SA.SaleDate) AS Hours
              ,TIMESTAMPDIFF(MINUTE, ST.DateBought, SA.SaleDate) AS Minutes
              ,TIMESTAMPDIFF(SECOND, ST.DateBought, SA.SaleDate) AS Seconds
              ,CONCAT(FLOOR(TIMESTAMPDIFF(HOUR, ST.DateBought, SA.SaleDate)
/ 24)
                    ,' Days - '
                   ,TIMESTAMPDIFF(HOUR, ST.DateBought, SA.SaleDate) % 24
                    ,' Hours')
                 AS DaysAndHours
FROM            stock ST
JOIN            model MD
                ON ST.ModelID = MD.ModelID
JOIN            make MK
                ON MD.MakeID = MK.MakeID
```

```
JOIN         salesdetails SD
             ON ST.StockCode = SD.StockID
JOIN         sales SA
             ON SD.SalesID = SA.SalesID
WHERE        YEAR(SA.SaleDate) = 2017
ORDER BY     Hours DESC, Minutes DESC, Seconds DESC;
```

Running the preceding query gives the results shown in *Figure 20.11*:

	DateBought	SaleDate	MakeAndModel	Hours	Minutes	Seconds	DaysAndHours
1	2015-04-30 12:00:00	2017-03-31T01:08:00.000+0000	Aston Martin-DB6	16813	1008788	60527280	700 Days - 13 Hours
2	2016-07-03 12:00:00	2017-11-01T05:36:00.000+0000	Porsche-911	11657	699456	41967360	485 Days - 17 Hours
3	2016-07-25 12:00:00	2017-03-31T04:08:00.000+0000	Aston Martin-DB6	5968	358088	21485280	248 Days - 16 Hours
4	2016-10-01 12:00:00	2017-02-12T04:02:00.000+0000	Triumph-TR6	3208	192482	11548920	133 Days - 16 Hours
5	2017-08-31 12:00:00	2017-09-20T02:32:00.000+0000	Aston Martin-DB2	470	28232	1693920	19 Days - 14 Hours
6	2017-01-02 12:00:00	2017-01-21T01:56:00.000+0000	Peugeot-203	445	26756	1605360	18 Days - 13 Hours
7	2017-09-02 12:00:00	2017-09-20T12:32:00.000+0000	Ferrari-Testarossa	432	25952	1557120	18 Days - 0 Hours
8	2017-03-12 12:00:00	2017-03-30T01:07:00.000+0000	Lamborghini-Jarama	421	25267	1516020	17 Days - 13 Hours

***Figure 20.11:** Using TIMESTAMPDIFF() and arithmetic operators to calculate time in hours, minutes, and seconds*

How does it work

This query begins by joining the tables that are needed to source the **`Make`**, **`Model`**, **`DateBought`**, and **`SaleDate`** fields. Then a **`WHERE`** clause is added that filters the records so that only vehicles that were sold in 2017 are displayed.

Five formulas are added to the **`SELECT`** clause to return as follows:

1. The time difference in hours, minutes, and seconds that the vehicle is in stock.
2. The hours in stock.
3. The minutes in stock after any hours are subtracted from the total time in stock.
4. The seconds in stock after any hours and minutes are subtracted from the total time in stock.
5. The days and hours in stock.

The preceding five formulas work like the following:

- **`TIMESTAMPDIFF()`**: The **`TIMESTAMPDIFF()`** function is used to return the time difference in hours, minutes and seconds between the sale date and the purchase date. As mentioned in the previous section, this function takes two parameters, first, the earlier date (the sale date) and second the later date (the purchase date).

- **HOUR**: The **HOUR** parameter of **TIMESTAMPDIFF()** calculates the number of hours in the time difference (calculated again using the **TIMESTAMPDIFF()** function) between the purchase date and the sale date.
- **MINUTE:** Here, the **MINUTE** parameter of **TIMESTAMPDIFF()** calculates the number of minutes in the time difference (between the purchase date and the sale date).
- **SECOND**: The **SECOND** parameter of **TIMESTAMPDIFF()** also calculates the number of seconds in the time between the purchase date and the sale date.
- **DAYS and HOURS**: The number of hours returned by a **TIMESTAMPDIFF()** function is divided by 24 to calculate the number of whole days between the two dates. The number of hours remaining after the elapsed days is calculated by using the % (modulo) function to return the remainder of the time difference in hours once the number of hours is divided by 24. These two figures are wrapped inside the **CONCAT()** function to make them more readable, and to add some illustrative text so that the days and hours are presented as a single output column.

Listing data by time of day

Now the sales manager wants to look at exactly when cars were sold to see if there are certain times of the day that are better for sales. You produced a list of vehicles sold in 2017 that includes the exact time the sale was made. The code for this is shown as follows:

```
SELECT     MakeName, ModelName, SalePrice, SaleDate
          ,DATE_FORMAT(SaleDate, 'hh:mm') AS TimeOfDaySold
FROM      allsales
WHERE     YEAR(SaleDate) = 2017
ORDER BY  TimeOfDaySold;
```

If you run the preceding SQL, you will see the output shown in *Figure 20.12*:

	MakeName	ModelName	SalePrice	SaleDate	TimeOfDaySold
1	Ferrari	Enzo	395000	2017-02-08T01:01:00.000+0000	01:01
2	Lamborghini	Jarama	305000	2017-03-30T01:07:00.000+0000	01:07
3	Aston Martin	DB6	45000	2017-03-31T01:08:00.000+0000	01:08
4	Ferrari	F50	255950	2017-05-12T01:15:00.000+0000	01:15
5	Mercedes	500SL	45000	2017-08-07T01:30:00.000+0000	01:30
6	BMW	Isetta	5500	2017-08-27T01:31:00.000+0000	01:31
7	Peugeot	203	1250	2017-01-21T01:56:00.000+0000	01:56

Figure 20.12: *Displaying records by time*

How does it work

As long as the source data contains a time element, you can display the time of an event (such as a sale) when querying data. Fortunately, the **Sales** table (used in the **SalesByCountry** view) contains the **SaleDate** field, which contains both a date and a time element. This query simply selects core information, including the **SaleDate**, from the **AllSales** table.

Isolating the time part of a field like this (a **TIMESTAMP** field) is as simple as selecting the **SaleDate** field and formatting the output from this field. The trick is to use the **DATE_FORMAT()** function. As you may have seen previously, the **DATE_FORMAT()** function requires the following two parameters:

1. **First**: The field to format
2. **Second**: The format code to apply

In this example, we used the **%H** and **%i** format codes. These codes display the output in a shortened time format with the hour, minutes, and AM/PM indicators.

The **DATE_FORMAT()** function lets you apply a series of built-in time formats. These are shown in *Table 8.6*.

Tricks and traps

The following are a few key points to note:

- You can extract the time element from the **TIMESTAMP** fields.
- The formatted output is converted to text. This means that you should not use it to sort the data or in-time calculations. Use the underlying data field to carry out these operations.

Aggregating data by hourly bandings

The CEO has been looking at some of the output that you have prepared for the sales manager and is convinced that sales staff need to be aware that certain times of the day produce better sales, so she has asked for a list of 2017 sales aggregated by hour bands. The following SQL delivers this:

```
SELECT
            CONCAT(HourOfDay, '-', HourOfDay + 1) AS HourBand
            ,SUM(SalePrice) AS SalesByHourBand
FROM
    (
     SELECT     SalePrice
               ,HOUR(SaleDate) AS HourOfDay
     FROM      salesbycountry
     WHERE     YEAR(SaleDate) = 2017
    ) A
GROUP BY    HourOfDay
ORDER BY    HourOfDay;
```

Running the preceding piece of code produces the output shown in *Figure 20.13*:

	HourBand	SalesByHourBand
1	1-2	1052700
2	2-3	106905
3	3-4	85000
4	4-5	829400
5	5-6	672900
6	6-7	605450

Figure 20.13: Displaying data grouped and aggregated for hour bands

How does it work

The heart of this piece of SQL is a subquery that isolates the hour when a sale was made. It does this by applying the **HOUR()** function to the **SaleDate** field of the

SalesByCountry view. This function can extract the hour from a **DATETIME** or **TIME** field.

To make this clearer, take a look at *Figure 20.14*, where you can see the output from the subquery (aliased as **A** in the SQL code):

	SalePrice	HourOfDay
1	45000	1
2	49500	5
3	225000	4
4	12500	4
5	22500	11
6	125000	11

***Figure 20.14:** Extracting the hour part of a DATETIME field using the HOUR() function*

Once the subquery has delivered the sale price and the hour of the sale, the outer query can take this information and use it as the basis for the final result.

The outer query simply aggregates the sale price by the hour. As a final flourish, it displays the hour band as a range by displaying the hour twice (by simply adding 1 to the hour figure). It does this using the **CONCAT()** function with the following three elements as parameters:

1. **First**: The hour of the day taken from the derived table.
2. **Second**: A dash (in quotes); this is purely decorative
3. **Finally**: The hour of the day taken from the derived table and incremented by 1

Tricks and traps

We have one idea to note, which is given as follows:

- You can wrap the whole query in a CTE or a subquery and then order by the aggregate amount to see the most profitable hours of the day to extract even more analysis from the data.

Aggregate data by a quarter of an hour

As a final part of the sales focus, the CEO wants to know which part of the hour is best for sales. You prepare the following piece of code to show sales for 2017 in quarter-hourly tranches:

```
SELECT      QuarterOfHour
           ,SUM(SalePrice) AS SalesByQuarterHourBand
```

```
FROM
    (
    SELECT     SalePrice
               ,FLOOR((MINUTE(SaleDate) / 15) + 1) AS QuarterOfHour
    FROM       salesbycountry
    WHERE      YEAR(SaleDate) = 2017
    ) A
GROUP BY   QuarterOfHour
ORDER BY   QuarterOfHour;
```

Running the preceding code snippet produces the output shown in *Figure 20.15*:

	QuarterOfHour	SalesByQuarterHourBand
1	1	3086360
2	2	2649600
3	3	1642115
4	4	490000

Figure 20.15: *Data grouped in quarter-hour bands*

How does it work

This piece of SQL consists of the following two queries:

- **An inner query**: That looks at every sale date and time for 2017 (using the `SalesByCountry` view as the source of the data). This subquery extracts the minute at which each sale took place using the `MINUTE()` function. Then, the number of minutes is divided by 15 to give each quarter of an hour. The 15-minute slot is then incremented by 1; otherwise, it would begin with 0. The entire calculation is then rounded down (to avoid fractions) using the `FLOOR()` function).
- **An outer query**: That aggregates the sales amount from the inner query (aliased as `A`) and groups the amounts by each quarter of an hour.

Reading dates and times stored as strings

As mentioned in *Chapter 8: Formatting Numbers and Dates*, dates are not always in a standardized format in the source data. Indeed, Databricks might not even recognize a date as useable and may treat it as a text (or a string of words). While this allows the data to be loaded, it makes date and time calculations impossible with Spark SQL.

The solution to this challenge is to convert unruly date fields to *proper* dates. This can be done using the **TO_DATE()** function. Refer to the following short piece of SQL:

```
SELECT TO_DATE('12/31/2024', 'MM/dd/yyyy') AS NewYears
```

Running the preceding code snippet will give the output shown in *Figure 20.16*:

	NewYears
1	2024-12-31

Figure 20.16: *Converting a non-standard date to a DATE datatype*

How does it work

The **TO_DATE()** function takes the following two parameters:

1. **The Date**: This is the string that can be interpreted as a date.
2. **The date format**: This is the date code that tells Databricks how to interpret the date.

In this example, the date that is passed as the first parameter is not in the standard YYYY-MM-DD format and so cannot be directly interpreted as a date by Databricks. However, the second parameter indicates that the format has the following:

- The Month, followed by a slash
- The day, followed by a slash
- The year

The date format codes are the same as those used to format date outputs. You can refer back to *Table 8.4* to find them.

Tricks and traps

A few comments will be added as follows:

- If a date cannot be interpreted correctly by **TO_DATE()**, then a **NULL** is output.
- You can set days and months as a single character or as two characters (that is, as MM or dd), and Databricks will still interpret days and months with one or two digits correctly. That is, if the dates do not have leading zeroes, they will still be read and converted correctly.

- If a string cannot be interpreted as a date or timestamp, a **NULL** will be returned for the record.
- The date format can be in single or double quotes.
- Date formats can also contain time format codes.

Conclusion

This chapter showed you a more advanced set of techniques to analyze data over time. You have learned how to compare data across different time periods, analyze how metrics accumulate over time, and break down timespans into their constituent parts. Using such advanced time analysis can help you discover trends in your source data.

When analyzing data over time, you need to be aware that Databricks can often solve a challenge in several different ways. This is why it is shown alternative solutions to problems in some cases. Indeed, you can also try using the solution suggested for one section in this chapter to other sections. In any case, what matters is the result. If you are obtaining the correct output in a way that you are comfortable with, then that is all that matters.

It is only fair to inform you that there are many more ways of analyzing data over time in Databricks that we have not covered in this chapter. This is because an exhaustive overview of every time analysis challenge would require an entire book. Hopefully, nonetheless, you have learned enough in this chapter to cover all your essential needs.

Core knowledge learned in this chapter

The keywords that you have seen in this chapter are listed as follows. Also included are the keywords you may already have seen previously.

Concept	Description
`LAST_DAY()`	This function returns the date for the last day of the month.
`DAYOFWEEK()`	This function returns the number of day of the week from a date.
`DATEDIFF()`	This function finds the number of hours, minutes, and seconds on two given dates.
`DATE()`	This function converts a datetime data type to a date.
`YEAR()`	This function isolates the year part of a date.

Concept	Description
`MONTH()`	This function isolates the month part of a date.
`DAY()`	This function isolates the day part of a date.
`MINUTE()`	This function extracts the number of minutes from a datetime field.
`HOUR()`	This function extracts the number of hours from a datetime field.
`SECOND()`	This function extracts the number of seconds from a datetime field.
`INTERVAL`	This parameter specifies the time interval to apply in a timespan calculation.
`TO_DATE()`	It is used with a date format; this function lets you convert a string to a useable date.
`TIMESTAMPDIFF()`	This function calculates the difference between two dates and times in a selected unit.

CHAPTER 21
Complex Data Output

Introduction

Often the way data is presented is perceived as more important than the data itself. So, you need to know not only how to analyze the data and deliver accurate results but also how to shape the output so that the essence of your analysis is immediately comprehensible. The techniques covered in this chapter help you present your analysis in various ways that can make the results easier to read and understand.

Structure

In this chapter, we will cover the following topics:

- Creating a pivot table
- Creating a pivot table displaying multiple row groupings
- Adding totals to aggregate queries
- Creating subtotals and totals in aggregated queries
- Creating clear tables that include totals and subtotals
- Replace acronyms with full text in the final output

Objectives

The techniques that you discover in this chapter include the following:

- Pivoting data to create crosstab tables
- Adding multiple separate subtotals and a grand total to an aggregate query
- Performing search and replace operations on the final output

The mentioned ways of enhancing the output from a query are practical and useful. They can make your results alluring and revelatory. In the real world, you may not use all of these techniques on a daily basis; nonetheless, it is probably best to know that they are available so that you can apply them when the need arises. What is more, these presentation techniques enhance your SQL skills. Indeed, you can apply several of the approaches that you see in this chapter to solve many other presentational challenges.

Creating a pivot table

The finance director has given you a new challenge which involves delivering a simple, compact table of sales by color for all the years that *Prestige Cars* has been trading. The finance director is adamant that this must be presented as a *crosstab* or pivot table. SQL can pivot data in this way, as the following code snippet shows:

```
SELECT      Color, y2015, y2016, y2017, y2018
FROM
            (
             SELECT      Color, SD.SalePrice, YEAR(SA.SaleDate)
                                                    AS YearOfSale
             FROM        Stock ST
             INNER JOIN  SalesDetails SD
                         ON StockCode = SD.StockID
             INNER JOIN  Sales SA
                         ON SA.SalesID = SD.SalesID
            ) SQ
PIVOT       (
```

```
        SUM(SalePrice) FOR YearOfSale
                        IN (2015 y2015, 2016 y2016, 2017 y2017, 2018
y2018)
        );
```

Running the preceding query gives the results shown in *Figure 21.1*:

	Color	y2015	y2016	y2017	y2018
1	Dark Purple	null	283000	219175	662640
2	Silver	89000	542205	1093900	926030
3	Green	216600	370750	655090	599540
4	British Racing Green	111500	663250	872340	566385
5	Blue	284600	423650	708420	1186400
6	Night Blue	57990	405500	457500	600830
7	Black	374490	1251410	3112550	1983695
8	Red	154795	442500	659150	932450
9	Pink	null	235950	54700	191600
10	Canary Yellow	132000	287070	104750	134045

***Figure 21.1:** Creating a pivot table using the PIVOT operator*

How does it work

Sometimes a simple list of data is not what you want. Comparing data in a list can be much harder than when it is presented as a table of intersecting rows and columns, as in a pivot table. This table style of data presentation is also called a *crosstab*.

What matters when using the `PIVOT` operator is realizing that it is there to display *three* pieces of data in different ways. It needs the following:

- **Row headers:** These are the data elements that appear in the left-hand column of the output table.
- **Column headers:** These are the data elements for each column. It is important to understand that these are not field names but data from the database.
- **Table data**: These are the aggregated numeric values that appear inside the final pivoted output table.

Therefore, the art of making a pivot table involves assembling these three pieces of data so that they can be used correctly to give you the desired result. Here is what is process used in this example:

- **Initially**: The inner query (which is technically a subquery) is defined to output the data elements that you want to see in the final pivot table. These are color, year of sale, and sale price. This is the core data that is used in the pivot table, and it contains fields from the Stock, `Sales`, and `SalesDetails` tables.

If you select the SQL for the subquery and execute it, you see something like the output displayed in *Figure 21.2*. This is a simple list query that contains hundreds of rows:

	Color	SalePrice	YearOfSale
1	Red	65000	2015
2	Blue	220000	2015
3	British Racing Green	19500	2015
4	British Racing Green	11500	2015
5	Red	19950	2015
6	Night Blue	29500	2015
7	Black	49500	2015
8	Canary Yellow	76000	2015
9	Blue	19600	2015
10	Blue	36500	2015
11	Blue	8500	2015
12	British Racing Green	80500	2015
13	Black	169500	2015
14	Green	8950	2015
15	Green	195000	2015

Figure 21.2: *The subquery that prepares data for the PIVOT operator*

- **Then**: You apply the **`PIVOT`** operator to the subquery. This is, in effect, another subquery. What it does is isolate two of the fields in the subquery for some special treatment (data to aggregate and column specification).
- **Finally**: A **`SELECT`** clause is applied that provides the row data for the output table. In this case, it is the **`Color`** field. Then you add the column headers that were defined as part of the **`PIVOT`** operator.

The **`PIVOT`** operator needs the following two elements:

1. **Aggregated element**: A numeric field is aggregated to be displayed in the body of the final output table. In this example, it is the **`SalePrice`** field.
2. **Column definition**: The content (in whole or in part) of another field is individually listed inside parentheses after the **`FOR`** clause to provide the column headers of the final output table.

A pivot table has to use an aggregation function to handle the values displayed in the table. This is because each intersection of a row and a column (several black cars sold in 2015, for instance) can have more than one value. You can use any of the SQL aggregation functions in a pivot table; consequently, you can just as easily use **`AVG()`** or **`COUNT()`** here to return the average sale price or the number of vehicles. If you are using **`SUM()`** or **`AVG()`**, then the field that you are aggregating has to be numeric. **`COUNT()`** can also be applied to text fields to return the number of values rather than the sum of the values.

Writing pivot table SQL is easier once you understand the process that the code represents. To help conceptualize this technique, refer to *Figure 21.3*:

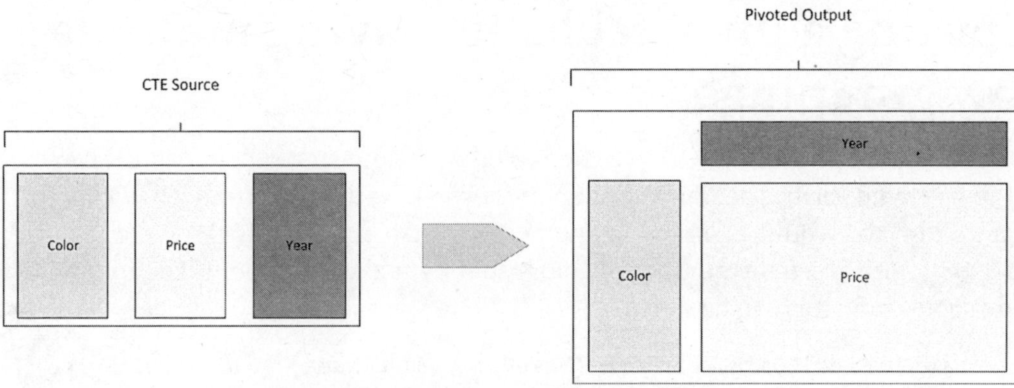

***Figure 21.3:** The concept of the pivot table*

Tricks and traps

Pivot tables require you to pay attention to the SQL being written, so be sure to remember the following points when you create your own pivot tables:

- The only tricky part of writing the SQL that creates a pivot table is selecting the data that will constitute the column headers. It helps if you start by isolating this list of individual data elements before you start writing the rest of the code. In this example, you can return the list of years used in the **`PIVOT`** operator *and* the **`SELECT`** clause with the following SQL snippet:

```
SELECT DISTINCT YEAR(SaleDate) FROM Sales
```

- This returns the years (shown in *Figure 21.4*) that you can then copy and paste to create the list of column headers.

	year(SaleDate)
1	2018
2	2015
3	2016
4	2017

***Figure 21.4:** Preparing the data for the column titles of the PIVOT operator*

The list of data elements to be used as the column headers must be aliased. What this means is that every data item (years in this example) must be attributed a column name (an alias) that will appear in the output from the **`PIVOT()`** function.

The column names that will appear in the pivoted output *must* respect Databricks column naming rules. So they *have* to start with a letter (numbers and underscores are not allowed). This is why the data for 2015 has the column header y2015.

Creating a pivot table displaying multiple row groupings

Fortunately, the finance director was delighted with your first pivot table. However, this has created further demands from him for yet more analysis from you. What the finance director would like now is another pivot table, only this time, the finance director wants to see the number of colors sold by make *and* model. The following code shows how this can be done:

```
WITH MakeAndModelCostByYear_CTE (MakeName, ModelName, Color, CostPrice)
AS
(
SELECT      MakeName, ModelName, Color, Cost
FROM        allsales
)
SELECT      MakeName, ModelName, Black, Blue, 'British Racing Green',
                           'Canary Yellow', 'Dark Purple', Green,
                           'Night Blue', Pink, Red, Silver
FROM        MakeAndModelCostByYear_CTE
PIVOT       (
                   COUNT(CostPrice) FOR Color IN
                          (
                            'Black' Black, 'Blue' Blue, 'British Racing
Green' 'British Racing Green',
                          'Canary Yellow' 'Canary Yellow', 'Dark Purple'
'Dark Purple', 'Green' Green,
                           'Night Blue' 'Night Blue', 'Pink' Pink, 'Red'
Red, 'Silver' Silver
```

```
                                )
                  )
ORDER BY    MakeName, ModelName;
```

Running the preceding query gives the results shown in *Figure 21.5*:

	MakeName	ModelName	Black	Blue	BritishRacingGreen	CanaryYellow	DarkPurple	Green	NightBlue	Pink	Red	Silver
1	Alfa Romeo	1750	1	1	null	null	null	null	null	null	null	null
2	Alfa Romeo	Giulia	3	null	3	null	null	1	null	null	1	null
3	Alfa Romeo	Giulietta	1	2	null	null	1	null	5	null	null	null
4	Alfa Romeo	Spider	4	1	null	null	null	null	null	null	null	null
5	Aston Martin	DB2	2	1	1	null	null	2	1	null	null	1
6	Aston Martin	DB4	8	null	null	1	null	null	1	1	null	1
7	Aston Martin	DB5	1	2	null	null	null	null	1	null	1	1
8	Aston Martin	DB6	4	null	2	2	null	1	2	null	1	2
9	Aston Martin	DB9	3	1	1	1	1	1	1	null	1	5
10	Aston Martin	Rapide	1	null	null	null	null	null	1	null	1	1
11	Aston Martin	Vanquish	2	null	null	null	1	1	2	null	null	1
12	Aston Martin	Vantage	2	null	1	null	null	1	null	null	null	null

Figure 21.5: A complex pivot operation based on a CTE

How does it work

Pivot tables can be more complex than the simple table mentioned in the previous example. For more detailed output where more than one column of aggregated data is required, a **Common Table Expression** (**CTE**) can help you simplify both the SQL and the way that you approach the problem. This query follows the same pivot function principles that you saw previously given as follows:

- Identify and select the columns to display.
- Identify the data to pivot as column headers and an alias for each column.
- Identify the value to aggregate and display in the table.

This query also begins by defining the source data for the pivot operation. This time, however, a CTE is used to do this. The CTE is based on the **`Make`**, **`Model`**, and **`Stock`** tables. If you select the query used in the CTE, you see a result like that shown in *Figure 21.6*:

	MakeName	ModelName	Color	Cost
1	Ferrari	Testarossa	Red	52000
2	Ferrari	355	Blue	176000
3	Porsche	911	British Racing Gr	15600
4	Porsche	924	British Racing Gr	9200
5	Porsche	944	Red	15960
6	Aston Martin	DB4	Night Blue	23600
7	Aston Martin	DB5	Black	39600
8	Aston Martin	DB6	Canary Yellow	60800
9	Porsche	911	Blue	15680
10	Aston Martin	DB5	Blue	29200
11	Porsche	944	Blue	6800
12	Aston Martin	DB6	Night Blue	36000
13	Bentley	Flying Spur	British Racing Gr	64400

Figure 21.6: *Using a CTE to return the data used in a pivot*

This CTE isolates the two fields that appear as row headers (`MakeName` and `ModelName`) and the field that contains the data elements that are to be pivoted as column headers (`Color`).

The query is then built into four sections, which are given as follows:

1. **`SELECT`**: This clause is where the output fields are defined: first, the two fields that make up the row headers are specified, followed by all the unique data fields from the color column that become the column headers.
2. **`FROM`**: This clause uses the CTE as the data source.
3. **`PIVOT`**: This clause first specifies the aggregation that is used, **`COUNT()`**, in this example. Then, it states the field that is aggregated, which is **`CostPrice`**. Finally, a **`FOR`** expression is used to indicate which field contains the column headers (**`Color`**) and to list unique data elements from this field (the list of colors) and aliases for each element that will be used as an output column name.
4. **`ORDER BY`**: Although optional, this clause guarantees comprehensible results by sorting the output.

All these elements together create the pivot SQL that you saw in boldface at the start of this section.

Tricks and traps

The following are two points that you must remember when pivoting data like this:

1. The second element (the alias) for each data point in the pivot list is a column name and so cannot contain spaces, only letters or numbers and underscores. Moreover, an alias must start with a letter.
2. Text output used in the pivot list (the first element in the pivot list) *must* be enclosed in quotes. You can use either single or double quotes.

Adding totals to aggregate queries

Although pleased with the lists of data that you can now deliver at the drop of a hat, the finance director wants one more thing. He prefers a more spreadsheet-like output that includes the subtotals in some cases; this will save him extra work in a spreadsheet. The following SQL snippet delivers exactly what he is looking for, that is, a list of sales by color and make including the grand total:

```
SELECT      MakeName, Color, SUM(Cost) AS Cost
FROM        allsales
GROUP BY    GROUPING SETS ((MakeName, Color), ())
ORDER BY    MakeName, Color;
```

Running the preceding query gives the results shown in *Figure 21.7*:

	MakeName	Color	Cost
1	null	null	17574360
2	Alfa Romeo	Black	74500
3	Alfa Romeo	Blue	37160
4	Alfa Romeo	British Racing Green	16840
5	Alfa Romeo	Dark Purple	17200
6	Alfa Romeo	Green	14000
7	Alfa Romeo	Night Blue	28152
8	Alfa Romeo	Red	6956
9	Aston Martin	Black	1151648
10	Aston Martin	Blue	284400
11	Aston Martin	British Racing Green	207508
12	Aston Martin	Canary Yellow	213080
13	Aston Martin	Dark Purple	91680

Figure 21.7: *Creating totals with grouping sets*

How does it work

You are familiar with producing aggregations with Databricks. So far, you have only seen how to deliver levels of aggregation or totals in *separate queries*; however, sometimes, you need to see not only the subtotals but also the grand total in a single query. This query extends the `GROUP BY` clause with an extension that is the `GROUPING SETS` clause. This new function allows you to specify exactly which totals and subtotals are returned in the final output:

- **First**: You begin with a perfectly normal aggregation query. In this example, the `Make`, `Model`, and `Stock` tables are joined, and the make name and color fields are output along with the total cost of vehicles purchased. As this is an aggregation query, any fields that are not aggregated must be added to a `GROUP BY` clause. In this example, these are the `Make`, `Name`, and `Color` fields.
- **Then**: The `GROUPING SETS` clause is added to the `GROUP BY` clause. This requires that you add parentheses that contain the fields to be aggregated. Each set of fields is inside its own parentheses. In this example, the make name and color fields are added so that the total for each combination of make and color will be calculated. Then, separated with a comma, an empty pair of parentheses is added inside the outer grouping sets parentheses. This tells Databricks to return the grand total for the dataset as well.

Reading the final result set is not completely intuitive, so we prefer to explain it. The total for each aggregated set of make and color is probably self-evident. However, the initial record without either a make or a color is probably less easy to understand. This is, in fact, the grand total. It is the record that is produced by the empty parentheses inside the `GROUPING SETS` clause. Because no fields are provided for the grand total in the `GROUPING SETS` clause, the grand total is represented by `NULL` objects in the make name and color fields of the output.

Tricks and traps

The following is one fundamental point to remember when creating grouping sets:

- When adding a grouping sets clause, you have to be careful to respect the sets of parentheses in the clause. There is always an outer pair of parentheses and then an inner pair for each aggregation that you add.

Creating subtotals and totals in aggregated queries

This time, the CEO wants a rapid report to see sales by make and color, along with subtotals for all potential makes and sales combinations. Writing the following code to provide her with this list:

```
SELECT      MakeName, Color, SUM(Cost) AS Cost
FROM        allsales
GROUP BY    GROUPING SETS ((MakeName, Color)
              , (MakeName), (Color), ())
ORDER BY    MakeName, Color;
```

Running the preceding query gives the results shown in *Figure 21.8*. Scrolling down this list will show the subtotals for other makes:

	MakeName	Color	Cost
1	null	null	17574360
2	null	Black	5357716
3	null	Blue	2066856
4	null	British Racing Green	1770780
5	null	Canary Yellow	506292
6	null	DARK PURPLE	36480
7	null	Dark Purple	895372
8	null	Green	1473584
9	null	Night Blue	1217456
10	null	Pink	385800
11	null	Red	1743116
12	null	Silver	2120908
13	Alfa Romeo	null	194808
14	Alfa Romeo	Black	74500
15	Alfa Romeo	Blue	37160
16	Alfa Romeo	British Racing Green	16840
17	Alfa Romeo	Dark Purple	17200
18	Alfa Romeo	Green	14000
19	Alfa Romeo	Night Blue	28152
20	Alfa Romeo	Red	6956

Grand total

Color totals

Make totals

Figure 21.8: *Adding subtotals with grouping sets*

How does it work

The totals for each aggregation and the overall total are not the only options when using SQL. It may also display any supplemental totals. SQL can assist you in seeing both the big picture and the intriguing details in this way.

This combination of high-level aggregate and low-level details is delivered via code that is fundamentally a basic aggregation query. Before displaying the total cost for each manufacturer and color, it uses the **AllSales** table as the data source. However, the **GROUP BY** clause is extended with a more complex **GROUPING SETS** clause that requests the following:

- **A grand total**: In the **GROUPING SETS** clause, the empty brackets are added to achieve this.
- **Total for make**: To accomplish this, add (**MakeName**) inside of its own set of brackets inside the **GROUPING SETS** clause.
- **Total for color**: To accomplish this, add (**Color**) inside of its own set of brackets inside the **GROUPING SETS** clause.
- **Aggregate totals**: For both color and make. The **Make** and **Color** fields are added, separated by a comma, as you would normally do in a **GROUP BY** clause to request these. These field names must be included in their own set of brackets, though, as this aggregation is a **GROUPING SETS** clause.

To fully comprehend what the **GROUPING SETS** query has produced, it may take some practice. More specifically, when applying grouping sets to an aggregate query, you need to pay special attention to the NULLs in the various columns to determine how the sub-totals are generated. Simply put the following:

- The row represents the total if all columns other than the value are **NULL**.
- When a **NULL** appears in a column with other components, you are examining the sum of those elements. For instance, if the **MakeName** column is **NULL** and the **Color** column is *British Racing Green,* then the total for that row is the color, *British Racing Green*. The amount displayed in the record is the total for the make *Alfa Romeo* if both the **MakeName** and **Colour** columns contain *Alfa Romeo*.

The **GROUPING SETS** operator conceptually acts in the manner shown in *Figure 21.9*:

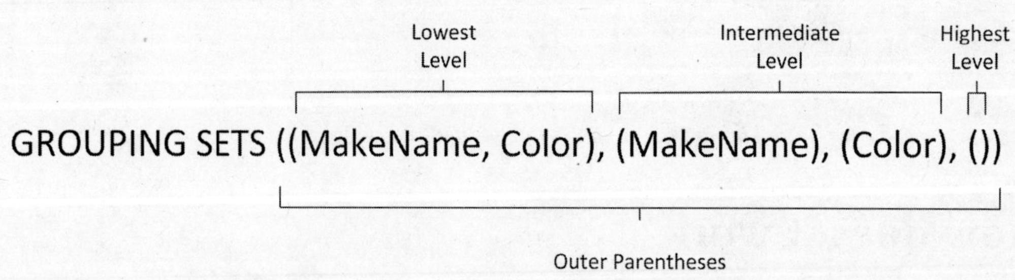

***Figure 21.9**: Anatomy of a GROUPING SETS operator*

Tricks and traps

There are two comments to note given as follows:

- Using grouping sets does not require adding an **ORDER BY** clause but doing so frequently gives a more comprehensive result.
- If you do not want to view the subtotals for each mix of make and color, you do not have to include the lowest level of aggregation in a **GROUPING SETS** clause. For instance, if you change this example's **GROUP BY** clause to read as follows:

```
GROUP BY    GROUPING SETS ((MakeName), (Color), ())
```

You only see the totals for **Make**, **Color**, and the grand total, as shown in *Figure 21.10*:

	MakeName	Color	Cost
1	null	null	17574360
2	null	Black	5357716
3	null	Blue	2066856
4	null	British Racing Green	1770780
5	null	Canary Yellow	506292
6	null	Dark Purple	931852
7	null	Green	1473584
8	null	Night Blue	1217456
9	null	Pink	385800
10	null	Red	1743116
11	null	Silver	2120908
12	Alfa Romeo	null	194808
13	Aston Martin	null	4082204

Figure 21.10: *Displaying the higher aggregation levels using a GROUPING SETS clause*

Creating clear tables that include totals and subtotals

The CEO was impressed by how quickly you answered the preceding subquery, which is good news. The CEO now wants the same data to be presented in a way that is easier for the board of directors to understand. The CEO wants something more explicit because she is concerned that the senior executives would not understand NULLs in columns.

You come up with the following code to resolve the query:

```
WITH GroupedSource_CTE
```

```
AS
(
SELECT
MakeName
,Color
,Count(*) AS NumberOfCarsBought
FROM        allsales
WHERE       MakeName IS NOT NULL OR Color IS NOT NULL
GROUP BY    GROUPING SETS ((MakeName), (Color), ())
)
SELECT AggregationType
,Category
,NumberOfCarsBought
FROM
(
SELECT   'GrandTotal' AS AggregationType, NULL AS Category
         ,NumberOfCarsBought, 1 AS SortOrder
FROM     GroupedSource_CTE
WHERE    MakeName IS NULL and Color IS NULL
UNION
SELECT   'Make Subtotals', MakeName, NumberOfCarsBought , 2
FROM     GroupedSource_CTE
WHERE    MakeName IS NOT NULL and Color IS NULL
UNION
SELECT   'Color Subtotals', Color, NumberOfCarsBought , 3
FROM     GroupedSource_CTE
WHERE    MakeName IS NULL and Color IS NOT NULL
```

```
) SQ
ORDER BY SortOrder, NumberOfCarsBought DESC;
```

Running the preceding query gives the results shown in *Figure 21.11*:

	AggregationType	Category	NumberOfCarsBought
1	GrandTotal	null	348
2	Make Subtotals	Aston Martin	77
3	Make Subtotals	Porsche	46
4	Make Subtotals	Triumph	37
5	Make Subtotals	Ferrari	29
6	Make Subtotals	Jaguar	25
7	Make Subtotals	Alfa Romeo	22
8	Make Subtotals	Bentley	20
9	Make Subtotals	Rolls Royce	14
10	Make Subtotals	Mercedes	14
11	Make Subtotals	Peugeot	10
12	Make Subtotals	Lamborghini	10
13	Make Subtotals	Austin	7
14	Make Subtotals	Citroen	6
15	Make Subtotals	Bugatti	6
16	Make Subtotals	Noble	6
17	Make Subtotals	Trabant	5
18	Make Subtotals	Delahaye	4
19	Make Subtotals	BMW	3
20	Make Subtotals	Lagonda	2
21	Make Subtotals	Reliant	2
22	Make Subtotals	Morgan	1
23	Make Subtotals	McLaren	1
24	Make Subtotals	Delorean	1
25	Color Subtotals	Black	114
26	Color Subtotals	Blue	37
27	Color Subtotals	British Racing Green	34
28	Color Subtotals	Red	33

Figure 21.11: *Displaying subtotals and grand total only with GROUPING SETS*

How does it work

No matter what data you produce, it is essential that you and your audience understand what you are looking at. Consequently, the next piece of SQL harnesses the power of grouping sets and adds some extra presentation tweaks to make the data easier to understand at first sight.

This query is essentially in the following three parts:

- **A CTE**: That aggregates the number of cars sold for each make, each color, and a grand total for all cars sold. This CTE uses the **`Make`**, **`Model`**, and **`Stock`** tables to isolate the cars that have been bought by Prestige Cars.
- **A subquery**: This is a derived table in the **`FROM`** clause of the main query. It isolates each type of aggregation (color, make, and grand total) by filtering on the NULLs in the **`MakeName`** and **`Color`** columns. Each type of total is a separate query that also adds a column specifying the aggregation type as text. The three queries are then joined in a **`UNION`** query so that they all appear in the same table structure. This table has three columns: the aggregation type, the make or color, and finally, the metric.
- **An outer query**: That selects the three columns from the derived table and adds a **`CASE`** clause to add some text (a string of equals signs in this case) to replace any NULLs in the output. This is purely decorative and has no value other than to highlight the grand total.

This query shows, then, how you can use CTEs, derived tables, and **`UNION`** queries together in a practical and useful way. It also shows how you can create your own table output on the fly and combine different data elements (colors and makes of car in this example) in a single column using **`UNION`** queries.

Replace acronyms with full text in the final output

The sales manager needs a quick report of all the company's clients. However, she wants you to make the list more presentable by standardizing some of the output to compensate for some shortcomings in the source data. SQL makes this easy, as the following code snippet shows:

```
SELECT      REPLACE(CustomerName, 'Ltd', 'Limited') AS NoAcronymName

FROM        Customer

WHERE       LOWER(CustomerName) LIKE '%ltd%';
```

Running the preceding query gives the results shown in *Figure 21.12*:

	NoAcronymName
1	Eat My Exhaust Limited
2	Glittering Prize Cars Limited
3	Posh Vehicles Limited
4	My Shiny Sports Car Limited.

Figure 21.12: *Using the REPLACE() function when outputting results*

How does it work

Corporate data policies may prevent you from altering the data in a table; however, you may need to clean it up for presentation in some way. This is where the **`REPLACE()`** function becomes useful. It replaces specified text anywhere in a field with other text. It is a little like the search-and-replace function in a word processor. You can add some data cleansing at the query output stage without affecting the source data. This SQL snippet uses the **`Customer`** table and then applies the **`REPLACE()`** function to the data in the **`CustomerName`** field.

`REPLACE()` is another SQL function that needs you to specify three elements for it to work. Experts call this *taking three arguments*. The arguments are as follows:

- **First**: The field whose data you want to modify
- **Second**: The text that you are looking for (Ltd in this example)
- **Third**: The text that you want to replace the search text with (Limited in this example)

As you can see from the code sample, these three arguments are separated by commas in the function.

There would be times when you want to replace multiple words with another word (or even with several words). In these cases, you need to nest several **`REPLACE()`** functions inside one another. The following example replaces **`Ltd`** with **`Limited`**, **`S.A.`** with **`Société Anonyme`**, and **`Corp`** with **`Corporation`**:

```
SELECT     REPLACE(

                     REPLACE(

                                REPLACE(CustomerName, 'Ltd', 'Limited')

                                 ,'S.A.', 'Société Anonyme')
```

```
             ,'Corp', 'Corporation') AS PrettierOutput
FROM         Customer;
```

Although not difficult, this nesting of functions does require you to be attentive to the structure and to ensure that each opening parenthesis has a corresponding closing parenthesis.

Tricks and traps

The **REPLACE()** function is quite simple. Nonetheless, be aware of the following when you apply it:

- As this technique only applies to a **SELECT** clause here, it has absolutely no effect on the underlying data, which is not altered in any way.

Conclusion

This chapter takes you on a whirlwind tour of some of the SQL virtuoso techniques that you can use to hone your query output. From pivoting data via concatenated lists to adding complex subtotals in your reports or even replacing text in the final output, you have learned a useful variety of advanced ways to present data.

This chapter also concludes the book and your introduction to Spark SQL in Databricks. We sincerely hope that you will put your learning to good use and have had fun learning Spark SQL with Databricks.

Core knowledge learned in this chapter

The keywords and concepts that you have seen in this chapter are as follows:

Concept	Description
PIVOT	This operator allows you to create pivot tables.
GROUPING SETS	This operator lets you add multiple subtotals to aggregate queries.
REPLACE()	The REPLACE() function replaces one or more characters with another string.

Index

D

S

T